Cilano

The Wedding Complex

Edited by Michèle Aina Barale, Jonathan Goldberg,
Michael Moon, and Eve Kosofsky Sedgwick

The Wedding Complex

FORMS OF BELONGING IN MODERN AMERICAN CULTURE

Elizabeth Freeman

DUKE UNIVERSITY PRESS *Durham & London* 2002

THE DISTRIBUTION OF THIS BOOK IS SUPPORTED BY
A GENEROUS GRANT FROM THE GILL FOUNDATION.

Contents

Preface

One can easily imagine ceremonies with a difference—in which people might solemnize a committed household, ironize their property sharing, pledge care and
inheritance without kinship, celebrate a whole circle of intimacies, or dramatize
independence from state-regulated sexuality. A movement built around such ceremonies could be more worthwhile and more fun than the unreflective demand for
state-sanctioned marriage. Indeed, some people already experiment in these ways.
Why do they get no press?
—Michael Warner, *The Trouble with Normal*[1]

Like many projects, this one began with an experience of cognitive dissonance. Even as I did activist work for same-sex partnership benefits at the
university where I began graduate work during the early 1990s, I felt dubious
about the politics of what I was involved in. I was certainly persuaded that
domestic partnership policies and even gay marriage might transform gender
as we know it. The marriage relation has historically worked to establish some
people ("men") as economic providers, and others ("women") as sexual, reproductive, and domestic providers under the law. So it seemed clear that
installing two people of the same sex into this structure might productively
dismantle "manhood" and "womanhood" as opposite and complementary
economic categories—though that work has in many ways been accom-

plished by reforms in domestic property law. It also seemed possible to me that same-sex marriage might productively muddle the gendering of parenthood, in which women are legally construed in terms of their supposedly prepolitical, "natural" relation to the children they bear, and their husbands are granted a legal form of guardianship that transcends and supersedes even the rights of the original male contributor of genetic material.[2]

Yet even as I recognized these possibilities, the rhetoric of the gay marriage and domestic partnership movements disturbed me. Its spokespeople often exalted sexual monogamy, shared property, and cohabitation as if they were the highest forms of commitment, frequently denigrating other ways of life as amoral or uncivilized.[3] Even as I believed that gay people deserved whatever rights straight people had, it seemed clear that domestic partnership policies or legalized gay marriages certainly wouldn't question the culturally privileged status of couplehood, or the dominant assumption that couplehood entails monogamy, shared living quarters, pooled property, and so on. More important, legalizing same-sex partnerships would not question the way that marriage law has intersected with a more general transformation of public resources into private perquisites over the past two decades. In the contemporary United States, that is, marriage may have less impact on the division between men's and women's *roles* than on that between coupled people's and uncoupled people's *access to public resources*. For marriage law ensures that privileges and benefits accrue to those who are willing to limit their outwardly acknowledged sexual relations to one other person, and to oblige themselves to the care and maintenance of that person and any children that result from this union, "forsaking all others," as the Protestant *Book of Common Prayer* puts it.[4] This last dictum is significant: marriage law may to a certain extent financially reward those who can limit the horizon of their social obligations, but it also allows the state to forsake the burden of caring for dependents. Why should any of us on the so-called Left be for *this*?[5]

So while I did work for policies that would equalize gay and straight partnerships at my university, I also increasingly doubted that economic or social privileges should attend to these kinds of relationships and not to others. Granting same-sex couples the benefits accorded to married heterosexuals would contribute—rather than criticizing or insisting on alternatives—to a privatized culture in which individual households are increasingly responsible for primary human caretaking functions such as physical shelter, health care, child support, and maintenance of the elderly, and in which people without such households are increasingly vulnerable. Partnership benefit laws might even increase people's likelihood of getting married or moving in together for economic reasons even if they would prefer to remain spatially or financially separate. Crucially, cultural and legal recognition of same-sex couples would do nothing to enfranchise the relationships that have also been fundamental to queer life: friendships, cliques, tricks, sex buddies, ex-lovers, activist and support groups, and myriad others.

What would the world be like if intimate couplehood did not have to function as an economic safety net for so many people? At the very least, I wished that if core human needs had to be met by private constituencies rather than public funds, people could share their perks within whatever small-scale social configurations they chose—in short, that institutions including the state would cease to make a singular form of love and sex into the matrix for its allocation of resources. What if one could have each of the things that marriage combines with a different person or small group? What if I could live with my mother, but still give my best friend hospital visitation rights and extend my health insurance benefits to my ex-lover?[6]

But imagine the paperwork. Like many cultural critics trained in literature, I'm not prepared to draft policy. Instead, I have come to wish, more simply, that there were no such thing as legal marriage for straight people, gay people, or anyone else—no mechanism that privatizes and automatically packages together such incommensurate elements as the sharing of material goods and shelter, expectation of ongoing sexual relations, extension of institutional benefits, and social recognition of a relationship. I do recognize that what historians Lisa Duggan and Nancy Cott have called the "disestablishment" of marriage from the state would bring special dangers to dependents (at the very least, women, children, and the elderly) who must turn to state law for help in cases of abuse and neglect in their household environment.[7] But the state could certainly address violence between intimates without privileging marriage—indeed, the state's increasing treatment of domestic violence in the same terms that it deals with violence between strangers has actually benefited vulnerable members of society. In the end, I have come to desire the final disappearance of what Michel Foucault labels the "deployment of alliance," or the state's maintenance of a social order by fixing the routes by which names, property, and other protected forms of cultural recognition travel.[8]

Yet the Foucauldian "deployment of sexuality" is not the endpoint I hope for either (nor is it Foucault's). The task is still, as he says, to imagine and put into practice new ways of being in relation, and I would add, to imagine representational possibilities commensurate with these new modes of connection: to produce something like a deployment of affinity.[9] I have come to wish that the more intangible benefits of social recognition and cultural intelligibility might accrue outside of state purview, and for a wide variety of intimate liaisons—the aforementioned friendships, cliques, tricks, sex buddies, ex-lover relations, activist and support groups, and beyond. But how? As I was thinking these things through, my most startling moment of cognitive dissonance came at a wedding. During the first of the two years that the activist group I was part of worked for domestic partnership benefits, we threw a mass "marry-in" in the university's central quadrangle. Some couples used this wedding as a public ceremony of commitment to one another and the idea that same-sex couplehood deserved institutional benefits. But all kinds of people who were more ambivalent about couplehood and/or marriage also showed up to symbolize and collectively affirm their shared histories, plans for a future together, and ongoing connections. As Ellen Lewin's ethnographic work on same-sex commitment ceremonies has demonstrated, many people use weddings to signal their ties to religious communities and extended families.[10] And many seemed to be at our marry-in to figure themselves as connectable and connected, period. For as anthropologist Robert Brain contends, Western culture lacks public modes of expression for emotional ties that fall outside of structured kin groups, but that do not constitute even informal couplehood, such as friendship dyads, love triangles, and extrafamilial intergenerational bonds.[11] At the University of Chicago, then, groups of roommates married one another, a woman married her motorcycle, pairs of best friends stood up together, and a sexual threesome marched down the aisle. This wedding did not, of course, permanently (or even momentarily) reorganize the *institutional* interrelations among sexual practice, material resources, and social recognition. Nevertheless, it did tap into what felt like a queer desire to imagine and represent something different from the social choices at hand, which at the time and even now, seemed to consist of isolated individuality, domesticated long-term couplehood, or membership in an abstract, homogeneous collectivity like the gay community or official nation. What felt queerest at the marry-in was the unpredictability of the small-scale alliances that organized people's lives, for which they clearly wanted to make a public claim and an aesthetic statement.

I was startled by my own and other people's attraction to the wedding form as a means for doing these things, when it seemed so directly metonymic of an institution that many of us found so politically suspect. Didn't the wedding mystify heterosexuality, making it look natural, inevitable, and sacred? Didn't it stage a scene of manufactured consent, especially by women, to compulsory heterosexuality? Didn't it separate the couple from their previous social networks, glorifying their relationship with one another over their ties to parents, extended family, friends, and other lovers past or present? Didn't it force its participants and audience members to spend time, emotions, and money with no guarantee of a return investment on their own relationships? If many of us felt that *marriage law* could not be queered, why did the wedding ritual seem to lend itself to such interesting fabulations? Even in the absence of all the gifts that are supposed to provide people's primary motivation to have a nuptial ceremony, what did it mean for so many of us to want a wedding, but not a marriage?

I began to gather texts in which the wedding did not necessarily instantiate a legal marriage but instead tapped into fantasies that were irreducible to the wish for long-term domestic couplehood recognized by the state. Rather than doing fieldwork (though I did go to a few bridal fairs and weddings) or interviews (though many cocktail parties I attended devolved into competitions for the most interesting wedding story), I accumulated primarily fictional literary, media, and performance texts, reading them alongside, and treating them as part of, both the material culture of the wedding and the history of Anglo-American marriage law. This was partly the default result of having been trained as a scholar of literature, yet what I found also contradicted much of what literary critics have said about the relationship between narrative and weddings.

Literary critics have long described the wedding in terms of aesthetic, social, and psychic closure. In theories of comedy, of which the "courtship plot" is paradigmatic, narrative itself moves inexorably forward toward a wedding, which situates the characters in their proper social relation to one another and quashes any unstable subplots that the narrative has generated along the way.[12] For example, as Joseph Boone notes of Jane Austen's *Pride and Prejudice*, the novel's final two words, "united them," tie the love knot at the exact same moment that they tie up the story's last loose threads.[13] In the "marriage plot," through which accounts of literary realism have been articulated, the action begins shortly after a wedding, and the text goes on to elaborate a state of connubial impasse, eventually ceasing to be a narrative at all.[14] In this view, the wedding halts both desire and plot, and minute descriptions of exterior details and interior psychic states substitute for the forward-moving dynamic of comedy. A crucial example here might be George Eliot's *Middlemarch,* in which Dorothea marries in one sentence at the end of chapter 10, only to find out by chapter 20 that "in the weeks since her marriage . . . the large vistas and wide fresh air which she had dreamed of finding in her husband's mind were replaced by anterooms and winding passages which seemed to lead nowhither. . . . "[15] As this rhetoric of spatial and psychological confinement implies, Eliot's portrait of a marriage is also one of narrative stasis, of a story that can go nowhere.

But compare these texts to the 1987 pornographic film *Sulka's Wedding,* directed by Kim Christy, in which a male-to-female transsexual celebrates her surgical self-realization with a wedding.[16] Sulka's transformation of herself into a bride allows her to cross the line between male and female, heterosexual and homosexual, and even between old and young—for she cheerfully has intergenerational sex with both men and women in her gown and veil. Or, in what might be a fairer comparison of similar genres, consider Shyam Selvadurai's 1994 novel *Funny Boy,* a gay male Sri Lankan Canadian émigré's coming-of-age tale. In the opening chapter, the protagonist Arjie plays a game called "bride-bride," in which he and his cousins dress up and enact a wedding. This game allows Arjie to imaginatively transform himself into, variously, a Sinhalese cinema star, a religious deity, and an ordinary grown-up woman—to migrate across the boundaries between the Sinhalese and Tamil ethnic identities that threaten to erupt into civil war, between domestic and public spaces, religious and secular iconography, male and female identities, adulthood and childhood. In fact, the game becomes the catalyst for a battle between Arjie and a female cousin who has been raised in Europe, and the two fight over the bridal sari. This might seem to be a rather simplistic use of the wedding, or more precisely the figure of the bride, as a representative of "traditional" culture embattled by Western norms—except that there are two brides, and the winning one is a boy obsessed with mass cultural icons rather than mythologized indigenous folkways. Indeed, Arjie's triumph as a better bride than the Westernized girl marks the beginning of his resistance to the sexual rules enforced by both the British Empire and the postcolonial Sinhalese state, a resistance that develops later on in the novel into a queer embrace of his own doubly minoritized, contradictory gay and Tamil identities.[17]

These texts use the wedding explicitly to reorganize gender. But their social imaginations also reach far beyond the mere neutralization of gendered economic and parental categories via same-sex marriage, or reforms in divorce and property law. They do not prioritize gender over other aspects of subjectivity or make its transformation contingent on a same-sex object-choice. Instead, they insist on connecting alternative possibilities for gendered embodiment to relationships between and among subject, family, nation, market, and other domains. *Sulka's Wedding* and *Funny Boy* do this partly by using the nuptial ritual as a device of narrative opening and semiotic linkage. As part of what Arjun Appadurai calls "a social *imaginaire* built largely around re-runs" in these texts, the ordinary wedding seems to provide neither psychic nor narrative closure, but rather an array of detachable narrative parts—characters, genres, story lines—that can be recombined into "proto-narratives of possible lives."[18] Not only does the wedding provide the representational toolkit for plotting an alternative life in these texts; it seems to provide the temporal dynamic for doing so as well. By using the wedding as a catalyst for "regressive" behavior of various kinds, *Sulka's Wedding* and *Funny Boy* also suggest that the wedding disrupts the Oedipal logic of "plot" itself, in which polymorphous desire yields to heterosexual object-choice, children succeed fathers, effect follows cause, and endings confirm beginnings.[19]

In short, though literary critics have punningly linked the dominance of "wedlock" with narrative "deadlock," when the wedding does appear in any sustained way in literary texts, it often produces anything and everything *but* closure. Even the word "wedlock" does not derive, as one might suppose, from the Old Frisian *wed,* "pledge" or "covenant," combined with the Old English *loc,* or "enclosure." Instead, the suffix "-lock" derives from the Common Teutonic *laiko,* "play," the High German *leich,* "song," and the Gothic *laik-s,* "dance." Thus wedlock means, roughly, "pledging by playing," or promising and thereby making a future by means of collective embodied performances.[20] The modern English word "wedding" actually disguises the kinetic, theatrical aspects of the nuptial pageant that, as I argue throughout this book, allow disruptive anachronisms to flicker forth, sometimes into flaming visions of unrealized social possibility.

The very form of a text, then, is part of how it works out the relations among suppressed or forgotten histories, the limitations or possibilities of a particular moment, and their imaginative transformation into a different future—the relations among has been, what must be, and what could be. This, too, is central to my understanding of queer politics: the idea that what has failed to survive, often most legible as mere residue in a cultural text, might be a placeholder for the not-yet.[21] Working with literary and filmic texts, I aimed to disinter two things: a history of the dialectic between the wedding form and the institutional control of heterosexual couplehood, and a future of possibilities for making minoritized or subjugated affinities between people more culturally legible. I ended up with an archive of "wedding texts" that began in the 1830s, when the elements of the Anglo-American "white wedding"—a bride in an eggshell-colored dress and veil, orange blossoms, bridesmaids and best men, engagement rings and honeymoons—began their slow convergence into a form that is now taken as the standard against which all other U.S. weddings seem to count as mere variations. The archive took me right up to the surfeit of wedding films and performances that appeared during the 1990s, about which I will say more in chapter 1.

To my surprise, the dynamics of works that centralized the wedding were quite different than that of the narrative courtship plot. In the latter, various alternatives to marriage are systematically deployed and then rejected or overcome, and the wedding finale signals, at best, acquiescence to a social order only slightly modified by bourgeois feminine values. But in the texts I'd gathered, when a wedding took over a plot, narrative and social chaos ensued. Many of the weddings in my archive of found objects seemed to grant their participants some kind of transitivity: the ability to be both black and white, for instance, both male and female, both child and adult; the desire to go somewhere else in place or time; the desire to extend beyond one's own bodily or psychic contours. And many weddings worked out fantasies about collectivity and publicity: the desire to be part of something publicly comprehensible *as* social, to create some group form for which the bourgeois couple was not metonymic but antithetical or just irrelevant. This suggested to me that the wedding might do cultural work at an interesting angle—perhaps slantwise—to that of marriage law. Indeed, in many of the texts I collected, the wedding actually served to demystify marriage, illuminating and critiquing the power of marriage law to maintain structures that do not seem immediately connected to it, such as the nation-state, racial taxonomies, and so on. Simultaneously, their weddings made forbidden (or forgotten) alliances tangible—as points of resistance to marital supremacy, and as figures for a different social order. And their weddings often scrambled the temporal sequencing on which not only the love plot but also the intertwined narratives of sexual development and racialized national progress depend.

This doubled work of wild fantasy and rigorous demystification seems to me to be fundamentally queer: to "queer" something is at once to make its most pleasurable aspects gorgeously excessive, even to the point of causing its institutional work to fail, and to operate it against its most oppressive political results. *The Wedding Complex* details these operations as they pertain in particular to marriage. Insofar as the word queer insists on sex practice as a central aspect of culture making, I'm not sure I would count every nonmarital or even failed wedding as automatically queer. But the social alternatives that are exposed by the excessive and/or failed weddings I will discuss do seem to resonate with a genuinely queer politics, one that insists on the mobility of identification and desire, on the ongoing production of shared meanings and unforeseen constituencies, and on exposing links between the "private" sphere and various "public" techniques of control. So far in at least some recent queer social theory, though, the magical sign for these kinds of commitments has been the flip side of the cohesive couple, the purely physical and often anonymous sexual encounter—and not the tangled network of ex-lovers, concomitant relationships, unconsummated erotics, and so forth that structure so many queer lives, and that often get homogenized as "just friends." Of course, the wedding is not the only possible form with which to "think" this social field, but its sexual meanings, its display of overlapping circuits of intimacy, its hyper-femininity, its improper, delicious self-aggrandizing dramatization of what is, after all, a relatively common event, resonates with experiences and sensibilities that in myself I can only identify not only as queer but deeply femme. All of this is to say that though gender is one aspect of the analysis that follows, the gendered lens through which I look is often femme rather than gender-neutrally queer or heterosexually female.

This book's point of departure is a hunch that there is a productive nonequivalence between the institution of marriage and the ritual that supposedly represents and guarantees it. I use literary and other cultural texts to disaggregate the wedding so that it becomes metonymic not of the timeless, transcendent nature of marriage but of a history of struggle among various institutions, and between these institutions and the subjects they engender, for control over the forms and meanings of intimate ties. Understood as a historically sedimented scene, the wedding has the capacity to suggest alternative futures to the one toward which U.S. culture seems to be moving, where long-term, property-sharing, monogamous couplehood accrues institutional benefits and social sanction, and other elective affinities cease to have any broad social meaning at all. It is toward any number of different futures that I launch this work.

Acknowledgments

For financial assistance during the writing of this book, I am indebted to the generosity of an Andrew W. Mellon Fellowship in the Humanities, a Mellon Summer Dissertation Research Grant, a Mellon Dissertation-Year Fellowship, two Marilyn Simpson Grants for Junior Faculty Development at Sarah Lawrence College, and the New Faculty Research Grant, Faculty Research Grant, and Dean's Publication Fund Grant at the University of California at Davis. I would not have been able to complete the manuscript without a Mellon Postdoctoral Fellowship at the Penn Humanities Forum, University of Pennsylvania, during the 1999–2000 academic year.

I am sure many of my colleagues and intimates would rather have put on a one-shot wedding for me than witness the seemingly endless writing of a book about the subject, but I thank them for their endurance. My graduate school mentors at the University of Chicago, Lauren Berlant and Bill Brown, lent their crystalline intelligences and faith to the dissertation version of this project. Elizabeth Helsinger and Candace Vogler asked important questions during my defense; I am also grateful for long-ago conversations with James Chandler, Miriam Hansen, Chris Looby, and Sherwood Williams. My graduate school colleagues helped me more than they know: Katie Crawford, Brian Currid, Patrick Larvie, Scott Mendel, Ann Elizabeth Murdy, Xiomara Santamarina, Dana Seitler, Nayan Shah, and Wilhelm Werthern all left an imprint on my intellectual life, as did Amanda Berry and Meryem Ersoz from afar. At Sarah Lawrence College, I was fortunate to be in a Faculty Writing Group that worked through some of my chapters: I thank Bella Brodzki, Lyde Sizer, Mary Porter, Bob Desjarlais, and Chikwenye Ogunyemi. My years in New York were also enriched by the Faculty Working Group in Queer Studies at New York University; I'd like to credit Paisley Currah, Ann Cvetkovich, Carolyn Dinshaw, Jill Dolan, Lisa Duggan, David Eng, Licia Fiol-Matta, Phil Harper, Janet Jakobsen, José Muñoz, Ann Pellegrini, Alisa Solomon, and Patty White for keeping me sane if not always sober. During my postdoctoral year at the Penn Humanities Forum, director Wendy Steiner and my fellow Fellows, as we called one another, were rigorous and supportive in equal measure, and Litty Paxton provided friendship and cross talk with her work on proms. At the University of California at Davis, Riché Richardson and Katherine Sugg have been my constant readers; Gayatri Gopinath and Gail Finney asked key questions during talks; and Don Abbott, Joanne Diehl, Margie Ferguson, Michael Hoffman, David Van Leer, Patricia Moran, and Linda Morris have been the kind of departmental mentors who help you get your work done. Judith Halberstam, Alison Shonkwiler, Jacqueline Stevens, and B. J. Wray each read my full manuscript at critical moments with wit, care, and clarity. The comments of my anonymous readers at *American Literature, Women and Performance,* and Duke University Press helped immensely; I also want to thank Rosemary Cullen at the Hays Library, and the archivists and reference librarians at New York Public Library, the American Antiquarian Society, and George Eastman House for their assistance in locating materials. Thanks also to my research assistants, Emily Sauber and Jocelyn Samson at Sarah Lawrence College, and especially the amazing Samaine Lockwood and Jodi Schorb at the University of California at Davis; more thanks to Eric Gudas for production work and to Samaine for the index. Ken Wissoker has been a model editor, tactful and generous, and his kindness has been a touchstone. Also at Duke University Press, Fiona Morgan and Rebecca Johns-Danes handled the manuscript with patience and precision, and Cindy Milstein provided exemplary copyediting. Miranda Joseph, Amy Robinson, and Shawn Smith have been my closest ongoing interlocutors as well as friends. I'm also indebted to the people who told me about their off-kilter weddings; they know who they are. Finally, Molly McGarry transcends any category I could generate here, and I want to thank her in her own special sentence.

In my life outside the academy, I have received emotional and material support from Camilla Enders, Andrea Lawlor, Sam Miller, Emily Park, Joanne Pendola, Annie Piper, Liss Platt and Claudia Manley, Deb Schwartz, A. K. Summers, Sylvia Sichel, Caitlin Sullivan, Nancy Tenney, and Dena Van der Wal. I would have chosen my family had they not been chosen for me, and I thank Caroline Freeman and Glenn Hoffman, Donald and Margaret Freeman, Roger Freeman and Mi-Sun Cho-Freeman for all they have done for me over the years. Diane Bonder saw me through the longest part; I will always be especially grateful to her. I met B. J. Wray latest of all, and I consider that a stroke of pure luck.

Chapter One

LOVE AMONG THE RUINS

What is marriage, is marriage protection or religion, is marriage renunciation or abundance, is marriage a stepping-stone or an end. What is marriage.
—Gertrude Stein, *The Mother of Us All*[1]

Between 1989 and the time of this writing, at least thirty-five Hollywood films, seventeen made-for-television movies, and eight national theatrical productions have put a wedding at the center of their plots. In a typical 1990s television season, eleven sitcoms opened or closed their series with a wedding; many national entertainment magazines produce "wedding issues" featuring celebrities; both network and cable stations regularly devote hour-long specials to home wedding videos and Hollywood weddings; talk shows and even the game show "Who Wants to Marry a Millionaire?" stage live weddings on camera; and new Internet wedding sites appear and disappear every day. Meanwhile, print and television ads pile up wedding images to sell things unrelated to marriage: a short list might include Pillsbury frosting, Visa Gold cards, Estée Lauder's Beautiful perfume, Loving Care hair dye, and MCI, with new ones appearing every time I try to finish this sentence.[2] This explosion of wedding images is different than, though obviously related to, the expansion of the bridal service industry or changes in the demographics of marriage. It looks like a national wedding complex in the psychoanalytic sense—America's terrible case of heterosexual exhibitionism, or perhaps its mass fixation on the primal scene of induction into that most insular relationship, the married couple.

Yet many of the weddings cluttering the national mediascape are actually gay: the documentary short film *Chicks in White Satin* (dir. Elaine Holliman, 1992) won an Oscar for its look at lesbian weddings; *Late Bloomers* (dirs. Gretchen and Julia Dyer, 1996) featured two women marrying; the television shows *Roseanne, Friends,* and *Northern Exposure* have all featured same-sex weddings; and cover stories in the national gay magazines *Out, The Advocate,* and *Girlfriends* have focused on the planning and styling of same-sex weddings. Even contemporary representations of "straight" weddings often focus on a gay participant whose presence in the ceremony and exclusion from its results seems to guarantee heterosexual marriage, as in *Four Weddings and a Funeral, Meet the Parents, My Best Friend's Wedding, The Object of My Affection,* and *In and Out.* This proliferation of gay weddings, and gay people *in* weddings, hardly reflects a mainstream commitment to the idea of same-sex marriage, which has been rejected in many popular polls and state voting referenda as well as in the 1996 federal Defense of Marriage Act that defines marriage as a union between "one man and one woman."[3] Even many lesbian and gay people, myself included, feel ambivalent about gay marriage. As I noted in the preface, some of us may believe that straight people should not have privileges that are denied to gay people but also feel that legalizing gay marriage would simply extend a set of privileges to monogamous, long-term, property-sharing couples at the expense of those whose lives cannot be so neatly packaged. A state that promotes marriage also disenfranchises people whose primary affinities do not get into the couple form and contributes to a culture that stereotypes these people as isolated failures, as immature and/or sexually indiscriminating, or as part of some mysteriously primitive social system.[4]

Yet if ratings and box-office numbers are any indication, many straight, gay, and even queer people may want to watch and participate in weddings for reasons that have little to do with a wish to obtain legal marriage. Audiences seem compelled by the legally nonbinding commitment ceremony, and willing to be both voyeur and witness to the fantastic ritual of people making promises with no legal contract to enforce them. This compulsion may be undergirded by a longing for inclusion or a wish to watch the ceremony collapse under the weight of its own solemnities, but in the case of queers, we may also identify with the expansive, figurally complex sociability suggested by some element of the wedding ritual. Many contemporary weddings, that is, suggest provocative visions of what the wedding itself might do beyond inaugurating a marriage; indeed, some of the richest contemporary images of weddings have little to do with gay *or* straight unions. Instead of featuring an ordinary couple with extraordinary accessories (as in the scuba, nudist, or bungee-jumping weddings of the 1970s and 1980s), quite a few mass-mediated wedding spectacles of the last decade or so dramatize ties altogether outside of, beyond, or even antithetical to couplehood itself.

For instance, the wedding has become a means of figuring and performing a relationship between persons and objects. A recent television ad for the Mazda automobile features a woman in full bridal regalia, sans groom, promising to "love, honor, and obey" in a vow that cuts two ways: in order to drive the car she must submit to its superior technology, yet that very technology enables the car to respond to her driving technique. This wedding registers the possibility of will, of intentionality, of savoir faire in a material landscape, of mastering consumer culture's vast terrain. Using the wedding to link people and objects seems also to create a space of permission to publicize other social ties—friendships, extended family, nonparental intergenerational commitments, subcultural alliances, and so on. For example, a TV advertisement for Nike women's sportswear shows a group of girls playing soccer, accompanied by a voice-over of females chanting wedding vows. Rather than a kiss passing from lip to lip, the soccer ball passing from Nike-clad foot to foot bonds the girls; the exhortation to "love, honor, and obey" portrays teamwork in terms of emotional ties rather than political or even athletic goals. Accompanied by another chant (say, the pledge of allegiance), the soccer game might be a figure for feminist activism in the civic sphere. But it would lose the erotic torque it gains from the wedding vows, which make the game into a specifically feminine expression of same-sex bonding, both suggesting and deflecting lesbian possibilities.

This overproduction of weddings seems odd in a country that has, since the formation of the New England colonies that count as the official beginning of its history, purported to follow a juridical rather than religious model in the making of its marriages. The civil courts have the last word on the validity of nuptial unions in the United States, and even the theocratic Puritans insisted that marriage ceremonies take place in secular spaces, in front of lay officials rather than clergy. Given this history, one would think that residents of the

United States could do without weddings altogether, simply registering partnerships the way they register births, voter status, automobiles, and patents; this is more or less the aim of the contemporary movement to extend legal and economic benefits to domestic partnerships or registered households. One might even expect to see long-term commitment dissociated altogether from state law, so that the decision to share living facilities, property, sexual pleasure, or child-rearing obligations with another person would be irrelevant to the governmental distribution of benefits and privileges.

Yet neither the reformist domestic partnership movement nor the more radical argument for disestablishing marriage takes seriously the need for whatever it is that weddings do: at the very least, they at once symbolize and multiply social ties, work in and with time, allow someone to be the star of a show, suggest the possibility of bodily and social transformations, and offer an elaborate series of visual icons to play with. Since the mid-1930s, the wedding industry has capitalized on these needs in order to promote an endless variety of goods and services. More recently, the national gay movement has tapped into these needs to advocate for the extension of rights and privileges to same-sex couples. Concurrently, the wedding seems to work as an emblem for the condition of belonging to constituencies *beyond* (if also sometimes constitutively connected to) the male-female couple: to proper gender, extended family, ethnic or religious constituencies, the nation, or a particular niche market. Yet, rather than producing these latter forms of belonging as homologous to couplehood—so that couplehood becomes, as Doris Sommer puts it, "the shorthand for human association"—the wedding often inadvertently plays forms of belonging against one another, so that the icons of one social configuration question the centrality of another.[5] Relatedly, some of the wedding's specifically temporal operations may actually undermine its seemingly monumental ability to reduce a variety of social matrices to mere extensions of the marital dyad.

One way to get at these possibilities is to separate the wedding, at least provisionally, from its ostensible purpose of inaugurating a marriage. For if marriage is still imaginable without a "proper" wedding—as in a common-law union or courthouse registration—a wedding is supposed to serve as the inevitable precursor to a marriage. Yet the examples above, and most of the texts this book examines, partially or completely sunder the wedding from its legal ramifications, reveling in the expressive, theatrical, and symbolic aspects of the ritual. Focusing on the wedding itself reveals possibilities that are lost when the purpose and result of "wedding" is presumed to be marriage as domestic law defines it: a monogamous, enduring, opposite-sex dyad with biological reproduction as its ostensible raison d'être. By undoing this presumption, texts that foreground the wedding as a production return to and rework the possibilities embedded in the ritual itself, asking in what ways the kinds of weddings people have, or dream of having, or thought they had, might be indices for forms of social life made possible in one domain but impossible in another, or in one historical moment but not another—or might even be avatars for changes in what Raymond Williams calls "structures of feeling," new senses of collective being felt viscerally, in advance of their institutionalization in discourse.[6] In short, the desire for the symbolic apparatus that is the wedding and the legal apparatus that is marriage cannot be reduced to one another. It is important to at least momentarily unchain the wedding from marriage or even couplehood and to explore the dynamic between weddings and the marriages they supposedly stand for or produce.

In 1991, Su Friedrich made a film that did just that. *First Comes Love* premiered at that year's New York Lesbian and Gay Experimental Film Festival, where some audience members complained that it was merely an advertisement for the gay marriage movement.[7] Shot in shimmery black-and-white, 16-millimeter film, this twenty-two-minute montage of four Italian Catholic weddings, interrupted by textual statements about same-sex marriage, does at first glance seem to traffic in mere envy of heterosexuality rather than critique it and to promote couplehood over other forms of intimacy. In its central shot, for instance, the bride and groom are seen from high above, standing at the altar, with the white aisle runner bisecting the frame and Richard Wagner's "Bridal Chorus" as the sound track. This music fades into the sounds of Gladys Knight singing "It Could've Been Me." Here, the filmmaker seems to "fall into line with the ritual," as one reviewer asserts, aligning bride and groom, image and sound, visual splendor and emotional fulfillment in exactly the way that marriage is supposed to align two people with each other and the state.[8]

The altar scene cuts to an intertitle that reads, "If two men or two women wanted to legalize their commitment to each other, for any reason, they would be denied this privilege in the following countries." This text is followed by a three-minute-long, alphabetized list of nations from Afghanistan to Zimbabwe. In a white typeface against a black background, the intertitle creates a column in the very center of the screen, exactly matching the white aisle runner, and then visually interrupts and replaces the wedding processional as the words stream upward and out the top of the frame. This text steals the whiteness and symmetry of the wedding to articulate what the viewer can now recognize as a new global political order. The alphabetical listing of these locales in a column aligns them along an axis other than the ones that officially conjoin nations, like geographic proximity, trade agreements, monetary systems, political theory, or religious ideology—specifically, that of monogamous heterosexual marriage. Depicting a "mass wedding" of individual countries into a world ordered by hetero-marital supremacy, *First Comes Love* is a momentary reminder that marriage is not only a relation between two people but also part of the process by which states ally with one another and create new citizens, especially through reciprocal immigration policies that naturalize "foreign" spouses.[9]

Thus Friedrich's elaborate engagement with the wedding ceremony might in fact serve a certain global sexual imperialism, promoting marital couplehood as a regime of sensation, subjectivity, and social affinity that can cut across existing registers of race, class, nation, and even sexual orientation to produce something like a spousal planet. But this possibility is exactly what the film slowly unsettles, for it actually dramatizes the wedding as a queer counterpossibility to what it has pointedly demarcated as a multinational association of hetero-supremacist countries. On the formal level, *First Comes Love* breaks down the wedding, providing opportunities for reading it as a scene in which identity and belonging can be complicated rather than simplified, and alternative affinities between people can be distinguished from rather than merged with a new marital world order.[10]

This breakdown begins with the film's opening. Over the words "First Comes Love . . . a film by Su Friedrich," children's voices chant a rhyme: "Lisa and George sittin' in a tree. K-I-S-S-I-N-G. First comes love, then comes marriage, then comes Lisa with a baby carriage." Narrating a male-female romance that ends as usual, with the woman doing all the child care, this chant is certainly a primer for compulsory heterosexuality. But the title "First Comes Love . . . " leaves the rhyme unfinished, substituting an ellipsis for the inevitable progression from kissing, to love, to marriage, to reproduction, to the asymmetrical allocation of gendered tasks. On the one hand, Friedrich certainly seems to intend the ellipsis to figure the lack of legal sanction for same-sex couplehood: for lesbian and gay partners, the title suggests, first comes love, then comes nothing. Certainly the chant that follows the title might be filled in with new content, like "Wendy and Lisa" or "Gilbert and George." Yet the ellipsis also creates a space of possibility wherein the temporal logic of the chant might be undermined: "First Comes Love . . . " and next, or before, comes what? In other words, what is missing is not just the legal status of "marriage" but the seriality and causal logic of "then."

Rather than simply repeating the chant with a lesbian difference, though, Friedrich undermines its progressive narrative with her camera work. She shoots the weddings from the position of what one reviewer calls "part anthropologist, part kid at the candy-store window."[11] As an "anthropologist," of course, she reverses the power relations of ethnographic filmmaking by voyeuristically examining the dominant straight culture from a marginal point of view. But as a "kid," she also aims to suture the viewer into the "before," the infantilized subject position of someone who cannot enter into the wedding's symbolics or fits imperfectly into its pageant.[12] From the sound of children's voices chanting a progression they cannot yet enact, the film segues to its opening shot of two children. Later, the image of a little girl climbing rather laboriously up the church steps cuts to one of the bridesmaids ascending much more smoothly. In other scenes, Friedrich focuses on details that only someone of a child's height would see straight on or she positions the camera from about three feet off the ground. *First Comes Love,* in short, uses the child as a figure for the polymorphous desires as well as prior personal and collective histories that marriage aims to erase. The point of view of the subject left below or behind, in a position of longing and incomprehension, halts the developmental logic of the playground chant, for that "first" point of view returns again and again.

But the figure of the child is merely a psychoanalytic intervention, a form of narrative disorientation and temporal regression that has no immediate public coordinates. Perhaps the film simply suggests that lesbians and gays are like children, stupidly falling in love with a social form that requires our abjection in order to maintain itself. Or perhaps *First Comes Love* means to point out that our history is intertwined with that of juveniles insofar as both children and adult queers have a long record of being legally barred from acting on their sexual desires. Although age-of-consent laws and laws against "sodomy" are historically and structurally interrelated, however, *First Comes Love* does not explore this phenomenon; that is simply not the project of the film.[13] Instead, Friedrich's sound track, floating disjunctively over her image track, suggests psychic regression to "childhood" as a means of reanimating lost historical moments and their corresponding kinship forms. The "juvenile" subject's displacement from the wedding, the sound track hints, is not merely a result of her emotional immaturity but of historically located institutional forces that promote married couplehood over other kinds of relationships.

With the film's sound track, Friedrich links her infantilizing camera work and images of psychological abjection to a horizon of historical and cultural displacement. The wedding footage is accompanied by a variety of bluesy songs from the 1960s and 1970s: Janis Joplin singing "Get It While You Can," Marvin Gaye's "Sexual Healing," and James Brown's "Sex Machine" over a shot of the virginally white-clad bride. Variously poignant and funny, these juxtapositions certainly interrogate the way that the wedding seems to sanctify heterosexual intercourse by erasing the individual erotic histories of the bride and groom: the songs interrupt the wedding ceremony with suggestions that the nuptial pair may have emotional and sexual ties that marriage law renders illegible, and that the ritual itself threatens to overwrite. But rather than simply celebrating a forbidden love object, these songs call forth sexual styles that monogamous gay or straight partnership cannot accommodate and that even mainstream gay culture seems to have renounced—ephemeral encounters, diffuse pleasures, flamboyant publicness, easy access to the technological mediations of pornography or sex toys. It is important, then, that several of *First Comes Love*'s songs come from the 1960s, an era whose vision of social justice was accompanied, some might even say propelled, by experiments in the forms and norms of intimacy. The songs also come from representatives of populations against whom marriage law has taken shape—straight black artists and queer artists of African and European ancestry, whose intersecting cultural history includes not only being barred from the privilege of marrying but also inventing and preserving associational forms other than monogamous nuclear families. The sound track thus expresses not only personal loss (the nuptial couple's loss of natal family, prior sexual ties, and peer culture; Friedrich's inability to marry her lover) but also the denial of kinship to whole cultures. In this way, the film implies that the wedding might work to consolidate not only heterosexual supremacy but more broadly, the hegemony of the Anglo-European nuclear family. The sound track also hints that the signs of the so-called white wedding—ivory gowns, pearls and diamonds, white flowers like orange blossoms and baby's breath, and long misty veils—encode racial meanings too, though the film does nothing with the suggestions. Yet at the same time, Friedrich's sound track makes the wedding into a scene for a certain *social* melancholia—melancholia for effaced forms and practices of *relationality* rather than a singular love object—and the insistent return of what has been effaced.

These disavowed possibilities are actually part of the Anglo-American white wedding's history and contemporary form. For crucially, the wedding ritual predates the state's control of marriage. The history of control over marriage suggests that the residual customary and religious elements in the ceremony might provide imaginary ways out beyond the state's promotion of monogamous, enduring couplehood. Other scholars have concentrated on the continuities among these institutions of control, on the way that each succeeding institution takes over and modifies aspects of the previous one so that the meaning and function of contemporary marriage seems dependent on a synthesis of patriarchal, Christian, governmental, and capitalist aims. But I am actually interested in the *discontinuities* between these three domains—on the dissonance within the nuptial ceremony produced by what each historical moment has foregrounded as the definitive sign of a valid marriage, and on the question of whether and how these discontinuities might be worked against marriage law and toward a recalibration of social life as we know it. And importantly, the present form of the white wedding is thoroughly saturated with commodity capitalism. Though the wedding industry seems to promote heterosexuality and link romantic partnership to material plenty, it also partakes in capitalism's unmaking of the nuclear family, a process in which shopping, consuming, and advertising actually create constituencies that compete with family ties.[14] For these reasons, the wedding might have a more utopian or emancipatory place in theorizing about social change than marriage possibly could.

Something Old: On History

Why does the white wedding make the couple, especially the bride, look sacred and untouchable even as it puts them on an often embarrassing regulatory display? Why does it englobe the couple in mystique, and yet also seem to make them run a gauntlet of spectators and pass a series of tests? Why does the wedding seem to flaunt the sanctity of couplehood and yet also display competing social connections? Answers to some of these questions emerge from recent ethnographies of twentieth-century "Western-style" wed-

dings in Asian countries, which emphasize the wedding's function of coordinating Anglo-American and Asian notions of subjectivity and social embeddedness, a couple's "Western" romantic involvement with one another and
their "Eastern" status as emblems for a broader set of communal obligations.
For instance, the anthropologist Walter Edwards argues that the Japanese
"new style," commercialized white wedding does not stress the mystery and
privacy of the couple per se. Instead, when Japanese wedding planners appropriate the stylized, abstracted, and detachable parts of the commercialized
Anglo-American wedding, they enhance the Japanese ideal of every activity
and pose as a gestalt, a form detached from other activities, and therefore
complete in and of itself.[15] At the same time, these weddings suggest the
incompleteness of the individual, interrelatedness of human beings, and
necessity of social respectability. While bodily gestures and actions are detached and folded inward, in other words, subjectivity and couplehood are
folded outward and merged with a larger order. This paradox need not depend
on an opposition between East and West, though: one can see in *First Comes
Love*'s movement between spectacle and candid camera, between shimmery
long shots and close-ups of rear ends, yawns, and other unsanctioned moments, that the Western-style wedding itself coordinates the ideal of an inviolable inward subjectivity with that of an ongoing outward responsiveness to
the demands of an audience, the production of a private zone for the couple
with the establishment of public authority over marriage.

Anthropologists have also noted the ways that Asian weddings, particularly Western-style ones, combine commercialized icons of "modernity" and
those of invented national or local traditions, with the bride's body as the
scene for these mediations. For example, Ofra Goldstein-Gidoni describes the
contemporary urban Japanese wedding as a production of modern "Japaneseness," and Laurel Kendall calls its counterpart in Korea a "rite of modernization."[16] Yet oddly, in these and other analyses, "kinship" itself seems to remain beyond cultural change. Even when anthropologists use the wedding to
capture the way that a given social group negotiates broad cultural continuities and discontinuities, they often treat the ritual as a relatively stable and
straightforward index for the small-scale organization of humans through
marriage and reproduction: each role in the wedding is presumed to express
an ongoing, structurally significant relationship, as though the ritual's end
product were always the same.[17] But no wedding works as such a transparent
window onto the social structure. At the very least, even in the most ordinary

wedding, ephemeral identities and affinities are suddenly and momentarily visible: In the Anglo-American wedding these include the maid of honor, bridesmaid, flower girl, best man, usher, secular officiant, and so on. For most couples, these "extras" have no ongoing role or legal status beyond the ceremony; their functions do not carry into the future even to the same extent as other extralegal ties such as godparenthood or ritualized blood brotherhood. But they do provide glimpses of older models whereby the couple was both more formally supervised and enmeshed in larger kin and peer groups, and of possible futures in which dyadic partnership might be one unremarkable social form among many. In fact, as the disjunction between sound track and image track in Friedrich's film suggests, the wedding actually vacillates between restrictive and expansive visions of the social, between elevating the couple and displaying alongside them the very things that compete with couplehood—ties with extended kin, social and religious movements, friends.

This dynamic is a result of specific changes in the function and meaning of Anglo-American marriage: once a means of subordinating a couple's relationship to a larger social framework, marriage has become more and more a means of separating a couple from broader ties and obligations.[18] The wedding's contradictory restrictive and expansive, privacy- and publicity-making qualities, then, condense a millennium-long history of institutional and popular struggle for control over marriage in Western Europe and North America. To sketch this history simply and schematically, marriage has been regulated—and weddings officiated—by an overlapping sequence of institutions. Before the Christianization of Europe, fathers, families, and community customs regulated marriage, to be followed by priests and the church, then by magistrates and civil law, now inflected by a commercial industry, with the couple's authority over the formation of their own marriage waxing and waning alongside these institutions. Prior to the eleventh century, parents, and to a lesser extent the local lay community, supervised the courtship and betrothal process; the nuptial ritual involved friends as well. Shortly after the first millennium began, the Roman Catholic Church began to take control of marriage, first overriding parental prerogative by sanctioning the couple's authority to marry themselves and then installing the priest as the crucial officiant; the number of participants necessary to validate a wedding narrowed to the couple and perhaps a handful of others. During the Protestant Reformation of the sixteenth century, the English state usurped this control, though only its American colonies actually exercised total civic power over marriage. Protestant colonists in New England kept to small weddings, but widened the apparatus of supervision over betrothal and remanded this supervision to the provincial government. Beginning in the mid-nineteenth-century United States, state and eventually federal governments renewed their supervisory role over betrothal and marriage, and the ceremony expanded to include large numbers of lay witnesses.

Yet the wedding form did not necessarily change in complete isomorphic response to these shifts in authority. At any given historical moment, that is, the ritual itself contained residual elements that resisted or complicated the dominant institutional meanings and functions of marriage. This is partly what makes it so difficult to frame even the Western wedding as an object of analysis, for the defining elements and actors differ across time. The formula for a "proper," modern, Western-style wedding, even a secular one, is familiar: a special costume for the bride that distinguishes her from both her groom and attendants, a gathering of witnesses, a processional, some words from an officiant, an expression of consent spoken by the bride and groom, a joining of hands and/or exchange of rings, a kiss, a recessional, a reception, the couple's departure, and the giving of gifts. But with the possible exception of the couple's consent (and then only under certain conditions), no one of these things by itself makes a legal marriage, let alone a wedding. And several elements have historically specific, incommensurate meanings.

For instance, the modern bridal costume, processional, giving away of the bride, and postnuptial departure suggest the bride's movement from childhood to a kind of demi-adulthood, signaled by her transition from one guardian family to another and facilitated by other people as participants rather than mere spectators. This aspect of the wedding—the community's active role in "trafficking" a relatively passive bride from one place to another—is among the ritual's most archaic set of symbols.[19] To take a specific example from the West, the ancient Greek wedding focused on the bride's change in locale and status. According to historian John Boswell, it included sacrifices to Zeus and Hera, a ritual cleansing for the woman about to be married, and a banquet at her father's home. The groom and his best friend then transported the veiled bride, followed by chanting guests, to her new home, where she was brought to her bridal chamber and the marriage was consummated to the tune of attendants singing an epithalamium.[20] Preserving this sonic element, the oldest European popular ceremonies that followed always included public noisemaking to attract the community's attention to the marriage.[21] Early

Germanic law also privileged marriages contracted by bride-price (payment from the groom's family to that of the bride) and denied the legal power of husbands over wives in the case of marriages contracted by elopement without parental consent—both laws figuring the bride as the object of transfer. The preferred form of marriage included an agreement between the suitor and bride's guardian, and the public carrying of the bride to the head of the groom's family.[22]

In contrast to the betrothal, processional, and costuming that signal the bride's and to a lesser extent groom's subjugation to parental or communal sanction, the modern kiss, rings, and expression of mutual consent focus on the couple's lateral bond. These elements have their roots in Roman rites. The Roman bride, like her Greek predecessor, began with a feast in her father's home, exchanged her girlhood costume for another (a special tunic and belt, flame-colored veil, and garland of flowers), and proceeded to her new husband's house showered with nuts and perhaps other fertility symbols while serenaded with bawdy songs. But the costuming and processional elements were considered to be outward manifestations of the couple's consent rather than extensions of the betrothal gift exchange between parents.[23] The central act of the wedding took place in the interior space of the bride's natal home, among the couple's friends, relatives, and dependents, sometimes presided over by a priest. A Roman couple stated their consent to the marriage, after which their hands were joined by a third party, they kissed, and they signed an optional contract.[24]

The modern kiss, handclasp, and exchange of rings are also vestiges of pre-Christian notions that words were not enough to bind bodies to one another, that people could be magically linked by joining extensions of their own bodies such as tokens, locks of hair, or even "love bites."[25] The Anglo-Saxons, for instance, put these fleshly signs at the heart of their nuptial transactions. At the betrothal ceremony or *beweddung,* which some historians have argued was far more important than the nuptial ceremony itself, the elders consented to the match and fixed a bride-price, sealing the bargain with a drink and kiss.[26] At first, the father or household guardian himself regulated the wedding ritual, or *gifta,* transferring his authority to the husband by means of objects such as his mantle or sword.[27] Yet by the eleventh century, by which time Anglo-Saxon daughters had acquired more power to choose their husbands and betroth themselves, the payment went directly to the bride at the gifta, as provision for her widowhood. The Anglo-Saxon ritual for self-betrothal included the promise of this payment, sealed by the groom's giving his bride a straw, pieces of cloth, a glove, an arrow, or another object, until eventually verbal oaths, a handclasp, and the betrothal ring substituted for these tokens.[28]

Despite all these differences, the prominent feature of pre-Christian marriage in Western Europe was its status as a social entity created by families as opposed to a religious or legal one created by the church or state; where family law existed, it addressed the aftereffects of marriage—inheritance, the legitimacy of children, and so forth—rather than its instantiation. Parental and communal control also meant that the betrothal process could take precedence over the wedding ceremony itself. This process, in turn, was concrete and material, grounded in a set of corporeal and sensory gestures. The second prominent feature of pre-Christian marriage, then, was a certain porosity of the boundaries between nuptial bodies as well as between the marital union and its surrounding social context.

Early Christianity inherited these dramas of fleshly binding, along with a tangle of consensual signs and signs of acquiescence to communal and patriarchal prerogative—ritual elements signifying the couple's turn toward one another and those soliciting the participation of an outside audience. But because earthly marriage was considered a secular estate and concession to carnality, the early church did not associate itself with weddings very much. Celibacy, not marriage, was considered the highest form of religious life, and one gained salvation by ensuring that one was in the right relation to a broad religious community: a parish of people praying for one's soul, priest administering the sacraments, sphere of unseen fellow believers, and so on.[29] Religious wedding ceremonies appeared sporadically as early as the first century A.D., and the Eastern church made the wedding ritual a necessary condition for marital validity in the ninth century. Historians disagree, however, as to when the Western Christian church began to require a nuptial blessing, and in any case it never seems to have been required for a valid marriage.[30] When nuptial masses finally became standard sometime around the first millennium, the church incorporated some of the existing customary elements— namely, the giving of the ring, the handclasp, and the exchange of kisses. Still, it reduced them from transubstantial acts that were customarily thought to literally transform the flesh of participants to consubstantial ones with a merely symbolic value in religious terms, for marriage was not a sacrament for more than a millennium into Christianity.

Only beginning with the Council of Verona in 1184 did the church pay serious attention to who married whom, codifying incest law, restricting adoption, prohibiting divorce and remarriage after annulment or the death of one partner, and condemning the Hebrew practice of polygyny.[31] When the Catholic Church finally got around to taking control of the nuptial ritual itself, declaring it a sacrament at the Council of Trent, it diminished the power of bodily acts to "make" a marriage, focusing on its aspect as a spiritual estate analogous though subordinate to the relationship between Christ and church, and frowning on the customary exchange of corporeal tokens and fertility rituals that had structured older betrothals. Indeed, the central contribution of the church was to center the wedding on a single sentence: "I do." According to the canon laws formulated during the second century of the first millennium, a marriage was effected not through bodily binding but solely by the couple's verbal consent in the present tense, with or without witness or officiant. Until the mid–seventeenth century in western Europe and even afterward in England, any marriage effected by the verbal consent of both parties in the present tense (*sponsalia per verba praesenti*) was valid unless impeded by prior conditions—even if it took place without parental permission, publication of banns (notices declaring the couple's intent to marry), witnesses, officiating authorities, or subsequent consummation.[32] Even sexual intercourse itself was binding only if preceded by a promise to marry spoken in the future tense (*sponsalia per verba futuro*). The words "I do," for the first time, were actually capable of severing the couple's relationship to any former context, for they took precedence over both the parental supervision of betrothal and secular community's raucous involvement in the nuptial ritual, and their status as the sole test of validity stood in clear opposition to the secular authority of the father or guardian.[33] This may be why the insistence on a consensual model was accompanied by a strict doctrine, unprecedented in European culture, that marriage was indissoluble except by church dispensation. For a bride and groom whose sacramental marriage also figured the primacy of their own bond over that with their families of origin or local community might, if separated, find themselves with nowhere to go for financial support except church charities.

Paradoxically, while the new possibility of valid clandestine unions certainly affirmed the sacred and inward nature of the marriage bond, it also expressed the couple's entrance into a spiritual fraternity considered to be much wider and less exclusive than the secular family or local environs—one potentially even universal. The church's primary emphasis on celibacy did not make marriage a requirement for entry into the church community; on the contrary, priests and nuns were required to eschew earthly marriage. But the Christian theological validation of the couple's mutual consent, and the triangulation of their relationship to one another with a relationship to God and an expanding sphere of fellow Christians, did promote elective bonds over inherited ones. By conflating two people's enjoinment with their relationship to God and congregation, the wedding had the capacity to metaphorize the importance of expansive religious affiliations over exclusive patrilineage and a spiritual over property-based alliance—potentially even beyond the boundaries of heterosexuality. For instance, historian John Boswell has discovered that a weddinglike church ceremony was sporadically used in Europe between the eighth and sixteenth centuries to perform same-sex unions between men; these ceremonies inaugurated a collateral set of spiritual vows.[34] With the disappearance of this male-male wedding as a means of formalizing bonds between two people and their God, we have lost not so much the same-sex civil marriage rights sought by modern gay marriage advocates (as Boswell suggests) but a means of symbolizing a set of horizontal obligations and affinities that only begin with the couple, and in fact extend to a potentially infinite sphere of fellow human beings.

The church, then, put several different kinds of pressure on the patrilineal model of marriage as a joinder of two families' property. It demoted marriage except as a metonym for spiritual community, elevating the latter over ties to the paternal household. And beginning with its system of impediments, it also increasingly seized the lost prerogative of the household head to regulate marriage. While couples had long been able to choose a third party outside the family to conduct their wedding ceremony, between the tenth and twelfth centuries, priests began to arrogate this officiating role. The church developed elaborate rituals for solemnizing the nuptials and introduced the bridal mass. By the start of the thirteenth century in all of Christendom except England, the couple no longer married themselves in the mere presence of a priest but were actually united by him with the words, "I join you in the name of the Father, the Son, and the Holy Ghost."[35] (In England, despite the system of impediments and rise of priestly authority within the wedding, the church preserved its theological emphasis on mutual consent and private nuptials until the Protestant Reformation, whereupon even the English Catholic liturgy began to include the priest's statement that *he* joined them.)

From a secular apparatus of "alliance" that relays power through the channeling of wealth down family lines, then, the nuptial ritual was becoming an apparatus for the production of new kinds of people: sacred spouses whose ties to one another, a spiritual constituency, and the church superseded those to their earthly family. This occurred through the stimulation and management of their bodily sensations and emotional drives, as Christendom appropriated and transformed the meaning of the corporeal gestures of older rituals, and finally made the nuptial ceremony into a sacrament, both an index to and a reenactment of the relationship between Christ and the church. Christianity effected its power over marriage not only through its complicated and often-violated canonical laws of kinship but also through the visual, affective, and spiritual sensations and impressions that forged a sense of belonging across earthly territorial boundaries. The marriage sacrament both focused on and regulated the body; it both isolated the opposite-sex dyad and made it a point of entry into a community based on practice and beliefs rather than property. "Sacramentality," it might be said, was a precursor to the regime of sexuality that Foucault describes emerging in the eighteenth and nineteenth centuries: the Catholic reformulation of the marriage ritual during the early modern era may have been a crucial hinge between ancient patrilineal "alliance" and late modern "sexuality."[36]

The Protestant Reformation brought yet another shift in the meaning of marriage. Theologically, the central tenet of the Reformation was the individual's unmediated relation to God, in which salvation resulted from faith alone rather than the agency of priests and fellow worshipers. Just as early Christendom had recodified marriage so as to sunder the couple's relationship with their secular family, early Protestants reworked it to sunder the couple's relationship to the Catholic Church, their embeddedness within its spiritual fraternity, and their dependence on its network of economic relations that included tithes, usuries, and indulgences. Under Protestantism, monogamous marriage became a figure for and means of engendering a relationship with God that was not mediated by any human community, and a set of property relations that were, ideally, much less institutionally regulated than they had been under the Catholic Church. Just as in the Protestant theological model spiritual property was held by the individual unbeholden to the church, in its marital model material property was held by the individual unbeholden to a large network of tithes and charities. As Janet Jakobsen maintains, Protestant marriage doctrine effaced the interdependence of the couple and community, substituting the figure of the individual whose sole acknowledged social relation was with a spouse.[37] As if in keeping with this minimalist ideal of semiotic and churchly mediation, Protestants aimed to simplify and downplay the nuptial ritual itself. The English Protestant ceremony, for example, had no set liturgy. Prior to the wedding, banns were asked in the chancel, and the ceremony consisted of vows and rings exchanged before the church door accompanied by a priestly declaration, after which the newlyweds came before the altar and received a scriptural reading and priestly benediction.[38]

But though the Protestants used marriage as a figure for unmediated spiritual relations and means of fostering unmediated economic relations, and included priests in the wedding, they actually shifted the intervening apparatus of marriage from the church to state. Rather than merely advocating for a return to true self-marriage uncorrupted by priestly officiants, as one might expect, Protestant reformers in Wittberg and Geneva argued that civic officials and not priests should unite the couple, and exhorted the church to restore an element of publicity to marriage.[39] While the Catholic Church saw the secular family as its primary competition, then, Protestants saw it as a primary ally, an extension of and an analogy for the state's authority. They retooled the wedding as yet again an outwardly directed event, advocating parental consent, banns announcing the engagement or a private license exempting the banns, a ceremony performed outside the home, and postnuptial registration with a parish or county clerk. Finally, they used civil marriage as a reenactment of the covenant with God, which interlocked the subject with God and secular authorities including magistrates, masters, fathers, and husbands. In this sense, though Protestant marriage seemed to release its participants from a tangle of institutional mediations, it actually just embedded them in a new set: those of the secular state. And while this state certainly did not make salvation a matter of purchase, it also did not have the same set of economic obligations as the Catholic Church had had to members who failed to be economically self-supporting.

In 1533, when Henry VIII seized jurisdiction over marriage in England from the church, the whole of English marriage moved officially from church purview to that of the state. Shortly thereafter, the Council of Trent not only distilled Roman Catholic wedding theology but also yielded to the Protestants by advocating public weddings, priestly authority, banns, parental consent, and registration in local parishes.[40] Even as the Catholic Church began to accede to Protestant demands for publicity, however, English Protestant heads of state adhered more to Roman Catholic than continental Protestant doctrine. In 1559, Queen Elizabeth's First Parliament promulgated a revised Book of Common Prayer, which standardized the ceremony for the solemnization of matrimony; it called for banns, a wedding at the parish church, and a service including requests for objections, ritualized oaths of marriage, wedding rings, a priestly declaration that the couple were man and wife, Christ's warning that "what God has joined, let no man put asunder," blessings and prayers, homilies, and the Eucharist. But by the late 1500s, the publicity-making elements of these reforms had failed. English law followed Roman Catholic theology. The English courts distinguished between betrothal, marriage, and consummation; codified various impediments of consanguinity, affinity, or precontract; and considered the couple's verbal consent the sole requirement for a valid marriage rather than parental consent, testimony of witnesses, publication of banns, ceremony in church, or sexual consummation.[41]

Except for the years between 1653 and 1660, when Parliament made civil marriage first mandatory and then merely permitted, the view of marriage as a private, couple-centered transaction prevailed in England until the mid–eighteenth century. During this period, a few elements of the wedding assumed their modern form. In the 1500s, for instance, white became established as the color of maidenhood (though not uniquely of bridehood), and during the 1600s elaborately iced and marzipanned, hard-shelled cakes began to substitute for the breaking of bread or showering of grain over the bride's head that had once symbolized her fertility.[42] Bridal white emerged in England during the mid-1600s, initiating the long historical process of distinguishing the bridal body from that of both the groom and her female peers. In beginning to separate and enclose the bride's body, both literally by color and perhaps metonymically in the form of the hard white casing that now covered the grain cakes, popular weddings may have been symbolically acquiescing to the Catholic Church's earlier attempts to appropriate and spiritualize the more carnal meanings of the wedding's popular elements.[43] But conversely, they may have been symbolically resisting the church's view of marriage as a sacred lateral bond between relative equals. As a symbol of the bride's body, the cakes may have encoded residual views of marriage as a communally authorized transformation in the bride's status and locale, and eating the cakes may have symbolically preserved the ability of the community to participate in her fertility and the magic ability of bodies to bind. In other words, these customs probably both acknowledged emerging forms of control over marriage and reanimated prior ones.

Certainly, the increasing production of the bride's body as an emblem of secrecy, through dresses, cakes, and eventually veils, partook in a general "clandestination" of the wedding itself. For after the Restoration, which re-established the hegemony of the religious ceremony, private weddings prolif-erated in England: the rich frequently married at home by special license, and the poor went to Fleet Street to be married in quick ceremonies.[44] In 1753, Parliament proclaimed the Hardwicke Act for the Better Preventing of Clan-destine Marriage, which required parental consent for minors under twenty-one, banns, and nuptials in an Anglican church for all British subjects except Jews and Quakers. The act thereby discriminated explicitly against Catholics and Protestant reformists, who were forced to adopt Anglican rituals, as well as against the poor, who were forced to pay church tithes.[45] Only with the Hardwicke Act did the English state adhere to a Protestant vision of marriage as a matter of public regulation—though marriages contracted by solely civil ceremonies were not valid until 1837. In response to the act, many English people went to Scotland's Gretna Greene for cheaper weddings, intensifying the view of marriage as a private, even secret arrangement. If the objects that have come to exemplify the modern wedding—veils and white dresses, pale flowers and satin slippers, rings and three-tiered cakes—now have a sense of secular as well as religious mystery, this may be partly a result of the British clandestine tradition.

In colonial New England, though, the dissenting Separatists and Puritans insisted from the first moment of settlement that marriage was solely a civil matter, a merely honorable estate rather than the holy one it had come to be described as in the Anglican Church. They objected strenuously to the Angli-can priestly officiant as well as the use of rings and communion and many of the popular secular rituals that preceded and followed the nuptial ceremony. Reemphasizing both the supervised betrothal process and the public nature of the marriage ceremony, many New England colonies required parents to convey their consent to the town or county clerk, the magistrate to post banns or issue a license from the governor and to solemnize the union, witnesses to appear, and the town or country clerk to register the marriage.[46] The cere-mony itself was vastly diminished: throughout the colonial period, most brides simply married in their best clothes, in their natal home, speaking simple words of consent before a justice of the peace (see figure 1).

Fig. 1. "The Country Wedding, engraved after Krimmel's painting," *Analectic Magazine* (Philadelphia), new series, vol. 1 (February 1820). Courtesy of American Antiquarian Society.

But in 1686, the laws that required civil marriage in Massachusetts were overturned and church solemnization was permitted in New England, as it had always been in the Anglican southern colonies. From the second Puritan generation until about the mid–nineteenth century, the courts that regulated marriage actually interfered minimally with it. Betrothal, ceremonial form, and even the validity of marriages were matters of custom and community supervision. Even banns dropped out of use by the eighteenth century.[47] The glaring exception to this governmental noninterference was the fact that when English colonists transformed the indenture system into a condition of lifelong slavery for Africans brought over to work, they preserved the rule that servants, being property, could not marry.[48] Whereas this law had simply delayed the age of marriage among the indentured, it reduced the enslaved black population to a condition of official kinlessness—to enforced reproduction without the ability to transmit names, property, or socially recognized family roles to their offspring. The laws against slave marriage developed into a prohibition of marriage between even free blacks and Englishpeople beginning in the southern colonies in the 1660s, with no precedent in English common law.[49]

Among blacks and other non-indigenous groups alike, though, colonial and early national weddings remained affairs between couples and ministers or justices of the peace (who often officiated at slave weddings). Marriages were frequently validated by communal recognition of a long-standing tie, which translated into legal status for every couple except enslaved ones—often including, until Emancipation, interracial couples.[50] In some ways, the de facto common-law system in the colonial and early republican United States looked more like the Catholic doctrine of mutual consent and self-ministry than like the English Protestant one of state-sponsored publicity. Governmental regulation of marriage in the United States intensified only in the mid–nineteenth century. At that point, the United States reestablished jurisdiction over marriage by reviving the policing function that banns had once had, developing a series of prenuptial tests that would determine the fitness of the couple to marry, and conflating fitness to marry with access to citizenship.[51] The first test was the patriotic loyalty of the wife. Beginning in 1855 with laws that insisted that a foreign woman's nationality would follow that of her U.S. husband, the federal government began to make marriage into a central technology of women's membership in the nation. In 1907, the U.S. wives of male noncitizens were automatically expatriated: women with unruly desire for "foreigners" were considered expendable citizens. Eventually, the laws that joined a wife's citizenship to her husband's were made gender neutral, resulting in the modern system whereby spouses of all U.S. citizens are automatically given preferential access to citizenship.[52] But the cultural production of wifehood as the female form of patriotic loyalty lasted at least through World War II, as I shall discuss in chapter 2 using Carson McCullers's *The Member of the Wedding*, a novel in which a young girl struggles to invent a relationship to her country without getting married.

2. The second set of tests focused on race. After Emancipation, the federally funded Freedmen's Bureau pushed African Americans into wage work and registered marriages—policies that aimed to reduce the state's support of impoverished ex-slaves by making individual families responsible for the maintenance of their dependents. Embedded in this essentially economic program was the question of whether African Americans could prove themselves suitable for U.S. citizenship. They could do so, the bureau argued, by embracing the family form of a male breadwinner who supported his dependent wife and children.[53] Simultaneously, as African Americans gained the ability to accrue and augment property, both African American and Euroamerican people were prohibited from marrying across racial boundaries and thereby "mixing" property. The U.S. states expanded, strengthened, and more regularly enforced state laws against interracial marriage—laws that were not overturned in many states until 1967.[54] The racialization of marriage subtends Chapter 3, where I explore William Faulkner's *Absalom, Absalom!*, a novel in which an African American man and white Euramerican woman separately struggle to imagine a connection that does not reinscribe the asymmetrical, legal taxonomies of race.

3. The third test was monogamy: in the 1860s, the U.S. government made couplehood the official sexual form of the United States by outlawing polygamy, a prohibition that continues to this day. Indeed, Utah gained statehood in 1896 only after the Mormon Church explicitly repudiated polygamy. The constitution of monogamy as the official kinship form of the United States enters into chapter 4 through Nathaniel Hawthorne's "The May Pole of Merry-Mount" and Joseph Kirkland's *Zury*, two texts in which lawful marriage threatens to collapse under covenantal and economic pressures that look suspiciously like polygamy.

By the early twentieth century, marriage was tied to the reproduction of a physically healthy population through state laws requiring tests for venereal disease and restricting marriage between blood relatives.[55] It also became a sign of legal adulthood through laws increasing the age of consent, a concern that I will take up in chapter 5 by examining a series of "perverse honeymoons" between adult male would-be citizens and little "native" child brides from Edgar Allan Poe to Vladimir Nabokov. During the first half of the twentieth century, marriage became the matrix for a system of federal taxation and the distribution of these resources in welfare, social security, and other benefits.[56] And most recently, by explicitly prohibiting same-sex marriage in the Defense of Marriage Act of 1996, the federal government has added heterosexuality to its official requirements for the monogamous couplehood that it had already installed as the legally recognized form of sexual intimacy. In fact, the Puritan regulation of civil marriage reappears in the modern treatment of marriage as a government-sponsored initiative for several things: the subsumption of women's entitlements into the household structure, maintenance of opposite and incommensurate racial categories, differential access to citizenship and/or social services, privileging of physically healthy people, and heterosexual supremacy. Having passed one or more of these tests, an engaged couple is given a license and left to wed more or less as it will, though the newlyweds must also register the marriage after the ceremony.

During the same mid- to late-nineteenth-century period when marriage was legally connected to race, nationality, monogamy, and physical health, the white wedding became standard in the United States. Not only had alabaster become the firmly established color for U.S. bridal gowns but rings of betrothal, attendants distinguished from other audience members by age, costume, and physical placement had come into fashion, veils made a comeback from earlier times, and new symbols like orange blossoms and double rings took hold. But do these elaborate trappings merely perform ideological dirty work in the service of marriage law, which has historically extended material privileges to relationships between no more than two bodies that are racially and nationally alike, physically healthy, and sexually opposite? Or do they resist or complicate this work?

Given that state control over marriage is relatively recent, and that the state has been relegated to the temporal outskirts of the actual wedding ceremony—the granting and signing of the license—the wedding ritual is more than just a tool of the state. Far from being reactionary, the vestigial religious and popular aspects of the modern U.S. wedding may reveal certain lines of flight beyond the social imagination of marriage law. For instance, several of

the wedding's religious elements I have described here (vows, the triangulation with God, priestly blessings) are a reminder that Christianity has many
antifamilial aspects. Perhaps this explains why *First Comes Love,* made by a
Jewish director, dwells so lavishly on the highly solemn, apparently Italian
Catholic nuptial ritual. Likewise, several of the wedding's popular or "folk"
aspects (rings, kisses, handclasps, garter throws, and bouquet tosses) express
the unruly physical body and call attention to relationships among friends
and neighbors—the specificities and attachments that individuals are supposed to forsake as they become citizens in a democratic nation-state. This
may account for *First Comes Love*'s use of the minor child and minority sound
track to register the presence in the wedding of those not quite "liberated"
from their bodies, to suggest the bride's carnality, and to record small-scale
attachments between people. Finally, the wedding's most "commercial" aspects (standard costumes, gift registries, souvenirs, honeymoon tours) create
social constituencies that actually de-center the couple form. That is, even as
the rhetoric and imagery of mass culture seem to promote heterosexual couplehood, its strategies of address and distribution bring other social possibilities to the fore.

Something New: Commodity Culture and the Wedding Form

The sound track of *First Comes Love*—not only its pop songs but "Here Comes
the Bride" itself—also registers the fourth and most recent institution that
now gives the wedding definitive form: the commodified world of retail goods
and mass media. The standard white wedding, consolidated during the same
period that the U.S. state took full control over marriage, is profoundly a
product of capitalism—and not solely, or even primarily, a collection of residual sacramental enthusiasms. The veiled bride in a white satin dress,
attendants in matching dresses, rings and bouquets, special music, and such
penumbral minidramas as showers, bachelor parties, large receptions, wedding gifts from people outside the immediate family, and a honeymoon, date
in the United States from the 1830s and onward. Before this period, middle-
class weddings were simple affairs, usually conducted in the home, unmarked by stereotypical costumes, and often planned as little as a week be-
forehand.[57] But by the end of the nineteenth century, most couples in the
United States followed a complicated cultural script including rituals of betrothal, special events such as showers and receptions, a white bridal gown

and veil along with specially costumed attendants, the giving and displaying of substantial gifts rather than just tokens, and a honeymoon. These changes were more than just an effect of marketing.[58] They registered fundamental changes in the relationship between intimate ties and economic production.

Two historians, John Gillis and Ellen Rothman, have connected the rise of the big white wedding to shifts in the economic and affective functions of couplehood relative to a larger network of kin and neighbors. For Gillis, who looks at England, the couple form became more ideologically central as it became more economically and affectively insular.[59] Aiming to distinguish themselves from both aristocrats and plebeians, both of whose weddings were big public affairs, the nascent middle classes of the early modern era held small ceremonies emphasizing the separation of the couple from their peers and natal family. By the mid–nineteenth century, the middle-class English wedding was marked by new aspects—the white dress, veil, honeymoon, father giving away the bride—that marked both the emotional seclusion of married love and highly polarized gender roles that enabled the marital couple to function as the smallest possible economic unit. But even the English lower classes eventually gave the big wedding up; poorer people's "little weddings" were an expression of their declining ability to form the broad, open households that had made big public weddings both necessary and possible. Only in the mid–twentieth century did the poorer classes "take back" the big wedding, using it to dramatize the inadequacy of nuclear couplehood. Even then, working-class people eschewed many aspects of the white wedding, especially the giving away of the bride. Groups for whom marital insularity is an impossible economic and emotional ideal, Gillis argues, still tend to use the modified big wedding to express and strengthen the ties necessary to sustain the couple.

Rothman and Gillis agree that the white wedding is an expression of middle-class ideology, but they differ in their interpretations of the big wedding. Looking at the United States, Rothman sees the large public wedding rather than the small private one as a means of consolidating middle-class domesticity. In her view, in the early-nineteenth-century United States, the rise of romantic ideology and the fall of parental consent laws and banns worked to relegate "courting" to the couple's discretion, separate engagement from the wedding proper, and exclude local clergy, kin, and neighbors from the process of betrothal. The latter people's participation was relocated and restricted to the ceremony itself, whose pageantry expanded to accommodate them. As the significance and function of extended family, friends, and neigh-bors waned, and that of nuptial couplehood waxed, Rothman contends, U.S. weddings actually grew bigger. Not only did the supposedly self-sufficient couple need a more elaborate and ritualized process to achieve the sealed-off mutuality that domestic ideology promoted; they also needed more material goods to set up the idealized household it celebrated. Among the middle classes, the big wedding acknowledged the larger community only briefly in order to launch the couple into economic and emotional autonomy: the "pub-lic" wedding now served an essentially privatizing function. By the mid–twentieth century, the big wedding, marked by mandatory gift giving and the presence of extended family, friends, and business associates, substituted the exchange of commodities for the forging of lasting emotional, physical, and financial obligations between unrelated people beyond the couple. As if both to compensate for and enforce the couple's newfound autonomy, the middle-class big wedding now constitutes not only the larger community's witness-ing and blessing of the nuptials but also the limiting of their participation in what follows. According to Rothman, "Young people [can] expect help in *getting* married—more help, in fact, than their grandparents had received—but once married, they [are] on their own."[60]

However they differ, both analyses reveal that the theological dialectic I described earlier—between patrilineal versus sacramental weddings in the Middle Ages, and between sacramental versus civil weddings in the early modern period—has been complicated by an economic dialectic between the wedding's privatizing and collectivizing functions, especially during the nine-teenth and twentieth centuries. In my view, the contemporary wedding indus-try, even as it seems to ideologically promote exclusive relationships, also produces expansive ones, although not quite in the terms either historian suggests: the field that the industry connects the couple to is not coextensive with their local acquaintances but rather traverses and moves beyond them. As soon as banns read in churches or posted in town halls gave way to wed-ding announcements printed in newspapers, brides could compare them-selves to other brides whom they had not met; wedding announcements, in a sense, created the first imagined community of brides.[61] Similarly, ladies' magazines of the antebellum era and beyond offered women access to images of bridehood and a sense of membership in an unseen collectivity (see figure 2). As the Euramerican wedding was increasingly standardized by the ex-panded production of wedding etiquette books, magazine lithographs and engravings, costume patterns and eventually ready-to-wear gowns, the bride's body was also genericized into an infinitely reproducible "type," substitutable for and linked to other brides. This is particularly evident in figure 3, which captures a pose that became popular in the wedding photography of the 1880s: rather than standing in isolation, the bride looks at a mirror that multiplies her image, an effect made even more dramatic by the photograph's printing in stereoscope format. The bride's female attendant is also included in this multiplication; she is both structurally necessary to the wedding and herself a potential bride. A scene that looks like a subject's induction into the gender normativity created by the heterosexual dyad, refracts into a proliferation of images and social connections between women.[62]

With a similar effect of proliferating bridehood and women's culture, "Bride's Rooms" or consulting salons in major department stores emerged in urban centers in the late nineteenth century, giving brides at least a theoretically communal gathering place (though in actuality, they hid the bride from view and brides from one another). It was with the rise of a national wedding industry itself—the second "wedding complex" registered by the title of this book—that the horizons of feminine sociability most dramatically refused to neatly close down once the bride got married and the wedding's clandestine elements were undermined even as they were rhetorically fostered. When *Bride's Magazine* was founded in 1934, retailers could finally advertise and distribute goods and services relating to the wedding in a centralized way across the nation. Initially called *So You're Going to Be Married!* and distributed free to women whose wedding announcements appeared in the society pages of New York, Connecticut, and New Jersey, the magazine changed its name and went national in 1936.[63] Like all mass-circulated products, *Bride's* constructed the new collectivity it purported to address and encouraged commodity-mediated ties extending beyond the natal family or conjugal unit. In the second issue, editor in chief Agnes Foster Wright stated that "in this issue we step out before a new audience. We hope you, the Bride, will applaud our initial performance because it delights, enchants, and satisfies you." Indeed, the word "Bride" was always capitalized in *Bride's,* as if to call this new consumer identity by a brand-new proper name. "Notice to Brides: No groom's cellar is complete without these fine old pre-prohibition whiskies," ran one liquor ad, while another hailed the bride more personally: "Do you, Doris, promise to care for this man in the style to which he is accustomed?" In a give-and-take process quite different from the unidirectional

Fig. 2. Wedding dress. Plate for
Cotton's Athaneum, 1829. Courtesy
of American Antiquarian Society.

Fig. 3. Bride and attendant. Found photograph, ca. 1880. Gift to the author from the personal collection of Molly McGarry.

prescriptions of earlier wedding etiquette books, brides were encouraged to share their experiences in such columns as "Brides Tell Us"—even as they were also urged to regulate these same experiences through the use of pullout "Bride's Reference Books," mail-order how-to "Booklets for the Bride," and charts on honeymoons detailing "Where to Go," "What to Pack," "What to Do," and "What to Buy."[64] This reciprocity and collectivity-building function is typical of magazine culture. But it is rather contradictory in a journal that was designed expressly to tell women how to leave peer culture behind and become part of an insular domestic couple.

Bridal magazines also expanded the bride's liminality—her suspension on the threshold between daughter and wife—into a form of more subversive sublimity. Within their pages, the bridal threshold became rather more of a theatrical platform, giving a woman a means of extended self-display and an identity beyond daughter or wife. Writing of "the Bride's Halo," one editor at *Bride's* claimed that "a Bridal veil seems like an inheritance from the saints. At no moment of her life does a Bride look so divine—so heavenly—so near celestial—as at the moment of her wedding," while another advocated that attendants dressed in jewel-toned frocks "set off the white Bride as a stained glass window does a Madonna." Bridehood was even linked to the visual production of celebrity: "The Bride is the central figure on this day of days," wrote one commentator. "Everything around her is the frame that sets her off and enhances her. As the focal point in the picture she must be at her love-liest." Another warned that "though you are the star performer, you can't carry the show without some support from the chorus."[65]

The bridal magazine, then, is paradigmatic of two aspects of capitalism. The first is the paradox whereby the rhetoric of consumer culture seems to idealize the nuclear household, while the conditions of capitalist produc-tion—the separation of men's and women's workplaces along with the rise of leisure activities outside the home—actually contest the dominance of the domestic nuclear family form. Even the modern lingerie showers that focus on equipping the bride for marital intimacy, for instance, not only bring groups of women together to shop and bond but also foster liaisons and gender performances that may expand the terrain of what "woman" means for participants.[66] The second is the paradox of consumerist self-making: by collaborating, in both senses of the word, with a production process rather more like the Fordist system for manufacturing automobiles and Taylorist system for disciplining the body of the worker, the bride actually gains access to a new kind of personhood and sense of connection to other such persons.[67] Changes in the groom's costuming are relevant to this process, too: as the bride's outfit became less and less like that of her bridesmaids, the groom also faded into the background, dressing more and more like his attendants as the nineteenth century progressed. Within the twentieth-century wedding industry as well, the groom became increasingly irrelevant as the wedding became a more and more lush means for both the remaking of the female body and for feminine expressivity. This process could be imaginatively continued as long as a woman chose to read bridal magazines—or more recently, to view her wedding video over and over again, go to wedding-themed movies, and buy products promoted with wedding imagery.

In turn, the commodities that bridal magazines promoted promised to extend the aura of bridehood and coupledom to all of the wedding's participants and witnesses. The personalized wedding souvenirs of napkins, matchbooks, cocktail stirrers, place cards, all imprinted with the couple's name, that appeared in the pages of *Bride's* during the 1950s and thereafter, allowed the guests to ritualistically consume couplehood, to carry it with them even after they left the reception. The visual "rhymes" that the wedding magazines increasingly insisted on—the expectation that the wedding party will all wear the couple's "official colors," the flower girls dressed as miniature brides, the guests seated in color-coordinated pews—installed bride and groom, family, attendants, and guests into a totalizing wedding world. In fact, for some women, the wedding has clearly come to signify self-completion, self-extension, and world-making even in the absence of a groom. As Reebok puts it in an advertisement for women's exercise equipment, "I take me, to have and to hold, from this day forward, for better or for worse, for richer, for poorer, in sickness and in health, to love and to cherish, till death do us part, so help me, god." The advertisement finishes with a spin on the slogan of Reebok's closest competitor, Nike: not "Just Do It" but "I Do" (see figure 4).

Something Borrowed: Performance Theory, or "Do What?"

I will return to the relationship between "Just Do It" and "I Do" in a moment. But first, a detour through "I do." J. L. Austin's *How to Do Things with Words* uses the marriage vow, " 'I do (sc. take this woman to be my lawful wedded wife'),", to exemplify performative language—language that *does* what it *says*, or inaugurates the state it seems merely to denote.[68] "I do," however, inaugu-

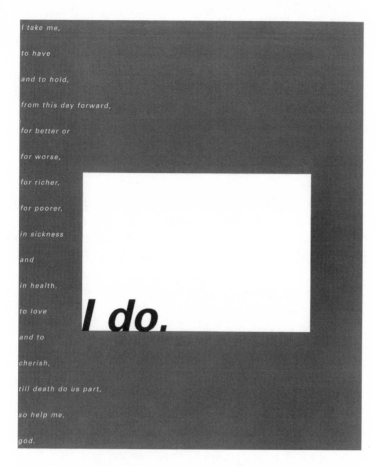

Fig. 4. "I Do," Reebok print advertisement, 1996. Reprinted by permission of Reebok International.

*Marriage
as
privileged
Subjectivity*

rates not only a marriage but a privileged form of subjectivity itself. As Eve Sedgwick suggests, lawful marriage, with its perquisites and privileges, its tacit and taken-for-granted nature, incarnates a stable subject whose very personhood ("I") and activities ("do"-ings) have been authorized by the state and bolstered by the logic of opposite-but-complementary masculinity and femininity.[69] Yet Sedgwick also observes that Austin repeatedly uses "I do" and "I now pronounce you" to demonstrate the possibility of infelicitous or unhappy performativity, of nullification caused by extenuating circumstances. In Austin, that is, the marital performance continually misfires (the couple is already married, the officiant who pronounces the marriage valid is not qualified to do so, the words themselves are merely an illustration for a concept, and so on). Why, Sedgwick rightly asks, does the central act of the wedding ceremony, repeated over and over again, actually seem to ward off the possibility of their speaker's ending up married? Why, I would add, does even the work of the *verbal* performance that is supposed to minimally secure marriage seem to be destabilized rather than reinforced by the semiotic performance of the wedding?

As I have argued, one reason is that the wedding's less remarkable, not-necessarily-verbal aspects tend to proliferate connections between people that would be illicit if they were to become sexual, and multiply possible subject positions. The wedding's linkage of commodities (through monogramming, for one) and bodies (through the duplication of brides with one another, flower girls as embryonic brides, guests coordinated by color and spatial arrangement) is a form of visual metonymy, connecting what was heretofore unconnected. In this sense, "I Do" is very like "Just Do It" insofar as "Just Do It" translates into a dare: both "I do" and "I dare you," as Sedgwick argues, are sanctioned by compelled witnesses; they depend on and constitute a public of witnesses that acts as an accomplice to the scene before it. Yet this public may not wish or be able to boil itself down to couplehood.

Another crucial reason that the wedding may destabilize "I do" has to do with the wrinkles in time evident in *First Comes Love*. The wedding purports to emplot bodies into linear time, to represent an unbroken chain of causal events continuing into an unchanged future: the flower girls will grow up to be brides, the couple were always meant for each other, this wedding recapitulates that of every married guest in the room and anticipates those of the unmarried ones, and so forth. Nevertheless, this doubled temporality—the self-conscious alignment of the present with prior moments on the model of allegory—contains the seeds of its own destruction. For the past is always radically Other. In contrast to the linguistic performative, which can only work by citing a past authority whose historical contingency it always aims to conceal, a ritual adorns bodies with the signs of disparate historical moments, putting them on display in incoherent relation to one another, calling their predictive or causal relationship into question.

Let me work through the necessary historicism of embodied performance by way of Judith Butler's theories of the relationship between performance and subjectivity. Connecting the linguistic performative to the gendered meaning of the human body, Butler has demonstrated that the repetitive everyday gestures of masculinity and femininity actually do what they purport to say, or create the psychic states they claim only to express. One of the several ways she arrives at this conclusion is to question the linear, unidirectional narrative sequence of gendered "development," in which the body's anatomy supposedly causes the corresponding gender role, and both anatomy and role then compel a heterosexual object choice. In contrast, for Butler, the performance of ordinary gender is actually narratively retroactive: the institution of heterosexuality comes first, and demands that subjects embody opposite and complementary gender roles; the enactment of these roles finally creates the illusion of naturally sexed bodies, core gender identities, and authenticating, originary, ahistorical states of "manhood" or "womanhood."[70] Thus, to dramatize identity as "performative" through the parodic theatrics of cross-dressing—drag—is also to disrupt this narrative sequence, to reveal that the "natural fact" of anatomical sex, a gendered sense of self, and even the supposedly universal categories of man and woman are not prior or primary essences but belated constructions, the aftereffect of repeated activities enforced by compulsory heterosexuality.

One thing that Butler's work might reveal about weddings, then, is how not only ordinary gender but dyadic couplehood itself is the effect rather than the cause of the wedding ritual, and how parodic overperformance of the sort enacted by Sulka or at the mass marry-in, or even more earnest representations such as that of Arjie or Friedrich, might reveal the psychic and historical contingency of monogamous love. While this seems theoretically plausible, it also seems to me that a politics of contingency has its own disadvantages, for calling into question the authority and originary status of any past threatens to efface the use of alternative pasts as a catalyst for possible futures as well. In contrast to the futuristic emphasis of *Gender Trouble*, Butler's later work allows for a consideration of the uses to which the historically sedimented quality of the wedding ritual might be put. For in *The Psychic Life of Power*, Butler suggests that ordinary masculinity and femininity not only metaleptically create the past but evacuate its specific forms by suppressing prior patterns of attachment and social being. Initially, this suggestion registers only in psychoanalytic terms: in a description of gender as fundamentally melancholic, Butler argues that a manly man preserves a prohibited, unmourned-for, prior homosexual love for his father in the form of his own present-tense masculine self-presentation; the manly man is "the archaeological remainder . . . of unresolved grief."[71] Drag, Butler claims, performs a certain kind of historicist genealogy, disinterring the lost object of attachment. She writes that drag "allegorizes" the process by which the disavowed love object becomes the source of gendered identity (perhaps the most obvious example of this is the way traditional gay male drag inscribes the mother's forbidden body onto the son's).[72]

But for the forbidden love object to be incorporated into the psyche as identity, and inscribed onto the flesh as properly gendered embodiment, its historical alterity must be evacuated: a man cannot turn the historically specific man he once desired into the form of his own body without looking slightly costumed, slightly theatrical, slightly less than manly. If allegory is the right word to describe the process by which drag exposes the melancholic aspect of gendered identity, then this is because the narrative mode of allegory works by keeping at least two disparate temporal levels visible, indeed, by putting a historically prior story into distorting competition with a present one.[73] A crucial kind of play with history, therefore, keeps drag shows from devolving into simple instances of "passing" to an unknowing audience: performers often wear an archaic form of gender on the present-tense body in the form of a fading or obsolete celebrity. During the 1960s, for example, many drag queens imitated Bette Davis; the early Madonna makes for amusing drag these days. As expressions of alternative masculinities, female theatrical cross-dressers (drag kings) have invested in exhausted icons such as David Bowie, Jerry Falwell, and LL Cool J.[74]

The "drag" in drag, then, is also temporal. Not only does drag disrupt the causal logic whereby anatomy determines role and desire; it also marks the body with signs that the meanings of "manhood" and "womanhood" are themselves historically contingent, and revives archaic gender forms to question the coherence of present ones. It is certainly plausible that "bride" might

allegory

work in a similar way not only for male-to-female transgender people like Sulka and perhaps Arjie but also for high femmes, precisely because it reanimates a fading model of (perhaps prefeminist) femininity as the means for contesting the dominant one. If "archaeological" can describe the residual presence of a renounced or foreclosed love object on the body itself, this is because not only the objects but the very cultural legibility of certain *kinds* of attachment is subject to violent foreclosure and erasure. Drag might be seen as a gesture toward lost kinship systems, imagined or real bygone patterns of exchange, dwelling, promising, and so on. In this sense, weddings in even their most earnest mode may fascinate those of us whose (trans?)genderism tilts toward excess femininity precisely because "bridehood" ornaments the contemporary female body with the signs of an era in which bonds between women, however desexualized, had greater cultural visibility.

Butler animates a genuinely archaeological theory of performance in her consideration of kinship in *Antigone's Claim*, where her focus on the performativity of gendered norms gives way to a consideration of a "family ritual" that productively disaggregates the present—in this case, a funeral that ends up as a wedding. Forbidden by the king to bury her slain brother, Antigone does so not once but twice, repeating the ritual, and then hangs herself in her family tomb with her bridal veil. Her verbal refusal to deny that she has buried her brother installs her into the legal apparatus as a criminalized subject. But the burial and her own wedding/funeral address and re-create a public realm other than the state—her dead ancestors and the chorus—within which her complicated, perhaps incestuous relation to her brother registers as a possibility not realized in or as "culture." Rather than preserving the prior, "prepolitical" sphere of kinship, as some critics have argued, Butler shows that Antigone disrupts the status of exogamy itself as the founding rule of culture.[75]

Though Butler does not use this phrase, it seems to me that with this use of the wedding/funeral ritual, *Antigone* allegorizes social melancholy, or a response to the process by which culture forecloses the possibility and even intelligibility of certain attachments as signs of the social. Antigone's nuptial tomb reverses the usual trope wherein a wedding becomes a funeral: it turns a funeral into Antigone's own wedding where, anticipating the bride of Frankenstein, she marries a collection of dead bodies. These bodies represent the extended family whom the laws of incest, especially once they have been expanded by the Christian church, will render increasingly impossible as

exogamy – take a wife outside of clan

objects of sexual desire. But her "wedding" to them also binds her both to multiple object choices and a "dead" or foreclosed social field. Rather than an example of the preservation of tradition, or the Bakhtinian "carnivalesque," a set of reversals that expose the limits of an official structure by parodying them, Antigone's act is a reversal that opens up an effaced, disavowed, or simply never-realized social field.[76]

It is this potential both to allegorize social melancholy and undo it precisely through the allegorical mode that I want to bring out in the wedding itself. That is, the alternative kinship systems or unofficial ties that marriage repudiates are actually congealed within the wedding ritual, not just in the haunting presence of repudiated Others in the form of bridesmaids and groomsmen but also flashing out in the play of customary signs against religious ones, religious signs against the apparatus of the civic sphere, all of these against the detritus of consumer culture, and so on. The wedding's often unintentional layering of anachronistic, incommensurate institutional and popular meanings suggests that the couple form is not inevitable—that, say, populist, religious, or capitalist "bonds" might actually contest kinship as we know it. While "I now pronounce you" cites a fictively coherent prior authority so as to secure a predictable future, then, the other more jumbled elements of the wedding ritual might detonate various lost pasts upward as the material for disrupting the present meaning of marriage.

Something Red, White, and Blue: On "America"

Finally, there is the question of why I track the wedding in U.S. cultural texts. As a form, doesn't it have a far longer history than this country and exist more cross-culturally than a focus on the United States can do justice to? Isn't the "ethnic" wedding in the United States a sign of belonging to a minoritized history, region, or religion, and the standard Anglo-American white wedding (whose participants tend not to recognize it as in any way specific) of belonging to that phantasm called "Western culture"? Don't both forms rather self-consciously elide the official nation? With the exception of the military ceremony and White House nuptial, when do weddings ever reference U.S. national culture per se?

More often than one might guess. Indeed, many U.S. texts that include the wedding—Anglo-American, "ethnic," or some combination—suggest that the ceremony itself is a portal both to national belonging and to other technologies of membership that exist alongside or even counter to those of the official nation. On one hand, the contractual, consensual aspects of U.S. citizenship seem to be perfectly figured by the voluntary submission of bride to groom, and the couple to domestic laws. For instance, the Ukranian orthodox wedding that constitutes the first half hour of *The Deer Hunter* (dir. Michael Cimino, 1978) seems to enact that town's metamorphosis from Eastern European to Ukranian American, local to national identification, kin- to state-based forms of membership. It is as if in this long wedding the town marries the nation, and then its young men, having achieved proper citizenship, go on a typically transcultural nightmare honeymoon to tropical Vietnam.

The use of a wedding to figure the incarnation of a polis has a long history in cultural representations of "America." What Doris Sommer argues about Latin American romances is also true of U.S. rhetoric about itself: "Eros and Polis are the effects of each other's performance."[77] In Puritan theology, the marital covenant between husband and wife also reinstantiated two interlaced ethical covenants: one between God and God's people, and another between magistrates and those whom they governed.[78] The latter would also be naturalized by the covenant between the husband and any children who resulted from this marriage; the birth of these children on U.S. soil seemed to make colonial authority over other native-born populations into a natural fact, too. The state thus authorized itself by sanctioning a particular kind of love. In turn, from as far back as John Winthrop's "Modell of Christian Charity," and later in the familial language of the American Revolution's rhetoric, "love" seemed to generate and sustain a particular kind of political engroupment, in which membership would be a matter of choice rather than coercion.[79] Hence, especially in the nationalist nineteenth century, literary and visual representations of the Puritan civil wedding—often between Pocahontas and John Smith or John Alden and Priscilla Mullins—seemed to emblematize the founding of an "America" distinct both from England and Native homelands.

Yet as I shall explore in chapter 4, where I examine a pair of nineteenth-century texts that use the Puritan civil wedding to connect the United States to its colonial past, the Puritan doctrine of civil, covenantal marriage actually haunts depictions of "founding" weddings. If the state must preapprove, witness, and record a marriage, it cannot thereby be founded by that same marriage. On the other hand, if the state is brought into being by a marriage, then the marriage that founds it is by the Puritan definition illegitimate, and the polity is actually founded on a sacrament, mere custom unregenerated by consent, or something even more sinister.[80] In other words, if Eros and polis are each effects of the other's performance, neither the foundation of marriage nor that of the nation can be guaranteed. Since the legacy of civil marriage that seems to make the wedding emblematize the beginning of the United States also undermines this very same project, the formation of a polis might be figured better by a religious or customary wedding. As *The Deer Hunter* shows, however, to take up popular and religious ceremonies is also to mobilize visions of affinity and belonging that actually contest the monogamous dyadic couple form through which the state reproduces itself, and question the way that the citizen is supposed to choose his or her country above all other social obligations. For the religious and popular aspects of this film's wedding constitute more than just fading folk "traditions" acceding to national "modernity," or the regime of kinship competing with that of democratic citizenship. They also suggest melancholic attachments to social forms that might contest the primacy of nationhood without elevating hetero-reproductive kinship: not just the family but in this case the village, high school graduating class, Eastern orthodox church, and factory as well. This is why the marital "joining" of bride and groom in *The Deer Hunter* can seem both to prefigure the military "joining up" of the groom and male attendants the morning after (its Anglo-American embellishments registering proper patriotic feeling), and to protest the war that follows (its customary and religious gestures registering dissent from national policy).

Along with the fundamental instability of the performative "I do," this specifically U.S. paradox may account for the fact that in many U.S. texts, weddings are marked by a dynamic of instability and repetition. *First Comes Love,* for example, consists of footage from four different weddings, each of whose elements are separated and recombined into a series; Friedrich thereby makes the wedding turn back on itself as if to rehearse each aspect of the ceremony rather than moving forward. Karen Tracey has recently described the "double proposal" plot in U.S. fiction, in which a woman's acceptance, repudiation, and then reacceptance of the same suitor's marriage proposal provides the text with opportunities to consider the politics of marriage itself.[81] Stanley Cavell has demonstrated in his study of Hollywood "comedies of remarriage" that though classical Hollywood films are certainly modeled on the eighteenth- and nineteenth-century British bourgeois comedies of manners that ended with a wedding, many of these modern films must produce a second wedding, a "remarriage," in order to affirm the legitimacy of the first one.[82] It is as if in an echo of J. L. Austin's unstable performative on the level of many U.S. literary and filmic plots themselves, the marriage contract in the United States disappears into the endless repetition of a wedding.

Finally, the wedding might also complicate one's view of how U.S. fiction used the affective register to consolidate a genuinely national culture. Critics have discussed the nation-making work of two mutually constructing nineteenth-century fictional genres in the United States: the feminine love story, and the masculine literature of frontier and travel adventure. These might be called, respectively, the American *romance* and *American* romance. The popular English sentimental novel, in many ways the precursor to the modern Harlequin romance, centered on female consciousness. Its primary aim was to substitute middle-class disciplinary power over proper feelings for aristocratic physical power of lords over subjects, and it figured these forms of power as the triumph of women's feelings over men's sexual rapacity.[83] Following suit, nineteenth-century U.S. authors such as Lydia Maria Child, Harriet Beecher Stowe, and Frances Ellen Watkins Harper offered up the home as a figure for a reformed national public sphere as well as a buffer against both the capitalist market and incursion of foreigners, and promoted heterosexual love and maternal pedagogy as crucial to the production of citizens and joining of these citizens into a nation.[84] Authors such as James Fenimore Cooper, Edgar Allan Poe, and Herman Melville, on the other hand, centered on movement away from civilization, "romancing" a vision of U.S. culture free from both the feminine disciplinary sphere and class stratifications that they displaced onto Europe—even as these novels also clearly invested in racial, territorial, and homoerotic social conflicts. Many male romancers produced alternatives to marriage in the rugged individual or male homosocial bond, and reconsecrated the visible male body as a sign of physical power.[85] In the domestic sentimental idiom, marriage was both the metonym for and means of achieving democratic freedom; in the idiom of the masculinist American Romance, marriage was the antithesis of this freedom.

But the wedding itself confounds the separation of culture into high and low art, public and private spheres, masculine and feminine genres, embodied and disembodied forms of power. As I have suggested, its religious and civil "high culture" aspects certainly mingle with its popular and commercial "low culture" ones, and even as the wedding seems to establish a zone of marital privacy that frees the couple from direct regulation of their sexual behavior, it also moves families out from behind "closed doors" and puts them on theatrical display. Furthermore, the wedding gives tangible, even visceral form to the dematerialized, sentimental, and feminized domain of feeling, turning emotions into a visual and tactile production, bringing bodies back onto the stage even as it ritualistically controls their expressivity. Indeed, domestic novels tend not to linger on the display-oriented apparatus of the wedding, which discombobulates domestic ideology and tests many of its assumptions—including the tacit and private nature of couplehood, the nuclear family as the primary and most elevated social form, and the secondary public role of wives. Yet if weddings are minimally evident in domestic novels, neither do they saturate masculine adventure fiction or the proto-modernist and modernist "Great American novels" that critics have seen as contesting domestic ideology. The wedding instead appears sporadically across a range of genres. And the sustained appearance of a wedding in a text often produces a generic rupture, spinning narrative energies, territorial and temporal logics, and subject positions elsewhere by spinning the couple form into disarray. In many of the texts I shall discuss, fantasies about social life do not even always appear as framed, recognizable wedding ceremonies; rather, fleeting glimpses of the wedding provide a variety of signs, semiotic linkages, and spatiotemporal rearrangements that multiply rather than reduce social and formal possibility.

This multiplicity may be especially significant to feminized subjects—not only girls and women but also men whose commitment to normative masculinity is in question to themselves and/or others. For the wedding releases the feminine from both the narrative confines of the domestic novel and social confines of the marital-reproductive nuclear family, without banishing women from the plot. Most often, the wedding's kaleidoscopic "spinning" is a specifically feminine gesture; since at least the eighteenth century, weddings have been controlled by mothers, brides, and bridesmaids, and the twentieth century has seen the rise of a wedding industry filled with women and gay men willing to risk the stigma of effeminacy. Rather than false consciousness, this embrace of the wedding form by at least two populations who are disempowered by marriage suggests that the wedding holds promises that marriage breaks. It offers a different form of power, different pleasures, than those heretofore linked to the production of U.S. cultural subjects in and through particular genres.

(And a final word or two)

What gets buried in theories of the wedding *complex* (the totalizing nature of the wedding industry; the narrative and psychoanalytic drive toward the closure of marriage) is the wedding com*plex:* the tangle of icons, semiotic transformations, and temporal rearrangements through which social being becomes *tangible,* if not strictly legalized. In keeping with the dialectical force of the form it examines, this book builds an archive for a set of incommensurate wishes that the wedding seems to give shape to and permission for, linking these wishes to both competing histories and unrealized possible futures. As Friedrich's *First Comes Love* suggests, these wishes include a different means of queer world making than the identity-logic of movement politics, the radical negation of this logic in utopian visions of anonymous public sex, or even the individualist deconstructive work of queer parody. As chapter 2 will demonstrate through an examination of how *The Member of the Wedding* uses the wedding to connect a queer child to World War II, the wedding indexes a wish to be private, unremarked on, and safe, to draw boundaries that could demarcate one's own particular social space—but also a desire to be officially recognized, to address spheres of power beyond family or nation, to be connected with, as McCullers puts it, "everybody. In the world."[86] As chapter 3 explores through a reading of Faulkner's *Absalom, Absalom!* that puts the wedding at the center of the novel, the wedding gives form to the possibility of a multiracial society engendered by something beyond just cross-racial, heterosexual reproduction. As chapter 4 discusses in relation to Hawthorne's "The May Pole of Merry-Mount" and Kirkland's *Zury,* the wedding may encode a specifically nationalist hope to ground the political contract in a prior one between man and woman, but it also encodes the threat that no contract is prior at all. As chapter 5 suggests through a discussion of man-girl honeymoons from Poe to Nabokov, the wedding's dreamwork includes the fantasy of a mode of genuinely *sensuous* sociability, one that might contest the modern liberal binary of the insular nuclear family that produces individual subjects and the vast, abstract "imagined community" that binds them as citizens. But this mode may have more to offer the male would-be citizen than the female whose role in the honeymoon makes that fantasy possible. As chapter 6 argues through an exploration of several contemporary wedding films and performances, the wedding can also seem to transform static and biological notions of being into dynamic, cultural notions of doing, extending the parameters of belonging—so that even when these parameters seem limited by race and sexuality, they can be operated against their most oppressive results.

The power of the wedding lies in its ability to make worlds through doing symbolic and aesthetic work on affiliation, attachment, and belonging, and in the way it preserves exactly what it claims to renounce: cultural possibilities for organizing social life beyond either the marital or mass imaginary. This constitutive contradiction between what weddings can do and what marriage law really does might be one reason people cry at weddings.

Chapter Two

THE WE OF ME: *THE MEMBER OF THE WEDDING*'S NOVEL ALLIANCES

"But what I'm warning is this," said Berenice. "If you start out falling in love with some unheard-of thing like that, what is going to happen to you? . . . Will you be trying to break into weddings the rest of your days? And what kind of life would that be?"
—Carson McCullers, *The Member of the Wedding*[1]

We must think that what exists is far from filling all possible spaces. To make a truly unavoidable challenge of the question: What can be played?
—Michel Foucault, "Friendship as a Way of Life"[2]

In *The Member of the Wedding* (1946), a twelve-year-old tomboy named Frankie Addams—who has a boy's name, a crew cut, and wears masculine clothes—suddenly falls in love with her brother Jarvis's wedding one summer during World War II. For the bulk of the novel, Frankie fantasizes about being part of the ceremony and even the marriage that follows it. But at the wedding itself, she is a mute spectator, and the newlyweds rather violently exclude her from their honeymoon getaway car.

Early critics read *Member* as a coming-of-age tale in which Frankie trades in the verdant, ambisexual imaginings of childhood first for illusions of feminine excess and then for a properly adult social life.[3] Indeed, McCullers originally titled her novel-in-progress *The Bride,* as if to foreground Frankie's future sister-in-law Janice as the figure with whom the protagonist identifies, and whom she will eventually replicate as bride and then wife.[4] This title registers the new centrality, in the 1940s, of the bride as a national icon; at the time McCullers was writing, the national wedding industry had taken off, early marriage had begun to replace "promiscuous" dating among adolescents in the United States, and U.S. "war brides" who married quickly before sending their husbands off to fight were seen as exemplary patriots.[5] Robert Westbrook's study of World War II pinups, for instance, shows how political obligations were figured as heterosexual ones: soldiers were supposed to fight not to end fascism but to get to rejoin their sweethearts, fiancées, and wives.[6] As part of this propagandistic war effort, three years prior to the publication of *Member,* McCullers herself had written a magazine essay that displaced America's obligation to fight fascism and its political connections with the Allied forces onto the obligations and emotions between husband and wife: "It is useless to deny that our love is threatened," she wrote in *Mademoiselle* under the pseudonym "A War Wife." "You are not only fighting for our own personal love, but for the rights of all human beings to love and live in a world of order and security."[7]

In the magazine piece, though, there are glimmerings of the much more complicated sense of relationality that would structure McCullers's later published fiction, especially *Member.* Even as the "War Wife" figures World War II as a fight on behalf of the conjugal couple, and getting and staying married as an act of patriotism, she also suggests that "all human beings" (and not, presumably, just married or heterosexual ones) have the right to love and "security," and even that equal rights for all kinds of lovers might be a worthy cause for battle. In this document, heterosexual marriage, supposedly the antidote to political oppression, begins to look like part of it. In fact, McCullers could hardly have seen marriage as a privileged patriotic cause, for she wrote the piece when she was divorced from Reeves McCullers, in love with AnneMarie Clarac-Schwarzenbach, and living in a group house that included Benjamin Britten, Christopher Isherwood, W. H. Auden, and various artists' collaborators and lovers. McCullers complained in a letter to her ex-husband that she could not assume her rightful persona, for whoever heard of a "Letter from a War Divorcée?"[8] Neither could a title for the magazine piece be generated by her involvement in a love affair with both Reeves and Clarac-Schwarzenbach for a time before the divorce, or by her marriage and remarriage to Reeves a total of three times: Letter from a War Bisexual? A War Triangulator? A War Bride-Bride-Bride?

In what seems to have been an effort three years later to figure affiliation without defaulting to heterosexual couplehood as its emblem, McCullers re-titled her novel-in-progress *The Bride and Her Brother.* This title foregrounds nonmarital social ties as well as autonomous identity—and its pronominal ambiguity suggests that Frankie might want to pair incestuously with her sibling groom. McCullers also briefly called the work *The Bride of My Brother,* which by adding a preposition, centers the question of relationship again. But here the bride is an object vis-à-vis the ungendered narrator's position as speaking subject—as if rather than becoming a war bride, Frankie could win one away from her brother. In this light, late-twentieth-century critics have read the novel as a classic "coming out story."[9] As with Ann Bannon's *Beebo Brinker* and other lesbian pulp novels that succeeded *Member,* Frankie's boy-ish body predicts her trajectory toward her newfound relationship with Mary Littlejohn in the last chapter, which represents the beginning of her recognition that she desires not weddings but other girls. A reading of *The Member of the Wedding* as a lesbian classic, perhaps even as a link between the lesbian relationships fostered by the all-female military and work environments of World War II along with the butch-femme bar cultures that succeeded them, would understand Frankie's obsession with the wedding of her brother Jarvis and his bride Janice as the misguided "before" to a happily lesbian, partnered "ever after."

But does *The Member of the Wedding* really assume that the wedding ritual produces either heterosexual or lesbian identity and nothing else? Though the novel seems to reroute Frankie away from an excess of fascination with hetero-ritual and toward a possibly lesbian partnership, "marrying" Mary Littlejohn (whose first name suggests the lawfulness of this union and last name the inferior status of a substitute groom, as well as incestuously echo-ing her cousin John Henry's name) actually seems to diminish Frankie's lushest fantasies and provides a disappointing denouement. In fact, after the wedding, the makeshift family with whom Frankie has spent the entire novel in the kitchen talking, utterly disintegrates. Frankie's African American nursemaid Berenice is forced to quit her job and marry her boyfriend when Frankie and her father move to the suburbs, the effeminate seven-year-old John Henry dies a horrible death from meningitis, and Frankie herself, in a change she neither instigates nor remarks on, becomes "Frances." Far from signaling her triumphant ascendance into either heterosexual marriage or its same-sex version, Frankie's involuntary reversion to her legal, given name registers a certain inability to use the law to make significant changes on the social terrain.

In another example of extralegal intervention, when Frankie finally arrives at her brother's wedding in the last chapter, she actually eschews the ceremony's official unit of protest: the moment when the audience is invited to object to the union. Instead, she intervenes after the ceremony, at the moment her brother and the bride are departing for their honeymoon: "The rest was like some nightmare show in which a wild girl in the audience breaks onto the stage to take upon herself an unplanned part that was never written or meant to be. . . . [S]he could only say aloud: 'Take me!' . . . She could only cry in the dust of the empty road: 'Take me! Take me!' " (MW, 138). Here she turns the end of the wedding itself into a funeral, throwing herself into the dust behind the honeymoon car as if it were a hearse and she a mourner. Rather than trying to stop the wedding, Frankie's reversal of wedding into funeral may be a way of attempting to make it go on forever. The funeral marks the symbolic death not of the wedding but of the child herself, and the imagined worlds that the wedding makes possible in this novel.

In short, neither accession to the laws of domestic couplehood nor absolutely outlaw interruptions of the wedding work for Frankie; her intervention into the symbolics of social life must take place somewhere else. For most of the novel's plot, then, Frankie does not want to be the bride and marry her brother Jarvis; nor does she want, as a lesbian might, to have the bride and marry his fiancée Janice. She wants, it seems, to remain outside of identity, but without sacrificing her own access to form. Even the wedding itself, as the novel's primary "object" of both identification and desire, is not stable enough to produce identity per se, for it survives only as an oscillation between sound and silence in the novel's concluding paragraph: " 'I am simply mad about—' But the sentence was left unfinished for the hush was shattered when, with an instant shock of happiness, she heard the ringing of the bell" (153). Mad about what? Like her desire, Frankie's final preposition has no stable object. In the novel's last two sentences, the bell seems to ring not in celebration of either an incipient heterosexuality or her relationship with Mary Littlejohn but in interruption of both: the bell chimes over what might have been Mary's name with the sound of the wedding that has reverberated through the novel.

It tolls as if the novel itself is mourning the wedding and its ability, for Frankie, to generate endless improvised investments.

If as Elspeth Probyn writes, queer desire conjoins radically disjunctive images, then an expansive symbolics of affiliation—ways of linking up disparate icons and people—is crucial to queer lives.[10] Though the bell might be a funeral bell sounding the foreclosure of Frankie's most fantastic horizons, or even mourning identity itself *as the very form of* social foreclosure, it also rings the very changes that the wedding is capable of signifying. It demands that the novel be read backward—toward the wedding itself, rather than away from it. Frankie's desire for the couple must be distinguished from either heterosexual or lesbian desire, her fantasy of the wedding from what she calls the "unmanaged nightmare" of the actual ceremony; and the focus of her fantasies as some social terrain beyond the mere sanction of her sexual object choice. As Frankie's nursemaid Berenice puts it:

> Frankie got a crush!
> Frankie got a crush!
> Frankie got a crush!
> On the *Wedd*—ing! (MW, 32–33).

Here, Berenice's singsong repetition syntactically duplicates Frankie's obsessive return, over and over again, to the figure of her brother and his bride. And the word "crush" suggests both a hopeless, passive longing and the more active wish to have a literal, physical impact on the ceremony. As Berenice's remark in the epigraph to this chapter shows, Frankie is not just "in love with" this complicated object; nor does she only want to "crush" it out of existence. Frankie wants instead to "break into" the wedding's identity-making work and turn the ceremony back into a scene of sociability itself—a field in which multiple and unpredictable affinities might take shape. Furthermore, the wedding offers Frankie a sense of self-extension not equivalent to the simple merging of one identity into another: "There was her brother and the bride, and it was as though when first she saw them . . . she had known inside of her: *They are the we of me*" (39–40, italics in original).

The title McCullers finally chose, *The Member of the Wedding*, reflects a different social and representational economy than that of either the marriage plot or lesbian coming-out story. Because it is grounded in performance, "wedding" foregrounds activity and transformation, instead of status and identity. In many respects, the white wedding Frankie is in love with is like the transsexual one discussed in my preface. For in the wedding, the sexual joining of male and female bodies is symbolized by the groom lifting the bride's veil, the finger entering the wedding ring, and the slicing of the cake.[11] Thus, Frankie's identification with the wedding might well signal her desire for genuinely "hetero-sexed" embodiment—a body that like the wedding, mixes male and female elements. If the word "member" is read in its explicitly sexual sense, perhaps Frankie's identification with the wedding registers a desire to simultaneously be and have the phallic member, even to be the "phallic" central term that can reorganize the significance of the wedding's other signs. All of this is to suggest that *The Member of the Wedding*, from its title onward, uses the wedding to elaborate the desire for, and indeed to create, a world in which object choice is not constitutive or determinative of sexual subjectivity, and the very form of bodies can change in response to new meanings.

But because it is grounded in conceptions of allegiance, "member" also insists on thinking about the *social* body, on the symbolics of connecting and belonging rather than just being or having. Hence, the title McCullers finally chose indicates possibilities for counterperforming not only bodies but also the meaning and forms of the ties that bind them. The novel's World War II setting, and Frankie's explicit concern with the relationship between the wedding and war, between private and public modes of alliance and obligation, register certain political problematics specific to the World War II era, when the question of whether, to what, and by what means the war might unify people in the United States was crucial. Frankie struggles to configure the relationship between personal and communal bonds in terms of love and war: "All these people and you don't know what joins them up. There's bound to be some sort of reason and connection. Yet somehow I can't seem to name it. I don't know" (*MW*, 115). The question of formalizing and making visible the way people "join up" complexly links domestic affiliations, like marriage and engagement, to civic ones, like "joining up" to the army or feeling properly American. But *Member* articulates a crisis in this simple homology. On the one hand, the novel registers, particularly for women, the dearth of forms other than marriage for actualizing (or even just conceptualizing) the relationship between self and social group, intimate and civic liaisons. On the other hand, though, the novel insists on not subsuming the feminine or erotic to what Benedict Anderson terms a "deep, horizontal comradeship," in which the fraternity of national citizens can be imagined neither as sisters nor an army of explicitly sexual lovers, or in which temporal layers simply disappear.[12] If *The Member of the Wedding* insists on the linkage between marriage and nationality, it also points to a connection between the wedding and forms of belonging both spatially and temporally slantwise to the nation.

In *Member*, then, redescribing the wedding does not mean simply avoiding, destroying, or stopping it—rather, the novel puts the ritual to new uses. For accompanying her desire to differently inhabit the couple form are any number of desires that don't logically follow it. Using the wedding to imagine changes apparently unconnected with Mary, or with marrying, she fantasizes about Berenice's statement that getting married will stop the growth spurt that so terrifies her, about the promise of going north to Alaska and experiencing snow, about becoming a vital part of the World War II effort. In this novel, the wedding has the power to guide Frankie from one "landscape," cultural climate, or social field to another; its field of transformation is not identity, sexuality, or gender per se but the entire symbolic field that heterosexuality accesses: its freedom *not* to focus on object choice, its way of telling stories, its colors, its gestures, the zones of psychic time it creates, its territoriality, its modes of publicity, and most of all its status as a blueprint for national belonging. As I shall explore in more depth below, it is this terrain Frankie seizes.

In thus calling the novel "queer," I mean not to resituate it as a lesbian coming-out novel but to emphasize its relationship to fantasized, acted-out, and lived transformations of historically specific public symbolic fields; as Michael Warner writes, there is no limit to what might be transformed by staging critical answers to the very local question, "What do queers want?"[13] For most of *Member*, Frankie views the wedding as the incoherent answer to this query. But to say that she wants a wedding is not necessarily to say that she wants marriage. *Member* makes it clear—and queer—that "wedding" might not only or always signify marriage and "membership" might not only or always signal assimilation. Frankie's relation to the wedding raises a few important questions: What does it mean to be in love not with a person but a couple, with the scene of couplehood and its pageantry? What does it mean to want to interrupt this scene without simply annihilating it, to adhere to it and in this very binding to change it? And how is *the we of me* a formulation for a queerer kind of social bond than couplehood, family, "community," or nation?

As the issue of gay marriage circulates internationally, the issues that *The Member of the Wedding* raises seem urgent. It is not clear whether the political advantages gained by legalizing same-sex marriage or the radical negativity of playing outlaw to the power of nuptial imagery will outweigh the possibilities engendered by following the lead of Frankie, who explores and inhabits the mode the wedding dramatizes in order to make other more seemingly phantasmic affiliations legible within it. The novel's queerness lies in its perverse use of the wedding as an opportunity to redescribe how intimacy, connection, or "membership" might be formalized and displayed. Finally, in its redescription of desire itself as the desire to join—and in joining, transform—a mode of public, collective identification, *Member* departs from the terrain of both the object-focused "lesbian" and less-gender-specific "queer," using the over-feminized form of the wedding to produce what might be called a female-inflected queer rearrangement of social life in the 1940s and beyond.

All Dressed in White

Before she hears about the wedding, Frankie can only imagine grotesque connections between people whose bodies seem to make the idea of connection impossible. She cannot, for instance, break her own long-felt alliance with the shape-shifting, immobilized freaks she has seen at a traveling side-show. Frankie has been obsessed with freaks—the Half-Man, Half-Woman, the Giant, the Fat Lady, the Midget, the Wild Nigger, the Pin Head, and the Alligator Boy—and worries about becoming one of them, "If she reached her height on her eighteenth birthday, she had five and one-sixth growing years ahead of her. Therefore, according to mathematics and unless she could somehow stop herself, she would grow to be over nine feet tall. And what would be a lady who is over nine feet high? She would be a Freak" (*MW*, 16–17). In the face of these monsters, the range of physical instabilities that threaten Frankie multiply: her body might remain Half-Man, Half-Woman, between the categories of male and female; it might lose its proportion to the rest of the world and take up too much space or too little, rendering her a Giant, a Fat Lady, a Midget; it might lose proportion to itself and turn her into a Pin Head. The inflection of her white identity by a more stigmatically racialized and sexualized southernness might take over, in the kind of degeneration that the Wild Nigger seems to represent to her, and from which she violently separates herself by referring to her African American caretaker Berenice as a "nigger" after the bride and groom leave for their honeymoon.

Not only is the threat that the freaks represent insistently physical; so is the way they bond with Frankie: "She was afraid of all the Freaks, for it seemed to her that they had looked at her in a secret way and tried to connect their eyes with hers, as though to say: we know you. She was afraid of their long Freak eyes. And all the years she had remembered them, until this day. . . . 'I doubt if they ever get married or go to a wedding,' she said. 'Those Freaks' " (18). Here the act of looking, literalized in the freaks' attempts to connect their "long eyes" with hers, unbearably sutures Frankie's body to theirs. Her involuntarily locked gaze with the freaks makes the cliché "it takes one to know one" into a physical bond, like the evil eye. Crucially, Frankie links their inability to "get married or go to a wedding" with their inability to affiliate in ways that transcend this merely corporeal exchange of glances.[14] The freaks, it seems, can only cruise.

Likewise, the portrayal of Frankie's cohort in the Addams' kitchen focuses particularly on eyes, which operate as symbols of the overembodied, underformalized mode of alliance that link John Henry, Berenice, and Frankie. The "long eyes" of the freaks, Berenice's single blue glass eye, the spectacles John Henry wears that she insists he doesn't need, and Frankie's gray eyes that Berenice refers to as "jealous," form a series of emblems of distorted vision that figure the inability of these three outsiders to produce stable, accurate images of themselves, which in Frankie's view seems to stem from their inability to inhabit a socially meaningful form of connection. The unmarried Berenice, for instance, "always spoke of herself as though she was somebody very beautiful. Almost on this one subject, Berenice was really not in her right mind" (MW, 79). In an even more condensed symbolic activity, John Henry labors over a "perfect little biscuit man" (8) that looks just like him, but swells to unrecognizable proportions when cooked (significantly, he eats it anyway). And when Frankie looks in the mirror, she sees only a "warped and crooked" reflection (2). These three nonmembers are locked into a dialectic that connects their mutual distorted gazes, their incomplete and out-of-proportion bodies, into something that Frankie feels is grossly unworthy of the pronoun "we."

On her brother's visit with his bride-to-be, though, the symbolics of the white wedding offer Frankie a way to reconfigure her body, and use this new body as a relay for connecting otherwise noncontiguous spaces and objects. Frankie first fantasizes about the change the wedding brings by imagining it in terms of the difference between northern and southern weather, as if the white wedding is powerful enough to be experienced as a climate: "So on the day before the visit [Frankie] only commented to Berenice: 'I think it's a curious coincidence that Jarvis would get to go to Alaska and that the very bride he picked to marry would come from a place called Winter Hill. Winter Hill,' she repeated slowly, her eyes closed, and the name blended with dreams of Alaska and cold snow" (5). The cold, white snow she desires might be read in opposition to the warm, red blood that will shortly announce her woman-hood. In this sense, wedding white liberates her body from the threat of puberty, mitigating the trauma of a tomboy getting breasts or menstruating by evoking the pleasure and relief of freezing. Mocking her growth spurt, "the hateful little summer children [holler] to her, 'Is it cold up there?' " (17), but the semiotic field of wedding-snow-cold promises her a release from the cold "up there" in her uncontrollable body. It allows her to project outward from her physical self to the United States and exteriorize the "up there" cold into a place at the top of the map to which she might literally escape: "She walked up a cold white hill and looked on a snowy wasteland far below. She watched the sun make colors in the ice, and heard dream voices, saw dream things. And everywhere there was the cold white gentle snow" (10). The imagined cold becomes a way of feeling change in a mode *other* than sexuality. It counters puberty with other sensations of bodily change, and registers the way a dif-ferent relation to place might also reterritorialize her body and reorganize its senses.[15] Within this representational economy, she neither is bound to her same old body nor altogether loses it to become that most abstract of subjects, the citizen. Neither does she appropriate what Lauren Berlant calls a prosthe-tic body, a concrete, iconic corporeal form that grants privilege and safety to its inhabitant.[16] Instead, the wedding grants Frankie something more like a prosthetic sensorium, a set of new bodily responses.

The register of cold, snow, and whiteness also express a way of bringing "things" into meaningful conjunction, into a different mode of narration, as in a "dream." The wedding allows Frankie to conjoin disparate places, to fantasize that her brother and his betrothed will marry in Winter Hill, where the bride is from, and honeymoon in Alaska, where her brother has returned from military duty: "Because of the wedding, these distant lands, the world, seemed altogether possible and near: as close to Winter Hill as Winter Hill was to the town" (*MW*, 67). In light of the wedding, her desire begins to work like the snow she fantasizes about, falling over all the objects and ideas that come into her domain and transforming them in her own image, thereby visually and affectively linking what once looked impossibly separate. This motion extends infinitely outward, so that the wedding ultimately allows her to transcend the boundaries between herself and the rest of the nation in a multiply gendered mode. For instance, as if combining the feminine fantasy of being in a World War II era vocal trio with the masculine fantasy of giving a fireside chat like then-President Franklin Delano Roosevelt, Frankie dreams about her connubial threesome broadcasting speeches together on the radio.

In marking these changes, the novel repeatedly invokes Alaska, though the linkage of weddings with a larger public and the nation itself could easily have been secured by general references to the North, cold, and snow (for example, though the rest of the novel's setting in Georgia provides a contrapuntal set of "hot" images, that state never gets named directly). Not only do Frankie's dreams of cold center around the specific locale of Alaska but she also fantasizes that Alaska will be the destination for a honeymoon that will include her. Frankie's fantasy of going to Alaska with the honeymoon couple certainly suggests the ease with which heterosexual people, particularly married ones, travel through national space: Alaska is the "polar" opposite of the way gay people with any desire for a wide social network have been restricted to local urban spaces. But more than the wish to travel, Alaska figures Frankie's desire for a broadly structural change in her relation to where she lives. For "Alaska" in the 1940s denoted an extremely incoherent space: not yet a state, it was a northern landmass physically disjoined from "America" proper and yet a center of national military operations.[17]

Paradoxically, Frankie's desire to join the union of her brother and his wife finds expression in her desire to go to a place that is both the most unjoined (physically) and the most almost-joined (conceptually) to the national Union itself—a place that is neither safely inside the nation's boundaries nor safely outside them, and figures neither full citizenship within nor absolute expatriation from the United States. In desiring Alaska, Frankie wants the kind of simultaneous removal/proximity that Alaska represents, the kind that will destabilize rather than stabilize or simply evacuate her relation to the nation. In short, Alaska is a different kind of frontier, a noncontiguous, seminational elsewhere. It is continuously linked with neither the geography nor history that precedes it, but ruptures the spatial and temporal continuum of "America" itself, and figures Frankie's hope to use queer desire to do so as well. The Alaskan fantasy-wedding suggests the deep connections between the formalization of erotic alliances and what Fredric Jameson labels "cognitive mapping," or the ability to comprehend the social system and one's place in it.[18] It reconfigures the cognitive mapping of places in terms of human relationships, the official nation in terms of less systematic forms of sociability indexed by the vocabulary neither of couplehood nor local community. In this sense, Alaska represents an "elsewhere" that is not merely a utopian "no place," a "somewhere over the rainbow," but a specific location from which to contest dominant structures of belonging.

Crucially, Frankie's fantasies about "Alaska," the U.S. territory thought most useful in the maintenance of U.S. national boundaries during World War II, open up into fantasies about the entire world:

> "Boyoman! Manoboy!" she said. "When we leave Winter Hill we're going to more places than you ever thought about or even knew existed. Just where we will go first I don't know, and it don't matter. Because after we go to that place we're going on to another. We mean to keep moving, the three of us. Here today and gone tomorrow. Alaska, China, Iceland, South America. Traveling on trains. Letting her rip on motorcycles. Flying around all over the world in aeroplanes. Here today and gone tomorrow. All over the world. It's the damn truth. Boyoman!" (*MW*, 111)

Here, becoming a member of the wedding might simply be the equivalent of a global passport; Frankie later declares, "We will be members of the whole world" (112). The wedding seems to enable Frankie to transform the imperialism of U.S. heterosexuality—its simultaneous defense and expansion of its own borders—into a vision of safe space expanding to enfold an entire (queer) planet. Where the three go, presumably, new social linkages will follow, in a simple expansion of frontiers. Similarly, when present-day queers argue, "We are everywhere," one imagines a kind of crazy quilt of gay-friendly and latently queer locales, infinitely expandable into a "queer planet" whose geography is transformed in the queering of its social relationships. Yet this "everywhere" threatens to look just like the regular map, with queer territory imagined as infinitely expandable.[19] The queer desire to reorganize social life itself must be reconciled with the U.S. frontier imagination—for in at least some queer U.S. politics and theory, the two seem intimate.

One vision of gay marriage rights only contributes to this liaison. For instance, in a recent article on the gay marriage debate, legal scholar Evan Wolfson quotes George and Ira Gershwin's "Love Is Sweeping the Country": "All the sexes, from Maine to Texas / Have never known such love before. . . . Each girl and boy alike, sharing joy alike, Feels that passion'll soon be national."[20] The queer charms of the Gershwins aside, what does the presence of U.S. nationality mean in a song about "love"? In an article advocating gay marriage rights, the lyrics have an odd effect: marriage is all-American; other affiliations can only register as threateningly communist (a dystopian future in which passion for any group formation smaller than the state is counter-revolutionary), or primitively "tribal" (an equally dystopian past of unrefined mating). In lectures around the country, Wolfson has commented that there is no moving away from gay marriage; he has claimed that "the ship has already sailed" in the case on marriage rights in Hawaii. Until December 1999, when changes in the Hawaii Constitution invalidated previous judicial decisions that outlawing gay marriage was unconstitutional, this ship was supposed to sail from Hawaii to the mainland United States, and from there to the rest of the world, like a gay Columbus.

Like Alaska for Frankie, Hawaii has seemed a model by which the entire planet can be queered since it is a state with a different "climate" whose social meaning is both racialized and sexualized in the national imaginary, and since it has a history of kinship forms and sexual practices that cannot be reduced to the Anglo-American nuclear family. But imagining Hawaii as a fantasy island for gay marriage rights depends on forgetting the history of how this territory came to be constructed in relation to the nation in the first place: during World War II this included martial law, the internment of citizens of Japanese descent as well as labor activists and "Communists," and the denial of statehood.[21] Lost in the debate on Hawaii is any sense of what its presence as a military launching pad for an army of gay lovers might say about the nationalism of gay politics. What would it mean for Hawaii to become a "gay" as well as "straight" honeymoon mecca? What kinds of local erotic and social practices, both homo- and hetero-erotic, would be devalued by the kind of sex tourism that honeymooning is, in which U.S. newlyweds flaunt their relationship while reveling in the "exotic" sexual practices of other cultures? Given the hegemony of marriage in New England Puritan culture, which I explore in chapter 4, it seems more fitting that Vermont has most recently emerged as the first state to make gay "civil unions" legal.

To return to Alaska, neither Frankie nor *The Member of the Wedding* explicitly register the fact that Alaska, too, was part of the U.S. military's Pacific triangle—a far less utopian triangle than Frankie's—during World War II. As mentioned earlier, her brother Jarvis has just returned from that state, from what is probably a tour of duty at one of the two air force bases constructed in Alaska after the bombing of Pearl Harbor in December 1941; Jarvis has been part of the following year's insistent and permanent Americanization of Alaska by the military. But if Frankie can imagine Alaska's impact on herself, she cannot simultaneously imagine the impact of her "we of me," her triangular world tour, on Alaska. The wedding form allows Frankie to move from a symbolics of monstrously connected bodies to one of alliance by shared climate and color, to one of the connections and spatial reorganizations forged by media culture; from an impossible and overembodied private status to a sublimely reembodied public one; from freak to celebrity; from regional southerner to imperialist national subject. Yet the novel only obliquely addresses the question of what forms of sociability even queer access to a national, not to mention global public sphere might erase.

Instead, for the most part, *The Member of the Wedding* uses the wedding to take a formalist turn. Moving from the inarticulate, overembodied world of the kitchen to the visual register of fantasy, and finally to pure sound, its wedding transports its members less to a stable semiotic field than a different representational economy—a change in modalities not reducible to political policy. In other words, rather than inaugurating a particular change, the wedding "rings changes," or provides a way of chaining metamorphoses to one another. It is a means of shifting from one conceptual place to another, an organizing form that says less about the particular fantasies of affiliation it organizes than what is necessary to organize a fantasy of affiliation.

I Now Pronounce Me . . .

As she contemplates the wedding, Frankie remarks that it is "hard to argue with a known saying," specifically the one, "Two is company and three is a crowd. And that is the main thing about a wedding" (*MW*, 73). Initially, rather than refuting the maxims of the wedding, she briefly articulates the desire to conjoin herself to other people and things in terms of blood kinship: "She decided to donate blood to the Red Cross; she wanted to donate a quart a week and her blood would be in the veins of Australians and Fighting French and Chinese, all over the whole world, and it would be as though she were close kin to all of these people" (21). But the Red Cross will not have her any more than the newlyweds will; consanguineous kinship will not save Frankie any more than conjugal kinship will. Instead, for Frankie, the wedding taps into an alternative economy to the "marriage plot," generating a use of language that both mimics and enacts the kind of social life she wants.

Berenice describes "a serious fault with you, Frankie. Somebody just makes a loose remark and then you cozen it in your mind until nobody would recognize it" (31). Here, the word "cozen" links the novel's narrative practice with its transformations of family structure and the uses of heterosexual formalism. In its relationship to "cousin," cozen emphasizes horizontal bonds, blurs the distinctions between marital and birth relations, and extends potentially infinitely outward from the nuclear family. But the original meaning of the word is also itself theatrical rather than legal or biological: "to clayme kindred for advantage, or particular ends; as he, who to save charges in traveling, goes from house to house, as co[u]sin to the owner of everie one."[22] In this definition of cozen, one gains relatives kinetically, by moving around in the world, and verbally, by making claims. Frankie's cozening is verbal *and* material; in contradistinction to the increasingly marriage-centered culture she is part of, she desires to be related to "everybody. In the world. Everybody in the world" (*MW*, 110). Even in this utterance, her syntax connects two phrases without a (marital) copula. Likewise, her narrative practice, transforming storytelling into the cozening of alliances that cannot be subsumed either by blood kinship or marital couplehood, aims to forge bonds between herself and other outsiders, and between herself and the world. Her cozening remotivates the "known saying" to fantasize both a love triangle and, correspondingly, different conception of public bonds and obligations.

This mode—the use of a "remark," a found verbal object, and the most banal of events, the wedding of a U.S. soldier and his bride, to cozen it into a narrative radically dissimilar from what engendered it—generates a novel whose detractors insisted it had no plot.[23] But rather than plot, the novel consists of a series of linked performances: fantasies, soliloquies, hallucinations, recounted tales. This structure allows McCullers to move from a vision of alliance grounded in the connection between bodies, to one imagined as a reconfiguration of family, to one performed as a narrative practice capable of differently articulating the relationship of U.S. subjects to one another and the nation.

Moving from the physical to the sonic, Frankie most complexly articulates the sense of alliance the wedding allows her to feel by changing her name to F. Jasmine Addams: "'J A,' said Frankie. 'Janice and Jarvis. Isn't that the strangest thing? . . . Both their names begin with J A. . . . If only my name was Jane . . . Jane or Jasmine. . . . I wonder if it is against the law to change your name. Or add to it. . . . Well, I don't care. . . . F. Jasmine Addams'" (*MW*, 15). Frankie's name change mimics the marital prerogative of renaming the woman, stealing the function for something far queerer, performing a "backward" renaming by transforming the first name, and submitting the Law of the Father to a kind of feminine hypertrophy by enlarging the "female" domain of the first name. She also refuses the model of self-renaming as mere cathexis onto a heroine, for she changes her name to F. Jasmine Addams, explicitly rejecting Jane Addams when she might have simply identified with this nationally known single, feminist, lesbian traveler.[24]

Instead of performing an identification as a way into identity, Frankie's name change makes literal and visual the novel's production of a narrative form for queer alliance. Name changes—diva names like Bertha Vanation, radical feminist names like Elana Dykewoman, and punk tags like Laura Sister Nobody—have been fundamental to contemporary queer performance precisely because they articulate a political affiliation by personifying it. Bertha Vanation makes the drag queen into a national subject; Elana Dykewoman aligns the lesbian feminist with a matriarchal lesbian genealogy; Laura Sister Nobody foregrounds the absurdity of both familial and feminist "sisterhood" to describe the punk zine writer's political and affective ties. Frankie's name change anticipates this gesture by linking her to a family without subordinating her to the Name of the Father and to a marital public without subsuming her into a couple. Unlike the current descriptions of drag as a means of allegorizing the theatrical status of normative *identity*, Frankie's name change allegorizes the idea of *alliance* itself. "F. JAsmine" does not merely transform one sign into another but changes a verbal into a visual emblem, insisting that the forms "J" and "A" signify in their material shape (in their visual alignment with Janice and Jarvis). Just as the wedding produces the symbolic forms by which legal marriage supposedly manifests and legitimates itself, "J A" produces the material form (alphabetical signs linked to produce sound) of an idea (linkage, joining, or "membership"). It is a counterperformance of the wedding's ability to personify the idea of intimate belonging by tarting it up as bride and groom, and World War II's insistent configuration of national belonging in terms of marital obligation.

Crucially, though, *Member* is not merely dedicated to an ethic of joining, as if one could merely join up with the correct social formation. "J A" instead reconfigures the act of joining itself. For *Member* registers a dialectic of what Walter Benjamin calls "dispersal" and "collectedness," which he links to a modern, antitypological form of allegory: "In the dialectic of this form of expression the fanaticism of the process of collection is balanced by the slackness with which the objects are arranged."[25] In other words, joining is undermined by the randomness of exactly what is joined (in this case, two disparate and meaningless letters of the alphabet); contiguity is not governed by a logic of subterranean sameness (as a metaphor might be).

The words "loose" and "caught" take on this Benjaminian charge in *Member*, articulating at once connection and separation, proximity and distance, freedom and restriction. Berenice depicts being caught as a restrictive mode: "I born Berenice. You born Frankie. John Henry born John Henry. And maybe we wants to widen and bust free. But no matter what we do we still caught. Me is me and you is you and he is he. . . . Everybody is caught one way or another. But they done drawn completely extra bounds around all colored people. They done squeezed us off in one corner by ourselves. So we caught that firstway I was telling you, as all human beings is caught. And we caught as colored people also" (*MW*, 113–14). Berenice cannot imagine a name change outside of marriage, and she will not remarry unless and until she has no other choice. In her vision, naming is destiny, and the name is both an emblem for the stigma of a collective racial identity imposed from without and a touchstone for survival. Berenice elides even the verbal state of "being" in her statement "I born Berenice," as if her own proper name is a metonym for both the "extra bounds around all colored people" that restrict the forms of being and the possibility of existing in another modality.

Frankie sees restriction differently, in terms of her own separation from any truly social bonds. She calls the world "huge and cracked and loose and turning a thousand miles an hour" (20); Berenice's foster brother Honey is "a sick-loose person" (35); and the soldier who asks F. Jasmine for a date and accosts her is "out loose on a three-day pass" (64). To Frankie, loose represents the worst possible state of alienation, and after deciding to attend the wedding she feels "connected with all she saw" (44). Her desire is to be caught, and caught up, in some hustle-bustle of belonging:

> "I believe I realize what you were saying," F. Jasmine said. "Yet at the same time you almost might use the word loose instead of caught. Although they are two opposite words. I mean you walk around and you see all the people. And to me they look loose."
>
> "Wild, you mean?"
>
> "Oh, no!" she said. "I mean you don't see what joins them up together." (114)

For Frankie, being loose is being too caught; she wants to inhabit a form of affiliation that is neither a segregated corner nor nomadic individualism.

Her solution to the problem is not to create community or couplehood but, as I have argued, to perform affiliation itself verbally, as if she can produce as image what fails her on the level of plot:

> *They are the we of me.* Yesterday, and all the twelve years of her life, she had only been Frankie. She was an *I* person who had to walk around and do things by herself. All other people had a *we* to claim, all other except her. When Berenice said *we,* she meant Honey and Big Mama, her lodge, or her church. The *we* of her father was the store. All members of clubs have a *we* to belong to and talk about. The soldiers in the army can say *we,* and even the criminals on chain-gangs. But the old Frankie had had no *we* to claim, unless it would be the terrible summer *we* of her and John Henry and Berenice—and that was the last *we* in the world she wanted. Now all this was suddenly over with and changed. There was her brother and the bride, and it was as though when first she saw them something she had known inside of her: *They are the we of me.* (39–40)

Rather than being contained in an object, the kind of desire "they are the we of me" articulates is a movement; it reconfigures the relations between objects such that the whole ("we") is contained in and subordinated to the part ("me"). Insofar as it allows for this shuttling motion between part and whole, prior and "secondary," major and minor, this motion follows the narrative logic of allegory, which plays with the relations between an emblem and its elaborations, an original text and its retellings. Yet insofar as it imagines and performs a new way of living social life, it is also distinctly queer. Patricia

White has suggested that Frankie's "we of me" is the primal scene of lesbian nonrepresentation, in which the subject is incarnated by her very exclusion from the scene in which she was conceived.[26] But I think "the we of me" is a figure for queer *para*-representation—representation "alongside of" the dominant, a self-extension that eschews the choices of self-annihilation or self-reproduction. For the phrase actually reverses the logic of conception in which man and woman produce a baby who is the "me" of their "we," and in the tradition of Walt Whitman, pictures social life as an extension of the self's very multiplicity.

As if to insist neither on representation in dominant terms nor a modernist antirepresentational economy, Frankie's mode of storytelling falls between radical antinarrative, figured by the unintelligible scribblings of John Henry that cover the kitchen walls, and conventional narrative, figured by Berenice's ability to tell the whole story of her brother's visit:

> "Oh," [Frankie] said. "They were the two prettiest people I ever saw. I just can't understand how it happened."
>
> "But what, Foolish?" said Berenice. "Your brother come home with the girl he means to marry and took dinner today with you and your Daddy. They intend to marry at her home in Winter Hill this coming Sunday. You and your Daddy are going to the wedding. And that is the A and the Z of the matter. So whatever ails you?" (*MW*, 3)

The "A and the Z of the matter" and even the peremptory renaming of Frankie as "Foolish" in the disciplinary mode are what the "J A" of the matter disputes. If Berenice can tell the story of the wedding in chronological order, with the beginning prefiguring the end, Frankie means to articulate these materials in a different relation to one another; she aims to knit the letters into something other than either a "loose" assortment of single, atomized vowels and consonants or whole, symbolic words like "Foolish," "colored," or "Addams," whose meaning is already "caught" in a web of impoverished social relations. In contrast, the "F" of Frankie–F. Jasmine–Frances and the "J A" of Janice-Jarvis-Jasmine are alphabetic, nonsymbolic, and gender occlusive—but emphatically connected. And Frankie's play with alphabetic rearrangements is also a kind of pictogram for the narrative structure of the novel, whose interlinked, lyrical flights of fancy do not correspond precisely to "plot."

"F. JAsmine," the wedding of Frankie to her brother's wedding, then, is something like the apparatus of "wedding" itself, but as a form of becoming minor, in a literally minor key.[27] Overhearing a piano tuner at work, Frankie remarks: " 'It is that last note," F. Jasmine said. "If you start with A and go on up to G, there is a curious thing that seems to make the difference between G and A all the difference in the world. Twice as much difference as between any other two notes in the scale. Yet they are side by side there on the piano just as close together as the other notes. Do ray mee fa sol la tee. Tee. Tee. Tee. It could drive you wild!" (*MW*, 103). Here, the "Tee. Tee. Tee" difference between "G" and "A" is the mark of the tuner's refusal to fuse them into a harmonious, major resolution. It sounds not only the name of Berenice's boyfriend T.T., with whom Berenice initially refuses the marriage plot's conventional ending, but the acoustic version of the unfinished "J A"—for these letters refuse to resolve into a proper name the three family members all might have in common, one that would make them legible as "family" according to an ordinary regime of signification. But they also refuse what Berenice recognizes as the privilege of "looseness" or autonomy.

By this insistently minoritizing light, Frankie's fantasy of using the wedding to go "everywhere" might also be read against itself, as a figure for the performance of a nonimperialist affiliation between the United States and the rest of the world, for an "America" whose "unfinished" nature signals promises not yet kept, rather than the infinite reach of its powers. For Frankie doesn't want to go to a "safe space" in which she can get married and from within whose closed borders she can then expand outward. She wants, as she points out, to "keep moving," to blur the distinctions between territory, country, and continent even as she traverses their boundaries. Her fantasies about rapid transit and universal access are framed by an even more fantastic form of mobility: the exclamations "Boyoman!" and "Manoboy!" that frame her long travelogue about going to China, Iceland, and South America.

This outburst articulates a different kind of locomotion, the kind her cross-dressing cousin John Henry cannot imagine when he asks of a neighborhood transvestite, "How did that boy change into a girl?" (77). As John Henry and Frankie sadly learn, "Boyogirl" and "Girloboy" cannot release them; neither their cross-dressing nor Frankie's fantasy a world where "people could instantly change back and forth from boys to girls" has an effect on the novel's symbolic order (92). But the inversion of child into adult and back again does: "Manoboy! Boyoman!" is less a transsexual than a transtemporal operation. It signals that Frankie recognizes the wedding as a performance not only of community, imagined as horizontal bonds between people, but of futurity, imagined as vertical bonds between generations. Her exclamation seizes this temporal domain—the assurance that the wedded couple will have a link to the next generation—as a mode of privilege and pleasure.

The wedding, in other words, does two things for Frankie. On the one hand, it organizes time in a linear way: after she decides to join the wedding, "her world seemed layered in three different parts, all the twelve years of the old Frankie, the present day itself, and the future ahead when the J A three of them would be together in all the many distant places" (56). On the other hand, "Manoboy!" and "Boyoman!" link up two generations (with a ring, no less) in a relationship of potentially endless slippage.[28] Neither permanent nor territorialized in the body's sex organs, this gesture links generations through something other than maternity, reproduction, or inheritance. It figures Frankie's insertion of herself into the wedding scene as a mode not merely of rewiring affiliation but reimagining eventuality itself, on a queer model—that is, refusing the developmental model in which children evolve into adults, never to return. It must be noted, though, that the relationship between girls and women offers her no such possibility.

This kind of thinking seems key to queering U.S. politics: to imagine social configurations and narrative forms that can refigure both the horizontal bonds between peers beyond couplehood and the vertical bonds between generations beyond parenthood. The powerful image of alliance and slippage between "Manoboy" and "Boyoman" might supplant the capitalist "manowar" even an army of lovers might use to queer the planet, and provides material for rethinking "queer" beyond the nationalist (now global) frontier mentality and progress narrative. The Benjaminian form of allegory replicated by the novel displays and complicates temporality itself, incarnating at once the infinitely receding horizon of history and the infinitely advancing one of utopia.[29] Or as the novel puts it, "That day alone seemed equally important as both the long past and the bright future—as a hinge is important to a swinging door. And since it was the day when past and future mingled, F. Jasmine did not wonder that it was strange and long" (MW, 56–57). If "progress" depends on the long march through a "homogeneous empty time," one might need the kind of transtemporal operations that The Member of the Wedding offers to rupture the developmental trajectory of even queer futurity.[30]

The Member of the Wedding, then, uses the wedding to simultaneously reformulate kinship and nationality, registering the wedding's most expansive possibilities on the level of narrative form. It links domestic and national culture by counterposing wedding fantasies and fantasies about World War II, suggesting that the dominant cultural images of "family" are also part of national and international "politics" proper. It transubstantiates narrative into visual emblems linked together by association, dominated by the sign of the wedding—yet the "minor key" within her new narrative also signals McCullers's refusal to resolve this practice into a representation of marital couplehood, gay or straight. Finally, *Member* implies that the wedding is capable of powerfully reorganizing relationships between past and future, child and parent, old and new. Rather than dramatizing either absolute continuity or rupture, the novel suggests a shifting, connected coexistence between different temporal moments.

The only other work of U.S. fiction that so completely inhabits the semiotic and temporal power of a wedding, while also pointing to the comparative representational and social poverty of inhabiting a marriage, is Faulkner's *Absalom, Absalom!* Both of these novels use the wedding to forge alternative conceptions of time, and to make visible affective ties between people who are denied legal sanction for their sexual desires and activities. In the case of *The Member of the Wedding*, these people seem to be primarily blood relatives, adult-child pairs, and women rather than the couples crossing the color line who populate Faulkner's novel, to which I return in the next chapter. As I noted earlier, when Frankie is left out of the wedding and honeymoon, her immediate reaction is to turn on Berenice and, for the first time, think of her in terms of "the mean word she had never used before, nigger" (*MW*, 135). Not only does the marriage that results from her brother's wedding not have room for Frankie; it also seems to engender her "proper" disidentification with a black woman, whom she replaces with the white Mary Littlejohn. And as Thadious M. Davis remarks, McCullers's stage version of *Member* even more violently replaces cross-racial homosociality with intraracial heterosexuality, diminishing Mary's role by reconciling Frankie with Barney McKeon, a minor character with whom she has earlier committed an unnamed sexual "sin" in her garage.[31]

The novel's and even more so the play's insistence on racial segregation may reveal something about marriage itself rather than about the wedding. In order to move the wedding inexorably toward marriage, and Frankie inexorably toward both conventional femininity and couplehood, the text must exile

Berenice, perhaps because Berenice herself has provided the most cogent arguments against marital couplehood by telling Frankie several cautionary love tales and stating her own disinterest in remarrying. In contrast, the most stunning work the wedding does in this novel is to connect Frankie to the improvised "family" she wishes to disavow. For in a crucial reworking of the wedding scene, Frankie resymbolizes her connection with Berenice and John Henry by triangulating herself into the "wedding" of a different couple:

> There was something sideways and behind her that had flashed across the very corner edge of her left eye; she had half-seen something, a dark double shape, in the alley she had just that moment passed. And because of this half-seen object, the quick flash in the corner of her eye, there had sprung up in her the sudden picture of her brother and the bride. Ragged and bright as lightning she saw the two of them as they had been when, for a moment, they stood together before the living-room mantelpiece, his arm around her shoulders. So strong was this picture that [she] felt suddenly that Jarvis and Janice were there behind her in the alley, and she had caught a glimpse of them—although she knew, and well enough, that they were in Winter Hill, almost a hundred miles away. (*MW*, 69–70)

The half-seen figures turn out to be "two colored boys, one taller than the other and with his arm resting on the shorter boy's shoulder" (70). This vision, a hieroglyph of blackness and boyness, peerness and queerness, points insistently at Frankie's relation to Berenice and John Henry. Just as the wedding reappears at the novel's end as sound interrupting sound, this couple appears as hallucinatory afterimage interrupting Frankie's fantasy image of the original bridal pair.

Like the dream of snow, this daydream exposes a wish for a scene of joining: the male, "colored" nuptial pair inhabit the couple form to illuminate not only the affective ties that Frankie wants with her brother and the bride but those made invisible by a national focus on racially pure, heterosexual nuclear families. The vision expands what Frankie calls "the wedding frame of mind" (69) toward the "terrible summer *we* of her and John Henry and Berenice" (39), for the phantasmic wedding couple is a kind of hologram for the homosexual, pedophiliac, and racial allegiances that the law proscribes, and whose underformalization makes Frankie's life unintelligible. These include forbidden same-sex connections—as between Frankie and Berenice, but also those registered by her crush on the bride, desire to join the girls' club that excludes her, and eventual liaison with Mary. They include the connections between children and across the adult-child divide prohibited by age-of-consent and incest laws—as between herself and John Henry with whom she begs to sleep in the same bed, herself and her father who has forbidden her to sleep with him anymore, and herself and Berenice's comforting body with its "soft big ninnas" (113). They include the intraracial connections among African Americans whose intimate ties were first threatened by laws against slave marriage and then by those that forced them to conform to the laws of middle-class marriage, as between Berenice and her boyfriend T.T., whom she refuses to marry until the Addams family effectively forces her to. And surprisingly, for a novel limited by what can only be called a racist vision of Berenice, the allegiances that *The Member of the Wedding* holds onto also include the interracial forms of kinship prohibited by miscegenation laws.

For the wedding fantasy in the alley actually solidifies connections between Frankie and Berenice's foster brother Honey, with whom Frankie is consistently cross-metaphorized in terms of body, language, and relationship to the nation: while Frankie is "unjoined," Honey is "a sick-loose person" (35); while Frankie "cozens," Honey "could talk like a white schoolteacher" (36), and the army has rejected both of them. After Frankie makes up her mind to join the wedding party and go to Alaska to shed her compromised white southern identity, she suggests to Honey that he "go to Cuba . . . and change to a Cuban" (125) so that he too can be relieved of his racial ambiguity. Despite the linkage of Frankie and Honey, these moments also seem to promote a vision of racial purity. But the alley wedding connects Frankie and Berenice without doing so.[32] In fact, as if to transgress all at once the boundaries of sexuality, age, and race, Frankie's hallucination of the two boys engenders both their first dialogue on love and Berenice's love story: "It was the first time ever they had talked about love, with F. Jasmine included in the conversation as a person who understood and had worthwhile opinions. . . . [Berenice] unwound the story of her and Ludie like a colored queen unwinding a bolt of cloth of gold" (*MW,* 94, 96).

Though the wedding momentarily and accidentally connects Frankie to the black woman who has been her only consistent source of intimacy, when Berenice herself gets engaged she moves out of the Addams household, and Frankie expresses no desire to see Berenice's nuptial ceremony. The wedding of Janice and Jarvis does become a marriage, which seems to reinstall Frankie into her all-white, nuclear family, and the cross-generational, incestuous, and intraracial connections engendered by the wedding dissolve. In *The Member of the Wedding*, surprisingly, it is marriage and not the wedding that creates racial hierarchy—despite the latter's surface "white" trappings.

Chapter Three

"THAT TROTH WHICH FAILED TO PLIGHT": RACE, THE WEDDING,

AND KIN AESTHETICS IN *ABSALOM, ABSALOM!*

O ceremony, show me but thy worth.
—William Shakespeare, *Henry V*[1]

In *The Member of the Wedding*, Frankie definitively disjoins the white wedding
from state-mandated heterosexual monogamy, gender normativity, and racial
purity. Her hallucinated and triangular wedding connects her to two African
American boys and through them to her nursemaid, thereby transgressing
the Jim Crow racial order of the World War II era South. Yet by the end of the
novel, an ordinary legal marriage between two Euramericans (Frankie's
brother and his bride) finally and irrevocably trumps Frankie's version of the
wedding. Not only do the novel's gender benders die or straighten out and its
children die or grow up, but its African American characters are also violently
displaced from the Addams household. In short, an *optically* white wedding
becomes a *racially* whitening marriage. Frankie must finally submit both to
the regime of lawful marriage and her culture's visual regulation of bodies,
where whiteness supposedly signals racial as well as sexual purity.

African American authors, on the other hand, have repudiated exactly this
visual form of regulation, primarily through the trope of the mixed-race body.
In the passing novel in particular, the biracial, visibly "white" but legally
"black" body belies the fiction of racial purity, registering instead a history of

transgressions against the supposedly inviolable boundaries between people of European and African ancestry. Hazel Carby, for instance, demonstrates that nineteenth-century literature's "tragic mulatta" encoded the history of white men raping black women.[2] Karen Sánchez-Eppler suggests that the mixed-race body could signify more than rape; the literary spectacle of light-skinned African American women choosing to couple with darker male partners both confirmed and disavowed the possibility of consensual cross-racial liaisons during and after slavery.[3] Even in present-day popular culture, the multiracial child, figuring the "mixed" status of all human beings, continues to serve as the emblem of a future supposedly beyond race.[4] Yet this paradigm for unfixing race is fundamentally evolutionist and even eugenicist, for it posits biology as a primary means of cultural transformation. As Robert Young notes, the concept of hybridity elaborated in theories of *metissage, mestizaje*, passing, and so on, is based on heterosexual procreation.[5] Focusing on the mixed-race body, it becomes difficult to imagine transgressions of "race" that don't have their origins or end in reproductive thinking, in the ideal of species progress. Still, to celebrate love or desire across changing racial boundaries in an attempt to move beyond a reproductive economy is to suggest that feelings and sexual acts are untouched by power except as the law represses them, and to posit an ideal, immaterial realm of transformation unmediated by social practice.

In contrast, insofar as images of African Americans getting married invoke the sphere of human-made, historically contingent laws, they actually do register transformations in racial taxonomy and hierarchy that follow neither evolutionist nor idealist models. Therefore, unlike *The Member of the Wedding*, many black women's writings of the later nineteenth century represent lawful marriage between men and women of African descent as a sign of freedom *from*, rather than induction *into*, the ideology of white superiority. Indeed, the equal protection clause of the Fourteenth Amendment that implicitly gave emancipated slaves the right to marry as well as more explicit state laws designed to legitimate unions formed under slavery transformed key aspects of the racial caste system in the United States. Legal recognition of their marriages gave emancipated slaves the right to transmit whatever property they could accumulate down family lines. It also made them human in the terms of nineteenth-century white middle-class domesticity. As Hortense Spillers points out, African American slaves had been torn from the kinship systems of their homelands and effectively barred from Anglo-American forms of gender and generation, both under law and in the representations that white people promulgated.[6] Not only did marriage bestow basic civic and economic entitlements, then, it also gave freedmen and freedwomen access to the structure of gender itself—for men, to masculinity defined as exclusive and ongoing sexual access to a woman, paternal rights over the children of this sexual union, and property rights with the corresponding economic responsibility to support his family, and for women, to femininity defined as sexual accessibility limited to one man only, the maternal right to socialize the children of this sexual union, and the expectation of spousal economic support with the corresponding domestic responsibility to maintain a home. For African American writers, the legalization of marriage thus made three representational regimes fully accessible: the novelistic "marriage plot"; the use of feminine "sentimental power" in which the civic sphere is reimagined as an extension of a well-ordered home; and eventually, the family dynasty novel in which the descent of generations reflects a group's forward movement in time.[7]

As Claudia Tate argues about the black woman's domestic novel of the 1890s, the heroine's successful attainment of marriage indicates "the fulfillment of enlightened black self- and group interest," and these texts thereby tend to conceive of civil justice on the model of a consensual heterosexual partnership and an entire people's progress on the model of familial history.[8] But if marriage is to work as what Tate calls "a domestic allegory of political desire," that allegory must efface the asymmetries built into marriage during the late antebellum, Civil War, Emancipation, Reconstruction, and Progressive eras, in which not even freeborn white married women held a national identity fully separate from that of their husbands. The marriage bond trumped the bonds of national belonging for women from 1855, when foreign wives of American men were automatically naturalized, through 1907, when American women who married foreign men were automatically expatriated in laws that were not fully dismantled until the 1930s.[9] Harriet Jacobs seems to recognize this paradox at the end of *Incidents in the Life of a Slave Girl*, when her autobiographical protagonist Linda Brent declares, "Reader, my story ends with freedom; not in the usual way, with marriage."[10] Tate contends that in this narrative marriage is the unattainable sign of Brent's final liberation and that Brent's declaration, which rhetorically counterposes freedom and marriage, is a retort to Jane Eyre's famous, "Reader, I married him."[11] Having earlier claimed that "there is something akin to freedom in having a lover who has no control over you, except that which he gains by kindness and attachment" (*1*, 55), Brent does not seem to see marriage as a route to liberation but as a rather limited way to conceptualize it. I would extend Tate's argument to suggest that Brent's distinctly nonmarital sense of mutual obligation—with her children, female benefactors, and grandmother—represents a set of bonds that competed with the middle-class, couple-centered model of marriage for African Americans in the antebellum era.[12] Even more important, Brent states that "the dream of my life is not yet realized" because she does not yet "sit with my children in a home of my own," rather than because she is unmarried (*1*, 201). Under the laws governing married women's property in the 1860s, marriage would not necessarily make her house "her own" in many states, but might remand it to her husband's control even if it had been purchased with her earnings.[13]

The sense that marriage provides an exemplary figure for liberation is even more problematic when it comes to "interracial" literature, or literature foregrounding sexual and familial alliances between European and African Americans.[14] For instance, Eric Sundquist has written that in Faulkner's *Absalom, Absalom!* marriage is the novel's overriding metaphor, a "perfect formal analogy" for the effort to "force into crisis," and by doing so "overcome the tragic divisions" of male and female, black and white.[15] But in order to symbolically overcome divisions between male and female, the trope of marriage must suppress the ways that marriage law actually *constructs gender* by affixing asymmetrical sexual and service roles as well as property rights to particular anatomies. Furthermore, in order to symbolically overcome divisions between black and white, the trope of "interracial" marriage must also suppress the ways that marriage law *constructs race* by affixing an unequal property base and a stigmatized sexuality to particular anatomies. For the history of statutes against marriage across an ever-changing color line makes it clear that in the United States, marriage has been a linchpin in the binary, hierarchical system of race since it appends ongoing economic disadvantage to particular ancestral lines, which is then naturalized through the discourse of inheritance.

To put it simply, after Emancipation, African Americans may have ceased to *be* property, but were still defined by their separate and unequal access *to* it. Though this was mostly effected by segregation, discriminatory hiring practices, and unfair banking policies, it was also due to the expansion and increased enforcement of state laws forbidding intermarriage—for these laws also prevented black people from inheriting or bequeathing any goods they held in common with a white lover. Because marriages and wills privatize the redistribution of accumulated wealth, intermarriage laws actually compounded other ways of disenfranchising African Americans. Until the Supreme Court's ruling in *Loving v. Virginia* in 1967, they helped ensure that African Americans would continue to operate from a racially bounded property base; though statutes prohibiting marriage between blacks and whites purported to preserve an inherent, biological separation, it was by enforcing continual economic segregation in the domestic as well as market economy that they actually produced the fixed binary race system they purported only to uphold.[16] And if the desegregation of legal kinship, achieved through the overturning of intermarriage and antimiscegenation laws, eventually effected a certain redistribution of property, it did not fundamentally challenge this system of family property itself.

In imagining the relationship between personal, intimate ties and more lasting interventions into the U.S. racial caste system, then, is it possible to depart from the reproduction-centered figure of the biracial child, dematerialized trope of "love," and property-centered domain of legal marriage? Faulkner's *Absalom, Absalom!*—the U.S. novel that most dramatically deconstructs the marriage plot—suggests that perhaps it is. Like McCullers, Faulkner uses the wedding as a centrifugal force out of which to spin social and narrative economies at odds with the marriage plot. But *Absalom, Absalom!* puts the U.S. racial caste system at the very heart of that project. Its weddings both critique the race-making work of marriage law and indicate social transformations for which marriage works neither as motor nor metaphor. For at least during the era of intermarriage prohibition that spans the novel's multiple historical settings (1830–1910), nonmarital declarations, claims, and performances of cross-racial social ties held a certain deconstructive promise. They transgressed racial boundaries without resorting to biology or privileging access to property; they renegotiated the social world through the body rather than transcending it for a dematerialized realm of "love"; they produced entangled pasts, ongoing commitment, and mutual futures without relying on class consolidation or the fiction of blood relations for their rhetorical power.

Though *Absalom, Absalom!* seems to focus on marriage, then, it actually posits the wedding as a performance of the kind of claim I am describing—as a vexed, but promising site for renegotiating "race." Thus, the antiracist work of *Absalom, Absalom!* depends on crucial differences between marriage and weddings. Marriage elevates couplehood over other relationships; the wedding brings these marginalized social forms into threatening view. Marriage demands what the novel's antihero Thomas Sutpen calls a "design," a re-scripting of personal narrative that both erases whatever does not lead up to the present relationship and eliminates certain possibilities from the future. In contrast, the wedding ritual defers progress and completion in favor of repetition and return, and in reordering time, brings an *unheimlich* past into destabilizing conjunction with the present. Finally, from colonization through the mid-1960s, laws against intermarriage enforced the fiction of sexually and racially pure white bodies whose conjoinment would presumably conserve white supremacy. But the folk and religious elements of the wedding, which preceded and continued in the era of intermarriage law and beyond to compete with the state's regulation of kinship, involve different fantasies about what bodies do when they come into proximity. Even as some elements of the wedding—such as the procession of generations and giving away of the bride—link the movement of time to biological reproduction, other aspects—such as the kiss and clasping of hands—suggest an instantaneous, horizontal binding of one flesh to another. Faulkner reappropriates many of the wedding's differential qualities as a means of dismantling racial categories: the competition between marriage and the wedding is, ultimately, his means for unmaking "race."

Sutpen's Plot

Colonial laws against marriage across the color line began in Maryland in 1661, to be followed by a 1691 Virginia statute, and then laws in Maryland (1692), Massachusetts (1705), Pennsylvania (1725), and eventually a majority of the colonies.[17] Rather than nullifying marriages between "Englishwomen" and "Negroes," these laws merely criminalized them. But during the antebellum years of the nineteenth century, and increasingly after Emancipation, many southern states automatically voided marriages between blacks and whites.[18] Under this new legal regime, it was impossible for a married couple to inhabit separate racial categories. If one member were black and one white, it wasn't a marriage; if it were to be a marriage, one member would have to change his or her race. This latter privilege extended only to white people, as in the case of Tempie James, who ran away with her father's slave, drank some of his blood mixed with whiskey, and apparently changed her race on the 1850 census, or in the case of an 1886 journalist's report of "a shriveled old white woman trudging down the lane who, when young . . . had her free-negro lover bled, and drank some of his blood, so that she might swear that she had negro blood in her, and thus marry him without penalty."[19] Theoretically, though, marriage to a white person could also change black to white—and this possibility haunts the minds of white characters in many "passing" novels. In *Absalom, Absalom!* Thomas Sutpen's disinherited mixed-race son Charles Bon is the most obvious representative of this fear: he is, as he puts it, "the nigger that's going to sleep with your sister," who seems to stake his claim to both white property and his white ancestry by affiancing himself to his half sibling Judith.[20]

The usual reading of this novel is that cross-racial reproduction unmakes the black/white binary in the United States, as the racial ambiguity of Charles Bon's body begins to seep onto all of the characters.[21] For at the end of *Absalom!* even the narrator Quentin Compson's Canadian roommate Shreve McCannon seems to be racially mixed; he finishes the story of Thomas Sutpen's life with the statements that there is "one nigger Sutpen left," these "nigger Sutpens" will take over the world, and "in a few thousand years, I who regard you will also have sprung from the loins of African kings" (A, 302). Yet this declaration actually registers the limits of reproduction across racial boundaries as a figure for the unmaking of "race," as it posits a *return* to only one of two races still imagined as opposite and originary: in Shreve's formulation, African ancestry will ultimately cancel out European ancestry. In fact, the novel often does seem to ascribe to a reactionary vision of cross-racial reproduction as both the ultimate mono-racial solution to the problem of "race" and final degeneration of the human species into animals. It finishes, famously, with the image of Sutpen's mixed-race great-grandchild, the "slack-mouthed" idiot Jim Bond, "arms dangling," howling amid Sutpen's burning estate (296). Jim's useless body and feeble mind certainly evoke racist images of devolution. But because his arms in particular are disconnected from both his own body and other people's, within the novel's own imagistic register they also suggest social isolation and ineffectiveness. In one of the novel's most frequently cited passages, Sutpen's legitimate daughter Judith declares that "you are born at the same time with a lot of other people, all mixed up with them, like trying to, having to, move your arms and legs with strings only the same strings are hitched to all the other arms and legs" (100–101). Here, the interconnection of "arms and legs" makes literal the idea that any one person's actions inevitably influence those of all others. Jim's paralysis, on the other hand—his inability to move his arms and thereby affect the social field as a whole—implies that the bodies produced by outlawed, interracial, heterosexual coupling cannot in and of themselves deconstruct the regime of "race." In this sense, Jim's damaged body might be read as a figure for the limits of reproductive thinking.

Jim's grandfather Charles Bon's claims on Thomas Sutpen do not represent an investment in a "pure" white identity either; rather, Bon seems to be seeking paternity of any kind. It is Sutpen himself who exploits the racially binarizing function of lawful marriage. Having discovered in 1831 that his first wife (Bon's mother, Eulalia) has African ancestry, Sutpen divorces her and two years later moves from Haiti to Jefferson, a town Faulkner ironically names for the president who authored this country's founding document of separation from its colonial past and about whom rumors of an unacknowledged black mistress had circulated for centuries.[22] Appearing in Yoknapatawpha County, Mississippi, as if out of nowhere, Sutpen understands that getting married will secure his previously tenuous status as a white person. For even if he is not literally of African or Native American descent (and there is quite a bit of textual suggestion that he might be), as the son of a West Virginia tenant farmer and then an overseer for a French planter, his own relationship to property has as yet barred him from any meaningful access to U.S. whiteness. Long before his arrival to Jefferson, Sutpen has been racially disinherited; fifteen years prior, in the novel's primal scene of initiation into the U.S. race system, a black servant has sent the adolescent Sutpen to the back door of his landlord's mansion. In the time between this event and Sutpen's recounting of it, Sutpen's own body has seemed to literally blacken as a result: he goes on to labor among Africans at a Haitian plantation, work alongside the slaves he brings back to the United States with him to his estate, wrestle with them in his barn, and take on a mud-bespattered appearance that makes him, "save for the teeth," indistinguishable from the men he owns (A, 16). To establish himself firmly as a white person after he comes to Jefferson, it is not enough for Sutpen to appropriate the labor of the "wild niggers" (4) he brings with him from Haiti, cheat a "tribe of ignorant Indians" out of that land (10), build and furnish a mansion on money he may have stolen from riverboats, and rape one of his slave women and produce a daughter. He needs, as he says, "incidentally of course, a wife" (212). Though he seems to fantasize about reproducing his pure-white self with only "incidental" female assistance, his own past is murky enough that his primary need is for a wife of impeccably Anglo-Saxon lineage. In order to ensure the racial purity of the son he so ardently desires, that is, he must first undo his own impurity.

To do so, he fixates not only on Ellen Coldfield and her Anglo-Saxon heritage but also "the big wedding, the full church and all the ritual" (38) that he assumes will secure whiteness for him. On Sutpen's wedding day, his bride's hyper-whitened face prefigures the transformation he hopes for in himself: she is not merely pale, with "no drop of blood in her face" (black, one can presume), but artificially powdered, which contrasts markedly with Sutpen's "face whose flesh had the appearance of pottery, of having been colored . . . " (A, 16, 24). This marriage, in other words, is explicitly figured as a racial makeover in which Ellen's whiteness will overwrite Sutpen's prior "colored" qualities. It is as if Sutpen rewrites the Christian doctrine that "they twain shall be one flesh" (Matt. 19:5) so that it has a racial meaning. Only marrying the propertied and pedigreed Ellen can grant Sutpen the whiteness he feels he has been denied; he understands that whiteness is a matter of *both* property ownership and conjugal respectability. Indeed, if the 1896 legal case of *Plessy v. Ferguson* demonstrated that whiteness is a property expropriable through the "theft" of passing, the literary case of Thomas Sutpen shows that whiteness is, at least imaginably, also a property appropriable through marriage.[23]

Sutpen's obsession with his own nuptials suggests that to focus on the mixed-race body is to overlook the system of marriage itself in making race, to privilege the outcome of reproductive activity across racial boundaries rather than the moment at which thresholds are literally crossed, and in their crossing also established. In contrast, *Absalom, Absalom!* makes threshold crossing into a recurring motif: a "Negro butler" prevents Sutpen from entering the front door of his landlord's house; Sutpen's black daughter Clytie twice bars his sister-in-law Rosa from going upstairs at Sutpen's Hundred; as he listens to Rosa, Quentin realizes that "he too could not pass" the same door Rosa was prevented from opening so long ago (A, 139). Insofar as crossing the threshold is a common expression for getting married, the repetition of this image makes literal the link between marriage law and the production of segregated, racialized identities: marriage law erects uncrossable legal barriers.

But does the wedding? Gina Hicks has productively argued that the Sutpen/Coldfield wedding ritual is emblematic of the nuptial ceremony's ideological work, which is to channel polymorphous desires toward a single object of the opposite sex and same race.[24] But this view of weddings assumes that they are always the successful agents of state marriage law. In actuality, as I asserted earlier, the domains from which the wedding gains its authority are incommensurate; law, canon, and folklore offer wildly different conceptions of what makes a marriage. Do citations from these disjunctive, competing aesthetic, discursive, and institutional domains really work to cordon off desire into a single territory? Or might the very multiplicity of authorities, modes, and historical moments brought forth as sources of legitimacy in such a complicated ritual actually disseminate both desire and narrative along trajectories that marriage cannot even imagine? Insofar as the motif of crossing the threshold evokes a rite distinct from and prior to the state control of kinship in *Absalom!* it also evokes passages that the wedding might make possible even as marriage law forbids them.

As much as *Absalom!* is concerned with the laws that prohibit interracial kinship, then, it is also just as extravagantly concerned with wedding rituals: it displays one proper "onstage" wedding (Sutpen to Ellen Coldfield) and lingers on two weddings that do not make a marriage (the wedding of Charles Bon and Bon's octoroon mistress, and the incestuous betrothal of Bon and Bon's half sister Judith). It also weaves in two disastrous proposals (Sutpen to Rosa Coldfield and then another character, Milly Jones, both conditional on the prior birth of a male child) and mentions several offstage weddings (Rosa's nameless aunt elopes, Sutpen marries his first wife Eulalia Bon, and their grandson Charles Etienne St. Valery Bon flaunts a marriage license that unites him with an unnamed "coal black" woman [*A*, 166]). While it could be argued that any dynastic novel of a family sustaining itself across time will have its share of weddings, it is less clear that these weddings need to be dwelled on as lavishly as they are in *Absalom, Absalom!* In particular, the narrative dilation around the weddings of Ellen Coldfield and Thomas Sutpen, Charles Bon and his "octoroon mistress," (75) and Charles Bon and Judith Sutpen, indicates that these rituals are not giving form and dynamic to the dynastic—that is, linking marriage simultaneously to the movement of narrative and to the transmission of social identities across time—in quite the way they are supposed to. Nor are they successfully installing the boundary between black and white. Instead, *Absalom* produces what Rosa Coldfield early on calls "that troth which failed to plight" (8), tapping into a history and developing a theory of weddings that do not end in state-sanctioned marriage, and yet do mutually implicate and merge black and white identities. Indeed, "to plight" descends etymologically from both "to endanger" and "to pledge." *Absalom* asks whether there lies beyond legal marriage a "troth," ("truth," and binding force) that does not endanger its participants by installing them into a singular racial category.

In part, *Absalom!* works through the difference between weddings and marriage by way of narrative form, specifically by examining a dynamic constitutive to storytelling—that between the spatial linkage of disparate elements and temporal sequencing of events. The novel begins with Quentin Compson listening to Rosa Sutpen's incantatory monologue of the Sutpen family story, which he describes as something like a dream, one that seems to occur "stillborn and complete, in a second" (15). Yet he notes that the dream, which collapses two events supposedly separate in time (birth and death), paradoxically achieves verisimilitude only by means of disavowing this collapse and acceding to "a formal recognition of and acceptance of elapsed and yet-elapsing time" (15). Even stillbirth, Quentin's metaphor for the condensation of two things that ought to be temporally separate, cannot be narrated without a sequential framework. Outside of time, undifferentiated by social markings, a stillbirth both competes with and depends for its comprehension on the stratification of past, present, and future, or what Faulkner later calls *"the was not: is: was"* (259). *Absalom, Absalom!* stages this relationship between simultaneity and sequentiality as a competition between bodily fusion and historical filiation *within* the wedding itself.

Let us return, then, to Sutpen's wedding, which he expects to perform a series of bodily and temporal reorganizations: it will make him white; it will replace his own racially mixed past with a "pure" one; it will erase his connection to Eulalia Bon and Haiti; and it will produce a predictable future in the form of racially pedigreed children. But instead, the Sutpen/Coldfield wedding joins Sutpen to the very flesh he expected it to expel from his own and mobilizes the past in ways that counter his vision of the future. First, the ceremony links Sutpen to Native Americans and African Americans, putting a series of illicit bodily interconnections on display. For among the few people who attend the nuptials are "two of old Ikemotubbe's Chickasaws" (41) and a "half dozen . . . wild Negroes" (39) whom he has brought over from Haiti. The Native Americans whom Sutpen has displaced from their land and black people with whom he has worked to raise Sutpen's Hundred serve as the wedding's ushers, standing at the door holding lighted pine knots. The visibility of their labor in literally illuminating his "white" wedding gestures at the centrality of a racialized labor force to the making of Sutpen's "white" identity.[25] Second, insofar as Sutpen's wedding actually includes more people of color than whites, it makes visible his prior sexual connections with blacks, not only his first wife, Eulalia, but the nameless Haitian slave woman on whom he has already fathered Clytie. Third, by including two sets of characters from populations with racial taxonomies that break the black/white binary—Chickasaws and Haitians—the wedding ambiguates rather than clarifies Sutpen's own racial identity. For the Chickasaws are neither black nor white, and their skin color and cultural practices seem to bleed onto later descriptions of Sutpen himself, whose "flesh had the appearance of pottery" and whose face is described as "faience," a term for earthenware decorated with opaque glazes (A, 36). Similarly, the Haitians, though "black" according to U.S. racial categorizations, come from a country with a three-caste racial system distinguishing enslaved blacks, free whites, and "colored" or free people of African descent; Sutpen's face is repeatedly portrayed as "exactly like" those of his Haitian-born slaves "save for the teeth" (16).[26] As Rosa puts it, "What [Sutpen] fled from must have been some opposite of respectability too dark to talk about" (11), not only in the literal person of his Afro-Caribbean first wife but in the racially admixed sex acts, property relations, and labor system that form part of his supposedly originless past.

Not only does this wedding fuse Sutpen more tightly with the Native American and African American bodies from which he aims to distance his own, it also performs temporal rearrangements quite different from the amnesia that the wedding seems on the surface to demand and that he seeks to will on the town. As if to mimic the history of U.S. expansionism, Sutpen's story begins in Jefferson, Mississippi, where he acts out a declaration of independence from his past, according to Ellen's sister Rosa Coldfield, by refusing to say "who and where and why he came from" (11). In particular, he effaces both his first wife and prior economic connections to Haiti, which evokes Thomas Jefferson's prohibition of trade between the United States and Haiti after Haitian independence. Sutpen moves outward to appropriate Indian lands, and eventually downward to New Orleans (historically, part of President Jefferson's Louisiana Purchase) in search of his son Bon's octoroon mistress and child. As Barbara Ladd demonstrates, it is as if Sutpen himself aims, just as the U.S. government did after 1803, to replace Louisiana's three-caste system with a black/white binary that would disenfranchise his eldest son and grandson.[27]

But rather than lifting Sutpen out of history, giving him a spotless past on which to base a pure-white future, his big wedding thrusts him back into a tangle of historical interrelations that implicate the United States itself. That is, the presence of Haitians at this wedding reinstalls Haiti into not only Sutpen's personal genealogy but also the history of the country for which he stands. For the Haitians at the Anglo-American wedding are a reminder that Spain claimed the island it called "Hispaniola" and landmass it called "America" during the same year of 1492, decimated the original populations of both territories, brought African laborers to both shores, and seceded parts of each territory (Louisiana and the western half of Hispaniola) to the French. Even as Sutpen's wedding reframes the U.S. and Haitian pasts in terms of one another, it also reimagines the future of the United States in terms of Haiti's. While the wedding is supposed to engender an image of the future as a conflict-free, biological unfolding of generations, the future that emerges from *this* wedding is emphatically political, already upon its participants in the form of Haitian-born Charles Bon, and immanent in sons and grandsons whose birth dates will coincide with a series of slave rebellions inspired by the Haitian Revolution. For each of Sutpen's male successors is born in a year marked by an uprising significant enough to enter the national consciousness and U.S. history books: his first son Charles Bon is born in 1831, the year of the Nat Turner rebellion; his second son Henry is born in 1839, the year of the Amistad mutiny; and his grandson Charles Etienne St. Valery Bon is born in 1859, the year of John Brown's raid on Harpers Ferry. Rather than tapping into and extending the Coldfields' Anglo-Saxon pedigree, then, the wedding actually ensnares Sutpen in a multidirectional time line of trans-Atlantic conflicts. Rather than a racially pure, nationally bounded past and future, this wedding makes visible a web of past relations among Europeans, Africans, and Native Americans, and an apocalyptic future of bloody interracial, international conflict irreducible to the Oedipal father/son drama or even the domestic Civil War. In sum, Sutpen confuses the race-, generation-, and citizen-making properties of legal marriage, which might indeed allow him to consolidate his white identity, properly banish his ancestral and political past, and unfold the future in terms of a stainless image of the present, with the work of the wedding itself. He might have done better to forget about "the big wedding, the full church and all the ritual," and just elope.

Bon's Plight

As if to repudiate Sutpen's misguided sense of what the wedding does, his son Charles Bon goes on to capitalize on the ceremony's insurgent ability to unmake the racial regime that marriage holds up. He does this by moving away from a model of lawful kinship, and toward affiliations that are performative and palpable—that is, achieved through a public act of embodied interconnection rather than a written document. This contrast between tactile and paper kinship is most apparent in Bon's search for his father. According to the novel's main narrator, Quentin, who along with his roommate Shreve disinters the racial secrets of the Sutpen legacy, Charles Bon's pursuit of his half sister Judith Sutpen begins as a way of claiming his rightful monetary inheritance: Bon's mother Eulalia hires a New Orleans lawyer to track the Sutpen family over the years, and this lawyer arranges for Bon to go to the University of Mississippi to meet Sutpen's legitimate son Henry, thereby gaining access to their sister and marrying into the financial legacy he deserves. But Bon seems much less interested in these legal claims to property than in some kind of customary acknowledgment of paternity from his father. He initially seeks not a birth certificate but a verbal statement, or failing that, a simple piece of paper with the name "Charles" written on it. Yet paper kinship "can be put aside," as Judith Sutpen later urges Charles Etienne St. Valery Bon to do with the marriage license that unites him with his coal-black wife (A, 168); indeed, paper is consistently thematized in this novel as ephemeral. As Shreve later retells the story, Charles Bon therefore turns away from paper and toward touch as a means of reestablishing his link to his father: "Because he knew exactly what he wanted . . . —the living touch of that flesh warmed before he was born by the same blood which it had bequeathed him to warm his own flesh" (255).

Earlier in the novel, Rosa has claimed that the power of touch causes "the fall of all the eggshell shibboleth of caste and color too" (112). In *Absalom!* the tactile act of sex between blacks and whites, siblings, and people of the same sex certainly undermines racial segregation, the boundaries between generations, and compulsory heterosexuality. But touch also has an *ordering* capacity in Shreve's depiction of Bon's imagination: to Shreve/Bon, it is physical contact, and not property or document, that will resurrect Bon's paternal ancestry. The restorative power of "touch" similarly allows Quentin and Shreve's tactile dialogue at Harvard in 1910, the "hushed and naked searching" (240) in which they shed their clothes as they rework the stories of their elders, to recapitulate the touch of Sutpen's flesh with Eulalia's, vicariously return the missing Sutpen touch to Charles Bon, and bring order to a scrambled narrative. Because Shreve, himself a Canadian and therefore not part of the history of U.S. racial taxonomy, insists that he too could be descended "from the loins of African kings," (302) the tactile episode between him and Quentin also gestures at interracial fusion. Yet by ending with Quentin and Shreve, the novel ultimately settles for a private, domestic version of this reordering touch, situating it in a closed-off room at Harvard. In the figure of Charles Bon, by contrast, the novel suggests that an unofficial though public realm of bodily acts, rather than either an official institution of law or a deterritorialized eroticism, might incarnate a different social order. In other words, in *Absalom!* public ritual, unlike sexual contact behind closed doors, acknowledges an audience and a specific cultural context, and unlike lawful marriage, produces racial multiplicity.

Long before Shreve depicts Bon trying to restore paternity through touch, then, Mr Compson alleges that Bon has already used the "one-flesh" doctrine in a way that directly opposes Sutpen's use of it, to stake claims for a racially mixed identity in a theatrical wedding rather than a legal marriage. On the surface, Mr Compson's version of Bon seems to dismiss his own wedding, the "ceremony which was still no marriage" (94) in New Orleans that, "vesting no new rights in anyone, denying to none the old," (94) unites him with a woman called only "the octoroon mistress" (93). Whereas Rosa has used the word "shibboleth" to describe the U.S. racial caste system, Mr Compson reports that Bon employs it to depict his own wedding; Bon calls the latter "a formula, a shibboleth meaningless as a child's game . . . a ritual as meaningless as that of college boys in secret rooms at night" (93). Yet the rituals of "college boys in secret rooms at night" are hardly "meaningless" to the workings of *Absalom, Absalom!* The homosocial hothouse of the pre–Civil War University of Mississippi is key to the novel's plot, for it allows Bon to erotically cultivate Henry Sutpen so that Henry not only invites him to Sutpen's Hundred but also encourages Bon to sleep with their sister Judith. And the Sutpen story only makes any kind of sense at all in the end because of the collaborative and sensual dialogue of Quentin and Shreve at Harvard in 1910. As Mr Compson's portrayal of Bon's morganatic nuptial ceremony in terms of college-boy rituals makes clear, Bon's mock wedding is *analogical with* rather than *antithetical to* Quentin and Shreve's "happy marriage of speaking and hearing" (253)—a key intervention into the black-white binary and the historical role of marriage law in its production.

The ceremony that unites Bon and his mistress has come about through the Louisiana French Creole system of *plaçage*, which loosely translates as "investment" or "placement." Under this system, white men went to luxurious "quadroon balls" in order to select free, light-skinned African American women as concubines, supporting them and their children in exchange for lifelong sexual access and fidelity.[28] According to Mr Compson, when Bon tells Henry about the ceremony that inaugurated this relationship between himself and the octoroon woman, he uses this mock wedding to lay bare the racist economics of lawful marriage, claiming that the latter is a more egregious form of prostitution than concubinage: " 'The night of a honeymoon and the casual business with a hired prostitute consists of the same suzerainty over a (temporarily) private room, the same order of removing the same clothes, the same conjunction in a single bed' " (93). In fact, Bon argues that it is the concubine's "white sister" who "must needs try to make an economic matter" of sexuality, not only by acquiescing to the terms of the marriage contract (92), albeit in terms mediated by Mr Compson's narration, but also by using the black woman's body to artificially raise her own price.

As Bon sees it, under the system of lawful marriage, white women secure protection from white men by tacitly approving the rape of black women: "The virgins whom gentlemen married" exist only because of "the slave girls and women upon whom that first caste rested and to whom in certain cases it doubtless owed the very fact of its virginity" (87). Since white women bargain their virginity for a husband, and all that safeguards the commodity of this purity and keeps its price high is the enforced sexual availability of black slave women, Bon views plaçage as a way of saving at least a handful of black women from exploitation by any number of white women as well as men, limiting their oppressor to just one white man. He seems to think that plaçage is rooted in a less racist political economy *between women* than marriage is: the octoroon mistress neither buys herself protection through the maintenance of a more exploited female caste nor submits to the violence visited on that caste. In fact, the history of Married Women's Property Acts in the United States actually supports Bon's theory of lawful marriage as deeply intertwined with the sexual exploitation of African Americans. Laws entitling a wife to maintain an estate separate from her husband's first emerged in the late 1830s in the South, and their function was to prevent a bankrupt husband's slaves from being sold off, thereby allowing him and his family to continue to profit from slave labor.[29] Louisiana, the state in which Bon performed his mock union, had historically had the most "liberal" statutes concerning married women's ability to maintain separate property.[30]

The relationship with the octoroon mistress, then, has a certain purity for Bon because he insists that it is "rooted in nothing of economics" for the octoroon mistress (A, 93), as he implies a marriage might be. Insofar as the octoroon woman is literally for sale and she or her family does profit monetarily from the arrangement, of course, he is absolutely wrong. Historical work on plaçage suggests that at best, the octoroon mistress or her family would have seen concubinage as a lesser form of slavery, perhaps more secure than marriage to an enslaved black man with only the master's consent to secure it, less dangerous than passing in a lawful marriage to a white man, and—at the outside—a means of gaining more economic independence and personal freedom than a conventional, domestic marriage to a fellow member of the free, "colored" caste.[31] Since the novel never affords the reader even a glimpse into the octoroon's mind, and Bon himself speaks only via Mr Compson one cannot know to what extent Bon legitimately speaks for her, or even for himself. But what interests me here is Bon's simultaneous critique of legal marriage *and* participation in an extrajuridical ceremony. He goes so far as to say that "the very fact that we acquiesced, suffered the farce" of a wedding ceremony, is "her proof and assurance of that which the ceremony itself could never enforce" (A, 93). Yet he (Mr Compson) is probably mistaken that it furnishes the mistress' "proof and assurance" of lifelong loyalty to him; neither man is a reliable window to her consciousness. Instead, the wedding ceremony seems to do something for Bon that marriage could not have done: it more clearly displays his own proof and assurance of fidelity to something besides maritally sanctioned white supremacy.

Bon's proof and assurance appears only in a shifting set of personal and relative pronouns. At the very moment that Bon explains the system of plaçage to Henry, he seems to be passing (or perhaps Mr Compson, who reports this dialogue to Quentin, distorts Bon's words because he simply does not know about Bon's African ancestry).[32] Momentarily claiming an identity as a white man, Bon declares, "We—the thousand, the white men—made them . . . we even made the laws which declare that one eighth of a specified kind of blood shall outweigh seven eighths of another kind" (A, 91). But then he switches to the third person: "But that same white race would have made them slaves too . . . if it were not for this thousand, these few men like myself" (91). He does not say "these few white men like myself," and indeed here he fleetingly distances himself from "that same white race" as if he were working against it to "save" a tiny handful of his fellow black human beings. Continuing with this shifty self-positioning, he speaks of the "perfectly normal human instinct which you Anglo-Saxons insist upon calling lust" (92), clearly distinguishing himself from Henry and other northerners. He describes the selling of black women "body and soul for life to him who could have used her with more impunity than he would dare to use an animal . . . and then discarded or sold or even murdered" (92), suddenly adopting the voice of an abolitionist. And he insists that "though men, white men, created her, God did not stop it" (92), again distancing himself from "white men." It is only when Bon revisits his own illicit, nonmarital wedding that he manages to maintain such a constantly shifting racial positioning, though Mr Compson misses the point entirely. Neither position is utopian from the mistress' point of view, for if Bon is part of the law-making white race, it is he who has made her "one eighth" African ancestry definitive; and even if he is part of a law-defying black race, his rhetoric positions her as waiting passively to be "saved" by a black man. Bon's lengthy justification of his wedding ceremony, however, does reveal that the economies of heterosexual marriage and racial slavery are linked, and repudiates both. In doing so, his soliloquy undoes Sutpen's mistaken collapse of wedding and marriage.

Bon's refusal to give up the "octoroon mistress," in fact, only makes sense as an unspoken declaration of his own multiple racial allegiances. For his concubine does not really further his plot to depose Sutpen, who could hardly incite Henry to kill Bon on the basis of the kind of illegitimate, perhaps ongoing, liaison that he himself has had with Clytie's mother. As even Bon's lawyer realizes, bigamy is not the issue here. Furthermore, though Bon leaves a photograph of the mistress and child in his pocket for Judith to see after he is killed, ostensibly so that she will know that he was "no good" (287), it is unclear that even Judith would be outraged by the sexual union, given that she has grown up alongside her black half sister Clytie and Clytie's enslaved mother. The problem is, as Henry sees it, "not the fact that Bon's intention was to commit bigamy but that it was apparently to make his (Henry's) sister into a sort of junior partner in a harem" (94). Bon's ceremony and refusal to divest from his mistress, then, constitute a public commitment to the black limbs of his family tree—one that does not collapse into a legal marriage that would reinscribe him into one race or another, though it certainly does not offer the same privileges to the mistress. In some ways, Bon's refusal to give up the mistress is more threatening than his son Charles Etienne St. Valery's legal reversion to a black identity, which the latter effects by marrying the "coal black" woman, for the extralegal plaçage ceremony allows Bon to remain racially liminal.

In the sense that it resists legal marriage without dissolving into social meaninglessness, Bon's illegal nuptial ceremony has affinities with another folk version of the wedding "threshold": the broom-jumping rituals practiced among slaves. These customary acts, recognized by slave communities as binding but by masters only when it suited them, had a dialectical force. They were certainly part of the denial of legal marriage rights to enslaved people, and may very well have sometimes been enforced on men and women paired for the purposes of breeding.[33] But when performed by African American slaves under their own auspices, broom ceremonies also gave evidence of binding ties and communal supervision of these ties even under the conditions of slavery, and of slave culture's ability to collectively support and regulate its own families. Jumping the broom constituted a form of marriage beyond the state's purview, not automatically recognized by it and not always cohering with the state's repressive definition of marriage as a set of private obligations that divested the wider community of responsibility for the maintenance of its members.

Once former slaves were freed, there was some competition between their own forms as well as norms of coupling and the state's definition of marriage. Recent historians have revised Herbert C. Gutman's assertion that slave culture consisted primarily of monogamous nuclear households, pointing to polygyny, serial monogamy, short-term coupling, and cross-plantation, non-domestic unions as equally viable social forms among slaves.[34] After Emancipation, southern legislatures moved quickly to ensure that unions between African Americans adhered to the laws of monogamy, shared domicile, and lifetime duration. Though some states automatically legitimated unions formed under slavery, others variously required a formal ceremony officiated by a justice of the peace, registration with county authorities, and issuance of a license. The work of historians Laura F. Edwards and Amy Dru Stanley suggests that this move to regulate slave marriages was not just the expression of a beneficent Union, nor was it unilaterally embraced by freedpeople. For the promotion of civil marriage was connected to the government's attempts to push former slaves into wage work, thereby abrogating any responsibility for the financial welfare of emancipated African Americans. In the eyes of the Freedmen's Bureau, that is, the wage contract was unenforceable without the reduction of diffuse support networks to couple-centered, domestic economic units; similarly, marriage ensured that private heads of households and not the public sector would be responsible for the upkeep of freedwomen and their children.[35] The legal scholar Katherine Franke contends that granting marriage rights to slaves even extended the state's ability to conscript freedmen back into nonpaying labor, as men who did not support their wives were incarcerated and forced to work on chain gangs.[36]

While the majority of freed slaves flocked to register their unions legally, then, some held that their folk marriage rituals or communal recognition of their various kinds of union were sufficient, and saw the demand that they marry as an imposition. Others actively resisted the state supervision of their domestic relations, refusing to marry legally.[37] Recognizing that legal marriage overwrote not only the master's will but also the slave community's methods of supporting, supervising, and maintaining intimate ties among its members, some freedmen even used the new registration laws to escape any further obligations to their partners. One freedman declared, "When we wuz freed, de slaves dat wuz married all had to git license an' be married over again. My pa quit my ma when he found dis out, an' wouldn't marry her over again. A heap ob 'em quit dat way. I recken dey felt free sho' 'nuf, as dey was feed from slavery an' from marriage."[38] Even slaves who did legally marry resisted the middle-class ideology of marriage as a set of private obligations and responsibilities by defining it as a means for accessing publicly held civil rights and entitlements. Both Claudia Tate and Laura Edwards, for instance, maintain that African Americans of the nineteenth century contested white liberal models of the family as disconnected from a wider public sphere. In doing so, they connected civil marriage to the communal systems of support that their jump-the-broom ceremonies had also obliquely referenced and demanded that the nation itself accede to this social vision.

Bon's plaçage ceremony is also connected to broom-jumping rituals in that the latter are mixed African European heritage. The popular books that have revived this ceremony among African Americans since 1976, when Alex Haley's *Roots* first portrayed it, have insisted on its African origins.[39] The post-*Roots* revival of jumping the broom has been part of a larger African American reclamation of the wedding as a declaration of alternate conceptions of kinship or, as one wedding handbook puts it, of the "African belief that a wedding is a community event."[40] If the white wedding always threatens, despite its potentially liberating connections with Christian and capitalist technologies of membership, to produce a cordoned-off domestic couple, the conscious use of an alternate tradition suggests a wider sense of obligation both to suppressed histories and collectivities imagined across the boundaries of the nuclear family. But as folklorist Alan Dundes points out, "The slave custom was not invented in the United States, and it is not derived from ancient African ritual. It is an undeniable borrowing from European folklore."[41] The ceremony, called a besom wedding in Wales, seems to have been brought by emigrants to the southern colonies in the 1700s and was perhaps even originally forced on slaves by their masters. Reclaimed in the 1970s and beyond as an Afrocentric act, the jumping-the-broom ceremony actually unites the popular kin-making rituals of two cultures otherwise seen as racially distinct: the Welsh who circumvented the English government's enforcement of church weddings in the 1700s, and African Americans who continue to resist Euramerican hegemonies of gender roles and nuclear family. Thus, the jump-the-broom ceremony has a certain promise as a figure for cultural rather than biological admixture.

Absalom, Absalom!'s numerous threshold crossings certainly evoke the jump-the-broom ritual, though they do not name it directly. Instead, the novel more explicitly invokes, repeats, and lingers on the handclasp—another archaic aspect of the wedding that precedes both church and state control over marriage—and makes this central feature of the Western wedding into an emblem of same-sex, cross-racial joining. As I have noted, Rosa Coldfield declares that the touch of flesh with flesh leads to "the fall of all the eggshell shibboleth of caste and color too" (A, 112). The word "shibboleth" directly links her statement to Bon's justification of his ceremony, where he uses the word too, and the events that she narrates after this statement constitute yet another of *Absalom*'s nonmarital "troths"—this one led by Clytie.

In 1865, Rosa Coldfield attempts to go upstairs to see Charles Bon, whom Henry Sutpen has just slain on learning that his best friend and future brother-in-law has African ancestry. But Clytie, Sutpen's illegitimate black daughter and the house servant, grabs Rosa's arm. Even as Clytie's motion of turning her own arm into a bar is yet another expression of racial barriers and the slave woman's suppressed rage and power, it also produces a threshold and challenges Rosa to cross it. Most important, and somewhat counterintuitively, this gesture is a kinship claim made through the medium of touch. For Clytie's motion evokes the "handfast" that has persisted as part of the wedding ritual since Roman times, when according to at least one historian, the bridegroom took the bride by the wrist to signal his power over and possession of her.[42] Eventually, the bride's right hand was merely placed into the groom's, but this action still formed the climax of the Roman ceremony. When the church resurrected Roman aspects of the wedding ritual in order to subordinate popular practices, it appropriated the handclasp, which as John Boswell asserts, "persisted throughout the Middle Ages as the single most critical act in unions of all sorts," and incorporated it into Christian sacramental logic.[43] But in popular practices, the handclasp continued to be part of a register of gestures that both figured and extended the sexual joining of bodies. John Gillis points out that up until the eighteenth century, "any physical contact, and especially with blood, was believed to have a powerful binding effect," so that courting and wedding were accompanied by love bites and ritual exchanges of "magical" tokens of the body like locks of hair; the handclasp was but one form of this binding.[44] As the state assumed control over marriage, the legal fiction of coverture, in which the man and woman became one economic and civic body (namely, the man's), replaced both the physical binding and sacramental transubstantiation of two bodies in one flesh. The handclasp and to a lesser extent the kiss, their sexual, magical, and even sacramental referents significantly diluted, remained the only corporeal scenes of binding. When the sentimental white wedding took hold in the nineteenth century, most of these bodily encounters gave way to more symbolic exchanges such as the ring and lifting of the veil, and to the mutual release of stored-up emotions in the form of tears.[45] But the handclasp remained.

In Christian liturgy, the knitting of two bodies into "one flesh" is symbolic rather than literal; in the legal fiction of coverture, the man's identity includes and subsumes the woman's; in sentimental culture the mutual expression of emotions overwrites the magical commingling of bodies. But Clytie's gesture seems to restore both female power and the archaic, pre-Christian power of touch to literally incarnate obligations between people. Surprisingly, it is the arch-racist Rosa and not Clytie who interprets this act as the transmogrification of two unrelated bodies into blood kin: she reports that the two stand "joined by that hand and arm which held us, like a fierce rigid umbilical cord, twin sistered to the fell darkness which had produced her" (A, 112). Clytie's arm both connects and doubles the two women into twin daughters ancestrally bound not only to the racially ambiguous "fell darkness" of Sutpen but also to Clytie's unnamed slave mother (indeed, an umbilical cord connects mothers, not fathers, to their children). Here, Rosa seems to assent to a black maternal lineage, metaphorically losing the racial purity she has claimed throughout the novel. Despite the otherwise implacable hatred of African American people that she displays elsewhere in the novel, here she stands "joined by that volitionless . . . hand," and cries, " 'And you too? And you too, sister, sister?' " (112–13).

This plea is the closest Rosa comes in the novel to saying "I do"; there is even a witness in this scene, for not only does Rosa insist that Quentin hear about it many decades later but Judith's voice also interrupts it at that very moment, calling out Clytie's name as if to object to the union. Rosa's cry also reverses and feminizes the biblical story from which the novel's title has been taken. "Sister, sister" reconjugates "Absalom, Absalom!"—itself a modification of King David's "my son, my son": "Oh my son Absalom, my son, my son Absalom! would God I had died for thee, O Absalom, my son, my son!" (2 Sam. 18:33). And Rosa's cry evokes the repetition of "my sister, my spouse" in the Song of Solomon (4:9).

The emblematically connective moment between Rosa and Clytie also links them to Quentin and Shreve, who are described as being joined by a "geologic umbilical" cord (A, 208), the continental trough that runs between Canada and the United States. This, in turn, effects a "geographical transubstantiation" (208) between the two men, much like the uniting of flesh supposedly inaugurated by the Christian marriage ceremony, which results in the only "happy marriage" in the novel (253). It is also in Rosa's narration of the scene between herself and Clytie that she uses the word "shibboleth," which now connects Charles Bon's narration of his mock wedding ceremony, the verbal games Quentin and Shreve play, and Clytie's gesture as three complex techniques of extralegal kin making. Shibboleth itself names precisely an embodied, though not precisely reproductive, means of belonging; according to the Old Testament, one proved membership as a Hebrew by correctly pronouncing this very word. The cross-racial connections between these three ceremonies of union—Quentin and Shreve, Charles Bon and his concubine, Rosa and Clytie—suggests that the rituals neither "whiten" their participants nor cast them out of the social field altogether. Ultimately, Clytie's handclasp, which cannot be reduced to reproductive sex, recapitulates and reignites the interconnections that destroy Sutpen's racist, heterosexist, repro-centric "design": the revenge of Eulalia Bon through her son Charles's homoerotic, incestuous, and fratricide-inciting claims on his father and brother; Henry Sutpen's homoerotic, cross-racial desire for Bon; and Judith Sutpen's incestuous, cross-racial desire for Bon.

This central event in *Absalom, Absalom!* evokes and feminizes the ceremony of eroticized, egalitarian binding between spiritual "brothers" that John Boswell has traced to premodern Europe, in which the handclasp was a defining act. In *Absalom!* the handclasp becomes a means for performing ongoing connections and obligations across both racial and heterosexual barriers. Boswell notes that in preindustrial societies, becoming brothers not only had erotic connotations but also "meant becoming a joint socioeconomic unit, recognized by and important to both society and the economy, with material and juridical consequences."[46] Following their "handfast," Rosa and Clytie too become "sisters" in exactly this sense, merging and triangulating with Judith Sutpen into *"one being, interchangeable and indiscriminate,"* (A, 125) who sleep in the same room and run Sutpen's estate for the duration of the war. Unfortunately, unlike Bon who will not give up the bond forged by his mock wedding, Rosa eventually sunders her tie with Clytie in the same corporeal way it started, by striking Clytie's hand away and then knocking her to the floor when she tries to block Rosa's passage up the stairs a second time, to see the dying Henry in 1910.

There are, then, two kinds of "touches" in *Absalom, Absalom!* There are sexual touches coded as private and even secret, such as Sutpen's rape of his slave woman sometime in the 1830s, his seduction of his sharecropper's granddaughter Milly in the 1860s, and even to a certain extent Shreve and Quentin's clandestine sex play at Harvard in 1910, which are the constitutive antitheses to the race-making technology of marriage. But there are also kin-producing touches; these draw from popular and even Christian notions of corporeal binding that predate the state's control of marriage, are made public by the spoken word and a witness, and extend beyond the couple-centered and reproductive logic of lawful marriage. It is arguable that Rosa and Clytie's handclasp is a rather attenuated "wedding," given that Clytie's gesture is an aggressive one and that when it is repeated almost half a century later, Rosa violently rejects it. Yet the status of their first handclasp as a wedding is reinforced by the fact that narratively, it leads directly to the novel's Song of Songs, Rosa's sustained and lyrical meditation on the engagement of Charles Bon and Judith. Rosa's description of what she calls her *"anonymous climax-less epicene and unravished nuptial"* (116) is *Absalom!*'s most redemptively antimarital wedding. This long, lyrical passage, an epithalamium of sorts, imagines how corporeal gestures unsanctioned by the state might reconstellate the social field in ways far beyond the taxonomizing logic of marriage law.

Rosa's Plaint

Speaking in 1910, having just told Quentin of her 1865 encounter with Clytie in the kitchen, Rosa suddenly modulates into a completely ahistorical narrative mode: "Once there was . . . " (115), she says, as if beginning a fairy tale. She then segues backward to the moment of her own fourteenth summer, in 1859, during which Charles Bon courts Judith Sutpen, and she herself begins sewing the garments for her sister's trousseau. As Mr Compson has told Quentin in his earlier version of the same story, with this act Rosa prepares for her own "vicarious bridal" (61). During the stretch of time she sews, which covers the Civil War years, Mr Compson portrays her as "losing the knell and doom of her native land between two tedious and clumsy stitches on a garment which she would never wear" (61). But as Rosa tells it, her sewing actually undoes the marital love knot; the act of stitching the bridal gown captures a kind of spacing, a deferral of both marriage and the "doom of her native land" as though the two were synonymous. (Indeed, insofar as Union rhetoric figured the reuniting of North and South as a marriage, they were.) Rosa can certainly be read as Mr Compson does—a spinster figure symbolizing a feminized South jilted, divorced, or widowed by the North; Mr Compson also figures the wartime sacrifices of southern women as a Confederate flag sewn from women's dresses (63). But the novel establishes in several different ways—most notably by Mr Compson's overlooking Bon's African ancestry—that Mr Compson is a bad reader. If Judith, for whom Rosa ostensibly sews the garments, is literally a widow before she is a bride once Bon kills Henry, Rosa is neither widow nor bride. Like her stitching, Rosa's role in the upcoming wedding stops time altogether and then moves it beyond the narrative as well as the legal economy of marriage.

Like Quentin, who in the novel's opening has counterposed "stillbirth" to narrative exposition, Rosa explicitly counterposes the wedding to linear time. For she declares that in sleep, memory cannot supersede the body: ". . . *The brain recalls just what the muscles grope for: no more, no less*" (115), and this "groping" she depicts as the "*sensuous marriage*" of a hand on a bedside table, threatened by the ordering work of the "*sleeping brain*" (A, 115). The fact that the "marriage" Rosa advocates is accomplished by a "hand" is key here, for it recalls the handfast she has just described between herself and Clytie. As if to escape once more the ordering mechanisms that have abstracted a narrative memory out of a tactile event, Rosa returns again to a time outside of history, repeating, "*Once there was . . .*" (115). This time, she aims to portray a "*world filled with living marriage*" (116), a form of relationality and temporal stasis that can achieve exactly the lambent properties of palm meeting table.

At first, the key emblem for this aspect of *Absalom*'s tactile project of remaking U.S. kinship seems to be a letter that Bon has written in black Yankee stove polish on heavy white French paper and sent to Judith from the front lines of the Civil War. The characters pass this totem of interracial and cross-regional binding from hand to hand and read it aloud, in a motion that Judith Sutpen claims is antithetical to the dead time of monuments. With the letter, Judith alleges, both human ties and narrative are created in the act of mixing flesh and language, reading and rereading, telling and retelling the "scrap of paper" that she insists " 'might make a mark on something that *was* once for the reason that it can die someday,' " as opposed to the "block of stone" that "cant be *is* because it never can become *was* because it cant ever die or perish" (101). Yet though Judith seems to think that the temporal contingency of paper has the capacity to change the past, she actually intervenes in history precisely in the monumental mode, by installing the tombstones of Charles Bon and his son into the Sutpen family plot. She also uses the ephemeral nature of "paper" in reactionary ways, insisting that paper kinship can be "put aside" by urging Charles Bon's son to destroy his marriage license to the unnamed "coal black" woman. In contrast, Rosa Coldfield really does put paper aside—for as the town's poet laureate, she could certainly tell the Sutpen story in writing rather than speaking it aloud to Quentin—to unite the connective properties of touch to those of sound. With Rosa, there are neither monuments nor letters, but only a series of physical and verbal claims on other people that transcend "paper" kinship and yet do not fall back on the fiction of "blood relations."

Significantly, Rosa's sense of touch is emphatically nongenital (or one might say, her sense of genitality relocates the key erogenous zones from penis and vagina to hand, mouth, and ear). She performs a binding of hands with Clytie; she dreams of a hand meeting a table. She claims that untouched *"by friction's ravishing of the male-furrowed meat,"* she does not become *"weaponed and panoplied as a man instead of hollow woman"* (117); she recognizes that the supposedly natural, "sexed" body is constructed by the regime of compulsory reproductive heterosexuality. Freed from that economy, and constituting her entire relation to other bodies first through the touching hand and speaking mouth, she imagines herself as *"all polymath love's androgynous advocate"* (117), falling in love like Frankie Addams with the mobile scenes of courtship and wedding and speaking endless lyrical monologues about them.

Rosa's liberation from the normatively sexed body is also freedom from the "developmental" body, another product of heterosexist and reproductively centered thinking. She claims that she has been *"held over from all irrevocable time"* (115) as she literally waits on Ellen, Judith, her father, and Sutpen. Her atemporal life involves *"not even growing and developing,"* a failure to accomplish *"the processional and measured milestones of the normal childhood's time"* (116). But the novel has already critiqued the milestone theory of history in Judith's dismissal of the "block of stone" (101) that cannot live because it cannot die. So when Rosa describes herself as a fetus caught in the womb, unable to be either aborted or born, she repeats Quentin's image of the stillbirth, suggesting that the narrative dynamic of *"was not: is: was"* cannot do justice to some bodies and lives. Outside the bodily economy of "sex" as well as narrative economy of marriage and reproduction, Rosa holds out for the economy of the wedding that repudiates the "processional," goes on forever without resolving into consummation, remains what she calls *"one anonymous climaxless epicene and unravished nuptial"* (116) in which alternative corporeal logics and an alternative temporal dynamic converge.

The final medium for this convergence is sound. If touch connects Rosa with Clytie across the bounds of race, sound conjoins Rosa to Judith and Bon across the bounds of both race and couplehood, just like the hallucinatory, triangulated wedding of Frankie Addams and the two "colored boys." For when Rosa enters into the marital aura that envelops Bon and Judith, she turns away from her persistent hand mindedness and toward a model of what might be called aural sex. That is, she substitutes *"the omnivorous and unrational hearing-sense for all the others"* (116), following Judith and Bon around eavesdropping as if to gain auditory entry into their connubial scene. With this scene and several others, *Absalom, Absalom!* seems to promote what is by now a theoretically rearguard conception of speech as somehow more present than writing. But it does so in order to imagine a mode of eroticized, corporeal connection that not only de-centers state-sanctioned marriage but also moves beyond either biological reproduction or genital sex. In *Absalom!* that is, speech is less a medium of bodily presence than a means of somatic and temporal fusion between bodies otherwise impossible to bind. For in this novel, speech is primarily about the sound of breathing and sharing of air, which connects characters and facilitates the novel's shift from one time period to another. When Rosa speaks to Quentin and Quentin to Shreve, the metaphor of breathing takes over; breathing transports Quentin from his own present to Rosa's past and allows Shreve to merge imaginatively with him at Harvard.

The basis for Rosa's recalibration of kinship is this dialectic, in sound and breath, between bodily presence and absence, immediacy and temporal delay. She sets her own "unravished," auricular nuptial in a transcendent springtime that she asserts consists of *"all springs yet to capitulate condensed into one spring . . . beholden of all betrayed springs held over from all irrevocable time, repercussed, bloomed again"* (115). Insofar as it registers a place outside of both dominant histories and historiographical modes, Rosa's place outside of official time might actually connect her to Clytie's mother, or Eulalia Bon, or Clytie herself, or even "that Porto Rico or Haiti or wherever it was we all came from but none of us lived in" (239)—all the African-derived people, places, and histories that the narrators repress as they construct the plot. But insofar as her "nuptials" take place in a springtime made up of past springs "repercussing" as well as future springs that have "yet to capitulate," this sense of timelessness does not merely put her outside of history. Rather, it suggests both the return of the repressed and a future not yet made over in the image of the present. The word "repercussed," that is, links Faulkner's critical theory of U.S. racial history to the sonic elements of his own writing, and both to the place of ritual in this novel.

As James Snead has argued, cultural repetition, in the form of ritual, is "not just a formal ploy but often the willed grafting onto culture of an essentially philosophical insight about the shape of time and history"—namely, a resistance to Western notions of time and history as progressive.[47] He points out that to Euramericans, repetition is perforce equated with accumulation, growth, and a transcendence of the past; certainly Thomas Sutpen aims to make his wedding do just these things. But in African American performances, Snead contends, repetition implies circulation, redistribution, and the reemergence of the past. In this sense, *Absalom, Absalom!* disrupts Sutpen's Eurocentric use of the wedding ritual with Rosa's (ironically) Afrocentric one. Not only is the novel insistently *oral* and collectively so, consisting as it does of a single voice and story disseminated across multiple narrators, it is also marked by the recurrence of motifs and phrases that neither advance the plot nor add up to produce cognitive breakthrough, but instead force a return to earlier textual moments.[48] Faulkner himself has famously noted that the very syntax of his sentences constitute his attempt to get the past into the present: not only every chapter but almost every sentence in *Absalom, Absalom!* literally "repercusses" something that has already been narrated before.[49] Rather than making Faulkner a "black writer" or Rosa a "black character," this technique reflects Faulkner's sense that the restoration of African history and culture to "America" demands both an aesthetic and a political revolution. Yet in the insistent pressure of the wedding on the text, its use of weddings to register diffuse, erotic sensory contact rather than reproductive sex or lawful marriage, this revolution goes beyond words to model what might be called a *kin-aesthetic* rupture of the boundaries between black and white, past and present—an embodied means of formalizing those very relationships that do not count as lawful kinship.

Sutpen's black servant Luster, apparently one of the least-important characters in the novel, succinctly states the terms of this project. When Mr Compson asks him to spell Jim Bond's last name, Luster replies, "Dat's a lawyer word. Whut dey puts you under when de Law ketches you. I des spells readin words" (A, 174). Refusing to spell out either a last name or a term denoting legal constraints, and privileging instead connections bound by the more corporeal act of speaking aloud, Luster elevates nonreproductive bodily relations over legal ties. Luster's preservation of a "readin" bond against a legal one makes some sense out of Rosa Coldfield's otherwise incomprehensible fixation on Quentin Compson, who as Shreve points out, is no kin to

her. In Rosa's nonreproductive, filiative economy, she and Quentin are connected through verbal transactions that extend across time, because as Mr
Compson remarks, Sutpen may have told Quentin's grandfather "something
about himself and her . . . your grandfather might have told me and I might
have told you. . . . So maybe she considers you partly responsible through
heredity for what happened to her and her family through him" (8). Here,
"heredity" is sonic and narrative rather than filial or property-based. Quentin
eventually acquiesces to Rosa's sense of kinship, not bothering as he has
consistently done to correct Shreve when the latter calls Rosa Quentin's
"aunt": " 'And so it was the Aunt Rosa that came back to town inside the
ambulance,' Shreve said. Quentin did not answer; he did not even say, *Miss
Rosa*" (301). Verbal performance here finally "repercusses" kinship in the way
Rosa has wished it to, reverberating it along a chain of sonic connections in an
auditory version of "inheritance." This model not only contests the visual
regime of racial typology that is so utterly unreliable in this novel but the
reproductive regime of ancestry itself.

In the end, *Absalom, Absalom!* privileges the actions of Quentin and Shreve
over those of Clytie or Rosa. In their pronounced fascination with and ven-
triloquization of the black male characters in the novel, Quentin and Shreve
suggest a model of cross-racial appropriation and investment that both breaks
the reproductive frame and remains accountable to history. As their dialogue
mingles the sound of their speech, the air they share, and even their bodies
not only with one another but also with Charles Bon, whose voice Shreve
resurrects, it becomes a form of cultural "miscegenation" somewhat like
minstrelsy as Eric Lott has described it.[50] That is, the dialogue of Quentin and
Shreve is an act of homoerotic "love" for Bon as well as cultural "theft" of his
voice, body, and culture. But unlike minstrelsy, their performance refuses to
substitute a healing myth of happy slaves for a history of violence. Instead, it
restores the latter history. The "secret ritual" of these "college boys at night"
not only produces a "happy marriage of speaking and hearing"; it also has its
own moment of consummation. Having heard Shreve retell the story such
that Bon's drop of black blood becomes the central motivation for Henry's
fratricide, Quentin "began to jerk all over, violently and uncontrollably" (288).
Yet as readers of Faulkner are aware, history's seizure of the subject is unbear-
able; *The Sound and the Fury* reveals that within a month of this episode,
Quentin commits suicide.

Rosa and Clytie meet no such fate; Rosa dies of natural causes and Clytie remains in her burning house to die, their longer lives perhaps suggesting that their interventions on racialized U.S. kinship have the capacity to create a future. What *Absalom, Absalom!* accomplishes with the wedding moments facilitated and imagined by these two women in particular, as well as with that performed by Bon, is to gradually strip marriage law away from the wedding, until the oldest form of the latter ritual emerges: the binding of flesh and speaking of words. The version of the wedding that is furthest beyond the state's imaginary—Rosa's, which engages the body and yet refuses to seal the couple off from their surrounding relations, to separate them from prior generations and imagine the future in reproductive terms, or to found a household on the act of forgetting—is Faulkner's model for reimagining a social field that might eschew biology, and yet still refute both the racial taxonomies constructed by the laws against interracial marriage and the privatization of property effected within even reformed marriage laws. *Absalom, Absalom!* makes clear the problematic legacy of marriage in the United States. The civil ceremony depends for its meaning and instantiation on folk and religious forms, which are drawn from modes of belonging that contest the hegemony of couple-centered marriage itself.

Chapter Four

"A DIABOLICAL CIRCLE FOR THE DIVELL TO DAUNCE IN":

FOUNDATIONAL WEDDINGS AND THE PROBLEM OF CIVIL MARRIAGE

this little bride & groom are
standing) in a kind
of crown . . .
. . . .

. . . this
candy crown with this candy

little bride & little
groom in it kind of stands on
a thin ring which stands on a much
less thin very much more

big & kinder of ring & which
kinder of stands on a
much more than very much
biggest & thickest & kindest

of ring.
. . . .
—e. e. cummings, "Poem 8"[1]

Though *The Member of the Wedding* and *Absalom, Absalom!* certainly invest in the florid sociability of the wedding, they also use the ceremony as a window onto the work of marriage law. *Member* suggests that lawful marriage produces domestic, cross-gender, dyadic couplehood as a metonym for and relay to national belonging. *Absalom!* connects this work to a U.S. history of white supremacy, asserting that laws against intermarriage enforced racial purity as the "natural" alibi for a continued segregation of property. Thus far, though, I have spoken as if lawful marriage were itself straightforward and internally consistent. A recent *New Yorker* cartoon by John O'Brien indicates otherwise. It shows a police officer escorting a woman into a courthouse, asking, "Bride or Groom?" (see figure 5). At the front of the room, seated at separate tables facing the judge's bench, a man and woman (presumably the "bride" and "groom") peer back over their shoulders at the guests. Next to each sits a lawyer; both of the lawyers face forward. The cartoon plays on the idea of a "divorce ceremony" to which one could invite celebrants or even command an audience. Yet the scene also looks somewhat like a civil wedding; only the police and attorneys mark it as a trial. The very convergence of wedding and trial on which the punch line relies is enabled by the conventions of civil marriage ceremonies—that a justice of the peace can be the sole adjudicator of legal marriage, that a man and woman may speak the marriage vows just as if they were taking the courtroom oath to speak the truth and end up legitimately married.

One obvious implication of the cartoon might be that a marriage unsanctioned by some further apparatus—religion, community authority, or even commercial trappings—will inevitably end in a divorce at the courthouse in which it began. Another might be that witnesses to any marriage are there more or less by force, commandeered as agents of the state whether or not they want to be, as the figure of the police officer usher implies. But the cartoon also presents a man and woman who look away from the judicial bench, a judge whose face is half in shadow, and the backs of two litigators, thereby signaling the difficulty of making visible the law that legitimates marriage.

If the foundation of modern marriage is state law, of what *positive* content does this law consist? The marriage contract certainly becomes visible in divorce court: many married couples only see its terms when they wish to dissolve it and find out that their wedding vows didn't quite specify their gendered financial, occupational, and sexual obligations to one another.[2] But

Fig. 5. © New Yorker Collection 1999, John O'Brien from
cartoonbank.com. All Rights Reserved.

in this cartoon, the state emerges most clearly in the figure of the police officer, who is the focal point of the drawing and the only authority with a legible face. His central role (of usher or perhaps even wedding director) and the gratuitous appearance of his gun imply that a civil wedding is always already, somehow, a crime scene. "Bride or Groom?" points to the problematic relationship between marriage and the nation-state: In what institution or apparatus does the "civil" status of marriage actually lie? From what source does the local or federal government get its authority over marriage? Might one find the substance of the marriage contract, its very foundation, in transgressions of the law that have nothing to do with the grounds for divorce? And how might the wedding expose this foundation?

A civil wedding seems overtly to confirm the state's power over marriage, as compared to that of parents, religion, or community norms. Even further, a civil ceremony figures the couple's bond as an agreement with their polity that supersedes those with natal family, church, or neighborhood. To say "I do" in a courthouse or before a justice of the peace is to explicitly subject oneself to a national kinship apparatus—though it takes the form of local state and county laws—that supersedes whatever patterns of affection and caretaking actually structure one's everyday life; in matters of inheritance, custody, hospital visitation rights, and so on, "husband" and "wife" trump "godparent," "neighbor," "roommate," and sometimes even extended "blood" family relationships. More than any other kind of wedding ceremony, the civil wedding also announces the existence of a body politic and makes explicit the induction of a couple as its disciplinary subjects. As Nancy Cott puts it, "One might go so far as to say that the institution of marriage and the modern state have been mutually constitutive. As much as (legal) marriage does not exist without being authorized by the state, one of the principal means that the state can use to prove its existence—to announce its sovereignty and its hold on the populace—is its authority over marriage."[3] Recent political theory has also shown that the link between marriage and state formation is more than merely rhetorical insofar as marriage law regulates the relations of legitimate birth that are constitutive of "natural" citizenship; thus, political membership in the modern nation is actually based on kinship.[4] In short, on the civil model, marriage and the state bring each other into being and marriage literally makes citizens, but citizens cannot make the rules of their marriages.

In the United States, the ability of the couple and country to mutually instantiate one another is also enhanced by the covenantal model of marriage that the Puritans brought with them from England. Though the New England Puritan concern with populating the colonies made them regulate *sex practices* according to the biblical injunction to "be fruitful and multiply," they did not conceptualize the *nuptial union* as primarily procreative in purpose. Rather, they treated it as a form of and figure for a covenantal social order, grounding their vision of marriage in the description of Eve as Adam's subordinate helpmate, arguing that the wife's consent was necessary to secure the husband's authority, and using this relationship to illuminate both the colonist's relation to the magistrates' authority and the elect population's relation to God.[5] The New England colonists also made the magistrate—and not the couple's verbal declarations, their parents' consent, or even a church blessing—the final arbiter of marital legitimacy. But rather than merely announcing the existence of the English state as a source of external control, the Puritan covenantal marriage ritually reincarnated the colonial polity itself, for it linked a couple to a community, members of a community to one another, and the community as a whole to God. The marital bonds extended both outward to enjoin members of a community to one another, and upward to oblige the couple to their secular governors and reaffirm the entire community's submission to God's will. These ties were certainly not egalitarian, for they constituted a set of hierarchical, homologous, and interconnecting relations based on the commandment to "Honor Thy Father and Mother." Yet they were, in a sense, plural, for Puritan marriage ceremonies conjoined and ratified the entire community.[6]

By the nineteenth century, this covenantal model had been overlaid with a contraction view of marriage as a private arrangement based on the will of the parties concerned, limited by statutes but not overtly supervised by the government.[7] Nevertheless, the colonial wedding continued to have a privileged place in later representations of "America," perhaps most famously in Henry Wadsworth Longfellow's poem "The Courtship of Miles Standish" (1858). Especially during the nineteenth century, the quaint colonial ceremony was a visible emblem through which the inauguration of the U.S. polity could be retrospectively imagined in terms of spontaneous, shared emotions rather than arcane charters and unfair bargains with Native Americans. In schoolroom tableaux, fictional sketches, and popular iconography, the wedding seemed to affirm that love was the primary basis for the establishment of a polity, creation of a new earthly domain, and binding of previously atomized individuals into a collective endeavor (see figure 6).[8]

Fig. 6. Colonial wedding pageant, 1911. Courtesy of Historic
Northampton, Northampton, Massachusetts.

Meanwhile, explicitly covenantal marriages were also used to ratify new communities during the Second Great Awakening and beyond. For instance, in the "complex marriages" at Putney, Oneida, and Wallingford, every resident was considered to be married to every other. Shakers discouraged marriage, promoting "sibling" relationships as a better model for collectivity. Fourierists focused their social energies on their "phalanxes" of 1,620 other people and practiced serial monogamy. Most famously, Mormons practiced polygny or men's taking of multiple wives (popularly referred to as polygamy). These activities suggested that polygamy may have been the most problematic (or utopian) horizon of the civic covenantal mode.[9] If the marriage ceremony could unify and incarnate the community itself, what prevented these bonds from being literally understood as a group marriage?

The contractual model of marriage that emerged from the covenantal one in the late seventeenth and eighteenth centuries appeared not to have this problem. Advocates for a contractarian view of marriage aimed to diminish the role of both state and family in supervising the marriage, and eliminate the function of marriage as an arm of the government—in short, to make marriage less literally political. The contractarian view of marriage drew a boundary between couplehood and larger social endeavors; indeed, John Locke relegated the nuptial union to a conceptual and legal place outside of "politics" proper.[10] But the contractarian model introduced a different dilemma: the question of why, unlike any other contract between two people, the terms of the nuptial union could not be adjudicated by the couple themselves. The vehemence with which jurists and the public rejected the claims of "marriage protesters" who wrote explicit marriage contracts that eliminated gender inequities—among them John Stuart Mill, Henry Blackwell and Lucy Stone, and Robert Dale Owen—provides a clue as to the threat that self-adjudication posed.[11] If the state comes into being and maintains itself by regulating sexual and reproductive relations, then the dissolution of marriage into a contract regulated by the couple threatens, at its most extreme, to dissolve the state. The purely contractarian model of marriage, that is, might nullify the very thing that the covenantal model seemed to ratify.

Thus, as Anglo-American juries shaped marriage, it became a contract that once entered into, established two status relationships: one between husband and wife, and one between the couple and state. As if to mediate this contradiction, nineteenth-century representations of "civil" weddings—by which I mean representations of weddings whose primary inflection is neither populist nor patriarchal, nor religious, but explicitly judicial—oscillated between the contractual and covenantal. The contractual model seemed to secure the "private," insular, voluntary nature of the marriage relation, while the residual covenantal model seemed to secure its ability to bring forth a political body.

A nuptial union central to U.S. literature exemplifies this shifting movement between contract and covenant, insularity and collectivity. In *The Scarlet Letter* (1850), Hester Prynne declares to her adulterous lover, Arthur Dimmesdale, "What we did had a consecration of its own. We felt it so! We said so to each other!"[12] What "consecrates" the union between Hester and Dimmesdale, or turns it into a marriage more valid than Hester's prior obligations to her legal husband, Roger Chillingworth? One possibility is the binding touch of bodies ("What we did . . . "), as in the pagan/popular model. Another is its status as an unwitnessed verbal transaction between two parties ("We said so to each other"), as in both the Roman Catholic and liberal contractual models. But emotions held in common ("We felt it so!") were increasingly central to the sentimental model and linked intimacy to the reformation of a larger public.

In fact, Hester's declaration, the only performance the reader sees of her wedding to Dimmesdale, is a private, even clandestine ceremony that paradoxically seems to reference and reinstantiate multiple versions of the Anglo-American polity: pre-Christian, Puritan, revolutionary, and antebellum sentimental. Her emphasis on "doing," on bodily consummation, points to pre-Christian rituals and connects her marriage to the novel's exploration of Salem witchcraft. Her sense of "consecration" also demands that the union in the woods be read as a figure for the Puritan covenant that authorized the "errand into the wilderness." But her suggestion that the union is legitimate on the contractual model because "we said so to each other" also figures her as a Christian subject breaking with a patrilineal order, a second-generation Puritan breaking with the founding fathers who made magisterial sanction the law of the land, and finally a genuinely "American" revolutionary subject breaking with her British forebears. For contractarian marriage was eventually tied to the colony's political secession from England; in revolutionary rhetoric, the marriage bond was a figure for a voluntary relationship between a government and population with equal powers. Thomas Paine, for one, argued from the point of view of "an American savage" that marriages in the colonies needed "no other ceremony than mutual affection," and used this

figure of self-marriage to indicate the primacy of love ties over prior obligations, need to separate from England, and rebalancing of powers between
government and populace.[13] As Jay Fliegelman maintains, "The point of the
Revolution would not be simply to dissolve an intolerable union but to establish a more glorious one founded on the most primary of social unions—the
voluntary marriage contract."[14]

Insofar as Hester is a figure for the emergence of a contractual polity in the
rupture with England, then, she does not really commit adultery but instead
enters into a true marriage with Dimmesdale that automatically invalidates
her previous one. But her insistence that the marriage is consecrated because
"we felt it so!" also draws from the postrevolutionary and antebellum emphasis on shared emotions as a binding political force. In monarchical Europe, marriage had been a means of allying families and consolidating the
tracts of land over which they held dominion into vast empires; in the republican United States, marriage became a gateway to these new affective modes
and a domain within which to refine them. As numerous critics have contended, the incipient U.S. middle class articulated itself by proliferating rituals and icons of feeling—taste, sympathy, mourning, and above all love. An
emergent bourgeoisie, that is, literally *felt* itself into communal being not only
as a class but also as a new nation. This articulation of feeling was not just
verbal, for the middle class redesigned some rituals and invented others,
making its own modes of affect concrete and available for group participation
and reworking.[15] Along with rituals of burying and mourning, those of marrying and courting allowed participants to collaborate in the making of shared
subjectivities.

In the antebellum United States, these emergent structures of feeling and
the tangible rituals that fostered them, linked the smaller society of the family
to the larger one of the nation in a way that was different than the Puritan
extension of governmental power to heads of household. While a Puritan
man directly exercised his civic power when he gave orders to his own family
members, an antebellum woman extended the "private" disciplinary work of
taming her husband's libido and shaping her children's character toward the
nation as a whole. She exhorted its citizens not just to vote but to emote
together and rhetorically reconfigured disenfranchised populations as "feeling" subjects who were worthy of political rights by the very strength of their
sensations. Thus marriage, though it could not literally ally states and remap
territories in the United States as it had in monarchical states, allowed the

subject to access, rehearse, and deploy a set of emotions that, in turn, served to bind him or her to a larger democratic entity.

Hester's momentary landing on emotions, "We felt it so!" thereby makes her marriage into a figure for several constituencies at once. Within the historical time frame of the novel, her declaration registers both the founding of the Puritan polity and presence of a dissident religious community, the antinomians who purported to experience God without the intermediary of ministers. Within the revolutionary era that provides Hester's acts with a nationalistic meaning, her pronouncement signals the affective reconstitution of a federation of atomized states into a national republic. Within the time of Hawthorne's own writing of the novel, Hester's words capture the white female reformer's mission of further reconstituting that republic through the power of love. Indeed, her statement suggests that the lateral bonds ratified by the Puritan covenantal model of marriage were in some ways close to the more porous bonds of communal feeling sought by sentimental reformers. Hester's declaration that the marriage is valid because "we felt it so" certainly recalls Governor Winthrop's metaphor, in "A Model of Christian Charity," of the bodily "ligaments" of love that join the colonists together into a new endeavor—and here is where the real trouble begins.[16] For if Hester's union with Dimmesdale is spiritually valid, it is also bigamous; under Puritan law, without a divorce it does not automatically cancel out her previous marriage. Furthermore, Hester's list of the factors that validate her union with Dimmesdale—"we did," "we felt," "we said"—does not include Puritan magisterial sanction, which was a matter of customary enforcement if not positive law before 1646, when the first statute mandating civil marriage entered the Massachusetts books.[17] Under the terms of the state it supposedly founds, then, Hester and Dimmesdale's "true" marriage is at best illegal and at worst void. The very union that seems both to prefigure and announce the existence of the Puritan political state is bigamous if it is valid, and threatens to nullify rather than ratify the colonial polity if it is not, and this has implications for the bourgeois-sentimental nation of Hawthorne's own moment.

What *The Scarlet Letter* suggests—at once, both the polyamorous possibilities inherent in covenant as well as the ability of voluntary contract to supersede state regulation and thereby nullify the state—is worked out most fully in two texts that might best be viewed as *The Scarlet Letter*'s nineteenth-century "bookends": Hawthorne's allegory of the beginning of Puritan political life,

"The May-Pole of Merry Mount" (accepted for publication in 1835, revised and republished in 1837), and Joseph Kirkland's novelistic exploration of how the Midwest might be properly incorporated into U.S. politics and letters, *Zury: The Meanest Man in Spring County* (1887). In these texts, the "civil wedding" necessarily fails to achieve its contradictory goals: to represent the "first instance" of the state and yet also prove the state's prior existence by submitting the couple to its regulation of the affections; and to forge ties among members of an entire polity and yet also establish a properly dyadic cross-gender marriage. Failing to properly adjudicate the mutual founding activity between marriage and the state, these texts move inexorably toward the very transgressions against which marriage defines itself. In doing so, they imply that nations themselves emerge neither through the loving consent of their members for which marriage is both figure and foundation nor through the state's prior authority to sanction only monogamous cross-gender dyads, but rather through the criminalization of sex. In the civil wedding, in other words, the state comes into being not through its ability to create a populace bound by proper feelings but through its ability to punish improper ones. As in the *New Yorker* cartoon above, in these two texts a civil ceremony is always also, in some sense, a sex trial.

A Maie Game of Marriage: Hawthorne's "The May-Pole of Merry Mount"

As Hester's complicated declaration reveals, the question of what "made" a marriage was in flux during Hawthorne's era: was it love or law? The increasing isolation of Hester and Dimmesdale from their social context also seems to ask, as according to Ellen Rothman the mid-nineteenth-century wedding ceremony itself did, if marriage were an emblem and extension of communal being, or figure for and means of withdrawal from the larger society.[18] Hester's statements indicate that the contractual model, which was certainly dominant in the antebellum United States, competed with residual covenantal energies that were both reanimated and transformed by sentimental culture. Moving outward from the primal national scene of Hester's union with Dimmesdale, I turn to Hawthornian texts precisely because Hawthorne himself was both a Puritan historiographer and part of a larger cultural reconstitution of the emotions during the mid–nineteenth century. His fiction not only diagnosed the residual Puritan elements of his own contemporary moment but also indexed and contributed to the antebellum production of privacy, interiority, and psychological depth—all of which were means for and signs of a specifically middle-class, implicitly white subjectivity distinguishable both from aristocratic displays of power and lower-class forms of embodiment. Yet for Hawthorne, these forms of "private" affect were intimately linked to the production of a national body politic.[19] It is no coincidence, then, that Hawthornian texts contain some highly politicized weddings.[20]

Hence, I begin with Hawthorne's "The May-Pole of Merry Mount," which may be North American literature's most straightforward use of the wedding as a figure for the founding of a polity: in this tale, "jollity and gloom [are] contending for an empire" in the New World, and the scene for this contest is a wedding.[21] Set in 1628, the tale revolves around Salem's Governor John Endicott, who crashes a nuptial festival in Merry Mount, the colony founded by Thomas Morton on the Shawmut Peninsula of Massachusetts. Endicott chops down the maypole around which the revelers have been dancing, thereby interrupting a scene marked by the multiple temporalities inherent in the wedding ritual: here, the dancers are dressed as Old English folk figures, "Gothic" monsters "of Grecian ancestry," animals, and Indians (*MPMM*, 361). Endicott banishes the officiating priest, orders punishments ranging from whippings and exile to death, and sends the newlyweds, Edith and Edgar, off to his own colony at Salem. By demanding that Esther "become a mother in our Israel," and that the couple go "heavenward, supporting each other along the difficult path which it was their lot to tread" (370), Endicott also installs Edith and Edgar into a strictly Puritan mode of typological history. Henceforth, they will move in a straight line from original covenant with God to earthly piety to salvation in heaven, their marriage both emblematizing and reenacting that founding covenant.

In short, in this tale Puritan marital "gloom" seems to triumph over the pagan/Indian/Anglican wedding's "jollity." The real-life Governor Endicott actually did mete out such a "family values" sentence at Salem in 1629, when he ordered all the colony's single men to form small households "grounded in religion," each with a head member.[22] But the fictitious Endicott's disruption of the wedding signals aesthetic commitments that go beyond his loyalty to the social form of the patriarchal family. He relies on the differences between marriage and the wedding to elevate reproduction over affection, historical over mythic or ritual time, and narrative over spectacle. In the figural terms of the tale, the wedding, with its streamers undulating around the maypole, is cyclical, pleasure-oriented, crisscrossed with lateral connections between people, legitimated by popular and religious ritual, and multitemporal. Under Endicott's direction, it gives way to the linear regime of marriage, figured by a sword aimed at a pillar, and to the "real time" of Puritan theology and politics. Here, marriage is vertical, disciplinary, characterized by hierarchical relationships, subject to the state's authority, and embedded in a forward-moving and ultimately protonational history.

In fact, the tale's third-person omniscient narrator has already anticipated Endicott's movement away from "mythic" and toward "historical" time. For even before the magistrate's arrival on the wedding scene, this narrator abandons it to "discover who these gay people were" (*MPMM*, 364) and instructs the reader as to Merry Mount's founding history. Recent Hawthorne scholars have followed this narrator's lead, moving away from readings of the story as a rewriting of other literary texts such as John Milton's *Paradise Lost* to viewing it as a comment on the writing of U.S. history.[23] Michael Colacurcio, for instance, has argued that Hawthorne's purposeful anachronisms are key to the critique in "May-Pole" of Puritan historiographical strategies. In the tale's most self-conscious anachronism, Governor Endicott shouts at the attending priest, " 'I know thee, Blackstone' " (*MPMM*, 367). But the narrator appends a most unusual footnote to the tale, stating that "did Governor Endicott speak less positively, we should suspect a mistake here. . . . We rather doubt [the Reverend Blackstone's] identity with the priest of Merry Mount" (367). With this famous footnote, Colacurcio asserts, Hawthorne highlights the distortion of facts within the most "historical" aspects of the tale: Hawthorne's historical frame break, and the footnote acknowledging it, calls attention to the way that chroniclers of New England history conflated separate events so as to produce political allegory.[24]

Colacurcio's work unpacks the tale's dizzying array of historical substitutions and condensations. As Hawthorne's narrator implies in his footnote, the real Endicott did not actually banish the Anglican priest William Blackstone from Merry Mount. Reverend Blackstone, who was the first English settler on the Shawmut Peninsula and claimed squatter's rights to the land, left of his own accord in 1635, and so he is clearly a substitute for someone else. The annals of Puritan history that Hawthorne consulted to write this story reveal that Endicott deported not Blackstone but rather Thomas Morton, the founder of the Merry Mount colony; these sources also make much of the fact that Endicott punctuated his moral lesson by chopping down the may-pole. But even these documents substitute Governor Endicott for Captain Miles Standish, the real governor who exiled Morton in June 1628 for selling guns to Indians and usurping the Plymouth fur trade. By September, when Endicott arrived to chop down the maypole (in an empty flourish probably performed without an audience), Morton was long gone. Hawthorne thus replaces Standish with Endicott just as his Puritan predecessors did, but he also replaces Morton with Blackstone and alerts his readers to the move, in order to critique the Puritan allegorists' earlier fudging of the facts—particularly their transformation of an economic battle over the fur trade into a theological quarrel over a folk icon. The maypole is the fulcrum of Hawthorne's critique; his narrator remarks that the whipping post "might be termed the Puritan May-Pole" (365), signaling that in destroying the maypole as a symbol of sin as well as in fetishizing instruments of torture such as the scaffold and stocks, the Puritans practiced the very idol worship for which they condemned Anglicans, Catholics, and Native Americans. As Colacurcio makes clear, the tale's commitment to revealing historical distortions suggests that it is a small leap from popish or pagan idol worship to a Puritan moral allegory that turns on a maypole.[25]

But to see the tale as an allegorical antiallegory fails to account for the lush presence of the wedding in this tale, and its quite different engagement with the promise as well as problems of allegory. Hawthorne could surely have told the story without having Endicott disrupt a wedding, dramatizing a confrontation between a self-righteous Endicott and an anachronistic Blackstone over a simple May Day dance. Instead, the historical personages and events shimmer up through the elaborate textual veil of the wedding, which Hawthorne seems to have produced out of whole cloth, for apparently nobody ever was married at the maypole nor by clergy at Merry Mount.[26] Historicist critics, limiting their conception of history to events and persons, have treated the wedding as sentimental frippery. Yet the wedding ceremony was a contested site for the Puritan battle against Anglican idolatry, and marriage was a defining element of Puritan theology: European Protestants elevated marriage over all other social relations, closing down monasteries and insisting that even clergy should marry, and the Puritans' covenantal model emphasized lateral bonds of consent as much as, and sometimes even more than, vertical lines of descent and authority.[27]

Finally, like Hester's declaration, Endicott's concern with binding the wedding ceremony to a new social order brings the tale into allegorical conjunction with Hawthorne's own time. "May-Pole" appeared during a period when lawmakers had just completed major codifications of marriage law in many states, and in which the precursors to the Married Women's Property Acts were just beginning to take shape in southern states and territories such as Arkansas.[28] Hawthorne also wrote the tale within a context of religious revival in which intentional communities and individual couples alike, including he and his wife, Sophia, debated the relationships among the public appearance of weddings, the spiritual essence of marriage, and collective social life.[29] At New Harmony, in communities like Oneida and Amana, and in transcendentalist collectives like Fruitlands and Brook Farm, wedding ceremonies were often self-consciously reorganized to align with principles of equality between the sexes and the communal sharing of property. Meanwhile, the weddings of ordinary men and women were starting to resemble the white wedding of today, providing a set of recognizable forms that articulated the emergent middle-class, nominally feminine power of feelings. Thus, to assume that the wedding is a mere organizing device that gives way to a more properly historical reading is to cede to the ideology that the wedding is "timeless," to assume that weddings neither have a history of their own nor intersect with other histories. In the case of Hawthorne's "May-Pole," the history of the wedding is at the center of the tale and slowly lays bare the incoherence of civil marriage.

In fact, the status of Edith and Edgar's marriage, and not the presence of an Anglican priest at their nuptials, is the most peculiar aspect of "May-Pole." Governor Endicott purports to end the wedding ceremony. Yet he sends the couple off to become members of his colony at Salem as " 'thou and thy maiden wife' " (MPMM, 369)—even though their marriage ought to be considered, at the very least, highly irregular, and perhaps even altogether invalid. The couple does not seem to have published banns, and the ceremony has not been performed by a civil magistrate, as all marriages were supposed to be in the Puritan colonies. It is not even clear that the priest has really married Edith and Edgar, as the narrator draws a rhetorical veil over the nuptial scene: "Now leave we the priest to marry them" (363–64), he remarks, and begins his lesson on the history of Merry Mount. He comments later only that the couple's "air of mutual support . . . showed them to be man and wife, with the sanction of a priest upon their love" (369). This is slim evidence, less in keeping with Puritan law than with nineteenth-century sentimentality, according to which the outward signs of love signaled the authenticity of a marriage. It does not seem unreasonable to suggest that as a magistrate, Endicott should not accept them as man and wife or that he should marry them in the civil mode just to make sure they are indeed married. While the solemnization of marriages by magistrates was not a positive law until 1646 and this tale is set in 1628, one might expect that a governor rigid enough to execute a dancing bear, as Endicott does, would ensure that his neophyte Puritan couple entered his own colony with no doubts as to the theological correctness of their own wedding.

Instead, Hawthorne's fictional Endicott gets sucked right into the pagan and Anglican aspects of the ceremony, mimicking the very rituals for which he has just punished the Anglican priest. He lifts a wreath of roses from the ruined maypole and throws it, "with his own gauntleted hand, over the heads of the Lord and Lady of the May" (370). This simple gesture carries far more freight than cutting down the maypole—in fact, at this point, the wreath completely usurps the maypole as the figural center of the tale. Binding the bride Edith and her bridegroom Edgar, the wreath becomes a makeshift wedding ring. And the ring joins more than just the newlyweds. It encircles the entire wedding party, for the wreath's shape is echoed in the "ring of monsters," the "circle" of onlookers who witness the disciplinary moment, and even the dancers moving around the maypole; the tale is structured, as John E. Becker notes, "almost geometrically, in concentric circles."[30]

Yet the literary Endicott is hardly practicing Puritan theology by introducing a ring, for Puritan objections to Anglican and Catholic weddings focused specifically on the use of this symbol. Puritan chronicler Cotton Mather was adamant that "in the Weddings of New England the ring makes none of the ceremonies."[31] In *New English Canaan,* the deported Thomas Morton's vengeful account of the colonies, even Morton condemned Puritan ministers for using wedding rings, which he called "relics of popery" and "a diabolical circle for the divell to daunce in."[32] Indeed, prior to these colonial expressions of distaste for the ring, the English Puritan "Admonition to Parliament" of 1572 had already claimed that the Anglican wedding was "wonte to be compted a sacramente, and therefore they use yet a sacramental signe, to which they attribute the vertue of wedlocke. I meane the wedding ring, which they fowly abuse & dally with all, in taking it up, and laying it downe: In putting it on, they abuse the name of the Trinitie."[33] In light of this Puritan manifesto, Endicott's performance with the wreath looks especially suspicious. "Laying it down," he chops down the maypole on which it is first seen hanging; "taking it up," he lifts the wreath; "putting it on," he throws it over the couple's heads, repeating with this move his prior acknowledgment of them as man and wife. If this performance marries Edith and Edgar at all, then, it does so with a pagan object and sacramental gestures. While the marriage may or may not be valid under these conditions, Endicott's priestly/pagan role-playing is surely suspect. As the narrator himself puts it in a seemingly innocuous description of the games the revelers play, "magistrates and all [have] their eyes bandaged" to what is going on here (MPMM, 366). It is Endicott who has participated in exactly what the Puritan reformers objected to in the "Admonition": the making of "rather a Maie game of marriage, then [sic] a holy institution of God."[34]

The wedding that seems to provide this tale's point of departure, then, simply will not go away—as with so many of the works this book examines, it takes over the text to call the work of lawful marriage into question. As in *Absalom, Absalom!* the wedding partakes in the more historicist, politically critical aspects of allegory: rather than homogenizing disparate temporal moments, it blocks any smooth transition into "modern" time by disrupting the coherence of the present tense with anachronistic events and meanings. But in *Absalom!* modern time is racial time, the era of a binary system central to the reactionary "reconstruction" of an Anglo-Saxon nation after the Louisiana Purchase. In this much earlier text, modern time is not only Puritan time but also national time, according to which the bonds of citizenship are supposed to displace both patrilineal and parochial attachments. By drawing Endicott willy-nilly into the role of priest, though, "May-Pole" undermines both the Puritan theocracy and antebellum civic sphere itself. Endicott's muddled performance involves some kind of repression that like all good repressions, returns to haunt the scene of the crime. What, then, can a nineteenth-century wedding superimposed on a Puritan one reveal about the legacy of civil marriage in "America"?

Hawthorne's peculiar insertion of William Blackstone into this tale, and his pointed suggestion that this character violates the temporal frame of the story, does provide an answer to this question, but in a different way than it has been treated thus far. Scholars have corrected the narrator's statement in "May-Pole" that Blackstone is "a clerk of Oxford" (MPMM, 362), noting that Reverend Blackstone actually studied at Cambridge.[35] Yet this "mistake" is yet another one of Hawthorne's purposeful temporal conflations, for which he seems to have taken permission directly from the scrambled New England chronicles Colacurcio describes. There really *was* a Blackstone at Oxford, albeit much later than the frame of this story would seem to allow for. Sir William Blackstone (1723–1780), the Vinerian professor of Common Law at Oxford and royal solicitor to the British Crown, was also the author of the four-volume *Commentaries on the Law of England*, which codified customs, statutes, and case precedents into a coherent body of English law for the first time since Sir Edward Coke's writings of the mid–seventeenth century. Blackstone's *Commentaries*, published between 1765 and 1769, were widely read both in England and the American colonies. The *Commentaries* were the most influential legal tracts in the Anglo-American eighteenth century and had immense crossover appeal: if Edmund Burke is to be believed, law books were second only to religious ones in popularity.[36] Blackstone also provided the basis for U.S. law, and even commentators of Hawthorne's own time were still hard at work recontextualizing Blackstone's work for the United States, with titles such as *Blackstone's Commentaries, with Notes of Reference to the Constitution and Laws of the Federal Government* (1803), *Commentaries on Blackstone* (1803), and *Commentaries on American Law* (1826–1830). Seeing the name "Blackstone," both U.S. and British readers would immediately have thought of the Enlightenment lawyer rather than the obscure Anglican clergyman.

Scholarly Blackstone chasers, then, have been too ready to assume that "May-Pole's" Blackstone must be a religious historical figure, when one of the many Anglican priests who wandered through New England would have done just as well for a purely theological conflict.[37] The matter at hand, like that of marriage itself in the New England colonies, is one of civil law rather than religious doctrine, of legal crime rather than moral sin. The method Hawthorne uses to get to the heart of this matter does indeed involve the collapse of multiple historical frames. But as previous chapters have shown, the wedding is the perfect form for effecting the temporal disruptions that go beyond the homogenizing kind of allegory that Hawthorne contests and even the antiquarian's restoration of the facts. Here, the tale's wedding performs a historicist critique of the way dyadic cross-gender couplehood and the state seem to legitimate one another. For in binding the Puritan couple to their sacrilegious peers rather than Salem, the ceremony that Endicott interrupts and then officiates in the forbidden "popish" mode both negates some aspects of the contract that were key to English imperialism in North America and links covenantal marriage to the very practices against which English political collectivity defined itself.

Among the many legal principles Sir William Blackstone outlined, his writings on marriage, property, and sodomy are central to his place in "May-Pole," and to the way the tale disaggregates civil marriage into a competition between covenant and contract, plurality and couplehood, sanctioned wedlock and criminalized sex. Most famously, Blackstone codified the ancient doctrine of coverture, in which the husband and wife are not just "one flesh" but one legal entity. Under the terms of coverture, a married woman could not contract or hold property separately from her husband. While in the United States, antebellum Married Women's Property Acts granted a woman somewhat more control over the material property that she brought into the marriage, these acts varied from state to state and did not fully guarantee economic independence.[38] Perhaps, then, the lingering presence of Blackstonian coverture in the antebellum United States accounts for the bride, Edith, "sigh[ing] amid this festive music" (*MPMM*, 363). Perhaps, in exiling the personification of coverture, Endicott becomes a protofeminist "marriage protester" like Lucy Stone, far avant la lettre.

But given Hawthorne's commitment to nineteenth-century domestic ideals, this seems unlikely. Instead, the fictional Blackstone—and even the way that the name's referent itself oscillates between a priest and lawyer—seems to represent a conflict between civil and religious control over marriage. For the lawyer Blackstone also defined English marriage as absolutely secular, writing that "our law considers marriage in no other light than as a civil contract," coincidentally echoing the Puritan Governor William Bradford's statement that marriage is a "civill thing."[39] By arguing for the civil nature of marriage, Blackstone seemed to be in explicit disagreement with the 1753 Parliamentary Act for the Better Preventing of Clandestine Marriage (Lord Hardwicke's Act) that made church consecration mandatory in England and Wales. In banishing the historical "Blackstone," the fictional Endicott is thus banishing the doctrine of civil marriage itself—the very tenet he is charged with upholding.

Perhaps Endicott intends to exile the contractarian Blackstone as a way of preserving Bradford's covenantal, "civill" model. Yet while banishing Blackstone might indeed secure the covenantal model of marriage, it undermines Puritan authority in another arena. For in dismissing Blackstone, Endicott

also preemptively dismisses a contractarian definition of *property,* over a hundred years before its time. Though Blackstone was a traditionalist about
coverture, he was not so about property. In his view, laborers held implicit title
to the land only for the duration of the period they actually worked it; any
permanent alienation was a matter of explicit agreement. His definition of
property disputed John Locke's earlier doctrine whereby laborers held automatic claim to the land on which they labored: by mixing the property in their
person with the land, Locke maintained, laborers gained title to that land.
Locke's naturalizing theory of property, outlined in *Two Treatises of Government* in 1698, seemed to retroactively legitimate earlier colonial claims to
Indian land and projectively guarantee any continued U.S. expansionism
after the Revolution. By contrast, under Blackstone's definition, many English claims in the New World (including that of the earlier Reverend Blackstone) would have been invalid.[40]

Long before Blackstone codified it, the idea that land could not be permanently alienated except by explicit contract was already being invoked by
competing claimants to the Shawmut Peninsula—especially Merry Mount's
founder, Thomas Morton. Indeed, the dispute between Blackstonian and
Lockean definitions of property enters "May-Pole" anachronistically, in Morton's uncanny, absent-yet-present persona. For the rascally Morton, whose
stay at Merry Mount is registered only by the maypole around which the
"diabolical circle" of scofflaws dances, was himself a lawyer who repeatedly
sought to invalidate the Massachusetts Bay Company's claims to their land.
Hounded and exiled by Miles Standish, Morton joined other complainants to
urge Sir Ferdinando Gorges toward a 1632 campaign that failed to produce a
verdict against Massachusetts. In 1634, though, Morton was part of a group
led by Archbishop William Laud and the Privy Commission for Foreign Plan-
tations, which found the Massachusetts charter void. In the transactions between Governor John Winthrop and prior claimants in England, Winthrop
stubbornly refused to produce the charter, alleging that it had been lost. By
1635—the very date that intersects wth the Anglican priest Blackstone's departure from the territory in question—Morton had been hired by the Council for
New England to bring a proof of warrant (claim) against the Massachusetts
Bay Colony's charter, which he successfully achieved.[41]

In other words, the date of 1635, hidden within the complex chain of
temporal and characterological substitutions in "May-Pole," marks not the
moral failure of Anglican or "papist" claims to Shawmut but the expressly

legal one of Puritan claims to it. Hawthorne surreptitiously transfers Morton's campaign against the Puritans into the tale, in the form of a marriage that may not be valid: a couple who may or may not have been married by a priest are (re)married by a magistrate who playacts as a priest in his remarrying of them, thereby calling the validity of the marriage into question yet again. By metaphorizing Morton's relentless campaign against the Massachusetts Bay Company as a potentially invalid marriage, Hawthorne suggests that what Endicott attempts and fails to banish is the unstable—and perhaps even fictional—status of the charter that legitimated his fellow Puritan planters' presence on the land they settled. The ambiguous legality of this marriage, which Endicott ends up fostering, figures the ambiguous legal foundation of the Puritan polity itself. Its civic sphere may have originated in covenant, but its territorial claims were justified by a contract that quite literally disappeared. Though the narrator describes the bride Edith's sadness as "high treason" against Merry Mount, the phrase more properly captures Endicott's relation to the Puritan polity he purports both to exemplify and inaugurate (*MPMM*, 363).

The lawyerly figure of Blackstone also transports the Property Acts of Hawthorne's own moment, which adjudicated competing material claims between men and women, backward into the moment of English settlement itself, which was fraught with competing territorial claims among men—Puritans, other dissenters, Anglicans, and Indians. When "May-Pole" is read as a dispute in which marriage law intersects with the definition of property to produce a crisis in the legitimacy of the polity itself, the intermingling of Anglicans and men dressed as Indians in the wedding party becomes more than just incidental. For the Puritans and their descendants would use proto-Lockean definitions of property to seize North American land not only from non-Puritan Englishpeople but also from other Europeans and Indians. In fact, Hawthorne wrote this tale in the aftermath of other invalid or suspicious contracts; in 1834 Andrew Jackson failed to secure a treaty with the Cherokees whose land rights he sought to overturn, and the subsequent Treaty of Echota was ratified with so few Cherokees present that even members of the militia complained that it was a fraud.[42] To exile Blackstone, then, was also to preempt the threat of future Anglo-American land titles becoming null and void.

In short, Anglicans and Indians had some of the same bases for disputing Puritan jurisdiction over territory, which is neatly represented by the tale's figure of an Anglican in Native American dress, a "counterfeit . . . Indian hunter, with feathery crest and wampum belt" (361). But this "Indian" also functions to render the marital *covenant* as unreliable a foundation for the polity as the marital *contract*. For he appears in a suspiciously polymorphous description of the wedding party:

> On the shoulders of a comely youth, uprose the head and branching antlers of a stag; a second, human in all other points, had the grim visage of a wolf; a third, still with the trunk and limbs of a mortal man, showed the beard and horns of a venerable he-goat. There was the likeness of a bear erect, brute in all but his hind legs, which were adorned with pink silk stockings. . . . Here might be seen the Salvage Man . . . hairy as a baboon. . . . by his side, a nobler figure, but still a counterfeit, appeared an Indian hunter, with feathery crest and wampum belt." (361)

Richard Slotkin has shown that sex between men, with animals, and across the Indian/Anglo divide counted not only as religious sins but also particularly heinous crimes against the Puritan civic order; and in this passage, the costumes capture all three violations.[43] Surrounded by multispecied bodies, English folk symbols of lust and cuckoldry, and a cross-dressing bear, the "Indian" becomes one in a series of sexual transgressors. And indeed, the Puritans punished Thomas Morton not only for his economic activities but also his erotic adventures: he and the servants who flocked to Merry Mount had sexual relations across both race and class barriers. While it is unclear whether or not the colonists actually practiced male-on-male sex or bestiality, Morton and his pamphleteering enemies implied that they did both by punningly referring to the colony as "Mare-mount," thereby conflating bestiality and phallic sexuality.

Yet they also called the colony "Marry Mount," pointedly suggesting that the aforementioned crimes against the civic order come dangerously close to the erotic and affective practices that supposedly constitute it. As Michael Warner demonstrates, the paradigmatic expression of New English covenant, Winthrop's "Modell of Christian Charity," also produced a model of the social based on affection, likeness, and affinity. The homosocial, plural erotics of that covenantal model were therefore "in tension with another model of the social equally important in the Puritan imagination—one based on natural order, hierarchy, the family, and reproduction."[44] Covenant could easily dissolve into a polymorphous associational model, into the sins against which marriage was seen as the very bulwark—in this case, not only cross-racial sex but homoeroticism and bestiality. The animals and "Indian" thus also regis-ter the third Blackstonian key to "May-Pole": the relationship between mar-riage and the sexual policing that the Enlightenment lawyer saw as a matter of civil law rather than religious mores.

The legal history of sodomy, in its imbrication with that of civil marriage, makes sense out of Hawthorne's otherwise idiosyncratic conflation of a wed-ding with a maypole dance rather than, say, the harvest festival that the narrator also describes the Merry Mounters celebrating. The circular wreath hanging on the phallic maypole is an obvious figure for heterosexual fertility, similar to the harvest ritual's "sheaves of Indian corn . . . wreathed . . . with autumnal garlands (*MPMM*, 365). But it is not clear that the maypole's sexual symbolism, in such close proximity with "Blackstone," involves only one orifice, and its wedding brings the history of relations between the marital hymen and other body parts into focus.

In his codification of British sex law, Sir William Blackstone revisited a legal decision that had been made more than two centuries earlier, in which sodomy itself became a civil rather than religious offense. He wrote that sodomy was an offense against "the personal security of the subject" and not solely an offense against God and religion.[45] Blackstone's statement called attention to and extended the redefinition of sodomy that began in 1533, when the very first sanctions against it appeared in English civil law. That year, Parliament defined sodomy for the first time as "the detestable and abomin-able vice of buggery committed with mankind or beast."[46] Not only did this definition make what had heretofore been a religious offense into a civil crime, it also left behind all of the other nonprocreative sexual practices that had counted as sodomitical under canon law—adultery, pederasty, masturba-tion, and so on. In short, as Ed Cohen has argued, the 1533 statute began to homosexualize sodomy. Eroticism between men therefore became the ful-crum of a long shift, beginning in the sixteenth century, from ecclesiastical to civil power over sex.[47] Extending this development, in his legal treatises of 1644, Sir Edward Coke defined sodomy as high treason against *the state*.[48] Coke's successor Blackstone refined sodomy law even further, for he began to sketch out the kind of *person* who would count as the representative of this state.

Blackstone's treatment of sodomy as a crime that injured the property of "personal security," something that newly constituted the subject, re-veals personhood to be a kind of back-formation, an implicitly heterosexual-masculine possession shaped in contradistinction to the increasingly homosexual, civil definition of sodomy. In this sense, Blackstone also put a sexual twist on the Lockean definition of property as something inhering in the body as labor power by insisting that the body also had the property of personal security itself, registered primarily by the absence of anal penetration. He even anticipated the transformation that Foucault depicts as a nineteenth-century phenomenon in which "identity" itself emerged out of secular institutions' engagement with human sexual practices. For under Blackstone, the "subject" materialized as such within a new state-created zone of personal security, or to put it more crudely, the subject was birthed through the ass that the state protected. While Enlightenment personhood—the basis for U.S. citizenship—is commonly understood as an abstraction defined by property rights, the link between Sir William Blackstone and Merry Mount brings out one of the stigmatized bodies against which this abstracting process also took shape. Hawthorne's substitution of the name "Blackstone" for the sexual polymath Thomas Morton links the colony of Merry Mount to the later, tandem emergence of the rights-bearing citizen who is taken to be the subject position protected by "America," and his negative body double, the criminalized homosexual.

As it turns out, marriage has intimately to do with this doubled construction of protected and criminal bodies. The statute on which Sir William Blackstone depended for his recodification of law and construction of personhood as heterosexual and masculine, also brings civil marriage and sodomy law into explicit conjunction. For England's first civil sodomy law appeared within, though apparently not explicitly connected to, the transfer of control over marriage from church to state. In 1533, the same year as it defined sodomy as male-male sex or bestiality, Parliament also passed the Act in Restraint of Appeals to Rome, which provided that all "causes of matrimony and divorces . . . shall from henceforth be heard and definitively adjudged and determined within the king's jurisdiction and authority."[49] In the same moment that sodomy became a crime against the state rather than a sin against God, marriage achieved civil rather than an ecclesiastical status. As Cohen puts it, "The criminalization of sodomy would seem to have effectively transferred the power to define and punish 'unnatural' sexual practices to the state and conversely . . . made the state—in this case coextensive with a king who sought to abrogate his wedding vows—the sole source for establishing the range of acceptable, legitimate, or 'true' relationships."[50] In other words, the purely civil definition of marriage in the New England colonies and eventually the United States, in which the state is the arbiter of legitimate kinship and enfranchises only monogamous, dyadic, cross-gender marriages, originally appeared in intimate contiguity with—and as a kind of reverse corollary to—the criminalization of sodomy.

Historically, then, the civil contract *of* marriage is also a contract *on* sex between men. In this sense, despite all of the Protestant attempts to define marriage positively, as an "honorable" secular estate and a basis for social order, its marital model was not all that different from the Catholic one of marriage as a necessary evil, a safeguard against a plethora of burning lusts. Protestants merely honed in on particular lusts. This may be why the police officer has the starring role in the "Bride or Groom?" cartoon: perhaps his question is really a demand that each guest name his or her object of desire, a way to call forth the state by sorting out the sex criminals just as Endicott does. It may also be why "May-Pole" makes the relationship between state-sanctioned marriage and the criminalization of other sex forms explicit, dancing the status of the Puritan colonies around the ghost of Thomas Morton, the sexually transgressive "divell" in a "diabolical circle" of suspect property relationships, missing contracts, and stigmatized erotic practices. The tale's wedding, supposedly the basis of an insular society grounded in covenant and controlled by the colonial magistrate, has at its very center the explicitly phallic, nonprocreative, egalitarian, and homoerotic maypole.

All of this makes the Merry Mount wedding into a highly unstable figure for the kind of covenantal marriage that would secure the couple's boundaries even as it installed them into a homologous hierarchy extending from household to church and state, as Endicott's rhetoric of typological couplehood would seem to insist. Instead, this wedding comes to instantiate a community that is lateral, interrelational, and infinitely expansive—figured not only by the maypole but also the wreath. Despite the sacrosanct terms with which Hawthorne described his own marriage to Sophia Peabody, his tale reveals that whenever "America" grounds its political order in the sanctified figure of the bride and groom, it is also simultaneously calling forth the bodies and sexual practices against which marriage supposedly inoculates both couple and nation. Perhaps the most hidden and potent of the many little rings of "Marry-Mount" are those interdependent symbols of sanctioned and criminal sexual activity that are contiguous both on the body and in the history of law: the hymen and the anus.

I have argued that the overpresent wedding in "May-Pole" does not secure lawful marriage but reveals the dubious status of the Puritan polis that seems to sanction marriage and that marriage simultaneously seems to bring into being. This instability is literal, a matter of contract and charter. It is also figural: the very relationship that seems to found the polity has no positive content and can become visible only in terms of what it is not—that is, not homoerotic, not interracial, not multiply amorous. If the core of civil marriage is its intersection with sodomy law, then the state's authority is guaranteed not by a positive definition of marriage but a negative definition of other forms of eros and affinity.[51] But as I suggested earlier, the wedding in "May-Pole" that will not go away is also a sign for a crisis contemporaneous to the tale's own production. For by the mid-1830s, when "May-Pole" was written, not only marriage law but the form of the wedding ritual itself had a new and different place in defining the functions and limits of marital couplehood vis-à-vis other social formations, up to and including the nation itself.

While the civil status of marriage was increasingly grounded in the laws against sex between men in England and its North American colonies from 1533 through the Enlightenment, and against sex across racial barriers from 1661 onward in the colonies, by the nineteenth century the foundation for civil marriage was yet another "sex crime"—namely, nonmonogamous marriage. For the federal government—which except in cases of interracial unions had essentially abandoned its proactive supervision of marriage—began to actively interfere with free white people's marriages again in the middle of the nineteenth century. The most dramatic incident of this renewed policing was a national campaign against Mormon polygamy that began in 1862, when President Abraham Lincoln signed the Morrill Act outlawing polygamy in all U.S. territories.[52] This act was the culmination of earlier state and country rulings that along with mob harassment, had driven groups practicing pantagamy, complex marriage, and polygamy from place to place. Thus, while the possibility in "May-Pole" that Edith and Edgar are really married not just to each other in a state-sanctioned Puritan civil marriage but to the entire "ring of monsters" in a plural marriage certainly reflects the contradictions inherent within covenant theology, it also registers the promises and dangers that plural marriage represented in nineteenth-century political thought. The tale was published before the Mormons publicly announced their practice of polygamy in 1852, but Endicott's interruption of the wedding at Merry Mount, his separation of the nuptial couple, and his execution of all other participants may also encode antebellum reactions to the complex marriages practiced by earlier religious sects.

Complex marriages were themselves a result of the intersection of religious and economic changes that reformulated the U.S. family. As the work of historian Mary Ryan has made clear, the economic shift from the self-sustaining agrarian home to a cash economy made the Second Great Awakening possible, for it freed some women from having to do farmwork, enabling them to form evangelical missionary and maternal associations.[53] These early societies threatened to replace parental and marital bonds with affinities between same-sex peers and undermine the patriarchal family and church as means of social control. As if in compensation for these dangers, though, missionary and maternal associations actually became the crucibles of nineteenth-century domestic ideology, for they fostered a vision of families themselves as structured by purely voluntary heterosexual affections, which the wife/mother was primarily responsible for inculcating and maintaining. By 1845, the "Era of Association," as Ryan calls it, had given way to the "cult of domesticity," and the home was disconnected from larger social networks.[54] Yet the most radical sects such as the Perfectionists and Mormons translated these economic and social shifts into a vision of expansive lateral association—a new form of "plural marriage."

In sum, the movement from filial to associational visions of community suggested a broadening of the horizon of the social. But this was offset by the movement from extended-patriarchal to nuclear-maternal households, which indicated a shrinkage of that horizon. The dialectical nature of these changes may have had an impact on the form of the ordinary, dyadic wedding itself, which began to mediate between expansive and restrictive social visions. For the same period that saw the waning of, first, the kin-centered, extended-familial household, and then the age of voluntary association that followed it, also saw the wedding change from a small ceremony in the home, attended by kin and neighbors, to an increasingly large, regimented, display-oriented one structured by gift giving. The middle-class white wedding symbolized the newly female-focused family structure by emphasizing the special status of the bride, who by the 1840s was distinguished from her peers with a white dress, veil, and attendants.[55] This restyled wedding also compensated for the smaller, increasingly less materially interdependent family by rescripting the ritual itself. To reiterate Ellen Rothman's contention, rather than expressing the couple's ongoing ties with extended family and neighbors as did the household-based, loosely structured weddings of the seventeenth and eighteenth centuries, the white wedding that emerged in the antebellum years enabled the couple to begin an economically independent life. Rothman shows that in the U.S. middle classes, the elaborate white wedding emphasized and supported a newly nucleated family. It ameliorated the increasingly isolated status of the couple and greater difficulty they would have in achieving economic self-sufficiency by giving them a onetime injection of collectively donated capital for their private use: the practice of asking family as well as neighbors to give gifts that helped the couple establish a separate domestic household began in the 1830s and was firmly in place by the late 1870s. Finally, while colonial and early republican families opened up the bride's house to friends and kin for extended festivities, antebellum couples went on a bridal tour with immediate family members, moving from house to house visiting their kin, as if to promote the affections that no longer came automatically in large, extended farm families. By the 1880s, the process of sealing off both the bride's body and couple's relationship culminated in the honeymoon that fostered nuptial intimacy and separation from the natal family.

From the perspective offered by Rothman's and Ryan's work, the danger of mid- and late-nineteenth-century plural marriages was that they took as literal and ongoing the momentary economic ties that the gift-giving big wedding substituted for the farm family's former interdependence between generations of kin and circles of neighbors, and sexualized the voluntary bonds of earlier associations. Radical religious and/or socialist sects made these fleeting economic and affective ties the basis for a new vision of "family," one grounded in a sometimes explicit, sometimes implicit return to the covenantal model in which a marriage incarnated and bound an elective community. In doing so, these groups took the tenets of both Puritan covenant theology and the antebellum age of association to their most radical conclusion, knotting the proliferating economic bonds and the new associative possibilities that the cash economy fostered into those of love and sexuality. The complex marriages at Putney and Oneida married everyone to everyone else and thus pooled property; the followers of French socialist Charles Fourier believed in multiple and transitory marriages; the Shakers discouraged marriage because it privatized property; and the Mormons allowed men to use polygamy as a means of accumulating vast tracts of land.[56]

Hawthorne's *The Blithedale Romance* (1852) concerns itself explicitly with these changes in the marriage relation. As part of a commune working toward "the millennium of love," the novel's narrator, Miles Coverdale, obsesses over whether or not one of his female compatriots is a virgin.[57] He asks "whether Zenobia had ever been married," whether "wedlock had thrown wide the gates of mystery," whether "Zenobia is a wife!"[58] As Lauren Berlant has shown, the taint of Zenobia's female sexuality threatens to undermine the homosocial brotherly love of a utopian community; the novel also links Zenobia to Fourier, who proposed a system of "consummated Paradise" in which work was seen as an extension of sensual life, people could act on all sexual desires, and marriage could be entered and exited at will.[59] But while Coverdale's nuptial language is certainly a metaphor for genital sex, it also suggests that Zenobia might adhere to a communitarian *marital* doctrine. Zenobia, in other words, is a figure for a paradox inherent in antebellum readjustments of the relationship between dyadic, possessive marriage and the collectivity-making covenant, between the privatization of property in marriage and its circulation on a newly emerging market. If spirituality "married" everyone to everyone else, if democracy subordinated family relations to the bonds between citizens, and if the self-sustaining family economy had given way to a system of unrelated laborers working side by side, what was to prevent polygamy and not monogamy from becoming the basis of social life? If the state were both invoked in every civil wedding and guaranteed by its regulation of marriage, would this threat of polygamy extend the nation infinitely outward, thereby eroding its boundaries?

These questions are not explicitly taken up in *The Blithedale Romance*. But they do arise in a later text that draws its energies from both the "polity-making" wedding explored in "May-Pole" and antebellum ceremonies of complex marriage that shadow *Blithedale*—Joseph Kirkland's *Zury: The Meanest Man in Spring County; A Novel of Western Life* (1887).[60] This novel situates the problem of the wedding in the same decade that informs "May-Pole," the 1830s, but adds ingredients particular to the 1880s and more explicitly connected to the nation than the colony of "May-Pole" or *Blithedale*'s commune: immigration from non-Anglo, continental European countries, territorial expansion into the U.S. Midwest, the federal regulation of marriage during the Mormon crisis, and the politics of the money form. In fact, while in "May-

Pole" the intersection between changing forms of marriage and those of property is visible only in the subterranean analogy between the marriage contract and Massachusetts Bay Colony charter, in *Zury* this intersection emerges in full force in the bigamous and polygamous possibilities that structure this overtly economic novel, published nine years after the Mormons attempted to defend their right to the property accumulated under this system of marriage, and lost.

A swift plot summary is in order for a novel that was a minor sensation in its moment, and yet remains out of print, untaught, and without much critical commentary.[61] *Zury* begins with the Prouder family arriving to farm a homestead in Wayback City, in Spring County, Illinois, a few years after the War of 1812. After his father dies, young Zury Prouder brings the farm to great prosperity through hard labor, penny-pinching, and marrying a woman strong enough to work alongside him. Sometime in the 1830s, the story's female protagonist, Anne Sparrow, arrives in Spring County to teach school. Anne has previously worked among other women in the textile mills of Lowell, Massachusetts, and has participated in the Fourierist movement— perhaps even to the extent, the novel suggests, of living in a phalanx. Shortly after her arrival, she sets out to acculturate Wayback City's midwesterners, predominantly European immigrants, by putting on a school pageant, the centerpiece of which is a Puritan wedding with herself playing the bride and Zury the groom. Unbeknownst to Anne, Zury's wife dies a week before the mock wedding, and after the performance the townspeople are scandalized at the possibility that the pageant may have created a real marriage. Shortly after the production the town holds a picnic, and a rainstorm forces Zury and Anne to spend the night in a cave, where they consummate their "marriage." Anne gets pregnant and quickly marries another transplanted New Englander, her longtime suitor John Endicott McVey, so as to avoid becoming the wife of the much older, miserly Zury. Equally terrified that the poverty-stricken Anne will claim rights to the estate he has worked so hard to raise, Zury marries his late wife's sister in order to appropriate her inheritance. Anne raises her twins alone after her husband dies on a mining trip to California, and Zury's second wife eventually dies as well. Along the way, Anne and Zury separately accrue a fair degree of wealth, and each falls gradually in love with the other without admitting it, but she repeatedly turns down his offers of marriage. The novel ends roughly twenty years after their mock wedding, "well on in the '[Eighteen-]Fifties,' " as the narrator puts it, with the twins grown up, and Zury and Anne finally married and raising their infant son (z, 509).

In terms of genre *Zury* is a liminal novel, containing elements of the domestic-sentimental "love plot" and the realist focus on the economics of the marital relation itself. But unlike later realists such as William Dean Howells, Edith Wharton, and Henry James, Kirkland does not use the bad marriage or domestic "deadlock" as a figure for and means of enacting formal innovations that break the frame of the bourgeois love plot.[62] Instead, he uses the Puritan wedding itself as the novel's centrifuge, to ask the question of what makes a marriage "real." Does the civil context (in this case, a town meeting hall) guarantee a marriage? Or is it actually secured by the "unreal," theatrical aspects of the wedding itself? Is a marriage instantiated by the approbation of the community, by verbal declarations, by consummation, or by some combination of these? What proper relationship to property can make a marriage "real"? In turn, what kind of polity does a "real" marriage figure, engender, or guarantee?

The novel's main female protagonist, Anne Sparrow, is a curious amalgamation of Puritan covenant theologist and antebellum utopian socialist. She is referred to more than once as a "transplanted Mayflower" and is clearly the novel's representative of New England culture. Yet her encounter with Fourierism and previous stint as a Lowell factory worker also connect her to the religious and economic transformations that undermined the New England corporate family once held together by church surveillance and domestic production. In Anne's quest to "Americanize" (or New Englandize) what she sees as an outpost of civilization, she inadvertently reveals that the connection between Puritan covenant and utopian socialist doctrine in the United States might be their mutual threat to couple-centered domesticity: under her direction, the covenantal Puritan model explicitly threatens to become the polygamous communal model. In the novel's broader analysis, however, polygamy and socialism are not actually opposed to capitalism either, for *Zury* shows the ideology of antebellum domesticity strained to the breaking point by capitalism's proliferation of bonds between debtors and creditors. *Zury* may use the Puritan wedding as a figure for the founding of a nation, but dyadic, domestic marriage ultimately becomes the least "American" of the many social forms explored by this novel.

Though Anne seems to represent Puritan culture at its most distilled, from the moment she arrives in Spring County she is also associated with sexual license:

> Society has created a cruel fate for lonely women. Every theory which seems to provide a place for the unmarried millions of the gentle sex finds a natural following of adherents among them. Even Mormonism is not coarse enough to repel the lower orders of the race, abhorrent as it is to the refined. Fourierism aimed at giving every human being an honorable chance to live; no wonder it gained passionate adherents from the ranks of New England women, Anne Sparrow among the rest. . . . As to Anne's part in it, we need not inquire how far from the beaten track her "broad views" led her. Whatever she did was not done from wickedness; it was in accordance with her honest opinions of right and wrong, and not in violation of them. Her lips are sealed; she had neither praise nor blame to bestow on her former friends at the time when she begins to be connected with our story. (z, 91–92)

In other words, prior to the novel's action, sexual frustration had led the unmarried Anne to a Fourierist community associated with what was then called "free love"—an explicitly racialized step above Mormonism in this passage, but nevertheless a serious transgression. As with Zenobia in *Blithedale,* Anne's former involvement with Fourierism gives her an aura of promiscuity: her "lips" may be "sealed" now, yet the narrator seems to doubt that she kept her legs crossed as she wandered "from the beaten track" and toward a suspiciously "passionate" collectivity.

But again as with Zenobia, Anne's transgressions may be a matter of civil crime rather than just moral sin, for the narrator's explicit mention of the Mormons suggests that her career as a Fourierist might actually make her a married woman several times over.[63] Indeed, Anne balks at labeling herself as "married or single" on her application for the job of Spring County schoolmistress. Before Anne will sign, she consults a justice of the peace, for she fears that "the marriage laws of some states are so different from those of others that a man might call himself married when in fact according to the law of Illinois he is single!" (z, 168). The hypothetical situation she describes seems to reverse her own: she may have counted as single in Massachusetts, but the laws of Illinois might make her married and therefore ineligible to be a schoolteacher. In Massachusetts, with its history of state-supervised weddings, sexual intercourse alone would not make her a married woman, but in Illinois, where immigrant cultures have brought their own kinship rules with them and consent makes a marriage, consummation might in fact tie the nuptial knot. Squire Brown assures her that to be married under Illinois common law, a couple must both vow that they are married in the present tense and live together publicly thereafter. Anne is relieved that *both* of these acts are required to legitimate even a common-law marriage in Illinois and signs as "single." But good Puritan descendant that she is, she declares that common-law marriage will not do for her: " 'I will never be married by anybody but a justice of the peace, Squire Brown' " (69).

Of course this conversation sets Anne up for a fall. After the novel has fostered all of these implications of marital transgression, the community is scandalized when Anne decides to put on a schoolroom exhibition of a famous colonial tableau, the Puritan wedding of Priscilla Mullins and John Alden (the production anachronistically re-creates Henry Wadsworth Longfellow's "The Courtship of Miles Standish," which was not yet written during the time frame of this episode). She does this in order to bring "A Scene from New England History" to a population of European immigrants whom she views as cultural barbarians. Indeed, she intends to use the wedding to renew the New England covenant in the Midwest, to unite and ratify a truly "American" people out of this motley collection of newcomers, as her hybrid Puritan/eastern European immigrant costume for the pageant makes clear (see figure 7). At first, planning to play the part of Priscilla Mullins herself, she asks the community's other archetypal New Englander, her suitor John Endicott McVey, to take on the role of John Alden. McVey, who has been in love with Anne since her arrival, gladly accepts. But a neighbor, Mrs. Anstey, advises her against producing the pageant:

> [Mrs. Anstey:] "Ye dunno, I don't mistrust, thet foolish folks is a-passin' the'r remarks abaout yer a-bein' a-goin' t' stan' up with Johnny McVey in a mock-marr'ge, as ye might say."
>
> [Anne:] "Oh, pshaw! McVey, indeed! Marriages are often displayed in theatres, and nobody in his senses ever takes them to mean anything!"
>
> [Mrs. Anstey:] "Ya-as—but then ye know th' school-haouse ain't no theayter; 'n' ef it wuz, perfessin' Christians, in course, would n't never go inter it, ner nigh tew it, nuther. It's a meetin'-haouse,—a haouse of God; 'n' marriages a many hez be'n performed thar a'ready. 'N' ef yew 'n'

Johnny wuz a-goin t'marry, thar's whar ye'd naytrally be, 'n' sayin' th'
same words, tew. . . . 'N'; then the' 's another thing: both on ye bein'
single and marriageable the' 's them as sez ye mought find yerself
marr'd t'Johnny, 'thaout never mistrustin' sech a thing!" (187)

Here, the Wayback community proves itself more Puritan than Anne the New
Englander, holding fast to the bias against theater and to the tradition of using
the civic space of the "meetin-haouse" to marry couples.

Hoping to avoid a misunderstanding, Anne demotes (John) Endicott
(McVey) to the role of the wedding's officiant, reversing "May-Pole" in her
insistence that an Endicott actually sanction a Puritan marriage by acting as a
magistrate. But in making her would-be beau into the officiant, Anne also
sets up a triangulated structure in which the witness/officiant threatens to
marry himself right into the couple (for in fact, McVey does end up married
to Anne later on). Furthermore, the pageant that Zury, Anne, and McVey
enact—the marriage of John Alden and Priscilla Mullins—itself depends on a
triangular structure that involves the state: according to the famous legend
they dramatize, the Puritan Governor Standish sends Alden to court Priscilla
on his behalf, whereupon the enterprising maiden asks Alden why he does
not ask her to marry himself. Perhaps the appeal of this legendary wedding to
nineteenth-century culture, as indicated by the later popularity of Longfellow's poem, is that it plays fort/da with the state: in the coupling of Standish
and Mullen, it seems to instantiate Puritan and hence nascently "American"
collectivity, while in the coupling of Mullins and Alden behind Standish's
back, it seems also to banish any governmental intermediary.

This aspect of the poem is evident in what follows, for the state's presence
or absence becomes crucial to the status of the bridal pair. Anne chooses
for her replacement groom an older married resident, none other than the
novel's eponymous hero Zury. The performance goes splendidly, but a day
later the news gets out that Zury's wife has died a week before. The townspeople immediately condemn the pageant in the language of providential history:
"Never c'd be a clearer case of a jedgement on play-actin' " (198). Because she
has spoken her marital vows in the present tense, Anne is horrified to think
that she might actually be married to Zury: "This was a new State. In Massachusetts she felt sure that no advantage could be taken of her accidental
predicament; but who could tell what might be the law and custom in Illinois?
The idea was horrible!" (199). Anne's anxieties are justified; by 1846, Illinois

Fig. 7. New England and immigrant culture meet in the wedding. "Anne Sparrow as the Puritan Priscilla," frontispiece to *Zury: The Meanest Man in Spring County*.

had established its willingness to police the marriage relation by driving the polygamous Mormons out of their capital city at Nauvoo.[64]

But Anne's outburst also breaks its 1830s' historical frame, alluding to an 1880s' movement to unify state marriage laws, and thereby to the subterranean role that polygamy played in this movement. During the 1880s, reformers called on the federal government to amend the Constitution so as to unify the marriage and divorce laws that varied from state to state. Reformers described exactly the sort of scenario that Anne finds herself in, in which crossing a state line could nullify or activate a marriage against the wishes of the people involved. One advocate of uniform marriage law protested that marriage should not be made a matter of geography, writing that "parties about to marry by crossing a river, a lake, or borderline may, through ignorance or design, pass from one jurisdiction into another having different and conflicting rules with regard to the mode of entering into the marriage contract."[65] The ostensible purpose of uniform marriage laws was not only to prevent the accidental instantiation or dissolution of a marriage but also to overturn various states' common-law doctrines that in reformers' eyes, made any union a potential marriage; in calling for a uniform licensing system they aimed to prevent interracial marriages, unions involving parties under the age of consent, and bigamy.[66]

The 1880s' advocates for uniform marriage laws officially lost, for the government simply asked states to voluntarily agree to standard doctrines. Still, the final defeat of the Mormons eliminated at least one form of the irregular unions they feared. The Mormons' exodus from Nauvoo to the Utah territories established that in order to continue to practice polygamy, Mormon leaders were willing to take advantage of the federalist ideal that each state or territory should regulate its own domestic affairs. Congress finally resolved the Mormon dilemma by assuming jurisdiction over marriage in the territories, ceding this authority only on a territory's ascension to statehood and requiring the prohibition of polygamy before making a territory into a state. In this way, they preserved the federalist model while also establishing the national government's prerogative to define marriage. With the 1882 Edmunds Act, the U.S. government disfranchised polygamists from voting, jury duty, and political office, thereby making monogamy an explicit condition of U.S. citizenship; in 1890, the Mormons were forced to give up polygamy as a condition of statehood, and Utah was admitted into the Union in 1896.[67] Yet the very title of the Mormon renunciation of polygamy, the "Declaration of

Submission," foregrounds the coercion inherent in the monogamous model, both for women who were potentially cut off from the female communities engendered by polygamy and for states whose "independence" was obtained through acquiescence to a single sexual standard.

Though federal law declared that monogamy was the official U.S. form of marriage, Kirkland's *Zury* seems to recognize that plural marriage was in many ways the *inheritor* of the Puritan covenant model. Unlike Governor Endicott, who in "May-Pole" gives the covenantal model ambivalent status in the question of what kind of kinship practices might effect a unified nation, the arch-Puritan residents of Springfield County seem to explicitly reject this paradigm, condemning Anne's New England pageant. But the covenant comes back to haunt these latter-day Puritans in the form of the plural marriages that their historical counterparts were on the verge of exiling from Illinois. Just as the illegitimate-yet-valid wedding in "May-Pole" reveals that male-male sexual practices purport to be antithetical to, and nonetheless (in the end) are foundational to the establishment of the marital civic sphere, *Zury*'s theatrical-yet-valid wedding extends this analysis toward the practice of polygamy: repeating and modifying Longfellow's triangular structure, this wedding both "marries" Anne to Zury and provides McVey a way to marry Anne.

The Puritan wedding pageant, that is, effects a common-law marriage between Anne and Zury as well as a bigamous union between Anne and McVey. For Anne and Zury consummate their mock wedding several weeks afterward, when they take refuge in an abandoned coal mine during a rainstorm. In the cave, terrified of the dark, Anne pleads with Zury, " 'If our mock wedding had been a real one, you would n't offer to leave me here—to die— now would you?' " (z, 222). Zury interprets this as a proposition, and the two have sex: indeed, Anne seems to seduce him by refusing to let him leave the mine and come back for her in the morning, and literally seizing him by the lapels. Among its many connections with "May-Pole," *Zury* has its own clumsy symbol of heterosexual intercourse: Zury drops his walking stick at the mouth of the abandoned coal mine. In the morning, a passerby sees the walking stick by the cave, and this display seems to satisfy the final condition for common-law marriage in Illinois—that a couple live together and are acknowledged as doing so by their community.

Nineteenth-century readers alert to biblical resonances might also have seen the cave scene as a recapitulation of Genesis 19 in which Lot, having been saved from the destruction that "rained upon" Sodom and having seen his wife turn into a pillar of salt, is seduced by his two daughters in a cave at Zoar.[68] Since Lot himself has not participated in threatening the angels with male-on-male gang rape but in fact offers the Sodomites his betrothed daughters in order to save the angels, by tricking him into incest they seem to punish him for secondhand adultery. This "punishment," however, produces Lot's progeny and thereby furthers the Israelites' history, in the form of their kin and mortal enemies, the Moabites. According to Genesis 19, then, the continuation of the Hebrew people occurs not only through the injunction to "be fruitful and multiply" that explicitly condoned the taking of multiple wives, not only through the destruction of "sterile" Sodom and a rejuvenating covenant with the procreative Abraham, but also through one of its own fathers' acts of incest, adultery, promiscuity, and abetting the rape of a virgin. In short, the story of Lot and the cave actually suggests that the nation of Israel came into being by simultaneously punishing sodomy and engaging in what are, by its own logic, a tangle of heteroerotic sins.[69] In *Zury*, the Anglo-Protestant "regeneration" of the frontier Midwest is similarly suspect. For though Christianity explicitly repudiated Hebrew polygamy and Protestantism elevated monogamy over even celibate communities, under Anne's direction the polity of Spring County seems to be ratified by complex rather than monogamous marriage. Pregnant by Zury, with whom she has said marriage vows, consummated them, and even "lived together" briefly in the cave, Anne quickly marries McVey. She is now not merely a potential bigamist like her "groom" Zury after he marries his dead wife's sister but a potential polygamist, especially in light of her history with Fourierism.

Zury has its own code word for the polygamy that both threatens the Spring County community and seems to provide its founding instance: "Universalism." After news gets out about the night in the cave, the community ostracizes Anne, whispering that "mebbe she's a *Universalist!*" and the scandal casts "a pall of 'odium theologicum' over both Anne and Zury, enfolding them *together*" (z, 236, 237). But Universalists did not practice plural marriage; they were a predominantly rural sect of poorer people whose beliefs included a Holy Spirit that operated freely among people without the need for interpreters, a nonhierarchical congregation, and women's freedom to speak in church.[70] The accusations of "Universalism" appear instead to connect Anne to another Puritan woman with whom she is analogized throughout the novel: the antinomian Anne Hutchinson. Zury himself calls Anne Sparrow " 'a reg'lar Salem witch!' " (z, 165), and the charge of Universalism links her to Hutchinson's beliefs in unmediated access to the Holy Spirit and a woman's right to preach. Both women, as it turns out, are also accused of a promiscuous disregard for monogamous marriage. Metaphorizing her religious meetings as orgies, John Cotton accused Hutchinson of "all promiscuus and filthie cominge togeather of men and Woemen without Distinction or Relation of Marriage."[71] But with Anne Sparrow, the causal arrows between sex and heresy are reversed. While Hutchinson's religious heresy earned her accusations of "carnal pride" and monstrous multiple births, Sparrow's Fourierism, possible multiple marriages, irregular wedding, and conception of twins with Zury earn her accusations of religious heresy. Like Hutchinson, whom Cotton reviles for "that filthie Sinne of the Comunitie of Woemen," Anne Sparrow too is eventually charged with usurping the prerogative of magistrates and forming a female public.[72] For after her "wedding" and consummation, a town mob terrorizes her for boarding female students in her makeshift home at the school and thereby, presumably, corrupting her charges with unorthodox ideas.

But what makes Anne Sparrow *different* from Anne Hutchinson is the social context in which Universalism specifically evokes the collapse of boundaries between marriage and other forms of social belonging—both the Fourierist "phalanx" of Sparrow's own historical moment of the 1830s and the polygamous Mormon unions that were under fatal fire during the time Kirkland wrote *Zury*. Anne Sparrow's Puritan wedding has produced a serious problem: the covenantal Puritan marriage, supposed to ratify Spring County as truly "American" on the New England model, has in the eyes of the townspeople produced a threateningly "Universalist" set of bonds that undermine both nation and patriarchal nuclear family. That Anne marries John *Endicott* McVey in an attempt to correct this view is no coincidence. Her husband's middle name registers Anne's capitulation to proper relations among state, family, and church (recall the historical Endicott's reorganization of Salem's single people into male-headed households).

If the novel stopped with Anne's marriage to McVey, it would simply work to reiterate the dominance of U.S. Protestant monogamy over the more radical aspects of Puritan covenant theology, New England's antebellum utopian socialism, and Mormonism alike. Yet though the narrator describes McVey as "a real New Englander," he also notes that McVey was "too slender in body and mind—too soft in head and heart" (z, 124) to contend with the Midwest. Eventually, the plot kills him off by dispatching him to California, where he suffers a mining accident. It remains not to the Puritan John Endicott (McVey) but to Zury to address the problem of proliferating affinities, relationships, or bonds—a problem that both figures a democratic nation and threatens to dissolve its boundaries altogether. *Zury: The Meanest Man in Spring County* undoes the Protestant ideology of monogamous marriage not by returning to Hebrew polygamy, Christian celibacy, or Mormonism proper but by connecting the cash nexus on which nineteenth-century social existence increasingly depended to transformations in kinship patterns engendered by a nationalizing economy.

In point of fact, the townspeople have already directly accused Zury of practicing heretical Universalism long before he meets Anne, which adds an economic twist to the novel's examination of Protestant theology, marriage, and the nation form. Zury's much less literal form of Universalism, though, is perhaps even more threatening than Anne's commitment to a covenantal model that turns out to be indistinguishable from plural marriage. For if the names Anne and Endicott signal the problematic legacy of Puritanism in this novel, the name Zury, short for Usury, signals the presence of money, a "universalizing" solvent that frees commodities from their original material form. Usury, or moneylending for profit, brings the financial contract and social contract into strange conjunction. As the historical use of the figure of usury to associate Jews with sexual perversion and domestic disorder suggests, usury is actually a radically "unnatural" form of binding or affinity that transcends the boundaries of birth and consanguinity alike. The Hebrews insisted that usury be exogamous; though Moses prohibited the Israelites from practicing usury within their own tribe, his Deuteronomic commandment permitted them to practice it on strangers. Seventeenth-century Catholics attempting to halt the practice among Christians, went so far as to analogize the taking of usury with the practice of polygamy.[73]

At first, then, Christianity, which saw all people as potential kin, prohibited usury. But a central act of the Protestant Reformation was Calvin's reversal of the logic that made usury a taboo, for he proclaimed that since Christians did not distinguish between brothers and strangers, they were permitted to charge usury to all.[74] Thus, the Reformation's lifting of the ban on usury would seem to extend the Roman Catholic vision of an expansive community of faith toward the secular sphere. Not only does usury reproduce money outside a productive labor economy, it actually fosters ongoing relationships of indebtedness between people, perhaps best captured in the word "interest." This contrasts with the simple exchange of commodities for money, which ordinarily depersonalizes, equalizes, and limits the relationship between the transacting parties. Yet when Protestants elevated monogamy above celibate devotional community, they seemed to counter, or at least disavow, the socially binding work of usury.[75] *Zury* reverses these relations, exposing the economic and affinitive entanglings that the Protestant model of monogamous marriage mystifies. The hero's very name asks the question that haunts *Zury*: under industrial and corporate capitalism, what will "family" be? Can anything mark its boundaries and guarantee its grounding in nature, rather than in human-made processes of production and socialization?

One way these questions are worked out is through the novel's analogy between marriage and the money form. In light of their occupations as farmer and former Lowell girl, the mock wedding between Zury and Anne is an emblem for the fiscal "marriage" between midwestern agrarianism (which needed eastern capital to finance its homesteads) and eastern industrialism (which needed homesteaders to settle territories and thereby expand the market for its goods). The pageant recalls the "Mountain Wedding" at Promontory Summit on 10 May 1869 that joined the eastern and western railroads with a gold "ring," a special spike driven into the tie that linked the two lines.[76] But from the point of view of a midwesterner like Kirkland himself, this connection might well be figured by a *mock* marriage that inadvertently collapses into a real one. For a central problem in the economic relationship between the East and Midwest was a conflict between the representational and "real" status of money. Easterners financed the homesteads and first crops of midwestern farmers with "soft money"—paper money not backed up by gold—but they demanded that they be paid back in "hard money"—specie adhering to the gold standard or gold itself.[77]

Zury addresses the question of whether money was to be hard or soft, real or representative, by remaking the terms through which a marriage becomes real—ultimately championing the theatrical and plural aspects of the "mock" wedding over the contractual and dyadic aspects of "real," lawful marriage. One might expect the conflict between representationalism and realism, soft money and hard, both to follow one another and line up in a series of gendered as well as geographically inflected dichotomies. Anne, who brings the sentimental love plot into the tale, is associated with the wedding, theatricality, the East, the factory system central to industrial capitalism, and a "writerly" style of speaking uninflected by dialect. Zury is associated with literary realism, "hard" marriages embedded in property relations, Spring County's bias against the theater, an agrarianism embedded in physiocratic notions of productivity, and a spoken midwestern dialect that is almost unreadable in print. Zury himself protests against soft money, exclaiming, "Banks can't print paper and make it inter money—it's only a promise t'pay money, arter all, 'n' sposen y'hev a pocketful on it 'n' th' bank can't or wun't redeem it,— wun't perform its promise—whar be ye?" (z, 348). He goes on to claim that "*money*'s a thing that can't be manufactured by a sharp in an office—it's suth'n' th't's got t' be dug aouter the graoun' 'n' then traded off fer suth'n th'ts growed a-top o' graoun'" (349–50). Here, dismissing writing and manufacturing alike, Zury establishes metonymic relations among spoken words, hard money, and farming, seeming in the end to literally "ground" money entirely in nature's dirt.

But in fact, Kirkland, as the son of homesteaders and himself a lawyer, would by necessity have been committed to what was by 1874 referred to as "fiat money," or paper money issued by government decree. For homesteader farmers like Zury had a vested interest in keeping soft money in circulation so that they could pay their debts. The very geographic terrain of Kirkland's realism, which purported to do away with the trickery of representation and give direct access to the U.S. experience, was also that of the most "representational" form of money, that which departed from the gold standard. Zury's love plot, seen by critics to undermine the novel's commitment to literary realism, adjudicates this paradox by displacing it onto a different discursive plane. The plot instantiated by a mock wedding aims to do what Zury suggests a bank might not: to "perform its promise," to make good on a representation. Writing becomes the novel's figure of and foundation for marriage, yet it is one that reduces neither to the state that stands "behind" civil marriage nor the state brought into being by it.

At first glance, Zury's statement that paper cannot be money seems to align with his contempt for any representation or performance of "love." Viewing his first two wives as labor-saving devices, and marriage as a means of extending his own property, he does not have a public wedding with either of the women he marries prior to Anne. Yet the mock wedding between Zury and Anne ultimately makes fiction into a constitutive element of the promise on which Zury suspects that banks might renege. Zury's remark about paper money reveals that paper money only works if it is kept in circulation and its "real value" deferred. Taken to the bank and redeemed for specie, it threatens to be worthless. His relationship to Anne is structured the same way, albeit with a *literary* and not a *legal* contract as its binding element. For long before Anne's arrival in Illinois, he builds himself a cabin, which he wallpapers with sheets taken from "a large bundle of 'Republicans'" (35). As a young man, he spends his free time reading the walls of his house, "full of tales, continued stories, political articles, news from abroad, advertisements, riddles, jokes, and such like familiar newspaper scraps" (35), but is frustrated when he encounters an unfinished serial story with the next page missing from his walls. When Anne sees the truncated story on the walls of this crude cabin many years later, she promises to write him the end of the wallpaper tale, aligning narrative closure with the fulfillment of heterosexual love: "Oh, I know the end of that story—and I'll write it out for you" (149).

But the end of that story is continually deferred. Likewise, Anne and Zury's wedding cannot be redeemed for the hard currency of a marriage license, domestic relations, or shared property. Even when he proposes to her some fifteen years after the pageant wedding, she turns him down: "One reason why we have hitherto got on so well . . . is that neither has had any power or authority over the other; neither has had to ask the other for money or for anything else. And that is the way it must go on" (507). Instead, Anne speaks vows with her daughter, explicitly following Ruth and Naomi:

> "Now what was it Ruth said to Naomi?"
>
> "'Entreat me not to leave thee, nor to return from following after thee.'"
>
> "Well, my daughter; 'Whither thou goest, I will go.' Now, you say the next."
>
> "'Where thou lodgest I will lodge.'"
>
> "'Thy people shall be my people.'"
>
> "'And thy God, my God.'"
>
> "Now, darling, listen to your mother while she vows a vow. 'The Lord do so to me and more also, if aught but death part me and thee.'"
> (503)

Though she makes good on this pledge to her daughter, Anne delays her promise to Zury through almost the entire length of the novel. Only in refusing to marry Zury—to fulfill and thus sever the narrative contract and write the "end of that story"—can she rewrite the marriage contract. Meanwhile, Zury, "the Meanest Man in Spring County," becomes a family man by surreptitiously supervising and financially assisting a marriage he is not part of: he watches Anne's children grow up from a distance and secretly pays off her debts.

When Anne and Zury finally are married, and she does offer Zury "the end of that story," he defers it even longer: "She says she 'll write it all daown afore she dies, 'n' I b'lieve her, 'n' so I wanter put it off till arter I'm dead" (533–34). At the same time, Anne never does cash in the stock certificate he sends her twenty years after their mock wedding as proof that his miserly ways have changed. Within the logic of this novel, in order to make good on their promise, both money and marriage need to remain performances; they cannot be allowed to collapse into the real. And the ceremony of commitment between Anne and her daughter also extends the bonds of "marriage" beyond the male-female couple.

Paradoxically, then, a "couple" whose mock wedding results in marriages to other people—and perhaps even in polygamy—becomes Zury's final figure for a real marriage. The novel transforms the frowned-on theatrical wedding, which does not yield a juridical marriage but instead fosters a series of potentially polygamous ties, from a state-centered covenant into an economically mediated infrastructure that fosters multiple social ties, within which Zury and Anne take over twenty years to find one another again. This, I submit, is the paradox of marriage in market capitalism: unable to produce the economically self-sufficient household it nevertheless promotes ideologically, capitalism must somehow bind the couple to means of sustenance that break the boundaries of natal and marital family—all the while denying these ties the cultural status of family. In Zury, the wedding levels the distinctions between relations that are mediated by commerce and the mystified relations that are supposedly untouched by it. Indeed, within the time of Zury's writing and publication, the elaborate white wedding had taken full cultural hold, superseding the plain civil ceremony, and adjudicating the paradoxes of family life in capitalism by simultaneously sealing off the couple and organizing a community momentarily around it. Only the grandiose, commodity-saturated, gift-mongering wedding could secure the couple's means of emotional and economic survival by binding them into peer, extended kin, and market relations. In Zury usury, writing, plural marriages, and the wedding itself intertwine to form this network of support, and the novel materializes them as both equivalent and foundational to the ordinary nuptial knot. While the very thing that appeared to give marriage a secure foundation—the juridical realm—seems in both Hawthorne and Kirkland to threaten marriage, the very thing that appears to undercut the reality of marriage—the wedding—is the only thing that can make social life feasible at all.

Chapter Five

HONEYMOON WITH A STRANGER: PRIVATE COUPLEHOOD

AND THE MAKING OF THE NATIONAL SUBJECT

"You will go a long journey,
In a strange bed take rest,"
And a dark girl will kiss you . . .
—Philip Larkin, "The North Ship"[1]

So far in the texts I have examined, the wedding has proven an unreliable guarantor of either narrative or social closure. Not only does it dismantle the narrative work of the courtship plot but also, neither its popular version nor its remaking as the figure for covenant or state-sanctioned contract can reliably guarantee a marriage or limit its members to two. As if to rectify these problems, a newer tradition has evolved to supplement the wedding: the honeymoon that physically separates the couple from peers and natal family, isolates them with one another and puts them into contact with a new place, and moves them along a narrative trajectory toward adulthood and (or as) dyadic heterosexual marriage.

Though the honeymoon began as a mere adjunct to the wedding, it has grown into a production that easily outdoes the wedding in cost and length. This is because the honeymoon actually promises to do what the wedding itself might not. By thrusting a male and female together into a supposedly "exotic" or "primitive" locale, the honeymoon seems to enfold heterosexuality into nature in a way that neither the theatrical wedding nor juridical marriage license securely can. By isolating the couple, the honeymoon also seems to make marriage into a matter of two and two only, escaping the polymorphous perversions that are latent in the wedding as well as the couple's triangulation with officiant and state that is inherent in lawful marriage. By focusing the meaning of marriage on sexual experiences and intertwining these with the sensory apprehension of a landscape often coded as a national landmark, the honeymoon substitutes the mutually structuring bonds of couplehood and patriotism for religious, local, and extended familial constituencies. On the honeymoon, erotic and emotional "contact zones" between man and woman seem to intermingle with spatial and cultural ones between couple and country. Ultimately, the honeymoon effaces the newlyweds' contract with the state apparatus and foregrounds instead their competence with bodies and landscapes, seeming to disconnect the pair's pleasures and privileges from mediations such as marriage, inheritance, and naturalization law.

As a standard feature of the white, middle-class wedding in the United States, the departure of the couple on a private postnuptial journey dates from the early nineteenth century.[2] During the eighteenth century, upper-class English couples began to embark on tours after their wedding; the innovation of arriving to and departing from the wedding in a closed carriage even further emphasized the private nature of the marital bond. But at that point, less wealthy newlyweds in both England and the United States were often accompanied to and from the wedding by large groups of peers making festive noise, and in the days following the ceremony, they simply received visitors in their new home. In both England and the United States, this practice was gradually replaced by the bridal tour, in which the couple, accompanied by other relatives, visited kin who had not been able to attend the wedding and enjoyed a piecemeal series of smaller celebrations. By the 1820s in the United States, as Ellen Rothman puts it, "bridal trips were [increasingly] planned around places as well as people," to Europe for the wealthy, and eventually for the middle classes, to famous U.S. sites such as Niagara Falls and Lake George.[3] By 1840, couples increasingly traveled alone.[4] The wedding journey had changed from a group excursion that integrated a couple into the extended kin and peer network, to a means of isolating the conjugal unit and suturing it to *place*. Especially for the middle classes, the honeymoon became part of a larger, emerging tourist industry that promoted U.S. scenery as a revivifying alternative to Europe and claimed that true

Americans would emerge through travel to places increasingly coded as "national."[5] In a sense, then, as an emergent backdrop for and means of fostering the nuptial relation, the U.S. landscape took on the role formerly occupied by the extended family. The nuptial relation, in turn, strengthened the role of the senses as venues for proper citizenship.

The shift from visiting people to visiting places also suggests that visual, experiential consumption of an unfamiliar environment became increasingly central to the production of nuptial privacy and to the project of distinguishing marriage from and elevating it above other affectionate bonds. Helena Michie has argued that the wedding journey was the culturally privileged site for the transformation of women's private experiences into public terms—for a sexual and sensual reorientation that dramatized a new relationship to the state.[6] But the relays also ran the other way. The public events and landmarks around which the bridal tour began to take shape also became elements of and means for nuptial privacy itself—for the couple's turn toward one another as the supposedly organic source of meaningful sociability, and away from more overt federal machinery of identity and belonging. Consider, for instance, William Dean Howell's *Their Wedding Journey* (1871), the story of a middle-class couple's bridal tour from their native Boston through Niagara to Quebec and back again. Basil and Isabel March move across the North American continent, understanding themselves first as Bostonians in relation to New York, and then as Americans in relation to Canada, precisely insofar as they also come to better understand themselves in relation to each other and consolidate the interior space of their relationship itself.

Isabel seems particularly sensitive to the way that the relatively new ritual of the honeymoon threatens to make the couple (particularly the bride) into sexualized objects as well as subjects of a tourist gaze. She insists on hiding her "public" status as a newlywed, and the reprivatization of this status allows her freer access to the sensory experience that her journey offers. As her husband reminds her, if the Marches are outwardly affectionate to one another, they will be restricted to the " 'bridal chamber' at all the hotels" and in the train cars.[7] By hiding her bridal identity, Isabel not only sleeps and eats where she pleases but substitutes the pleasures of her own, often frankly erotic visual consumption of people and places for the embarrassment of being an object of titillating gossip among travelers and members of the tourist industry. The Marches' freer access to tourist sights, in turn, enhances their intimacy with one another and their fellow nationals. The novel finally pivots on its own title: "Their" wedding journey, one controlled by the growing honeymoon business and structured by the voyeurism attending a more display-oriented heterosexuality, actually creates the enclave of couplehood that enables them to reclaim the pronoun "they." "So you see, my dear," Basil observes at the end of their trip, "our travels are incommunicably our own. We had best say nothing about our little jaunt to other people. . . . [E]ven if we tried, we couldn't make our wedding-journey theirs." Isabel's reply transforms the public properties of both marriage and landmarks into the private property of a "relationship": " 'Who wants it,' she demanded, 'to be Their Wedding Journey?' "[8]

Howells himself wrote that *Their Wedding Journey* offered him his first chance to translate the travel and character sketches of his earliest work into a new form of realist fiction, in which invented characters would view "actual" places and their inhabitants. In this model, the negotiation of tourist pleasures would foster the development not only of characterological interiority but new forms of collective being. His version of literary realism aimed to produce circuits of shared experience and understanding between people that reduced neither to dangerously erotic sentimentalist bodily bonds nor dangerously abstract juridical citizenship, and that could bridge the post–Civil War United States's burgeoning social gaps between rich and poor, men and women, and native-born citizens and their disenfranchised immigrant, black, and Indian counterparts.[9] The honeymoon offered a perfect rubric for Howells's first experiment with this paradigm. As Michie notes in her discussion of British Victorian honeymoons, the wedding journey gave middle- and upper-class couples "a time and place for the shifting of bodily and geographical territories, for the checking of bodily coordinates against maps and expectations."[10] The very journey that would bind the couple to one another only, then, was also supposed to give them a sensory relationship to the landscape and inhabitants of their country, serving as a relay to new forms of being and belonging.

Another reason the honeymoon may have offered Howells his best chance to move from travel sketches to the kind of full-length novel that might challenge the dominance of sentimental literature in U.S. culture, is that this new ritual promised to "marry" the nuptial ceremony to a forward-moving narrative dynamic controlled by a man. Though the honeymoon seemed to mutually transform only the sexual and legal status of the bride by ceremoniously deflowering her in a liminal space and allowing her to test her new name on strangers, it also transformed the husband from suitor to tutor. For the honeymoon made male sexual and cultural know-how, rather than female domestic competence, into a decisive sign of adulthood. Earlier couples, in moving directly from the wedding ceremony to the new home, or in having the ceremony in their homes, had transferred the newlyweds into a domain in which the bride had more skills than the groom. The female-centered bridal journey to visit faraway relatives had similarly acknowledged the lines along which authority might be transmitted between women. But as twenty-seven-year-old Isabel sees clearly on her wedding journey, her skills as an adult woman are unintelligible according to the logic of the honeymoon; as an "evident bride," she will be eroticized and infantilized. The couple-centered honeymoon put the husband in charge of both erotic knowledge and knowledge of life beyond home and immediate community, and in charge of moving the bride toward both. Until the 1950s, the husband was in charge of paying for, picking the site of, and orchestrating the honeymoon, and honeymoon destinations were often chosen for their primitive or natural aspects rather than their ability to mimic the domestic life that would follow the journey.[11] This suggests that the honeymoon served especially to produce a new man, whose relationship to the state as "husband" was reinflected as cultural and sensual competence outside the home.

In sum, the honeymoon evolved from the need to "straighten out" the transition from childhood to adulthood, from the larger family of origin to dyadic couplehood, from local environment to the social horizon of the nation itself, from female- to male-dominated spheres. Though Howells exploited this function to produce a male-centered narrative realism, in other literary texts the honeymoon seems to further scramble these domains. The historical changes I have outlined here inflect a genre of U.S. literature that I call the "pedophiliac picaresque": the honeymoon journey in which the bride is not only infantilized but literally a child, in which man and girl have an explicitly tutorial relationship that is not only sexual but geographic and cultural, and whose directionality is reversed such that the girl comes to run the show.

Paradoxically, the linked figures of man and child-bride mingle the roles of parent/child and husband/wife—the very thing the honeymoon was designed to separate. This collapse of natal and conjugal relations in the honeymoon narrative suggests that travel creates a certain crisis in kinship itself, a violation of its founding laws of generational separation and exogamy (Isabel, for instance, is outraged when she is mistaken for Basil's sister rather than his wife).[12] And indeed, since the honeymoon stressed contact with unfamiliar places and their inhabitants rather than extended family, it inevitably allowed the couple to witness or imagine the pleasures, kinship systems, and sex practices that U.S. marriage law disallowed; as Isabel remarks on her honeymoon, "Basil, dear, don't be jealous . . . but I'm in love with that black waiter at our table."[13] In the pedophiliac picaresque, which makes explicit and plays out the logic of all that *Their Wedding Journey* both implies and manages to contain, kinship relations, spatial logics, and pleasures call one another into question to produce changes and crises in white, masculine, heterosexual U.S. subjectivity. The honeymoon with a little girl encodes a wish to have both a "prepolitical" relationship with the land on the analogy of a blood relation and a "political" relation to the nation-state on the analogy of a marriage. But the analogy with "blood relations" founders on the fact that these are, precisely, political relations created and managed by the state—while the little girl's insistence on foregrounding the mediated nature of the subject's relation to the land calls its prepolitical status into question as well.

Two startlingly resonant scenes from literary texts otherwise separated by genre and period combine wedding imagery, travel, and man-girl relationships in the manner I have described. In Hawthorne's "Little Annie's Ramble" (1835), a man and little girl take a walk around their village.[14] Their journey is elaborated by such nuptial imagery as "rings . . . or the costly love-ornaments" (LAR, 229); "those little cockles, or whatever they are called, much prized . . . for the mottoes which they enclose, by love-sick maids and bachelors!" (230); "bridal loaves at the wedding of an heiress" (230); and "those sweet little circlets, sweetly named kisses" (230). The tale comes to an abrupt end when the travelers encounter a spanking scenario, figured by slapping noises and a disembodied cry: "a shrill voice of affliction, the scream of a little child, rising louder with every repetition of that smart, sharp, slapping sound, produced by an open hand on tender flesh" (233). Just after this displaced moment of violence, they hear the town crier reveal that a little girl has "strayed from her home" and "her afflicted mother" wants her back (234). All along, then, this "ramble" has really been an abduction. Over a century later, Nabokov's *Lolita* (1955) makes the violence of the man-girl travelogue explicit.[15] Trapped on an endless journey with her stepfather Humbert Humbert after her mother's death, Lolita attempts to escape when they stop in a small town. When Humbert catches her, she claims to have been window-shopping, pointing to a storefront whose display also registers the damage of a man-girl liaison. There Humbert sees a fully dressed bride mannequin "quite perfect and *intacta* except for the lack of one arm," a bald and limbless child mannequin, and a man vacuuming the floor around "a cluster of three slender arms, and a blonde wig." He reports that "two of the arms happened to be twisted and seemed to suggest a clasping gesture of horror and supplication" (*L*, 224).

These works connect wedding imagery to both tourism and something like pedophilia, the merging of adult and child bodies in a tableau of damage. But both texts go on to reverse the direction of the tutorial relationship between man and girl. When the nuptial imagery leads to the crisis-laden scenarios I have detailed above, both narrators abjure their positions as tour guides. The narrator of "Little Annie" returns the child to her mother, and pointedly suggests that he has lost both his spatial and moral compass: "After wandering a little way into the world, you may return at the first summons . . . and be a happy child again. But I have gone too far astray for the town crier to call me back!" (*LAR*, 234). Humbert addresses his child companion even more directly, ironically insisting that she and not he can properly interpret the storefront emblem: "Look, Lo," he says. "Look well. Is not that a rather good symbol of something or other?" (*L*, 224). In fact, these reversals assert that all along the little girl has been the mentor: Hawthorne's narrator has needed Annie to show him how to enjoy the pleasures on sale in their village, and as *Lolita* goes on, Humbert cannot negotiate the mass cultural spaces of the 1950s United States without Lolita.

These works, and the other texts I shall examine in the remainder of this chapter, invert the honeymoon's typical initiation structure, in which the groom teaches the bride how to have sex. Instead, they portray a "child bride" on her honeymoon, who teaches her male partner how to have a proper bodily relationship to the spaces, landscape, visual culture, and consumer pleasures of her native land. Hawthorne and Nabokov frame a span of time between the mid-1830s and mid-1950s, from the moment that the honeymoon first gained cultural foothold among the white middle classes, through the era in which the honeymoon became a standard feature of the U.S. wedding. Within this time period, Edgar Allan Poe and the nineteenth-century adventure writer Captain Mayne Reid, the other writers I will discuss, also connected travel, man-girl nuptials, and the cultural competence of the white male in the United States. Hawthorne and Poe were contemporaries;

Reid met and befriended Poe; Poe and Reid both married child brides; and Nabokov admired Poe and Reid.[16] This literary history is therefore less a genealogy of influence than a rather incestuous literary kinship web consisting of generically liminal or hybrid texts (Poe's and Hawthorne's "sketches," Reid's Westerns, and Nabokov's case-study-*cum*-romance) that infuse the U.S. travel narrative with a man-girl nuptial fantasy. According to all of the texts this chapter examines, the pedophiliac "honeymoon" articulates what eventually become nationalist concerns about space, family, and cultural assimilation.[17]

The literature whose contours I limn here borrows structurally from the male-narrated, episodic picaresque, from the captivity narrative, from the female-centered sentimental novel, and from the didactic "geographic history" of nineteenth-century juvenile literature. It is also connected to, but not coterminous with the ways that other, more dominant literary genres link sexuality and space. For instance, these pedophiliac "honeymoon" narratives borrow from typical travel narratives' descriptions of the New World in terms of the female body, as in "virgin territory."[18] But the texts I am concerned with here focus on the redistribution of sensibilities rather than the appropriation of territory, inserting the Anglo-American female right into the landscape and using *her* relationship with it as a relay to new forms of male subjectivity. They also partake in the imperialist imaginings of British children's literature, in which the boy-adventurer restores a "lost" psychic and material empire to the adult. In substituting a girl for the boy, though, they focus on the project of the adult's acculturation and subject formation as opposed to his imperialistic conquests.[19] In fact, the novels of Reid and Nabokov in particular draw from the sexual energies of earlier captivity narratives, in which "Indians" provide the material for critiquing English kinship systems, gender norms, and erotic practices, but they exploit this genre to suggest new heterosexual possibilities inflected by race. Finally, the works I will discuss here revise the archetypally American cross-racial, male-male bond that develops outside of feminized domestic space, reworking it into a heterosexual liaison that makes some races whiter, and some bodies more "American," than others.[20]

In the explicitly pedophiliac honeymoon narrative, which foregrounds the girl's semiotic activity rather than her passive status as metaphor, and uses age difference to coordinate racial and cultural taxonomies, a little girl leads her partner productively "astray," taking the affective technology of sentiment out of the home and on the road. The genre, if it can be called that, implicitly argues that the U.S. culturescape is properly experienced by a traveling romance with a little girl. This female child's sexual, sensual, and critical sophistication—albeit one sometimes enforced by her male partner—licenses her to bestow on this partner a sense of cultural belonging that supersedes (and even in some cases substitutes for) mere juridical citizenship. The trope of the nuptial journey with a child bride allows three cultural changes to crossarticulate: the male relationship to an emerging consumer culture; the separation of nuptial from familial "love"; and the transformation of nationality into a proper form of feeling achieved by combining the child's sensory apparatus and bride's ability to consent. Hawthorne's "Little Annie's Ramble" examines a rising consumer culture and its effect on family form. Poe's "Three Sundays in a Week" explores the temporal erotics of preindustrial travel and trade. Two novels by Reid, *The Scalp-hunters* and *The Child Wife*, seize on this erotic logic, making the child bride into a coordinator of Manifest Destiny and global policing. And *Lolita* brings elements from all of these texts together into what is perhaps the quintessential nightmare honeymoon of U.S. literature. In all of these texts the child bride, trapped within the logic and structure of a honeymoon, must make the country intelligible and available to the male subject who cannot rely on the romantic cult of nature, asexual and familial sentimentalism, or frontier logic to secure his relationship with "America."

Marry-Time Travel, or, the Traffic in Little Girls

Hawthorne's "Little Annie's Ramble" was published in 1835, the same year as his travel sketch "My Visit to Niagara."[21] Both texts slightly anticipate the late 1830s, the earliest date that historians have established for the popularization of the private honeymoon in the United States; yet in a third work published the same year, "Sketches from Memory," Hawthorne mentions "two young married couples, all the way from Massachusetts, on the matrimonial jaunt" to the White Mountains.[22] Clearly, Hawthorne was at least aware of the couple-centered, distance-traveling nuptial tour by the time he wrote "My Visit to Niagara" and "Little Annie's Ramble," and these two pieces articulate a set of problems that the honeymoon itself would shortly begin to manage. In "Niagara," the narrator travels solo, and struggles to have a genuine experience of a national landmark despite its being overcoded by commercialism and prior artistic representations. Niagara is revealed here as a place one comes to have one's *own* feelings, indeed, to create a self by having an experience unmediated by antebellum culture's numerous literary and pictorial depictions of the site. But though the narrator of "My Visit" purports to seek an unsullied experience of the sublime, he is initially quite unwilling to consummate his desire to see the waterfalls. When he first hears the roar of the water, he closes his eyes; after arriving in town, he seeks out the dining room rather than the cataract; at the entryway to the waterfalls, he becomes engrossed in the museum and gift shop; even atop the Table Rock, he is as interested in people watching as he is in the wonders of nature. He declares that on seeing Niagara, "a wretched sense of disappointment weighed me down," anticipating Oscar Wilde's famous statement that Niagara Falls must be "one of the earliest if not the keenest disappointments in American married life."[23] Finally, Hawthorne's narrator learns to appreciate the landmark only by dreaming of it nightly, whereupon he finds himself "gladdened every morning by the consciousness of a growing capacity to enjoy it."[24]

In short, though "My Visit to Niagara" is not really a honeymoon narrative per se, the narrator's initiation into the sublime does happen in bed, anticipating a certain sexualization of both tourism in general and Niagara in particular that the honeymoon would help produce. Yet "Little Annie's Ramble" solves what might be called the Hawthornian narrator's commodity-induced sensory impotence—his failure to engage with his native environs—by giving the traveler a partner, a female child who works as a different kind of tour guide from those rejected in "Niagara." In "Little Annie," Hawthorne also moves the journey into a village. Rather than overwriting nature with culture like the guidebooks and paintings that the narrator of "My Visit" dismisses, or leading the man out of the village and into nature like the Wordsworthian romantic child, Little Annie insists that marketplace pleasures can foster an awakening of the senses. Because Annie's connection with the bachelor narrator is festooned with wedding imagery, it seems fair to read "Little Annie's Ramble" in terms of the honeymoon's evolving merger between tourism and heterosexual intimacy.

At first glance, "Little Annie's Ramble" seems to engage more directly with the rise of juvenile literature than with marriage. For Annie is a veritable maven of an emerging nineteenth-century juvenile reading culture, "deeply read in Peter Parley's tomes" (LAR, 230), the travelogues for children of which Hawthorne himself wrote at least one. He revised "Little Annie's Ramble" for republication in 1837, a year after writing *Peter Parley's Universal History*, in which an old man leads fictional children and real readers through history by moving them through geographic space.[25] Because Samuel Goodrich, the publisher of the *Peter Parley* series, intended the books to be a properly U.S. substitute for the dangerous fantasies unleashed by European fairy tales, the books emphasized the didactic framing work of the elderly narrator/tutor. The ancient Parley takes his child tourists through a series of descriptions of foreign countries rigorously sequenced from "primitive" to "modern," Asia to the United States.[26] Some critics have read "Little Annie" as a recapitulation of Parley's journey, signaling Hawthorne's final acceptance of an "ennobling partnership" between his own art and U.S. juvenile literature.[27] Yet in this tale, the partnership between adult and juvenile literature looks suspiciously like a meeting of adult and child libidos.

"Little Annie" does clearly borrow from the *Peter Parley* series. But Hawthorne's short tale engages with local as opposed to world geography, and travels through a marketplace rather than landmarks and historical events. The avuncular bachelor narrator pairs up with a little girl whom he meets on one of his habitual rambles, and the two visit a dance on the church steps, a jeweler's shop, a bakery, a bookbinder's, a toy shop full of "gilded chariots" (LAR, 230) and dolls, and finally a zoo. Here, "Little Annie" steals the developmental logic of the travelogue to depict the stages of an antebellum, white, middle-class female life—the tale outlines a progression from courtship (the dance) to engagement (the rings at the jeweler's), to the wedding (the bakery with its big white cake), to a bridal trip (the chariot), to maternity (the dolls and animals). Nevertheless, the tale is ultimately concerned with masculine rather than feminine subjectivity: by fantasizing that he is on a wedding journey, the narrator acquires a set of legitimate forms with which to articulate a new and confusing set of sensations. The wedding imagery, in turn, seems to sanction marriage in a new way—not through popular consent or religious blessing but by conjoining it with the pleasures of spectacle, travel, and consumption.

Throughout the tale, Hawthorne uses the form of the travelogue to confound the very distinctions on which the *Parley* series depends: between child and adult, pedagogy and pleasure, then and now, here and elsewhere. The two ramblers also move through spaces that alternate between domestic and market, *heimlich* and *unheimlich*, innocent and sinister. As the journey progresses, the normal is revealed as only one of many fantasies, capable at a moment's notice of turning into something grotesque. At each instructional "stop," ordinary scenes and objects turn perverse, changing commercial into familial relationships, child into adult sensibilities. For instance, confronting a dance in the town square, the narrator realizes that Annie's potential partners, quite possibly including himself, are too old. The jeweler's shop provokes unseemly comments about "rings of the wedlock" (LAR, 229); the confections at the bakery are described in sexualized terms as "kisses" and "bridal loaves" with bosomy "summits deeply snow-covered" (230). The dolls and parrots in the toy store begin to "walk and speak" (231); the circus monkeys' "ugliness shocks [Annie's] pure, instinctive delicacy of taste" (233); and the town square becomes the scene of public chastisement that I have already detailed above.

The tale's most elaborate and strange fantasy is engendered by the bookshop: "What would Annie think, if, in the book which I mean to send her, on New Year's day, she should find her sweet little self, bound up in silk or morocco with gilt edges, there to remain till she became a woman grown. . . . That would be very queer" (230). Even setting aside the way this image of bondage, entrapment, and perpetual childhood resonates with modern queer sensibilities, the narrator's question does suggest that the mutual consumption of goods, perhaps most especially literary ones, has the capacity to both stop narrative time and collapse generations; he envisions Annie yoked to her own child self in perpetuity. Toward the end of this journey, this logic is furthered when the two travelers collide with a scene straight out of the fairy tales that Goodrich contested: man and girl see "the very same wolf—do not go near him, Annie!—the self-same wolf that devoured little Red Riding Hood and her grandmother" (232). This moment utterly dismantles the age and gender divisions central to the *Parley* series. For if Annie can be situated as the Little Red Riding Hood of this scene, the narrator seems to identify with both the feminized, protective grandmother and the "self-same," sexually devouring wolf. By the time the pair of ramblers reaches the circus and zoo, relations between animals serve as emblems for the breakdown of all kinds of social boundaries, perhaps especially those between generations. To cite only one example, when the narrator sees a hyena and a bear in the same cage, he rather too anxiously asks whether there are "any two living creatures, who have so few sympathies that they cannot possibly be friends?" (232–33).

In the end, the tale's scene of crisis—the screams, slapping, accusations of kidnapping, and narrator's admission that he has gone *too* far "astray"— override his pious moral that "the pure breath of children revives the life of aged men" (234). Ironically, even this "moral" is figured as mouth-to-mouth resuscitation, a kiss the child initiates. Should he, or we, experience the kiss of his child-tutor as parental, marital, or sexual? As *Zury* also seemed to recognize, here the "binding" activities of mutual consumption might proliferate in and intensify other kinds of relationships, including in this tale, that between a strange man and the little girl he takes from her doorstep. Indeed, "Little Annie's Ramble" conjoins traditional courtship images and the language of sensation novels, signaled perhaps most clearly by the slightly pornographic wedding cake at the bakery, whose "summits deeply snow-covered" echo the period's racier depictions of women's bodies. This conflation implies a certain eroticization of the family and a confusion of tongues within it.[28]

In its merging of affects, the tale is a study not only of the mutual influence of an emerging consumer culture but also the flowering nuclear family. The narrator's fleeting wedding fantasies, occurring as they do within the marketplace, serve as an important index for the relations among changes in family form and structures of feeling, modes of production, and technologies of identity and belonging. Historians initially traced changes in familial affect in terms of a shift from the paternal power to punish, to a maternal power of "influence" exercised first through moral suasion, then later through proper patterns of consumption and household management. But children, too, have their place in this shift of disciplinary modes. Paula Marantz Cohen, for instance, contends that by the nineteenth century, the daughter of a household functioned as a mediator for the father's dual role as breadwinner outside the home and parent within it, becoming the ideal audience for a reformulated fatherhood.[29] Karen Sánchez-Eppler, in a related argument, explores the role of the child in temperance literature, in which eroticized scenes between a child and its drunken father allowed men to embrace nineteenth-century domestic values without seeming to acquiesce to women.[30] Likewise, the narrator's contact with Little Annie is supposed to teach him not only how to experience consumer pleasures outside the home but also how to practice the increasingly significant intimacies of family life, or what he calls the "native feeling" of children (LAR, 234). Even this short phrase suggests the combination of emotional, sensual, and cultural competence now attributed to the child.

The emerging ritual of the honeymoon had a crucial role to play in these changes, for it seemed to grant a sequence to a confusing morass of sensations. As a combined narrative structure, literary genre, and initiation rite, the honeymoon took on some of the same functions as Goodrich's travelogues, using travel as a tutorial that produced sanctioned feelings through a particular experience of environment. More specifically, the "honeymoon" structure of "Little Annie's Ramble" capitalizes on a wish that the eroticized and market-mediated pleasures that cemented a marriage might still be imagined as somehow prior to and outside the domestic sphere. The narrator of "Little Annie" therefore removes Annie from her biological family and fosters intimacy with her by showing her a village, attempting to link the geographic tutorial of the travelogue with the sexual one of the wedding night—and then returns Annie to the domestic space occupied by her mother. But significantly, the tale refuses to simply reproduce a father-daughter dyad or contain the child in the household. Though Annie seems to have no parents when the narrator finds her on her doorstep, he does not for a minute fantasize about adopting or parenting her. Neither does she reproach him for straying from the home, as the child of temperance literature might. Instead, she uses her newfound cultural authority to lead him toward rather than away from the various pleasures for sale in the village, and the tale, like the narrator, goes relentlessly "astray."

The narrator's interest in the "native feelings" of children also figures the child as someone born into a particular place whose sense of connection extends beyond the boundaries of home to an exterior environment, landscape, or region. Yet Annie does not stabilize the opposition between the home and dangerous, immoral city, nor does she suture home neatly to nation. Rather, the tale's spatial ambiguities actually both stand for and produce confusion between parental and marital intimacy, natural and commodified experiences. At the same time, the tale has no equivalent to the sexualized national landmark that Niagara Falls eventually became, or even to the explicitly regional White Mountains of "Sketches from Memory"—instead, its backdrop is only a generic small town. Though certainly a tutorial that draws energy from the reinscription of time and space in the didactic travelogue, sentimental culture's focus on teaching family feeling, the new sensations provided by commercial amusements, and the increasingly important position of the honeymoon in mediating these changes, "Little Annie's Ramble" is not a tutorial in a subjectivity that can really be called national. It remained to Edgar Allan Poe to reconnect the *Peter Parley* series' comparative sense of national history with the "time difference" between a girl and an older male.

Although he may be the U.S. pedophiliate laureate, Poe is not usually connected to nationalism or imperialism. For instance, his most famous paean to erotic girl-loving, "Annabel Lee" (1849), situates childhood off the map, in mythic time; the "highborn kinsmen" who lock Annabel away and envious angels who kill her are unmarked by nationality. The poem's famous repetitions and doublings ("Can ever dissever," "chilling and killing") render the past utterly inaccessible, and defer consummation indefinitely.[31] But an earlier piece, the slight, riddling sketch "Three Sundays in a Week" (1841), contains the material suppressed in "Annabel Lee," allowing a male adult to have contact with a female child by using a different model of time—not the spacing and temporal deferral of repetition but the switch points and temporal collapses of coincidence.[32] The sketch situates these coincidences within a plot whose climax involves maritime travel, or in this case "marry-time" travel; unlike "Annabel Lee," "Three Sundays" relates man-girl love to historical changes in transportation and trade. Crucially, it brings the dis-combobulations of "Little Annie" into a global frame, suggesting that the contraction of time and space brought about by revolutions in travel, communication, and consumerism produced a new sexual imaginary.

"Three Sundays in a Week" uses the conceit of international time zones to make the difference between a child and adult relative—in all senses. At the story's opening, the twenty-one-year-old narrator Bobby prepares to speak to his elderly uncle Rumgudgeon about marrying his cousin Kate, who is "barely fifteen" and whom the uncle has forbidden to marry until what he calls her "plum" is ready (TSW, 119). Rumgudgeon is a literalist, famous for adhering to the letter of the law even as he breaks the spirit of most of his vows. He also resolutely insists on the separation of past, present, and future in an economy of delayed gratification: "To every request, a positive 'No!' was his immediate answer; but in the end—in the long, long end—there were exceedingly few requests which he refused" (117). When Bobby asks for the precise date when he will be allowed to marry Kate, the uncle replies that the young man shall have her and the mysterious sexual/economic prize of her "plum" when three Sundays come together in a week. Bobby's challenge is to find a situation that will exactly coincide with Rumgudgeon's words.

Three weeks later, Kate and Bobby accompany two world navigators, Captains Pratt and Smitherton, on a Sunday visit to Rumgudgeon. Pratt, who has sailed westward around the world, insists that the next day will be Sunday; Smitherton, who has sailed eastward, asserts that Sunday was the previous day. Because Pratt operates by a time zone one full day behind the current Sunday and Smitherton one full day ahead of it, three Sundays have indeed converged in a single week. The pubescent Kate first interprets the situation and figures out its mathematics, seeming to be a willing analytic partner to the temporal conflations that will enable her to marry an older man. The captains and Bobby eagerly follow her lead: "It is positively clear that we are *all right*," argues Smitherton, "for there can be no philosophical reason assigned why the idea of one of us should have preference over that of the other" (123). Rumgudgeon, following this theory of relativity to the letter, consents to the marriage of his two relatives. Two trips around the world override the Law of the Uncle.

In short, here the "time difference" between adult and child as well as the spatial separation necessary to exogamy are both overcome by global traveling rather than local rambling. Though the sketch predates by over forty years the establishment of Greenwich mean time and world time zones in 1884, international trade was already transforming spatial distance into temporal difference, such that the collapse of distance could also seem to dissolve temporal boundaries.[33] "Three Sundays" registers the moment when it becomes literally possible for "today" to touch "yesterday." Caught between earlier models of circumnavigation and the nineteenth-century division of the globe into standard time zones, Poe seems to recognize that linear time has become anachronistic. The coexistence of past, present, and future in a single moment opens up the possibility of communion between disparate temporalities, and the meetings enabled by temporal coincidence become explicitly sexual in his sketch.

While not precisely a honeymoon tale, "Three Sundays" advances travel as a way of turning blood relationship into erotic intimacy, generational barriers into sexual connections. Poe's successor, the Irish American writer Captain Reid, exploited this possibility in two mid-nineteenth-century novels whose pedophiliac project is explicitly connected to newly emerging racial paradigms and to a progress narrative now coded as explicitly "American." In Reid's work, the rubric of erotic child-loving manages explicitly nationalist concerns about how to conceptualize and coordinate the differences among European immigrants, native-born white colonists of the Southwest, and indigenous groups with prior claims to this territory. A best-selling author in his day, Reid was both a lover of young girls and prolific producer of semi-autobiographical Westerns. His adventure tales about United States territories were marketed to men, but avidly read by juveniles abroad (especially in Russia, where he is still considered a classic of U.S. literature), and Reid eventually crossed back over into the juvenile dime market in the United States. His works served simultaneously as travel narratives and adventure tales, scientific treatises on botany and dirty books, fictions of the Americas for a European audience and fictions of the West for a U.S. one.[34]

In *Speak, Memory*, Nabokov describes Reid's work as integral not only to the development of his desire to go to the United States but also to the formation of his sexual fantasy life. Rereading Reid's 1865 novel *The Headless Horseman*, he relives his reaction to a sexually explicit passage: "With still more excitement did I read of Louise Poindexter, Calhoun's fair cousin, daughter of a sugar planter. . . . She is revealed in the throes of jealousy . . . standing upon the edge of her *azotea*, her white hand resting upon the copestone of the parapet which is 'still wet with the dews of night,' her twin breasts sinking and swelling in quick, spasmodic breathing, her twin breasts, let me reread, sinking and swelling."[35] Notice the complexly transcultural architecture of this writer's desires. Syntactically mimicking the autoerotic reader who reads and rereads the juicy parts, Nabokov also calls attention to the way his sexuality developed in relation to a "foreign" nationality. He recalls (and perhaps repeats) being aroused by images of Spanish colonial buildings, whose details take on the characteristics of a sexually responsive female body. Indeed, he adds the phrase "her twin breasts . . . sinking and swelling" to the original passage as if to bring out the latent eroticism of Reid's portrayal.

By the time the young Nabokov was panting over Russian translations of Reid's work, the frontier was closed, and the U.S. Wild West had been circulating abroad for almost fifty years in dime novels and Buffalo Bill shows. In fact, Reid's successors downplayed relations with women, presenting an "America" rich with homosocial possibilities.[36] But in Reid's work itself, the Southwest is a place in which it is possible to imagine having a different kind of *heterosexual* sex. He not only helped pioneer the vision of the hypermasculine white adventurer that was to be a major export for the next century but also made the consensual liaison between man and girl into an aspect of U.S. Manifest Destiny. A nineteenth-century Humbert, Reid introduced himself to his future wife, Elizabeth Hyde, in 1851 when she was thirteen and he thirty-three, saying to her, "You are getting old enough to have a lover and you must have me." He married her two years later.[37]

Since Reid gives every indication that the heroes of his novels are auto-biographically based, his own problematic citizenship is relevant to the meta-morphoses in national subjectivity that his novels imagine. As he remarked in 1863, "I am half an American in nationality, and wholly one in heart."[38] Born in Ireland in 1818 and arriving in the United States in 1839, claiming Irish or U.S. citizenship according to whichever was convenient at a particu-lar moment, Reid seemed to consider his marriage to a teenage (albeit Brit-ish) girl, service to the United States in the war with Mexico, travels in the Southwest, and involvements in the European revolutions of the 1840s and 1850s to be mutually informing sources of U.S. cultural legitimacy. Across three novels, he figures erotic development (explicitly denoted as puberty in two), his own development as a national subject, and the territorial expansion of the United States as simultaneously political and sexual, reworking racial and national categories to delineate a kind of precocious female desire that can initiate and legitimate various forms of U.S. imperialism. Ultimately, Reid links the child bride to the political unification of Spanish creoles and newer immigrants to the United States against the indigenous populations of the Southwest, and then transforms this linkage into a sense of global Man-ifest Destiny. He himself eventually developed into a rabid foe of colonialism and imperialism in Europe, but remained a fierce advocate of U.S. expan-sionism fueled by European immigrants, writing that "every soul—Saxon or Celt—landed on the American side of the Atlantic is a gain, not only to America, but to Humanity."[39]

In *The Headless Horseman*, the novel that seems to have most directly influenced *Lolita* and Nabokov's other works, Reid's attraction to female chil-dren appears only indirectly, as a pedagogical technique for encountering space.[40] This work treats the Texas landscape as shifting scenery in need of decoding—not conquering by force but taming by reading properly. Within the frame of a heterosexual courtship plot, the novel promotes an aesthetic of trailing, apparently taught first by a Native American to the white male hero, Maurice Gerald, the dispossessed descendant of Irish aristocrats, and then by Maurice to the Poindexters, French Creole settlers from Louisiana. Rather than relying on European cartography, in which map readers understand the landscape in relation to an exterior key, trailing involves an indigenous prac-tice of reading the signs of nature in relation to one another, or what William

Boelhower calls "chorographic" mapping.[41] In this novel, the failed European semiotic of landscape produces sexual failure and a properly "native" relationship to the land brings sexual success. In a statement that links his love for the Poindexters' daughter Louise to his capacities as a horse trainer, Maurice remarks, *"She will regard you as her tamer, and ever after submit to your will, if you but exhibit the sign that first deprived her of her liberty"* (*HH*, 72; italics in original). With both Louise and the mare, "signs" are supposed to coordinate power. In the end, though, only the reader who can use them in a Native American way gets the woman. For Louise falls for Maurice not because of the indexical sign system that he uses on the mare but because he uses his indigenous relation to the land to mark a trail across the prairie, rescuing her family from their endless circling around a burned stretch of land. In contrast, the tale's villain, Cassius Calhoun, is a bad user of signs. Initially unable to chart a course over the burned-out prairie, he later seeks revenge on Maurice for usurping his romantic prerogative with Louise. But he mistakenly stalks and kills Louise's brother Henry, who is wearing Maurice's cloak and hat, and his series of semiotic mistakes leads eventually to his capture.

As Nabokov was to recognize and repeat in his onanistic reading practices, then, landscape and libido are connected. Geographic acculturation is always also sexual acculturation; assimilating to a new place means becoming differently eroticized (and perhaps vice versa). Yet only in Reid's other novels, *The Scalp-hunters, or, Romantic Adventures in Northern Mexico* (1851) and *The Child Wife* (1868), does the "trailing" plot mobilize sexual energies across generational as well as geographic boundaries. Reid's earlier "child-bride" novel, *The Scalp-hunters*, figures the tutor who enables this process not as an Indian but as a little white girl who, like Little Annie and Kate before her and Lolita afterward, possesses amazing interpretive powers. Emerging from Reid's adventures in the war with Mexico, *The Scalp-hunters* reverses *The Headless Horseman*'s movement from landscape to body, holding out the promise that if the (male) immigrant can learn to read the young female body by properly responding to its sexual rhythms, he will obtain a new relationship to place. This transformation is different than the unmediated fusion of self and landscape elaborated by earlier authors from Thomas Jefferson to Ralph Waldo Emerson, which Myra Jehlen labels "incarnation," for it involves an actual female as a third term.[42] It also differs from Annette Kolodny's reduction of the woman to a rhetorical figure through which the conqueror experiences "the lay of the land."[43] For a girl's active sexual energy literally retrains the conqueror, giving him a new body and therefore a new experience of space. The process of "naturalization by sexualization" translated, for Reid, into a proimmigrant vision of how the U.S. empire might grow: not by plundering the new territories but by acquiring more sensually adept male inhabitants trained by precocious little girls who embody the best characteristics of white women and Indian men.

In *The Scalp-hunters*, Reid figures this "gain" through a native-born child of European parentage whose artificially induced puberty, brought about by learning to read and then rewiring her immigrant male teacher's sensory apparatus, enables this "teacher's" competent relation to the United States. This novel, set just prior to the war with Mexico, aims to reconfigure Europe's relationship to the United States in a way that both legitimates and follows the logic of an imperialist heterosexual desire—here explicitly imagined as erotic girl-loving. At first, the novel's most unbridgeable distance is that between the hero, Henry Haller, newly arrived to the States from Ireland to join a trading expedition, and his beloved, the thirteen-year-old French Creole Zöe Seguin, whom he meets along the way: "From day to day, strange reflections passed through my mind. Could it be she was too young to understand the import of the word love? too young to be inspired with a passion?"[44] But Haller transforms Zöe into someone who can read the signs of *his* arousal, thereby legitimating it. In contrast to *The Headless Horseman*'s sexually passive Louise, Zöe must be an active professor of her own desire: "With her there will be no reservation, no reasoning, no caution, no cunning. She will yield alone to the mystic promptings of nature" (*SH*, 56). And Haller discovers a hermeneutic that gets nature to prompt, promptly.

Whereas the hero in *The Headless Horseman* must learn an indigenous form of geographic decoding, in *The Scalp-hunters* the decoding is explicitly sexual. Erotic communion between adult and child occurs almost instantaneously, without verbal mediation, and at the girl's apparent instigation. As Haller sketches for the child, attempting to map her face, "the sketch was held jointly between us" as though it were cocreated. Yet "no pen could trace [his] feelings at that moment," and Haller's writing hand soon becomes a sex toy, "wander[ing] over its surface, until the unresisting fingers of [his] companion were clasped in [his own]" (57). Haller insists that Zöe is "yielding," that "there was no resistance," and that theirs is "a kiss of reciprocal love" (57). Immediately after the kiss, however, he also announces, in italics, "*I was lord of that little heart*" (57), troping his sexual conquest in monarchist terms. He also alleges that the kiss literally causes Zöe's puberty, giving her "the form and outlines of a woman," so that "her form had become more developed, her bosom rose higher in gentle undulations. . . . It was the mystic transformation of love" (58). It is as if in a strange twist on the Pygmalion story, he has drawn Zöe and kissed her into being, only to see her complete the sketch by drawing herself with breasts.

Haller here becomes the catalyst for a puberty reconstructed as precocious yet utterly natural, dormant yet somehow jump-started by his presence. Crucially, he accomplishes this not only by literally drawing Zöe but also by rhetorically recasting her as Mexican. Whereas in *The Headless Horseman* Louise remained a French Creole, in *The Scalp-hunters* Zöe "was but twelve years of age, but then she was a child of a sunny clime; and I had often seen at that age, under the warm sky of Mexico, the wedded bride, the fond mother" (56). The "mystic transformation" he induces and witnesses, that is, is more national than sexual. "Hispanicizing" Zöe—but also keeping her identity resolutely separate from that of Indians, as we shall see—allows him to imagine her as the agent of precocious desire rather than the victim of his lust.[45]

In *The Scalp-hunters*, the child bride becomes a U.S. national—and also sexually available—by embodying the distinctly Mexican character of the Americas in a kind of racially inflected puberty. Nubile creole sexuality simultaneously stands for what must be preserved in the United States (its infantilized "innocence") and what must be controlled (its feminine and racial "excess"). In turn, this strategy figures one of the anti-European-imperialist, but pro-U.S.-imperialist projects of Reid's novel. For *The Scalp-hunters* explicitly aims to recapture the Spanish creole culture of the southwestern United States. The novel representationally reorients this population back toward a reciprocal, hierarchical relationship with Anglo-"America" in order to disaffiliate it from the surviving indigenous people. As Zöe's father, the scalp-hunting Seguin, explains, "Unless some other race than the Iberians [Spanish] take[s] possession of these lands, the Apaché [*sic*], the Navajo, and the Comanche, the conquered of Cortez and his conquerors, will yet drive the descendants of those very conquerors from the soil of Mexico" (SH, 71). Haller's communion with Zöe, then, metaphorizes some of the contradictions of the author's position on the New World. Insisting that immigrants from the British Isles can rescue white Spanish culture in the Americas, he offers the latter site not for direct economic exploitation but for overwhelming semiotic and sensual experience. He recodes this takeover as submission to a Hispanicized, creole American child's seduction, elaborating on the "Spanish" rather than the Indian qualities of the Southwest to lure British and Irish immigrants there, and yet differentiating the latter newcomers' response to the region from Spain's prior imperialist project.[46]

In effect, Reid modifies a paradigm described by Werner Sollors, in which couples legitimated their break with parental authority by "going native" to tourist sites associated with Indians, such as Niagara Falls, thereby mystifying the innovation of isolated couplehood with an appeal to the customs of an "ancient" people. As Sollors puts it, "In the world of nineteenth century white fantasies, it was as if the Indians had invented the new love and the whites had learned it from them."[47] But Reid's couple, one might say, goes creole. By insisting that Zöe is of Spanish descent, the novel strengthens rather than bridges the racialized boundary between Europeans and Indians. As Reid observes in *The Headless Horseman*, "There are, indeed, two borders. One that separates two nations termed civilized [and] . . . the other border . . . beyond which roams the savage Comanche—the Ishmaelite of the prairies" (HH, 455). *The Scalp-hunters* uses man-girl love to solidify that border, first linking Zöe to Mexico in order to make her a viable sexual object for Haller, and then using intergenerational sexuality to connect her back to Spain, healing any possibility of racial difference between Spaniards and other Europeans. Pedophilia thus both reflects and enables the creation of a race somehow "in between" Native American and Anglo, but (in Reid's view) properly aligned with Anglo. For in the travel plot central to *The Scalp-hunters*, the creole child bride works to reposition Native Americans as absolutely Other. Discovering his daughter Zöe and Haller in an embrace, Seguin demands as his bride-price that Haller join him on an expedition to rescue Zöe's older sister Adele, who has lived most of her life as a captive of the Navajo. During their rescue mission Zöe too is captured, so the posse must pursue both girls. Uniting the Irishman Haller and French Creole Seguin, this joining also unites lover and father, creole and immigrant in warfare against indigenous Americans. The rescuers merge these identities by trailing the child bride through the land-scape; if not precisely a honeymoon, this journey at least merges intergenera-tional sexuality and conquest.

The Scalp-hunters manages its threatening collapse of fatherly and sexual pursuits by recasting race—instead of blood kinship or age—as the ultimate barrier to sexual contact. The posse discovers that sister Adele has become an Indian: Her "hair was dark, the skin browned, and there was a wildness in the expression of the eye" (SH, 157–58). Even after the hunters reverse the American captivity narrative by dressing as Indian warriors and imprisoning Adele back within her own family, Adele does not remember white people's ways. Haller worries that Zöe, who remains in captivity across a canyon that is now literal and spatial rather than temporal, might undergo not only rape but also a similar racial conversion process. He reimagines the gulf between himself and Zöe not in the previous terms of their ages but of a threatening future in which she might lose her sense of racial identity. In the same language he has earlier used to depict the sexual tension between them, he now mourns for Zöe: "A love like ours, tantalized by proximity, almost within reach of each other's embrace yet separated by relentless fate, and that forever; the knowledge of each other's situation; the certainty of my death and *her* dishonor: these and a hundred kindred thoughts rushed into our hearts together" (189). These "hundred kindred thoughts" could easily describe the possibility of the liaison between himself and the twelve year old to whom he has now assumed a fatherly relation by bonding with Seguin. But here the insurmountable distance is racial, for Zöe's "relentless fate" would be to disappear, like Adele, into an Indian identity.

Yet the same instantaneous "love" that brought on Zöe's puberty also brings back her sister Adele's racial memory, which awakens when she sees her old lover, Haller's fellow rescuer St. Vrain: "What memory, friendship, entreaties had failed to effect, love had accomplished in a single instant. Love, mysterious power, in one pulsation had transformed that wild heart; had drawn it from the desert" (206). While Zöe's newly Hispanicized ethnicity has previously provided the necessary bridge between adult and child, here love erects the proper boundaries between a white girl and the "wild" races of the "desert." Both sexual awakenings become cultural ones in which little girls with hybrid identities recognize themselves as properly aligned with European culture, while native-born and immigrant white men unite into a truly "American" force by annihilating the "Indians." Simultaneously conflating adult and child, Anglo and Spanish, intergenerational love makes insurmountable only the difference between European and indigenous people.

In sum, in *The Scalp-hunters*, only a love that combines paternal and sexual affection can enact the mutual cultural awakening of the child (as creole national) and adult (as immigrant national), aligning them with one another. What has been invented is a form of "white" heterosexual desire that is neither precisely interracial nor simply an appropriation of indigenous child marriages. Instead, it is a newly sanctioned form of pedophile sexuality that purifies diverse European cultures into a single white race, managing nationalist concerns about how to engage with indigenous North Americans (wipe them out), native-born Mexicans (use their Spanish roots to align them with Europe rather than their indigenous kin), Spanish creoles (instill a sense of nationality separate from, but affiliated with Europe), and European immigrants (align them with Anglo-American creoles and their descendants). Intergenerational love, Reid seems to maintain, strengthens the United States by "uniting" them into a nation capable of conquering its previous inhabitants while allowing newcomers to be culturally seduced. To put it succinctly, the man-girl travel narrative allows everyone to be a native—except Native Americans.

Since Zöe has already asked Haller, "Enrique, tell me, what is *to marry*?" (sh, 60), all that remains for him is to teach her by marrying her, reestablishing the proper hierarchies despite his "submission" to her. Similarly, for Reid, once the American Southwest had been revalued by and for creoles and immigrants at the expense of indigenous Americans, its very sublimity demanded regulation by white people and repatriation by other European immigrants such as his fellow Irishmen. The love that Haller feels for a creole child combines a paternal/imperialist attitude toward Mexico and an erotic/democratic stance toward fellow white (immigrant and native-born) North Americans. It also justifies a coalition of conquerors, who can appreciate the region's sensual sublimity, against both an indigenous population that merely lives there and does not "love" it, and a previous European conquest that explicitly depended on plunder. Indeed, *The Scalp-hunters*, initially subtitled *Romantic Adventures in Northern Mexico*, was given a new subtitle, *A Romance of the Plains*, on its release by New York's dime novel publisher Beadle and Adams, thereby arrogating its very setting to the U.S. empire through a representational rather than a military tactic. The sexual politics of this kind of imperialism lies in a tourist ideology of "taking" a virgin land by leaving it untouched, appropriating not its raw materials but its meaning— just as the lover of children aims to "take" the object of his desire without despoiling her and thereby making her no longer a child.[48]

Reid's second child-bride novel, *The Child Wife*, resituates this project in global as opposed to domestic terms. Set just after the Mexican War, during the European revolutions of the late 1840s and 1850s, this novel redescribes man-girl love as a relation between two people of pure Anglo blood, figuring the transformation of Manifest Destiny into global policing as a whiter, more intraracial pedophilia. Indeed, this novel deracinates its Irishman, the clearly autobiographical Captain Maynard, by marrying him to a twelve-year-old, blond-haired, blue-eyed, full-blooded English girl named Blanche (explicitly modeled after Reid's wife, Elizabeth Hyde, whom he called "my little Zöe" when he met her and claimed as an example of life imitating art).[49] But lest her name is not enough, Blanche is racialized as hyper-white by consistently appearing alongside of her black maid, Sabina, and (de)sexualized as a super-virgin by the association of this maid's name with the Roman legend of the rape of the Sabine women. If Sabina stands for nations too damaged for the Reidian hero to rescue, Blanche represents a Europe in sexual danger from various nondemocratic regimes, and her seduction, Reid's politics in the war with Mexico, now exported abroad.

Within the novel's complicated and somewhat incoherent plot, Maynard intervenes in a Bohemian rebellion, helps restore the empire to the people of France, and works for the Hungarian independence movement. Meanwhile, Blanche has been forbidden by her father from having any contact with Maynard. When Maynard informs his friend Roseveldt of his intent to marry the girl, Roseveldt replies, "*Cher capitaine!* . . . The girl's only an infant; and before she can be ready to marry you, all Europe may be Republican, and you a President!" (*cw*, 121–22). He speaks as if Europe's acceptance of U.S.-style democracy will automatically make Blanche available. The nationalist and heterosexist equations of *The Child Wife* are summed up by its last sentence: "And to win such a wife, *who would not be true to the people?*" (400; italics in original). Here, "such a wife" is a child, and "the people" is a global class of workers, European and Euramerican, on the proletarian side of the revolutions of the mid–nineteenth century, for whom U.S. postrevolutionary republicanism serves as a template. Join the fight for democracy, the ending seems to say, and you too can marry a little girl. After restoring republican governments in European countries, Maynard settles down with Blanche, and they live happily ever after as man and child wife.

In Reid's most explicit child-bride novel, travel across the interior of the United States gives way to international travel, in which "America" serves not just as a compendium of scenic wonders for Europeans but a political blueprint available to them for transforming the home front. The reward for adopting U.S. political policies becomes a kind of sex that is different and interesting, though still heterosexual and racially pure. The child bride, re-articulated as whiter than white, comes to represent the synthesis of Anglo superiority and democratic idealism in an "America" defined in opposition both to European monarchism and Indian territorial claims. In the end, acquiring the semiotic and sensual competence necessary to have sex with a child inaugurates a kind of political and cultural legitimacy that goes beyond juridical citizenship: what ultimately matters is not the length of the Reidian hero's sojourn in the United States but what he can do with it.

But although Poe's "Three Sundays in a Week" and Reid's novels use travel as a way to reconfigure sexuality, they do not present true honeymoons—for their child brides remain relatively immobile while the male characters travel. It is only in *Lolita* that the energies I have described—mobility across geographic and generational boundaries, racial reconfigurations, commodity culture, and privatizing refigurations of citizenship—come together.

Lolita Rediviva

Let us return, then, to the child Lolita, standing in front of the bridal shop, looking at a bald and armless child, an amputee bride, and a man vacuuming. While in Hawthorne the wedding to a child provides a momentarily safe image of communion with consumer culture, and in Poe and Reid it is the reward for conquest and adventure, in Nabokov the fusion of bride and child causes a horrific blast. Yet as the presence of the man cleaning up around the mannequins suggests, this blast is the occasion for Humbert's self-remaking. The fractured mannequins emblematize what Frances Bartkowski terms his "private combinatory" out of which Humbert must make "the fictive nation where a mirror scene can take place": in other words, the combination of child's body and bridal trappings are the semiotic materials for Humbert's national subjectivity.[50] Like his predecessors in pedagogical travelogues, Humbert learns U.S. history and geography, but through the looking glass rather than in front of the mirror: with the frontier closed, he trails Lolita through a maddeningly self-referential landscape of riddles, anagrams, and puns. This postmodern experience of the landscape is intimately linked to the commodification of the wedding, and particularly to the consolidation of the honeymoon as the consummate union of sexual intimacy and tourism.

Nabokov's first version of *Lolita*, a novella titled *The Enchanter* (written in 1939, yet unpublished until 1986), contains a wedding but no "America," suggesting that the elimination of one and addition of the other might be connected. In *The Enchanter*, an unnamed narrator marries a terminally ill woman in order to gain access to her daughter.[51] After the mother dies, the narrator brings the girl home from school to live with him, and on the way home they stop overnight at a hotel. He molests the girl in the night, she awakens screaming, and the man runs from the hotel and throws himself under an oncoming car. The story's unnamed nymphet heroine is French and its setting is a sparely sketched Provence. Its primary literary allusions are not to U.S. texts but to "Little Red Riding Hood" and other fairy tales as well as *King Lear*.

But in *Lolita*, Nabokov transformed these allusions into contemporary signs, specifically those of twentieth-century U.S. domestic tourism. Reworking the materials of his unpublished novella, he resituated its tale of incest in the contemporary United States and thrust it into motion by portraying its characters traveling in a car rather than being hit by one. The earlier jaunt through Provence is replaced by *Lolita*'s two extended road trips across the United States. Nabokov also added specifically U.S. elements to the basic pedophiliac plot. *Lolita* constantly alludes to Poe's "Annabel Lee," and *The Enchanter*'s blurrily childish French schoolgirl becomes an American pre-adolescent exactly twelve years of age. Lolita, whose name is short for Dolores, is also Hispanicized in the same way as Zöe Seguin: conceived in Monte Cristo, Lolita lives in a house filled with "Mexican trash" and gets molested to the tune of a song about Carmen. Humbert even calls Lolita "my little Creole" (*L*, 171)—as though her U.S. identity, reconfigured as a racialized creole one, explains why she seduces him instead of vice versa. Humbert's courtship depends not on *The Enchanter*'s "storybook images (the pet giant, the fairy tale forest, the sack with its treasures") but on manipulating and partaking in Lolita's susceptibility to male Hollywood stars and consumer pleasures.[52]

At the same time that Nabokov added "America" to *Lolita*, he also subtracted *The Enchanter*'s wedding from it. In the earlier text, the wedding between the narrator and the schoolgirl's mother is "a civil ceremony and a moderately festive dinner."[53] The scene is abbreviated and without details, but definitely visible. *Lolita* recapitulates that scene in Humbert's marriage to his first wife, Valeria, described as a "brief ceremony at the *mairie*" (*L*, 26). Yet the novel elaborately negates this wedding in his second marriage to Lolita's mother, Charlotte, in which Humbert reports that "the bride may dispense with a tiara of orange blossoms securing her finger-tip veil, nor does she carry a white orchid in a prayerbook" (73–74). This is a wedding of "nots," perhaps to make eminently clear that it is only an expression of Charlotte's acquisitive personality as well as Humbert's manipulative lust. But also, between the two works, the self-contained wedding disappears into a kaleidoscopic set of images, interchangeable with one another as well as other visual fragments. For instance, Lolita is obsessed with both newspaper pictures of movie stars and wedding announcements, described as "photographs of local brides, some in full wedding apparel, holding bouquets and wearing glasses" (163)—as if the mediating and advertising work of newspaper and camera on the wedding itself is reproduced on the bride's body as yet another set of lenses. Lo consumes brides, celebrities, and comic strip characters with equal satisfaction, and her own "wedding photo," the triad of two mannequins and a figure of industrial manpower, is literally framed by a store window. Still, the disassembled child and bride mannequins suggest that the wedding can neither hold the family together nor negotiate the impact of mass culture on the family form. Lolita eventually shatters the wedding into a honeymoon, as if the latter can do what the former cannot.

In sum, between Nabokov's two novels about sexual communion with a child, The Enchanter and Lolita, the travelogue becomes national rather than local, and the wedding seems to explode outward across a landscape of commodities, disappearing altogether into the honeymoon. In Lolita, the wedding gets recoded into a tourist trip across the United States, a moveable feast of consumption in which "if a roadside sign said VISIT OUR GIFT SHOP—we had to visit it, had to buy its Indian curios . . . copper jewellery, cactus candy" (L, 146). The wedding ceremony disseminates into a honeymoon that encompasses the vast zones of time and space that Humbert must somehow rearrange into an image of a self, a nation, a national self.

Lolita, then, is the quintessential honeymoon narrative because tourist travel in the United States controls the logic of its sexual drama and sexual drama controls the tour: "Far from being an indolent partie de plaisir, our tour was a hard, twisted, teleological growth, whose sole raison d'être . . . was to keep my companion in passable humour from kiss to kiss" (152). In fact, Humbert drags Lolita on a parody not only of the honeymoon but the 1950s' family vacation—a cultural form that updates and expands on the honeymoon in its insistence that mutual consumption of the U.S. landscape is the key to intimacy, that the family that camps together stays together. Humbert tries to use travel to retrain Lolita's sexuality, and the novel consistently thematizes this as *her* U.S. education: "By putting the geography of the United States into motion, I did my best for hours on end to give her the impression of 'going places,' of rolling on to some definite destination, to some unusual delight" (150). Yet in the end, it is Lolita who turns the screw of national subjectivity, using "the geography of the United States [in] motion" to teach Humbert a lesson.

Throughout the novel, Humbert boasts of his mastery of semiotics: first those of nymphet sexuality and later those of the cryptic paper trail that Clare Quilty leaves when he rescues Lolita from Humbert. Humbert the literary critic offers the tantalizing possibility of a "master text" by which one might read both novel and nymphet allegorically: "In a volume of the *Young People's Encyclopaedia*, I found a map of the States that a child's pencil had started copying out on a sheet of lightweight paper, upon the other side of which, counter to the unfinished outline of Florida and the Gulf, there was a mimeographed list of names referring, evidently, to [Lolita's] class at the Ramsdale school. It is a poem I know already by heart" (51). The children's names on the class list rather obviously allude to other plotlines and moments of wordplay within the novel. Humbert himself also points out that the list serves as an emblem for Lolita, whose name appears between "Hamilton, Mary Rose," and "Honeck, Rosaline": "This 'Haze, Dolores' (she!) in its special bower of names, with its bodyguard of roses—a fairy princess between her two maids of honour" (52). He indicates that a close reading of this wedding emblem will open up the novel as a whole: "What is it? The tender anonymity of this name with its formal veil ('Dolores') and that abstract transposition of first name and surname, which is like a pair of pale new gloves or a mask? Is 'mask' the keyword?" (52). Inserting himself between bride and bridesmaids, lifting the veil, noting the displacement of Lo's "Christian" name with the state-sanctioned surname that as stepfather and husband he is endowed with the power to change yet again, and reducing her to one of a "pair," Humbert suggests, as Haller also does with Zöe, that to read is to teach is to marry.

But as with the previous works, it is Lolita who turns out to be the educator. Humbert's tutorial entirely fails to read the most important sign. Not having gone to graduate school in the 1990s, Humbert forgets the "outside" of the text: on the other side of *this* wedding tableau lies an unfinished map of the United States drawn by Lolita herself. He does not flip the paper over and ask a more significant question: "Is 'map' the keyword?" For the emblem that Humbert so smugly overreads is literally the other side of something much less formally bounded: an outline of the United States drawn by the child bride herself, and left unfinished. The unfinished outline suggests what Lolita has refused to grant Humbert—a legible, complete identity. Her marks on the paper mimic the novel's unending movement not only across the United States but among narrative modes and the kinds of public person-hood that she inflicts on Humbert as she calls him "Dad" (114) and "dirty old man" (115) and herself "daisy-fresh girl" (140) and "juvenile delickwent" (113). His travelogue, in turn, lurches uncontrollably between romance and court-room testimony, and its narrator never stabilizes as either lover or pervert. Displaced to the borders of his own narrative, in the first and last chapters that frame the story he tells, Humbert tries to will *Lolita* into one of the two conflicting genres of case study and romance: "Ladies and gentlemen of the jury, exhibit number one," he begins as a juridical subject, "is what the seraphs, the misinformed, simple, noble-winged seraphs, envied" (9), finish-ing the sentence in the language of courtly love. Were he contained within a lawyer's document, he might at last settle into the category of pervert. Were he bound between the covers of a romance, he could pass as normal. The fact that he is denied final placement, that the two are inextricably intertangled, that Humbert seems condemned to imaginatively stagger across U.S. spaces and genres even from his jail cell, is Lolita's triumph.

More than a "key" to the novel, this childishly scrawled map of the United States serves to make visible the literary and historical outline I have de-scribed. The child, figured as female and bridal in Hawthorne and Poe, creole in Reid, and all three in Nabokov, must take part in a honeymoon that remaps U.S. spaces and sexual practices for its would-be subjects, figured as male, bachelor, and culturally unanchored. By doing so, she promises to remake these men as legible U.S. subjects—consumers in Hawthorne and Poe, pa-triots in Reid, criminals, fathers, or just ordinary lovesick guys in Nabokov—whose Americanness consists precisely in its ability to supersede the appara-tus of citizenship itself. *Lolita* exploits the paradoxes of the honeymoon, on which the male traveler seeks to frame his own body and its desires in terms of both marriage and nation even as he also de-coordinates space and time to experience conflicting forms of intimacy in thrilling conjunction. By not finishing the map, Lolita leaves Humbert terminally "astray," refusing to

indulge his wish to use her body as a means of transforming sensual competence into a framing device that would at last seal him safely within the
borders of the nation.

Lolita Repetida

In May 1995, when I was drafting the dissertation version of this chapter, I
was living in New York, reading the *Daily News*, and following the latest
"Lolita" story. Glenn Harris, a thirty-three-year-old Manhattan schoolteacher,
had run away on 8 March 1995 with his fifteen-year-old student Christina Rosado in search of a state that would grant them a marriage license.[54] Whereas
Humbert drove from hotel to hotel painstakingly combing through guest
register books and deciphering Clare Quilty's anagrams and puns, the FBI
fugitives unit tracked Harris and Rosado across the country using records
from automated teller machines.

Like Humbert, Harris also took Christina on a shopping spree; she later
remarked that "all we did was have fun. We went from hotel to hotel. We went
to amusement parks. He bought me toys. He bought me sneakers."[55] On
10 May, the *Daily News* released perhaps the most arrestingly *Lolita*-esque
image of the chase: a map of the United States showing the couple's stops in
Washington, D.C., Missouri, Alabama, Georgia, Texas, California, and finally
Caesar's Palace in Las Vegas, Nevada. Inset over the map was a picture of the
Casa Clara Motel in Santa Clara, California. Why a photo of the Spanish-
named Casa Clara and not the Madison Hotel or Great Western Inn where
they also stayed, or the Baker's Square Restaurant where they ate, or even
Great America, the amusement park they visited in Santa Clara? Insets with
these place-names over the map would threateningly reveal that the pedophiliac picaresque is, as I have suggested, a feature of Anglo-Americana.
Instead, this inset implied that Mexico was the important part of this story.

The story was, in fact, subtly played as a Latino community interest story,
with the *Daily News* assigning several Latino/a reporters to the case. One
paper even quoted Harris as saying that child marriage was legal in his native
Mexico, while others blamed the teenage girl's traditionalist, "Hispanic"
grandmother for causing her rebellion. The Mexicanization of this story—
the use of Casa Clara instead of Great America to emblematize Christina's
deflowering by an older man—suggests that this story was somehow un-
"American," rather than quintessentially so. Even more markedly, the lan-

guage of the tabloid headlines implied that intergenerational sex is an ordinary, banal feature of nonwhite, working-class culture and only properly shocking to middle-class, white "Americans." The *Daily News* dubbed Harris "Romeo" for a moment, but headline writers settled on "Classanova"—a nickname that combines a connection to Europe with the role of pedagogue, yet also adds the sarcastic implication that his desire for a young girl lacks the moral integrity associated with being middle or upper class.

Yet since Don Juan Casanova was merely promiscuous and unscrupulous with adult women, the name Classanova also eliminates any intergenerational resonances, and puts Christina in the structural position of an adult woman with a sleazy male lover. I have argued that Anglo-American culture needs this fiction of the Hispanicized little girl with adult knowledge who, while her adult male companion shows her a good time, shows him how to experience American culture. In this instance, though—in a historical moment when the demonized child abuser serves to deflect attention from this culture's insistent sexualization of the child—it is crucial that a relationship between a man and little girl *not* end up granting symbolic cultural enfranchisement to the would-be American male.[56] While the map that Lolita drew was unbounded, offering at least a potential route for the immigrant male to enter or exit the conceptual geography of the United States, Classanova's map achieved closure and situated the Latino male outside its parameters even as it traced his movements within them.[57] As long as the child molester is un-American, it implied, "America" is safe from itself.

The Classanova story ended anticlimactically with Harris surrendering to the authorities and accepting a three-year probationary period during which he was free to see the girl as long as they did not flee. The court ruled that Harris was merely committing "custodial interference" and not statutory rape, and banned him from teaching in the city of New York. Ironically, as if to follow in the footsteps of his fictional predecessors, the "trailing" experts Maurice Gerald and Henry Haller along with the butterfly-collecting Humbert Humbert, Glenn Harris went on to declare his stake in the U.S. landscape, noting that he was looking for a job in "wildlife and conservation."[58]

Chapter Six

THE IMMEDIATE COUNTRY, OR, HETEROSEXUALITY

IN THE AGE OF MECHANICAL REPRODUCTION

We chose to make a public thing of our marriage, because we hadn't yet gone beyond demonstration and be-in in inventing the forms that will show us what we are becoming.

—Michael Rossman, *The Wedding within the War*[1]

In 1839, the same year historians establish for the advent of the couple-centered honeymoon among the U.S. middle classes, the daguerreotype was invented. Newlyweds could now purchase portraits of themselves taken on or close to their actual wedding day (see figure 8). But unlike the honeymoon that at least tantalized its isolated couple with possible connections to unfamiliar spaces and temporalities, the daguerreotyped wedding portrait suspended its subject(s) outside of historical time and effaced social contexts wider than the individual or nuptial pair. As Shawn Smith has persuasively argued, the very conventions of daguerreotypy helped construct antebellum heterosexuality and middle-class privacy in one another's terms. The visual language of the daguerreotype elaborated feminine sexual innocence as a quality of the spirit that manifested itself through face, eyes, dress, pose, and the artifacts of domestic life, and figured masculine sexual prerogative as the cameraman's or picture buyer's ability to "see" into this deeply concealed feminine interior.

Daguerreotypy also limited the bride and/or couple's exposure to the penetrating eyes of others: this technique produced a single image, which circulated solely between lovers or among immediate family members. In sum, the iconographic rhetoric and reception practices of daguerreotypy enclosed a heterosexual couple in its own privileged visual circuit—a scopic version of the secluded sphere that marriage was also becoming.[2] Extending Smith's analysis to the photographic wedding portrait in particular, it might be said that the latter combined the honeymoon's ability to eroticize the spatial isolation of couplehood and the daguerreotype's ability to grant an aura of privileged interpsychic intimacy to male-female relationships.

Both the honeymoon and photography also translated family feelings into extralegal, sensory forms of national belonging. Honeymoons, as I asserted earlier, linked erotic competence between a male and an infantilized yet precocious female to ways of seeing and interacting with the "American" landscape. Likewise, photography helped produce a distinctly *corporeal* sense of engroupment. For instance, Smith demonstrates that the imaging technologies that succeeded the daguerreotype turned the visual signs of masculinity and femininity along with the reading strategies that conjoined them into the syntax for a larger unit: the racial "family." When negative/positive imaging techniques emerged in the late 1850s, photographers could distribute multiple copies of the same image, and "scientific" portraits of racial types appeared in such public exhibition arenas as rogues galleries of criminal mug shots and published albums of composite photographs. In the visual language of racial typology, facial expressions and bodily poses became signs that criminals and people of color lacked the inner subjectivity supposedly evident in photographs of middle-class people. Galleries and albums abstracted these people's faces, subjected their images to public possession, and effaced their kinship bonds, portraying them as individuals dangling in fatal isolation or as an indistinguishable mass.[3] By contrast, the white bourgeoisie could imagine its own racial specificity in terms of structured families, signaled by the conventions of family portraiture. It could control the distribution of its portraits among other families. And its members could picture themselves as part of an ever widening circle of racial kin. Circulating in potentially infinite reproductions, the negative/positive photograph linked its subject and viewer to others by a process of visual metonymy in which facial features, clothing, and poses turned into signs connecting people who

Fig. 8. Unidentified Female in Wedding Dress, c. 1850. Daguerreotype, Southworth and Hawes. Courtesy of George Eastman House.

had never met. Photography seemed to reveal lines of connection that transcended the boundaries of individual domiciles, to make the U.S. populace visible to itself as an extended family of Anglo-Saxons.[4]

In short, by the end of the nineteenth century, racial, class, and national "kinship" depended not only on marriage, legitimacy, inheritance, and spousal immigration laws, and not only on the visual consumption of a landscape and other tourist sites, but also increasingly on the visual medium of photography—the primary tool with which social groups could make their members look and feel inevitably and naturally conjoined. Indeed, in his seminal treatise on nationalism, Benedict Anderson fleetingly suggests that the circulation of photographs, specifically those of the wedding, might both complement and complicate the construction of a community. Anderson's well-known thesis that "*amor patriae* does not differ . . . from the other affections, in which there is always an element of fond imagining," is followed by a brief remark on the power of a wedding photograph. "This," he says, "is why looking at the photo-albums of strangers' weddings is like studying the archaeologist's groundplan of the Hanging Gardens of Babylon."[5]

While Anderson's comparison remains frustratingly undeveloped, it is notable for several departures from his formulation of nationhood as an "imagined community" forged through the practice of reading mass-produced literature in a standardized language. First, here he puts forth a model of *envisioned* communities rather than *spoken* or *read* ones. He turns momentarily away from his focus on the printed word as the primary technology of national fantasy to hint that images may also be crucial to the formation of constituencies unbounded by locale.[6] Second, Anderson departs from his insistence that the nation is constituted by the homogenous, empty time of synchronous actions such as those of a populace that reads the newspaper or sings the national anthem at a baseball game. The subject here instead enters the social frame as a genealogist by coordinating historical moments into an organic logic of planning, planting, and growing (the unspoken metaphor in his remark seems to be the family tree). The photo albums of strangers demand a kind of armchair archaeology, an exegesis of pictures to find resemblances between oneself and others not only horizontally, across the boundaries of face-to-face community, but also vertically, across the boundaries between historical eras, indicated by the "before" of blueprints and the "after" of the garden. Thus the activity of "looking at the photo-albums of strangers" in order to feel a sense of membership involves two processes. The viewer must substitute visual correspondences for narratives of cause and effect—but then, the practice of reading from a photo album reanimates a narrative as the viewer turns this paratactic array of photos into cumulative and sequential evidence of individual or collective ancestry.[7] Finally, the fact that this genealogical project is analogized to a *wedding* photograph contests Anderson's implication throughout his *Imagined Communities* that family relations are the prior, more natural material—the "groundplan"—on which nationality can simply depend for its emotional resonance. For while "Mother Russia," "fraternity," the "mother tongue," and other nationalist metaphors depend on the naturalization of bonds that are actually regulated by the state, here the photograph of a wedding is an insistent reminder that "family" is also produced by representational technologies.[8]

In Anderson's remark, "the affections" that connect one person's intimate relations to a broader social field are anything but natural, for they actually rely on delicate negotiations among bodies, representational conventions, and media apparatuses. At the very least, for the wedding photographs of strangers, these operations would include the staging of the wedding pageant, its portrayal in photographs, the insertion of these pictures into an exhibition format that demands a narrative connecting them to one another and prior moments, and the "fond" pictorial and historical imaginings of the viewer. This chapter therefore moves toward visual representations of the wedding that are self-consciously aimed at an audience of strangers, viewers with no past or future face-to-face connection to the marrying couple. I ask: If we can (or cannot) conjure up the Hanging Gardens of Babylon by looking at a blueprint, then what exactly is facilitated (or blocked) by looking at pictures of strangers' weddings? What is it that looking at the weddings of strangers is supposed to do for viewers? When and how does "looking" at a wedding also solicit participation, or doing, and what does that "doing" do? What tangle of affinities does the image of some unknown couple's wedding call forth, or fail to, and how does this structure relate to Anderson's primary site of inquiry, the nation? What do various and sometimes competing visual technologies do to the construction of a national, counternational, para- or peri-national "we"?

To answer these questions, I focus on moving rather than still portraits— on cinematic, video, and theatrical productions of weddings—to claim that moving portraits of weddings facilitate the transformation of "race" into something like "culture." If archaeologists' drawings stimulate one's imagination to re-create the lush flowerings of a garden, and still photography entreats one to connect visual features into aspects of genetic lineage, then moving pictures of strangers' weddings may conjure forth a social status somewhere between biological "race" and legal citizenship, a social space somewhere between the confines of a family and the vast horizons of a nation. Moving portraits also install their subjects into a temporal sequence, embedding whatever they are doing into a narrative. To represent a group not by suspending its bodies outside of time and space but by putting its rituals on moving display within a social context is to suggest that group identity is not a matter of being but one of doing, not a matter of biology but one of praxis—of performing certain activities and then transferring them across time through repetition.[9] In the contemporary wedding pageant, mediated as it is by theatrical, filmic, or televisual conventions, the "natural" facts of heterosexual love and filial devotion are detached from sheer biology, from the brute logic of phenotypic sameness and genetic inheritance, and turned into a sequence of obviously human-made signs and gestures. To invite others to witness or even join this process is to extend the reach of a group identity potentially infinitely, on a model of religious conversion or acculturation rather than biological inheritance.

At the same time as the moving wedding seems to facilitate the release of a group's identity and continuity from biology, it also still seems to offer a formal mechanism of joining that is more visceral than citizenship. Particularly for the white middle classes, visual representations of weddings that move beyond still photography and the motion picture, to the increasingly interactive modes of live television, home video, and experimental theater, substitute the sensual signs of culture for the comparatively less materialized ones of official national belonging. In this sense, Michael Rossman's comment, in the epigraph above, is especially suggestive: ". . . we chose to make a public thing of our marriage . . . because we hadn't yet gone beyond demonstration and be-in in inventing the forms that will show us what we are becoming." He implies that the wedding pageant, extended beyond the audience of immediate family, has the power to remake a public: to refashion "us" by showing us in visual and kinetic language what it is that "we are becoming." In his eyes, the spectacle of strangers' nuptials offers access to a form of collective subjectivity, an anthropological "we" distinct from the national "we" evoked by demonstrations and be-ins. In some ways, this seems quite reactionary: while the demonstration constitutes its participants and audience as collective subjects by reminding them of this country's history of political dissent, the wedding has the more conservative function of grounding group identity in generational descent and heterosexual consent.[10] But on the other hand, the bonds dramatized in the wedding do transcend the abstract connection between subject and state, drawing strangers into relations that feel immediate, tactile, and intimate.[11] Witnessing or joining the performance of the wedding of a stranger, we are asked to imagine that we too might, by taking up these activities, belong to the group these strangers are part of, bypassing both hardwired genetic inheritance and the recondite machinery of legal citizenship.

My primary contention here, then, is that mass-mediated wedding spectacles offer groups the opportunity to experience themselves, in a transvaluation of Anderson's organic metaphor of the Hanging Gardens, as "cultural" and more specifically "ethnic." By ethnic, I mean possessing a distinct collective identity that is distinguished from both biological notions of race and juridical conceptions of citizenship (though it is also clearly propped up by both), and less explicitly sexualized than the one I described in the previous chapter. Wedding pageants aimed at a mass audience of "Americans" promise to transcend the overembodied signs of race, especially for stigmatized groups. In particular, representations of the weddings of strangers allows one to see the recalibration of kinship norms as central to what William Boelhower calls "ethnogenesis," or becoming ethnic.[12] Racial (and sexual) constituencies become ethnic groups by performing the signs of kinship itself; the wedding in many ways provides a visual grammar for this transformation. Even "whiteness" disappears as "race" in the wedding pageants of actual white people, metamorphizing into a sense of (benignly) cultural, but always already familial, belonging. Mass-mediated weddings also even more problematically promise to transcend the underembodied signs of citizenship for dominant groups. For they transcode an abstract form of belonging and a set of privileges connected with it into a display of concrete, sensory signs that seem equivalent to those of others, mere variations on the surface displays of subordinated groups. When the "ordinary" white wedding addresses and includes an unbounded set of spectators—an infinite group of "strangers"—the family form provides a basis for recoding power relations as harmless differences.

Asking what happens when dominant racial groups use the wedding to turn themselves into ethnic ones, I focus here on a series of "generic" Anglo-

American filmic, televisual, and theatrical weddings: the 1950 film *Father of the Bride*, a series of weddings of presidential daughters in the era of the Vietnam War, the wedding of Prince Charles and Lady Diana Spencer in 1981, and the off-Broadway show *Tony 'n' Tina's Wedding* (still running at the time of this book's publication). I treat these weddings primarily as productions of *situational* ethnicity for the white middle class. That is, I see them as opportunities for a dominant group to experience itself as embodied and specific, as bearers of "traditions" and producers of uncommodified cultural signs, without seeming to revert to the Anglo-Saxonist, racial paradigms of the earlier twentieth century.

The Wedding without the War: Father of the Bride

Shortly after World War II, the spectacle of a commercialized, high-"Victorian," U.S. wedding pageant became available to a mass public addressed both as anonymous strangers and potential fellow participants in this ritual. Film critics identify *Father of the Bride* (dir. Vincent Minnelli, 1950) as "one of the first Hollywood productions to use the wedding celebration as a plot device that helped the audience to identify characteristics of a segment of American culture"—namely, Anglo-American, Protestant, white middle-class suburbia.[13] The film revolves around a father's loss of control over his daughter's enormous and complicated wedding. Seen from within a history of the wedding form itself, *Father of the Bride* registers the fact that by the 1950s, the big white wedding was an expected feature of middle-class female life, and a commercial industry had come to dominate its representation and production. Yet the film also appeared right after World War II had effected one of the largest demographic reorganizations in U.S. history, a moment in which the United States was traversed by ever larger numbers of nonwhite refugees, immigrants, migrants, exiles, expatriates, and people caught in neocolonial territorial remappings.[14] Though it is nowhere spoken in *Father of the Bride*, the word "ethnicity" was resurrected from linguistic obsolescence during this postwar period, after revelations about the Holocaust discredited the eugenicist implications of the term "race."[15] Viewed in light of this context, then, the film seems to follow up on and extend the "culturalist" turn of the United States of the 1930s. Before the war, the works of anthropologists such as Ruth Benedict and Margaret Mead were best-sellers, and public intellectuals aimed to describe an "American way of life" separate from the products of mass culture. After the war, it became imperative to portray an "American" identity grounded in something other than biology.[16] The community that *Father of the Bride* constructs is neither a race of Anglo-Saxons nor a homogenized mass culture, but an insular set of family ties that competes with, and triumphs over, both the threat of foreign interlopers and the commercialization of its rituals.

Though it is certainly also an example of classical Hollywood cinema, *Father of the Bride* plays with a few elements of ethnographic documentary as well. Accompanied by the explanatory voice-over of someone who acts as a participant-observer (Stanley Banks, the eponymous father), it presents a festival as the quintessence of a particular culture and a window onto its meaning.[17] Through visual penetration, *Father of the Bride* offers access to this culture's "back region," moving from the opening shot of the banquet table decimated by the reception, back to the making of the festival itself, and detailing the labor and tension involved in this production.[18] The film initially theorizes the middle-class WASP wedding as a rather primitive economic exchange: the bride, Kay Banks (Elizabeth Taylor), engaged to a man named Buckley Dunstan (Don Taylor), is the subject of a merger between her father's "Banks" and her fiancé's "Bucks," their identities further doubled in the names "Stan" and "Dunstan." The central irony of the story is the wedding for which Stanley Banks (Spencer Tracy) must pay in order to be robbed of his only daughter: "What does Buckley's family give?" he asks his wife, Ellie (Joan Bennett), "Just Buckley?" Compared to the price of the wedding and the $1K—or one "Kay"—that he must give up, this seems to Stanley like a raw deal. His challenge is to experience the wedding, and the white suburban culture for which it stands, as something besides a set of economic transactions.

In the moment when the United States had emerged as a world power, the U.S. nation might be expected to fulfill this need. But in this film, "America" no longer quite works as the essence of or alibi for white culture either; it appears only briefly in this film, though notably at the wedding ritual. Stanley has been clumsy throughout the preparations for the wedding—to list only a few examples, he rips his tuxedo, insults his daughter's future in-laws, and sprays soda all over himself at a prewedding party—but the ceremony itself goes so perfectly that in his voice-over, he likens it to a military maneuver. Kay "waited for the proper moment with the calmness of a general watching his forces deploy into battle. . . . Buckley, on the other hand, had the haggard look of a man who had just completed a bombing mission." In this momentary conflation of wedding and war, one might expect the bride leaving her natal household to serve as a figure for the various kinds of displacement that World War II had effected—soldiers leaving home, families broken up, or even cultural practices transformed by migration. Yet here, it is Kay who seems to uproot Buckley, while her father empathizes with the groom's fatigue and powerlessness. By casting Kay as a general and Buckley as the foot soldier whose movements she commands, this military analogy reverses the traffic in women that the wedding, with its focus on the father, would otherwise seem to represent. In this ceremony, the film's men experience their own irrelevance and incompetence as national subjects in relation to postwar forms of power that are troped as feminine.

Instead of locating this feminized power only in the U.S. suburban home, though, the film links it to the twin threats of mass culture and homosexuality, coded as foreign. Kay may act like a military man at the moment of her nuptials, but the film's most controlling character is the caterer, a suspiciously fey "Mr. Twingle" with an exaggerated upper-class British accent.[19] To Stanley especially, he seems to represent several kinds of foreignness at once: before the wedding, Twingle comes across as a specifically British, antidemocratic advocate of stronger class boundaries, advising the Banks family to invite fewer people or move the wedding. But paradoxically, he also represents the commercial extension of the aristocratic big wedding to the middle classes: Stanley struggles to resist his sales pitches for cakes, reception tents, and other mass-produced signs of nuptial propriety. On the wedding day, Twingle metamorphoses into a more generically foreign intruder who breaks into the family home and causes catastrophic social promiscuity. He has urged the Banks family to rent a catering hall, but they have insisted that they will not leave their home and can accommodate all of their guests. Twingle retaliates by moving all of their furniture out and taking off the doors between the rooms. At the reception, Stanley gets lost in his own home and cannot reach the doorway to say good-bye to his daughter, who is leaving the country for her Nova Scotia honeymoon. The postwar, U.S. nuclear family form, predicated on patriarchal privilege and domestic insularity, has been utterly discombobulated here by the feminine/gay, "foreign," commercialized, and crowded event that Twingle has turned this wedding into.

In the end, however, this same wedding is the controlling technology for the respecification of wasps on a cultural model rather than an avowedly racial or national one. The film distinguishes the Banks family from for-

eigners and the feminized masses alike, through a logic of generational conflict and resolution in which generations themselves are reduced to parents
and children. Kay continuously argues with Ellie and Stanley over the wedding: she tells Ellie that "if you want to go through all that old-fashioned
rigamarole, that's fine," yet is horrified by Stanley's suggestion that she elope;
she accuses her father of turning her wedding into a business function, but
revels in the presents sent to her by people she has never met. In this film, not
only are there few signs of extended family (who make telephone calls and
send presents, but do not participate in the making of the wedding), there are
also few signs of friends or siblings, and even the relationship between Kay
and Buckley themselves is lightly sketched. Culture making therefore consists not of negotiating the boundaries between broad, extended kinship networks or peer groups but of the child's acceptance, rejection, or modification
of parental values; what makes wasp culture legible is the central importance
of the parent-child relation that can be superseded only by the relationship
between husband and wife. As in the honeymoon narratives I have described,
wasp culture making also consists of the young female's greater competence
with a commercialized form, transferred back to the older male: if Stanley
gives away his daughter, Kay gives him in return a renewed membership card
to his own culture itself, a revitalized sense of belonging to something. Despite his fears and difficulties, Stanley does pull off the wedding, and Kay
telephones her father from the train station to say good-bye and thank him,
ending the film on a note of continuity rather than conflict. To ensure that this
continuity is understood as extending beyond the boundaries of one particular family, the film moves back to the ethnographic-documentary mode; the
camera pulls back out across a banquet table littered with the debris of postwar consumerism and prosperity, and the sound track returns to Stanley's
weary, though satisfied voice-over.

Father of the Bride, then, presents the wedding as what William Boelhower
labels an ethnic "type-scene": "an instructional gestalt composed of a pre-
fabricated script, a fixed amount of semantic data, and a specific set of role
slices, actions, settings, and goals." Boelhower claims that the type-scene is
the raw material for the production of ethnicity: "Because the type-scene is
structured as a performance, its spatio-temporal organization is associated
with typical capacities, events, and roles, embodies a specifically ethnic perspective, and reveals an ethnosemiotic interpretive calculus."[20] According to
Father of the Bride's type-scene, white middle-class identity is distinguished by

the preeminence of the nuclear family over other social groupings, resistance to both European aristocratic pretensions and mass-produced objects, and the wish to recode economic transactions as exchanges of feeling. Through the wedding, the film represents that identity in terms of "doing" (ritual, costume, food, and festival) and changes to that identity in terms of "generations" (parents and children, tradition and rebellion)—and extends that representation to other white middle-class people. This is a significant departure from the way that earlier visual technologies constituted shared identities such as race, class, and nationality in the image of "family." For rather than portraying the characteristics of the white middle class as inherited and transmitted by blood, as in the late nineteenth century through at least the 1920s, the cinematic cultural self-portrait of *Father of the Bride* depicts these features as contingent—as things to be embraced, rejected, or transformed by a new generation.[21] The film's use of a conversational voice-over sutures the viewer to Stanley, who is the bearer of standards and expectations that turn out to be neither generic nor timeless, but in need of continual renewal by the young. *Father of the Bride*'s momentary allusion to war also suggests that the link between white, suburban, middle-class families and national culture itself must be forged differently: that daughters and not fathers, practices and not bodies, are the source of a revitalization now understood as cultural, in contradistinction to biological or legislative.

Father of the Bride solicits its audience to recognize "themselves" rather than consume an exotic spectacle of otherness. In this sense, it asks for a certain kind of participation, if not in the ritual, at least in the shared understandings that the ritual represents. Even by the late 1960s, this sense of the wedding as having the potential to renew the nation in cultural terms was still in force, as is clear not only in activist Michael Rossman's aforementioned remark but in the classic wedding film of that era, *The Graduate* (dir. Mike Nichols, 1967). In this film's most famous scene, Benjamin interrupts the nuptial ceremony of his beloved Elaine Robinson, who flees from the altar. She does so less out of desire for Benjamin than out of hatred for her mother's society, now explicitly coded as American in the film's theme song, "Mrs. Robinson": "Where have you gone, Joe DiMaggio? A nation turns its lonely eyes to you." Though the lyrics of this song appear to condemn Ben and Elaine's parents' haute-bourgeois society, the song's original title was "Mrs. Roosevelt," implying that the nation itself had disappointed in ways that only a different kind of wedding could renew.[22] With Elaine in full bridal gear, then, the runaway couple board a local bus rather than the usual private car or limousine. Here, the bride and "groom" occupy a genuinely public space, as if to renew the covenantal use of marriage as coterminous with a people's political engroupment. The film ends with Benjamin and Elaine eloping toward a new national future, figured in terms of both a consensual marriage and a generational break. But the couple also sits in the rear bus seats refused by southern blacks in the 1950s, so this future is figured as a transfer of countercultural authority from black civil rights protesters to white hippies as well. And it is a private utopia consisting of only two. As grounds for protest, race disappears; as horizon of change, the nation does too. What is left is love and (sub)culture.

The Weddings within the Wars: The White House Weddings, 1966–1971, and the Royal Wedding of 1981

Twice in between *Father of the Bride* and *The Graduate*, and once shortly after the latter, the United States was entreated to turn its "lonely eyes" to a series of weddings that promised to remake an explicitly national sphere as "cultural" in the ethnicizing terms of generations and customs, and seemed to offer a scene of direct, though avowedly nonpolitical participation. President Lyndon B. Johnson's daughter Luci married in 1966; her sister Lynda wed in 1967; President Richard Nixon's daughter Tricia tied the knot in 1971.[23] The weddings of White House daughters, and the publicity surrounding them, explicitly repudiated the dissident energy and emerging authority of the young white people represented in *The Graduate*. In the White House productions, loyalty to fathers became a basis for remaking the national sphere. The coverage of Tricia's wedding especially emphasized the continuities between the presidential father and his daughter: "As startling as it may seem in her generation, Tricia is capable of complete filial piety," wrote one journalist.[24] Another commentator remarked on "Tricia's sense of tradition and family loyalty—pre-eminently Nixonian qualities."[25] But at a time when people in the United States were extending the parameters of civic participation into everyday life through demonstrations and protests, these White House weddings were also opportunities to reshape the terms of public and private, active and passive, political and personal, to the advantage of a government increasingly less accountable to its citizens. The Nixon wedding was perhaps the most cynically manipulative of the three. While Tricia said that she and her fiancé "both thought it fitting and appropriate to share [the wedding] with so many of the American people," her father directed his chief aide "to begin a totally oriented commitment of relating everything we do [in the wedding] to the political side, without appearing to do so."[26] The Johnson weddings were more subtle. Luci's wedding at the National Cathedral, a Catholic mass according to the preferences of her husband-to-be, was not televised, perhaps because it was too religiously and culturally "minor" to enfold the U.S. public. But Lynda allowed news journalists into her military White House wedding, and the press made much of her status as a "war wife" whose groom would soon be a U.S. soldier in Vietnam.

White House weddings typically have a tricky time negotiating the relationship between marriage and nationalism.[27] They are opportunities to put the official nation on lavish display: "It may be the closest thing Americans have, or want, to a royal occasion," newscaster Dan Rather declared during the broadcast of Tricia's wedding.[28] Yet they are not supposed to be "state affairs," lest they seem to waste taxpayer funds, or worse, replicate the monarchical use of marriage to consolidate political alliances and territorial mergings. They must also transcend display—which always threatens to distance performer and audience—to produce a sense of participation on a democratic model, with each witness acting a part. An ordinary citizen who sought the pleasures of aristocratic spectacle through the democratizing medium of television, for instance, wrote to the Johnson family on Luci's engagement, "Please [broadcast the wedding]! Each home will have the TV on when the Princess of our United States is going to be married."[29] Thus, these weddings aimed not only to present "America" with a flattering spectacle of itself—again through fathers and daughters—but also, crucially, to reinvent the terms of participation in national life. Their dissemination in the national media reinvoked the covenantal aspects of the "founding wedding" discussed in chapter 3 that connect people outside the bonds of domestic family into a genuinely political body. But like the honeymoons explored in chapter 4, the White House weddings also made the sensory reorganization of individual bodies into a meaningful basis for explicit, official national belonging. The result was a regenerated "public" sphere whose members were distinguished by the fact that they used private channels to interact with the nation and that they felt themselves to be part of a culture rather than an electoral constituency.

In all three weddings, the White House appeared to answer to ordinary citizens' desire to be part of the festivities. For instance, after protests, Luci's wedding gown was commissioned to a U.S. manufacturer. The Johnsons asked the taxpayer-supported White House marching band to play at Luci's wedding, and LBJ's gift to his youngest daughter was a loan to his own treasury in the form of a U.S. savings bond. Tricia Nixon chose the army strings to play for her wedding because "the Nixons feel that the Army has had to suffer so many indignities of late, so much attack from within, that this is one small way to honor it."[30] She also used the news media to give the U.S. citizenry a chance to vicariously participate in at least one element of the ceremony itself, printing a mistake-filled recipe for her lemon wedding cake, and then a corrected version, in newspapers across the country.

The primary work of these weddings, then, was to give sensual form to the nation itself by merging state apparatuses such as the military, treasury, and legislature with "folk" elements such as costume, food, and music. They transformed aspects of the federal bureaucratic sphere into techniques for displaying and celebrating the native culture not of, say, Protestants, politicians, or white East Coasters but of "America" itself through its festivals. Furthermore, the weddings seemed to extend the boundaries of this culture outward, drawing the public into its frame as the domestic manufacturing sector sewed Luci a dress and loans to the treasury made up her dowry, taxpayer funds supported the music at all three weddings, and the media disseminated Nixon family recipes and decorating ideas. Yet even as these events opened the wedding outward to "Americans," soliciting them as witnesses and participants, the First Families also insulated the wedding against "foreigners." International heads of state and diplomats were not invited to Luci's wedding because as the Johnsons insisted, they did not "consider Luci's wedding an affair of state, but rather a family and personal occasion."[31] They nevertheless belied this rhetoric by inviting the presidential Cabinet, Supreme Court justices, and congressional leaders, such that the federal and familial spheres merged and the international sphere was left out of both. As comedienne Edie Adams remarked of Luci's wedding, "Only the immediate country" was invited.[32] This joke captures the dynamic of all three of these White House nuptials, which simultaneously extended an invitation to all members of the public to affirm their "American" qualities by witnessing and participating, made the federal sphere feel "immediate" (sensual, proximate, and warm), and rhetorically exiled the uninvited and/or uninterested to a space outside the nation.

Particularly in the weddings of Lynda Bird Johnson and Tricia Nixon, the mass media formed a key part of this project. Lynda's military wedding to Captain Charles Robb was the first White House wedding ceremony to allow journalists in as witnesses, and the protocols of "live" coverage as well as military ceremony fused this marriage to the Vietnam War:

> Officials agreed to let small groups of reporters be herded inside, in relays, for quick glimpses of the proceedings. . . . The procedure with photographs was to send them to a laboratory, where a White House censor was assigned a five-hour vigil to cull out unflattering shots. Then the photos would go to news media to be flashed around the world. . . . Regular briefings of presidential magnitude were scheduled for every phase of the wedding on such subjects as "the procession," "the cake," "the first fifteen minutes of the receiving line."[33]

The limiting of press coverage to "small groups" hurriedly ushered in, the "censors" who weeded out shots, the sense of an ongoing "vigil," the "flashes" around the world, and the press briefings: this wedding presented itself according to the speed, precision, and flattery with which the media also tried to depict the war. In a gesture that revisited the analogy between marital and military prowess in *Father of the Bride,* Lynda's groom cut the cake with his sword, and after the wedding his tour of duty replaced their honeymoon.

In Tricia's wedding, which was with the exception of the actual ceremony taped and broadcast after a one-hour delay, the conventions of public news coverage met those of private portraiture. The broadcast had the feel of a home movie, a genre that endows its viewer with greater access to heretofore forbidden zones than a still photograph ever could. The Kennedy family had already used this model to grant these privileges to the U.S. public, taking television journalists on tours through the White House.[34] Tricia's televised wedding promised to move the viewer even further inward, penetrating the inner sanctum not only of the White House Rose Garden, where the wedding was held, but also of Nixonian personal relationships. Barred only from the ceremony itself, television cameras portrayed the entrance of the wedding party, including the bride on her father's arm, and broke for commercials only after the two reached the altar. CBS then substituted watercolor illustrations—which looked oddly like courtroom sketches—accompanied by a voice-over describing the nuptial kiss that Tricia received on her cheek. The network then returned to videotape for the recessional, with the voice-over describing an unseen Nixon dancing with his wife. But as the competing newspaper coverage of Tricia's wedding and what are now called the Pentagon Papers on the next day made clear, whatever the public had gained in terms of access to the private lives of the presidential family, it was swiftly losing in terms of access to information about matters of national policy.[35]

Indeed, though these mass-mediated weddings promised the public greater access to the private White House, along with the greater ability to participate as taxpayers, newspaper readers, television watchers, and cooks making miniature versions of the wedding cake, they also expressly limited access to the tools of participatory democracy. As Daniel Dayan and Elihu Katz note about the broadcast of live events, media coverage of celebrations in general tries to incite a contagion of minifestivals in which viewers gather to watch the event communally, watch themselves watching it, and perform imitative events of their own. But on the street, in public space, these forms of pseudoparticipation sometimes erupt into carnivalesque or even belligerently oppositional displays, threatening to divert attention from the event itself—which is particularly verboten in the case of a wedding.[36] Thus, while the White House weddings claimed to include the "immediate country" by multiplying opportunities for mass witness and participation, they also circumscribed the forms that participation could take, asking the country to mediate its contact with the federal arena solely through sanctioned wedding activities. In honor of Luci's wedding, for instance, Congressman Wayne Hays introduced a bill prohibiting antiwar demonstrators from coming within 500 feet of any Washington, D.C. church. Because Tricia's wedding took place at the White House, the Nixons did not even attempt such unconstitutional legislation. Instead, Tricia Nixon's response to the possibility of a genuinely democratic, civic performance addressing her wedding was dismissive; when asked what she thought of student plans for an antiwar demonstration at the White House on her wedding day, Tricia replied "blandly," according to one reporter, "It's a free country. . . . I hope we don't infringe on each other's rights. I know we're not planning to [interfere]. . . . Do you think there should be a right to have a wedding?"[37] Analogizing the nuptial couple and demonstrators through the trope of "rights," she seemed at first to suggest that the wedding might be a form of political expressivity like activist Michael Rossman's. But the effect of Tricia's statement was also to make the form of the demonstration seem merely expressive, to change the legal right to assemble and speak into just another rite—a performance of local affinities and personal interests rather than an invocation of the most fundamental guarantees in the United States and a variant of other collective though not civically inflected celebrations such as the parade or fair.

Thus far, I have argued that the Vietnam-era U.S. media used the wedding to rescript political changes into generational conflicts and continuities, remake the federal sphere itself as a kind of local culture, and transform democratic participation into sensory consumption of this local culture. This process reemerged in the wedding of Prince Charles of England and Lady Diana Spencer on 29 July 1981. Though it is not an "American" wedding per se, I include it in my discussion because the U.S. media was so fixated by it, and because it has been credited with the resurgent popularity of lavish white weddings in the United States during the 1980s and beyond.[38] By allowing the entire event to be broadcast live on BBC and CBS, the royal couple blurred the distinction between the ceremony in which only some people are performers and its "reception" via television, which extended the role of witness to transnational constituencies and encouraged them to act out within the bounded spaces of their own homes. In the United States, this merging of ceremony and reception, witness and participant, offered a distraction from the activities of labor unions; air traffic controllers would walk off their jobs just five days after the wedding. In England, the schisms were generational as well as class based; Charles and Diana's romance took place in the context of massive Labour Party unrest and protests by unemployed working-class youth, both native born and immigrant. The British media had therefore already portrayed the couple's courtship as an intergenerational love affair between an older British establishment (Charles, with his love of opera, history, and typically British weather) and an emerging, more multicultural and consumerist youth culture (Diana, who loved discos, romance novels, and Caribbean cruises).[39] On the wedding day, television cameras lingered on a sign held by a fan outside of Buckingham Palace that succinctly registered this "wedding" of nationalist filiopiety and youth culture: "Rock and Royal."[40]

Lauren Berlant has described the 1980s and 1990s in terms of a shift away from demands for the "civil rights" of access to the public sphere, predicated on claims to equal citizenship, and toward the "intimate rights" of economic, juridical, and bodily protection in a symbolic private sphere, predicated on claims to privileged forms of feeling.[41] If Tricia's momentary question about the right to a wedding expressed this shift as a wish in 1971, ten years later the royal wedding acted it out as a promise. During the actual ceremony, the

Archbishop of Canterbury claimed that "all couples on their wedding day are regarded as royal couples," suggesting that political authority might spring from the mere fact of heterosexual couplehood (rw). He went on to assert that "all of us are given the power to make the future more in God's image, and to be kings and queens of love." Here, he reanimated the monarchy's obsolete power to "make the future" through policy, refiguring it as a broad-based heterosexual power to make the future through biological reproduction. His rhetorical readjustment of power implied that the public and monarchy might be disenfranchised in the civic sphere in similar ways—for why invoke their mutual power to make the future unless this power could no longer be taken for granted? In retrospect, it seems fair to suggest that this wedding completed the British monarchy's transformation into a genuinely *mass* monarchy—more accessible to the general population not only through tabloid and television coverage but also through soliciting popular identification with its own political obsolescence by rescripting it as personal vulnerability: the monarchs, like the masses, were helpless. By the mid-1980s, this had constellated around Princess Diana, the bride betrayed.[42] And of course by Diana's death in 1997, this process of redescribing political impotence as white, feminine, emotional fragility had culminated in the oxymoron of a "people's princess."

In many ways, the royal wedding predicted this oxymoron. The archbishop concluded Charles and Diana's ceremony with a benediction that transformed this new coupling of a mass monarchy and monarchical public into a form of passively "participatory" democracy: "May the burdens we lay on [Charles and Diana] be matched by the love with which we support them in the years to come, and however long they live, may they always know that when they pledged themselves to each other before the altar of God, they were surrounded and supported not by mere spectators, but by the sincere affection and the active prayer of millions of friends" (rw). Initially, this blessing links marriage to aristocratic noblesse oblige, fusing the "burden" of the royal family's status as figureheads with the "burden" that all marriages supposedly have to be a public example to others. It also implies that a marriage merits automatic "support," using this imperative to solicit public emotional investment in the monarchy itself. Political subjects here become "friends," bonded in relations of equality to their anachronistic leaders through the ties of "sincere affection." But the blessing also figures the wedding as a scene that can regenerate the public from passive bystanders into engaged actors in collective life. Rather than transcend their status as "spectators" through the public activities that maintain the civic sphere, the archbishop suggests, people ought to do so through the more intimate, religious and emotional activities that will maintain the royal marriage. In keeping with this vision, the ceremony included the hymn "I Vow to Thee My Country," as if not only to marry the British to their nation but also to reconstitute the marital promise itself as an act of patriotism.

In England, then, the royal wedding transferred the scene of consent from political state to cultural nation, by transforming the monarchy into family and citizens into friends. British subjects were asked to perform their Britishness not by demonstrating competence with state-centered practices like voting or civil disobedience but by witnessing a "typically British" ritual, the high-Victorian wedding, and participating in its reception on national television. In the United States, this wedding had a different function: its logic of "cultural" regeneration reemerged just in time for the Reaganite 1980s. People in the United States watched Charles and Diana's wedding live from abroad early in the morning Eastern Standard time and were not expected to participate by vowing or praying in private, or even by celebrating in public. Instead, on this side of the Atlantic, media coverage of the wedding aimed to regenerate white Americans' sense of racial kinship with England in cultural terms. For example, in one of several U.S.-made videos that supplemented cbs's live coverage of the wedding, the voice-over claimed that "collaterally, [Diana] has been worked out to be an eighth cousin seven times removed from George Washington" (rw). Another video reminded U.S. viewers that "wherever we come from, some part of us feels, we come from England" (rw), a message that Native Americans, African Americans, Latinos, and descendants of immigrants from other European countries as well as continents other than Europe surely found surprising. "We may sometimes laugh at each other," commentators admonished, "but in a funny way, we're kin" (rw). But kinship became a matter less of ancestry than of responding with laughter or tears, of renewing an emotional investment in cultural patterns somehow "ours." As it was solicited by the U.S. media, mass witness to the royal nuptials was precisely the looking at photos of strangers' weddings that reorganized a sense of transnational identity around Anglo-Saxon, Protestant whiteness, without ever calling it by name.

This kind of commentary recalibrated U.S. ethnicity in the way that Werner Sollors has contended is constitutive of "ethnicity" itself—that is, through a third-generation narrative in which a group denies the possibility that it is more assimilated to a new culture than its immediate ancestors, by cathecting onto a set of even earlier, often fictive ones. This "revolutionary genealogy," for instance, allowed early colonists to claim Native Americans as the political ancestors of freedoms that their British "parents" had corrupted.[43] Yet by the early 1980s, the newly elected Reagan administration needed something more like a counterrevolutionary genealogy, in which U.S. citizens would reject both their southern Democratic "parents," the Carters, and the claims of nonwhite groups to have made fundamental contributions to U.S. culture. "Americans" would instead attach themselves to Anglo-Saxon "ancestors"— the grandparently Reagans themselves, perhaps even the Nixons, and more broadly, the English.

In sum, in England the royal wedding ultimately posited heterosexuality as a form of "royalty" that superseded not just class interests but national boundaries and origins, and U.S. commentators capitalized on that transnational linkage to invite Americans to participate in the remaking of "our" personal histories as always already Anglo whether or not our ancestors really did come from England. Not long after this spectacle reanimated the white wedding as a technology for remaking Anglo-Saxon whiteness into a benign form of cultural specificity, a show opened off-Broadway that removed any lingering taint of Anglo-Saxon supremacism or aristocratic display from this project. It did so by refiguring whiteness *as* ethnicity itself, specifically that of Italian Americans. *Tony 'n' Tina's Wedding*, which opened in New York in 1986, has grossed $2.5 million annually by tapping into the desire to belong to something by going to the wedding of a stranger.[44] As a way of uniting "Americans," it offers up a kind of vicarious, mythological "Italianicity" that provides a counterpoint to the solemn Anglophilia of the high-Victorian wedding.[45]

The Wedding within the Culture Wars: Tony 'n' Tina's Wedding

Tony 'n' Tina's Wedding draws from a long history of carnivalesque uses of the wedding to temporarily invert gender, sexual, age, and class hierarchies, and by doing so to consolidate them. The show is somewhat reminiscent of a rural North American ritual called the "womanless wedding," an all-male performance that both mocks and affirms heterosexual models of masculinity and femininity.[46] *Tony 'n' Tina's* examination of ethnicity and class also seems to derive from the vaudevillesque mock wedding playbooks that were marketed to U.S. community theaters and churches during the 1920s and 1930s. These productions included both single- and mixed-gender casts, and dramatized multiple and intersecting inversions (men in women's clothes and vice versa, whites in blackface, adults playing children, and incongruous pairings of short and tall, fat and thin).[47] The few blackface vignettes that appeared among early-twentieth-century mock weddings represented African Americans as particularly incompetent in matters of courtship and ceremony, suggesting the linkage between the racialization of a group and distortion or effacement of its kinship structures. But most of these productions were actually racially neutral and made fun primarily of unsophisticated, small-town folk rather than specifically ethnic or racial "types." Nor did they explicitly address national culture. Instead, the rural, shabby, klutzy weddings they depicted seem to have served as foils against which even small-town audience members might imagine their own marriages as cosmopolitan and modern.

At the same time, early-twentieth-century mock weddings emphasized the popular elements of the wedding ceremony as opposed to the commercial and standardized trappings of which a "modern" wedding now consisted. The makeshift costumes and absurd props of the playlets confirmed the superior status of the white wedding, and yet also critiqued its materialism and pomp. In contrast to the distancing spectacle of the bourgeois white wedding, which all of the performances I have addressed so far ameliorated through the use of mass-mediated forms of participation, these earlier mock weddings integrated their audiences right into the wedding spectacle by featuring amateur actors, usually members of the audience's own community (one production even merged performers and spectators altogether by using a lottery system to cast characters from the audience).[48] They thereby provided the opportunities for heckling, improvisation, and other ruptures that had been exiled from the wedding ritual; their primary charm seems to have been that they were interactive. In short, the target of all of these productions was not marriage itself, but the prim white wedding marketed by department stores and bridal magazines: its expense, its solemnity, its demotion of peers and extended family to the status of mute spectators. *Tony 'n' Tina's Wedding* follows up on this project, but links the more participatory wedding with a revitalized sense of whiteness.

This late-twentieth-century contemporary reanimation of the interactive mock wedding stars professional actors who play working-class Italian Americans with exaggerated genders, overblown sexualities, and loud mouths. But *Tony 'n' Tina's* Italians are not merely the representatives of a race-, class-, or region-inflected failure to uphold heterosexual proprieties. Rather, they also promote themselves as avatars of a truly democratic social horizon; in this production, "ethnicity" is the sign of a promise to make the audience member feel part of an imagined whole. By including audiences in the production, as wedding guests with whom the players mingle, the show's creators aimed to make the Italian American wedding into the sign of an infinitely expansive social field and a regenerated community. "Everybody becomes part of a family," enthuses producer Joseph Corcoran, "The adversaries and conflicts are resolved and joined in marriage."[49] The director of one *Tony 'n' Tina's Wedding* remarks, "It's Margaret Thatcher who said there is no such thing as a society. Conservatives have given up on the idea of one nation," linking participation in these weddings with a revitalized sense of universal nationality marked as American by its rhetorical contrast to the parochial British.[50] Some commentators go so far as to depict the interactive mock wedding as a good multicultural education: a writer from the *Nation* solemnly intones that "to be plunged into a simulated environment is not only good entertainment but sound social psychology," arguing that these weddings engender empathy for working-class people and immigrants, and serve as a rehearsal for real intercultural contact.[51]

But why are *Italian* American "family" weddings now so important to the reconstitution of one nation under the sign of marriage? For knockoffs of the production have included *Joey and Maria's Comedy Wedding*, *Frankie and Angie's Italian Comedy Wedding*, *The Original Mario and Mary's Wedding*, *Mario and Mary's Wacky Italian Wedding*, *The Godfather's Meshuggener Wedding*, and *Joey and Mary's Irish/Italian Comedy Wedding*. Though they edge toward other white ethnic groups, these weddings nevertheless seem to privilege "Italian-ness," with even the one gay imitation, *Tony 'n' Tony's Wedding*, preserving the Italian aspect. The utopian element of these productions may lie in the way that they seem to privilege marriage, thereby affirming "traditional" notions of family, while also drawing energy from the most persistent stereotype of Italian American culture itself: "mob family values" as they were dramatized in Francis Ford Coppola's *The Godfather* (1972).

Marriage and immigration are usually analogized by way of the bride who severs her ties with more expansive family forms represented as patriarchal, oppressive, and haremlike, thereby entering the nation via the consensual paradigm of couple-centered marriage.[52] But *The Godfather* actually critiques the way that "modern" marriage isolates a couple. Thomas J. Ferraro has argued that *The Godfather*'s orgy of killing is a metaphor for the violence of capitalism on immigrant men, but the film's opening sequence implies that New World marriage is a form of violence as well.[53] For *The Godfather* begins by crosscutting an outdoor scene of a wedding with indoor scenes of mob transactions. Cutting between the sunshiny backyard where Connie's wedding takes place and the dim interior of her father Don Corleone's office, *The Godfather* seems at first to suggest a dramatic contrast between "good" wedding family values and "bad" mob family values. Yet this simple distinction is undermined by the fact that the wedding is filmed mostly from a distance and the office scenes in close-ups, as if the latter were actually more intimate. In fact, while Connie's husband later beats her savagely and randomly, Don Corleone protects his Mafia clan unless they cross him, demonstrating that mob family values actually have more integrity than nuclear ones. For Italian American men, then, the mob generates forms of masculinity and social alliance that counter the isolation and degradation of the low-paying wage work offered to immigrants. Nevertheless, the film also reveals the violent logic at the heart of the analogy between the bride and immigrant: Connie, who as a woman is barred access to the alternative affiliative structure represented by the mob, assimilates to "America" by restricting her social horizons to a spousal loyalty that turns out to be lethal.

Tony 'n' Tina's Wedding takes *The Godfather*'s assertion that the U.S. family form is a cultural straitjacket right into the scene of the wedding itself. Like *The Godfather*, this show promotes "Italian" family values by staging the boundaries of "family" as shifting and permeable, extending beyond the reproductive and marital to embrace not only extended family but also the honorary familial ties fostered by organized crime (the Mafia reappears in the figure of the reception hall owner) and the bonds fostered in capitalist transactions (one joins this family by buying a ticket). *Tony 'n' Tina* also emphasizes, like *The Godfather*, that joining a family is as violent a process as being excluded from one: rather than a wedding that smoothly merges the Nunzio and Vitale families, audience and play, and/or Italian and American culture, the show portrays a wedding that disintegrates into a cocaine-snorting, drunken melee of blows, epithets, and accidents. The production's very genre, interactive theater, mimics the interpellating work of "family" itself:

audience members find themselves hailed into roles over which they have no choice or control. Like the family in general and wedding specifically, interactive theater works by violating the bodily and psychic boundaries of unwitting entrants, forcing them to play along whether they feel like it or not; one journalist on seeing *Tony 'n' Tina* reported, "I had the powerful feeling that I really was at the wedding reception of people I neither knew nor liked, that the party had turned boringly strident, and that I just wanted to go home."[54] And actor James Altuner told one reporter, "We get a lot of people [who] say, 'This isn't very funny. It's just like my wedding.' "[55]

Thus the very form that purports to merge difference into "family" on the Italian model also follows the rules of Anglo-American kinship a bit too closely: one is forced to take up a role—one cannot just "opt out"—but the opportunities for improvisation are rather limited. Indeed, like that of White House and royal weddings, the *inter*activity of the show is actually strictly controlled. The playbook, which audience members do not have access to, insists that compelled participation can only run in one direction:

> As soon as the word gets out about how much fun the audience can have at the wedding, some of the audience will go too far. They will come dressed as brides, as nuns, as mobsters and pregnant bridesmaids saying that Tony is the father. Remember! They do this in a spirit of "It's audience participation, isn't it?" The reality is . . . yes, it's audience participation and the audience has a certain way it should participate. Don't let anyone stay at the wedding who is inappropriately dressed. . . . Other audience members will think they are part of the show and focus on them and not on timeline events. . . . Ask them to tone down their dress and if they can't, ask them to leave.[56]

This rhetoric is hauntingly similar to the gentle admonitions that many of us receive not to take attention away from the bride by bringing our same-sex lover, wearing nongender normative or overtly sexual clothing, or being "out." To become part of this family whose "Americanness" seems to be regenerated by its polymorphous and expansive "Italian" aspects, one must agree to subject oneself to whatever kind of participation the actors compel, mute one's own expressivity, and have one's attention and actions regulated according to a particular sequence whose culmination is the wedding ceremony—in short, to adhere to middle-class, heteronormative, Anglo proprieties even as the actors purport to abandon them. This regulation of bodily behavior and temporal sequence governs not only the play but its double logic of ethnicity: a limited amount of "acting out" will heal the wounds of generic, abstract, cultural nonbeing for audience members who are not consciously connected to an immigrant past. But the ability to control the body and follow an ordered series of events is paramount, and will presumably absolve the pain of racial, class, and even sexual markings for any audience members who have not shed their "alien" ways. Thus, the honorary ethnicity that the show extends to its audience consists at once of expanded family feelings and of diminished bodily and performative opportunities.

The relation of this mock wedding to the process of ethnogenesis is clearest in the play's self-conscious jokes about multiculturalism and immigration. Donny Dulce, the leader of the mock wedding band Fusion Donny, tells the cast and audience (by now mingling on the floor), "Stay on the dance floor, 'cause we're gonna take you around the world without even leaving the room with the magic of music. . . . We are going to Israel. It's Hora time. Here we go!" (TTWP, 92) He breaks out into "Hava Nagila," and the playbook instructs the groom and his little brother Johnny to "end this section with a Cossack-style dance." Donny then shouts, "OK. Let's go to Mexico!" (92). The characters perform a "Mexican Hat Dance" in which Tony's father and Tina's mother pantomime a bullfight. Donny cries, "Tina and Josephina! Let's go home to Italia!" (93), and the cast performs a tarantella. The role of Fusion Donny, clearly, is to create a hash of stylized ethnic signs.

Donny finishes this section by joking, "We want to thank you for traveling on our Fusion Jet. I hope no one has any trouble getting through customs. If you know what I mean" (93). Of course the phrase "getting through customs" evokes the cocaine that the wedding party has been snorting throughout the event as well as the routine detainment of Italian Americans who get mistaken for Mexican drug smugglers. In addition, it suggests that the drunken bride and groom might not get through the "custom" of the honeymoon night. But the phrase also points out the vertigo induced by the play's rapid whirl through other cultures. Does the three-minute medley really get the audience through the customs of Israel, Mexico, and Italy, especially when Israeli dances collapse into Russian ones and Mexican rituals morph into those of southern Europe? Is this wedding really enough to get the audience through the customs of working-class Italian Americans? Finally, who doesn't get through customs, becoming American by becoming ethnic by joining the wedding?

As it turns out, only one character is stopped at the borders of this festi-val—the one who controls neither his body nor his relationship to the show's narrative timeline. Toward the end of the play, confronting the chaos in the reception hall, the groom Tony demands loudly of his bride, Tina, "Is this the wedding you wanted? I got the flashbulbs going off in my eyes. I got the video guy up my ass" (113). The "video guy" is Rick DeMarco, the wedding videogra-pher and boyfriend of Tina's brother Joey. The playbook confirms that Rick is this wedding's only real outsider: "Today Rick is miffed because Joey would only let him come to the wedding 'under cover' as the videographer. Although Joey explains that this way they can be together without people thinking they are 'together,' Rick sees it as a cowardly move. As the evening wears on, he begins to see Joey in a new light . . . [of] disgust" (43). But Rick's ability to get "up the ass" of the groom is not merely a result of his homosexuality, for the Nunzio family already has a gay member whom they have incorporated into the wedding: Joey is described in the casting notes as "not flamboyant" (9), and he sings in the choir and directs the wedding's female members in their lip-synched reception performance. If Joey's form of homosexuality supple-ments and supports heterosexual couplehood, Rick's relentlessly threatens it. Why?

At first, Rick's status as videographer would seem to support heterosexual privilege along the same lines as Joey's performances. By centering on and fetishizing the couple as objects of significant knowledge and pleasure, the camcorder also constitutes them as subjects with psyches, feelings, and inte-riors. In a show in which characters and audience are sometimes indis-tinguishable, the video camera might be a crucial tool for maintaining the couple's privileged position: they, not the audience, are "shot" into meaning-ful subjectivity. Furthermore, the video camera controls the intermingling of media forms that threatens to literally *dis*integrate the contemporary wedding and its subjects altogether; in *Tony 'n' Tina*, for instance, live bodies refuse to pose for photographs, the players scream "dick!" instead of "cheese!" the videographer jostles the photographer, the band competes with the brawlers for attention, the bridesmaids cannot properly lip-synch or dance to their prerecorded song, and audience improvisation threatens to destroy the time-line. The camcorder flattens out all of these competing media into what Siegfried Kracauer has called a *Gesamtkunstwerk* or "total artwork of effects," and once edited properly, the wedding video coordinates a disjunctive series of actions into an Aristotelian plotline.[57]

Yet there are indications all along that visual media somehow menace ordinary heterosexual love. Tony describes the photography as an assault on his "eyes," implying that still photos denaturalize the wedding and interfere with organic vision. Though the shooting may reveal the representational labor necessary to make heterosexual love look natural, the still camera is embodied in the merely annoying figure of Sal Antonucci, who is "40, pushy, eccentric, bored with his job" (TTWP, 10), yet seems to do it properly. But the Video Man, rather than enhancing the couple's mystique, smoothing over the cracks in the plotline, or synthesizing various levels of mediation, flaunts his own status as artificer. Impresario of a representational *mise-en-abyme*, Rick directs a dream of a dream of a dream: a live actor representing a character uses film to capture other characters, who act out an artificial version of a ritual that is itself a representation of the inaccessible Real that is "love." In the performance of *Tony 'n' Tina's Wedding* that I saw, the Video Man, as he was played by Colin Magill Somers, was actually the show's biggest de-coordinating force. He distracted the live audience from the event, sticking his camera in their faces and blocking their view. He also refused to direct his future video-watching audience's attention at all. Zooming up and down the aisles, jerking his camera around spastically at whatever details caught his attention, he pointed it at a blank expanse of wall or single fork on a table, or stood mesmerized, shooting nothing at all. Moreover, he committed the infraction that most destroys the wedding's aura of sealed-off perfection: he intruded into the videotape itself, shooting parts of his own body and asking audience members to shoot footage of him.

James Moran maintains that wedding videographers "reinvent the genealogical traditions of family and domestic culture that, ironically, they have been hired to preserve"; that is, they shoot and edit the traditional family into being as such, whether or not the wedding participants conform to such a model.[58] The Video Man's insertion of himself into the ceremony and its representation does not merely reinvent but altogether dismantles the family tradition. He restores a certain cruisey, distracted gaze to the wedding spectacle, decentering the bride and groom, and undermining the narrative sequencing and integrative movement of both conventional videography and the ritual itself. Stripped bare of their aura, the bride and her bachelor enter the Video Man's production as just two of many equivalent people and commodities, their "private" moments turned into scenes of dumb opacity, the wedding's sacred details turned into narrative chaos. In short, the Video Man—at least as one actor performed him—subjects Tony and Tina to a regime of de-signification, depersonalization, disconnection, and de-subjectification. Per-haps there was not even any film in Rick's camera, in which case he may be the figure for a cyborg desire, beyond representation, which within this wedding at least, cannot be framed at all. In turn, the actor Somers's body language merged sexuality and technology into a series of jerky, repetitive, robotic dance moves reminiscent of the early 1980s, so that his own body actually syntaxed the technological threat that Tony describes (see figure 9). No wonder the groom feels something up his ass.[59]

In contrast to Joey the gay choreographer, then, Rick the Video Man can be called absolutely queer insofar as that label captures the intersection of sexual stigma with other forms of alterity. For as we have seen, Rick's outsider status is figured in technological, narrative, and sexual terms. It is also a matter of nation and economy: while the logic of marriage and reproduction allows the Nunzios and Vitales—even Joey—to count as "ethnic" and therefore nascently "American," Rick remains "international" and thus permanently and unas-similably "foreign," and the playbook makes this explicit. It advises that in dressing the character of Rick DeMarco, "If you can get a copy of the *Interna-tional Male* clothing catalogue, it will help" (TTWP, 146). This catalog of sexy men wearing scanty clothes posed in "exotic" locales, marketed to gay men, links gay male sexuality with global cosmopolitanism and perhaps even sex tourism. The *International Male*, that is, cuts across the national frame to suggest a group identity founded on sex and consumerism—one increasingly unintelligible as the couple-centered, child-focused marital unit performs the fantasy work of "naturalizing" immigrants and gays alike, whether through immigration laws that automatically grant preferential entry to the spouses of citizens or the mainstream gay movement's rhetoric of gay marriage as a form of citizenship. The Video Man's outside status is constituted by the fact that the show represents him not in terms of the laws, feelings, and naturaliz-ing visual rhetoric of "family" but in terms of artifice, consumerism, and nonreproductive sex.

I would also submit that the Video Man is more than just an abstract figure for the queerness of international tourism. For his multiple kinds of outsider-hood converge into a particular racial stereotype. Because he is an effeminate loner, overinvested in his camera to the extent that his very body moves like an automaton, capable of using technology to rhetorically effeminize the

Fig. 9. Colin Magill Somers as the Video Man, Piper's Alley Theater,
Chicago, 1994. Personal collection of the actor, courtesy of Colin
Magill Somers.

working-class, white-ethnic male, Rick implicitly marks the limits of ethnic belonging less in strictly national terms than in those of a stereotyped Asian masculinity. The show has no overt discourse on whiteness, U.S. nationality, racial characteristics construed as Asian, or any particular Asian nation or region. Instead, the one character who is not invited to this wedding as a guest, whom white U.S. ethnogenesis cannot accommodate, embodies a combination of sexual, technological, and national features that have been central to anti-Asian racism. Italians' access to U.S. whiteness and "Americans' " access to multicultural pleasures emerge through the exclusion of this particular body. In other words, though the show—and by implication the wedding—has room for select mechanical interventions, narrative variations, homosexual object choices, and international differences, the limits of its assimilating work are subtly marked by race.

But for this viewer at least, Rick was also the show's most promising aspect. To run the argument the other way around, the Video Man's queer, "international," technologized, and racialized body productively threatens the merger of family and community into ethnic American "culture." His presence in the play undermines this particular wedding's attempt to alchemize group identities as "family," with evidence that family, like any other group identity, is constructed in and through representational conventions whose disjunctivity to one another can be exploited. If kinship increasingly depends on visual technologies that can merge the ritual of the wedding itself with the chance resemblances captured in still photographs, to produce what looks like an effortless unfolding of generations linked vertically through time and horizontally through synchronous practice, this dependence is also the Video Man's point of intervention. His activities make it clear that modern kinship itself is profoundly unnatural, produced within the shuttling movement between narrative and spectacle that also forges the patriot's "affection" for the nation—and he insistently throws the switch on this movement.

The Video Man reveals that when an unmarriageable person enters the scene of the wedding itself, he or she can manipulate the most disjunctive aspects of the event to reveal that the family, supposedly the raw material for national sentimentality, is just as fictive. His work as videographer serves as a reminder that systems of affinity and alliance that run alongside of, but do not always reduce to familial and national imaginings—local cultures, religious ties, consumer identities, even same-sex love—are sedimented in the history of the wedding itself. Seen through his lens, the wedding, latticed with multiple temporal modes, confettied with incommensurate signs, and fashioned within multiple technologies, has the capacity to become a site for dissecting and transforming, rather than reinforcing, the supposed isomorphism between straight U.S. kinship and U.S. nationality.

Coda

Throughout this book, I have argued that the wedding can call forth social possibilities that do not necessarily reconcile with or reduce to the legal construction of marriage as (at various historical moments) heterosexual, adult, domestic, asymmetrically gendered, exogamous, property-based, racially pure, monogamous, and/or indissoluble. I have claimed that the wedding can conjure up sites other than the state within which relationships of many kinds might become visible and preserved in cultural memory—not only those of gay couples but nonparental ties between adults and children, connections that transcend the household or split various kinds of sharing and caretaking among several people, sibling or other bonds that are forbidden to count as sexual because they involve "blood" relationships, attachments that refuse racial taxonomy, polyamorous liaisons, and even brief erotic encounters. I have suggested that religious, capitalist, and other systems that simultaneously bind people to one or more others and incarnate a group as such do not necessarily follow the rules listed above, and that their residual or emergent presence in the wedding questions the post-Reformation, Western, state-sponsored form of lawful marriage even as the ceremony appears on the surface to sanctify it. In sum, I have held out the possibility that other forms of belonging, appearing fleetingly within the wedding, might offer some traction against the state's control of kinship.

At the same time, several of my chapters have shown that while the wedding seems to offer a relay to differential forms of belonging, when it circumvents marital law but still remains tethered to the symbolics of national belonging, it does seem to leave some familiar corpses in its wake: the "ethnic" wedding of "Tony 'n' Tina," especially, looks like the funeral of an abjected sexual, racial, and technological subject whose only escape from the representational mechanisms of familial citizenship seems to come from a rigorous play with formal techniques specific to video, such as shooting, editing, and framing. Indeed, my readings of various cultural productions have privileged the textuality of the wedding within texts themselves, revealing how the wedding not only critiques marriage and encodes other affinitive possibilities but also enables the lyrical antiformalism of Frankie Addams, Charles Bon, and Rosa in their soliloquies; the antifoundational historicism of Hawthorne's narrator; and the commodity-mediated interventions of Zury, Lolita, Little Annie, Poe's plummy Kate, and the Video Man. But if the wedding's possibilities suddenly erupted into practices off the screen, stage, or page, what might this look like?

In the final days of the year 2000, the dialectical potential of the wedding as a form suddenly flashed forth, though beyond the borders of the United States that have thus far framed this book. On Sunday, 10 December 2000, Reverend Brent Hawkes of the Metropolitan Community Church of Toronto (MCCT), Ontario, momentarily de-centered the nuptial "I now pronounce you." He put in its place another, almost obsolete performative statement: "I publish the banns of marriage between Kevin Bourassa and Joe Varnell." Since nobody present at the services objected to the impending marriage between the two men, Reverend Hawkes told the congregation, "Hearing no legal cause raised this day, we will continue to publish the banns the next two Sundays and we will celebrate the marriage on January the fourteenth." He proceeded to repeat the same set of proclamations for a lesbian couple, Elaine and Anne Vatour, who had already taken the same last name prior to the announcement of their upcoming ceremony.[1] On the second and third Sundays, several conservative Christians suddenly appeared in the congregation and objected to the nuptials on theological grounds. Reverend Hawkes ignored these challenges because the unions violated neither any scriptural proclamations about marriage nor the doctrines of the Fellowship of Metropolitan Community Churches, nor the provincial statutes of Ontario. On Sunday, 14 January 2001, despite a bomb threat and a woman proclaiming herself to be a messenger from Jesus, the two couples were joined in the church.[2]

In following this procedure, Hawkes drew on an obscure and little-used section of the Ontario Marriage Act, which declares that "any person who is of the age of majority may obtain the license or be married under the authority of the publication of the banns, provided no lawful cause exists to hinder the solemnization."[3] The publication of the banns, which historian George Elliott Howard dates from fifth-century France and which the church had enforced all over western Europe by 1215, consisted of a minister announcing a couple's intent to marry three weeks in succession, thereby giving parishioners a chance to reveal any obstacles to the union.[4] If there were no objections, the couple proceeded to wed and the marriage was valid; subsequent discovery of impediments did not automatically invalidate the marriage but did allow the couple to petition for annulment. The keys to Reverend Hawkes's intervention seem to be not only the ungendered language of the Ontario Marriage Act but also its parallelism between the declared "authority" of the church's system of banns, which does not prohibit the union of same-sex couples, and that of Canada's governmental licensing bureaus, which have repeatedly denied the applications of same-sex couples.

Hawkes and the lawyers for the MCCT sent the paperwork to the Ontario attorney general for formal registration of the marriages. The registrar general refused to register the unions, and in November 2001, the MCCT challenged the province on the basis of religious discrimination.[5] A judgment is expected within the month I write this, January 2002. Yet as the Mormons found out in 1878 when they lost *Reynolds v. United States* on the same kind of appeal, it is the state's control over kinship rather than its refusal to tolerate heterogeneous religious beliefs that may invalidate the MCCT's claim.[6] Under the Canadian Constitution Act of 1867, the federal government has the right to define the term "marriage," and provincial governments supervise the administrative procedures and name the set of obligations between the spouses by formulating the grounds for divorce. Religious and other organizations merely have the tacit privilege of determining the shape of the wedding ceremony. Just as the U.S. government did in *Reynolds*, and then again with the 1996 Defense of Marriage Act, the Canadian government has also exercised its de facto right to define the meaning of the word "marriage." The preamble to Canada's Modernization of Benefits and Obligations Act of 2000, which extends full benefits to same-sex couples, states that "the amendments made by this act do not affect the meaning of the word 'marriage,' that is, as the lawful union of one man and one woman to the exclusion of all others." MCCT lawyers argue that this preamble is not equivalent to a formal legislative act and does indeed affect the meaning of marriage, heretofore undefined by Canadian federal law, precisely by limiting its participants.[7] But when the federal government has the constitutional prerogative to define the term as it pleases, this may be a moot point.

The Toronto case highlights one way that the modern, liberal state protects its own definition of marriage: precisely by separating the bonds of family *from* those of religion and other forms of sociability, and making only the latter "private," or inconsequential for citizens' claims to rights or privileges and governmental claims on citizens. Relations among the *members* of established families may count, like the relations among members of a given religion, as "private" insofar as the government claims to interfere only minimally with the ways spouses treat one another or parents treat their children. But the *form* of the family, unlike that of a congregation, is emphatically public insofar as only one specific kind of family has rights and duties determined by the state. Paradoxically, the form of long-term spouses and their children that the state promotes is, in the end, grounded in Protestant doctrines about monogamy, reproduction, shared domicile, and indissolubility. Even when Canada's comparatively liberal domestic partnership system uses dyadic, enduring, and household-based relationships between adults as a channel for benefits and taxation, it distributes public resources and extracts dues along channels at least partially cut by Protestant theology—or by explicitly abjecting the kinship systems of non–Judeo-Christian populations. Thus, as Lisa Duggan has suggested, it would make more sense for the lawyers to claim that as long as the state uses its control over kinship to privilege Protestant beliefs over other religions, church and state are not properly separated.[8]

Instead, what the MCCT did succeed in doing at least momentarily was to use state-based law against the state itself. It reanimated an archaic transfer of power over kinship from one institution to another, and by doing so, at the very least it revealed the historical contingency of modern, state-based kinship rules. For banns themselves were the residue of earlier rituals of betrothal governed by the family and local community, who were most concerned with the extensive network of interfamilial relations that would result from the wedding. When Protestants and later the post-Reformation Catholic

Church enforced the reading of the banns, particularly as a substitute for the more corporeal rituals of betrothal, it signaled that it had seized control over the formation of ongoing sexual unions. Though its system of impediments to endogamous marriage narrowed the horizons of the secular family, the Christian doctrine of universal kinship expanded the heavenly family. By transforming the banns into the marriage licensing and registration system, and increasingly linking these to health and other tests of fitness not only for marriage but citizenship itself, the post-Reformation state produced the narrowest family of all. Reverend Hawkes simply threw a historical switch the other way, reanimating the church's wider vision of what might count as kinship in the service of contesting the state's narrow one. Indeed, in at least one interview Hawkes alleges, apparently referencing John Boswell's work on male-male unions in the early Christian church, that he wished to reclaim this church's comparative latitude in matters of kinship.[9]

Yet the church is not the only sphere of sociability toward which this wedding gestured. Kevin Bourassa tellingly remarked that although he and Varnell had already had a "holy union," the prospect of a state-sanctioned marriage inspired his mother to go to five bakeries asking for a set of plastic grooms for the top of the cake.[10] The commercialized wedding, perhaps the only compensation for the restrictive kinship forms and schemes of bodily management authorized by the state, seems to have released Bourassa's mother into a kind of giddily polymorphous sociability unmatched by the marital form it supposedly served; imagine an elderly woman chatting with bakers, handling miniature couples, perhaps even flirting a bit. Thus, the events in Toronto also whisper the question of what might happen if, rather than seeking entitlements from the state for gay unions, queers agitated *both* for a more widespread cultural refusal to recognize the state as the arbiter of kinship, *and* for a corresponding investment in the mechanisms of binding and belonging specific to non–state-based institutions, rituals, and events.

For instance, in Hawkes's reading of the banns, the complicated interplay between the performative "publishing" of the couples' intent to marry and charged silence of the witnesses brought an alternative public sphere into being. "I publish the banns of marriage between Kevin Bourassa and Joe Varnell" is a performative statement more like "I dare you" than "I do," for "I publish the banns" rather suddenly enlists spectators as potential threats to the upcoming nuptials. In the dare, the silence of spectators amplifies a threat; in the reading of the banns, silence diminishes it. But the performative in both cases establishes a public of potential collaborators in the events that follow. As long as the same-sex nuptials of Bourassa and Varnell, the Vatours, and the other couples who have wed by the banns remain unregistered, then, they unite the couple and others in a collaborative relationship of ongoing mutual witness and performance. Prior to being registered, those marriages do not exist outside the parameters of the congregation that recognizes them—a public that extends beyond the boundaries of the MCCT to include supportive members of the Universal Fellowship of Metropolitan Community Churches, and various interested, sympathetic, or just curious readers and Internet surfers who "witnessed" the ceremony and ensuing events.

Yet the form of this constituency itself is neither that of the democratic state nor another couple. It is instead a group whose affinities with one another could never be telescoped into monogamous, enduring, domestic couplehood—gay or straight. Indeed, the most interesting aspect of Reverend Hawkes's performance is the way it combined the energies of and revealed interdependencies among an obscure, residual, almost anachronistic law originating in small European villages, a cosmopolitan gay population consolidated in the twentieth century, and a technologically mediated network that took shape in the 1990s and that exceeds any strictly geographic boundaries.[11] Right now, the couples and this mass-mediated public of supporters need one another to exist; each is the "we" of the other. The Bourassa-Varnell and Vatour weddings, miniature versions of the mass marry-ins that marriage rights activists have staged at city halls every Valentine's Day in many cities, figured and formalized this dependence.

The MCCT and couples ultimately want to trade in the worlds evoked and instantiated by their wedding for the narrower set of privileges and obligations enforced by marriage. As groom Varnell put it in an interview, "[Many people think that] I'm trying to undermine the institution of marriage. I'm not! I'm trying to uphold it, and make sure that it is what it is supposed to be— a union of two committed individuals who love one another."[12] This very "upholding" extended to his and Bourassa's willingness to substitute for another gay male couple, Tom Atkinson and Tom Alworth, who had been approached first as a possible test case for the MCCT challenge to Canadian marriage law. Because one of the two Toms had been married before, the reading of their banns would have left room for a legitimate theological objection, presumably because their union violated the doctrine of lifetime, indissoluble unions and was therefore bigamous in religious terms.[13] To simultaneously contest the exclusion of Atkinson and Alworth's relationship from theological validity within the Metropolitan Community Churches system, and to use it as a wedge into the civic sphere, would have been a different, much messier project. And yet it might have better honored the serial partnerships, polyfidelity, and discontinuities of both identity and sex practice that are as regular features of queer life as the falsely opposed, mutually constitutive paradigms of monogamy and "promiscuity."

Varnell's partner, Bourassa, spoke in slightly different terms about the intervention he was part of: "For me, it's almost a social issue. . . . I found that marriage is . . . an institution with certain rituals, with certain rights and one of them is the gathering of your family and friends to celebrate the marriage . . . not only to celebrate but to offer their on-going support. . . . Unless we can have full status as a married couple, its [sic] hard to get full recognition of our relationship in the eyes of the community, in the eyes of our family, in the eyes of some of our friends."[14] In practically one breath, Bourassa moves from rituals—which bind people by virtue of mutual spectatorship and bodily participation—to rights—which constitute people as abstract, disembodied individuals worthy of public resources (if not automatically granted them) and not bound by any particular ties—to recognition—which accords symbolic validity to bodies previously stigmatized or unthinkable, and establishes someone "as a full partner in social life able to interact with others as a peer."[15] By naming all of these sites of possible enfranchisement, Bourassa inadvertently offers up the possibility for disentangling them and seeing them in relation to one another.

Marriage grants the couple form unequal access to resources and privileges; rather than demanding our "right" to what is indeed a form of special treatment for couplehood, it seems quite possible to demand the final demise of state-regulated marriage. Recognition, on the other hand, cannot be legislated per se; as Nancy Fraser has cogently argued, when the state mandates economic redistribution on the basis of specific identities and social forms it tends to leave the existing representational field intact, reinforcing existing stigmas and differences.[16] Rites, I would add, accord their actors not only visibility but also status as participants in group forms not reducible to the state. Hence, recalibrating the forms of belonging and the subjectivities forged within rituals may involve challenging not their institutionalization, which is inevitable, but their primary institutionalization *in the state*. In fact, queers could work to genuinely socialize the distribution of public resources by decoupling this system from marriage, thereby deinstitutionalizing marriage; deconstruct the valuation of couplehood by showing its simultaneous reliance on and exclusion of other affinitive possibilities; *and* multiply the sites, scenes, and rituals within which small-scale affinitive possibilities can come to feel and be understood as legitimately "social," as bases for participation in larger group endeavors. Rather than looking to the state for "recognition," or even seeking to transform religious mechanisms for joining people into state or federal laws, queers might be better off proliferating the terrains of recognition and exploiting the possibilities that alternative frameworks for recognition such as religion provide.

I finish with a final vision of this sort of wedding: Essex Hemphill's poem "American Wedding" (1986), from his 1992 collection *Ceremonies*. The work appears second-to-last in a series of poems and essays, the majority of which treat a black gay man's participation in sanctioned and unsanctioned, holiday and everyday, witnessed and secret rituals—basketball games, trials, hazing activities between adolescents, funerals, family gatherings, and especially, sex between men.

"American Wedding"

In america,
I place my ring
on your cock
where it belongs.
No horsemen
bearing terror,
no soldiers of doom
will swoop in
and sweep us apart.
They're too busy
looting the land
to watch us.
They don't know
we need each other
critically.
They expect us to call in sick,
watch television all night,

die by our own hands.
They don't know
we are becoming powerful.
Every time we kiss
we confirm a new world coming.

What the rose whispers
before blooming
I vow to you.
I give you my heart,
a safe house.
I give you promises other than
milk, honey, liberty.
I assume you will always
be a free man with a dream.
In america,
place your ring
on my cock
where it belongs.
Long may we live
to free this dream.[17]

In its opening line, "American Wedding" transforms the trope of the national nuptials, seizing the central symbol of the wedding to sanctify not love, not affinity, not engroupment, but queer sex: "In america, / I place my ring / on your cock / where it belongs." Here, the speaker rejects the homology between marriage and nation, displacing "america" and uniting himself and his partner to the public S/M scene where cock rings are not only symbols of passive belonging but tools for participating. Along the way, he reveals the links between witness and surveillance, evoking both the Ku Klux Klan and official military interventions into the sex lives of African American males: "No horsemen / bearing terror, / no soldiers of doom / will swoop in / and sweep us apart." He suggests that governmental neglect, a lack of sanction, might be positive insofar as it can provide a screen behind which to foment rebellion: "They don't know / we are becoming powerful." Finally, he decouples that rebellion from any nationalist project, moving from the nuptial ring to a kiss that is transubstantial with a world in the making, a wider social landscape not only saturated with but also animated by eroticism: "Every time we kiss / we confirm a new world coming." In the climax of the poem, Hemphill's "we" simultaneously kisses, performs a ritual of acknowledgment with explicitly Catholic overtones (a confirmation), and ejaculates; in turn, the world seems to reach orgasm and emerge into being as the partners kiss.

Afterward, the poem's speaker does move from utopian world making back to national space: he vows to give his partner not a cordoned-off piece of property but another body part, "my heart, / a safe house," and pledges unnamed things "other than" the clichéd "milk, honey, liberty" that the United States has promised and denied to its inhabitants. Instead of a generic U.S. promised land, the speaker evokes the civil rights era and constituencies it engendered, and binds this public to the contemporary sexual one that this couple is a part of. And he releases his personal claims to his partner at the very moment they are bound, connecting him to their shared political ancestry by invoking Martin Luther King Jr.: "I assume you will always / be a free man with a dream." Only after this move does the speaker shift to the imperative, commanding his partner to seal their own bond: "In america, / place your ring / on my cock / where it belongs." At the poem's end, he embeds the partnership back into a collective project rather than a larger form of passive engroupment, and infinitely expands the partners' "we": "Long may we live / to free this dream."

Bourassa's fantasies about witness, acknowledgment, and celebration are, ideally, what a wedding brings to any liaison—but Hemphill's poem suggests that a queer sex public may be a better witness than the state, the liaisons it enables broader, more historically accountable, and more complicated than the domestic household. Hemphill's wedding is like several other anecdotal "American weddings" that I collected in conversations about my research: a pair of twin sisters, for instance, who booked themselves a honeymoon suite, dressed up and ate cake, read vows, and put together a photo album. Or a nonmonogamous lesbian couple who went outside and wrote their names in wet pavement on a public sidewalk so that, as they put it, their primary relationship was "written in stone" even when they slept with others. If one argues for detaching the distribution of material goods from couplehood, one need not secede the terrain of cultural recognition for the lives people create together, whether in pairs or other kinds of groupings, domestically or not, involving caretaking across generations or not. What if the MCCT loses its case, and Bourassa and Varnell decide to dress up, appear before spectators, and renew their pledge to one another every year, change its terms when they choose, or fold new people into it? What if other constituencies decide to use the form of the banns, shower, processional, blessing, rings, kiss, recessional, reception, honeymoon, and so on to make claims for their varied modes of ongoing erotic or affectional relation to other people—and this act did not determine their subsequent economic condition or status as citizens? What might any of this show us about what we are becoming?

Notes

PREFACE

1   Michael Warner, *The Trouble with Normal* (New York: Free Press, 1999), 133–34.
2   Though this too is rapidly changing as DNA testing establishes the "natural" basis of fatherhood.
3   See Bruce Bawer, *A Place at the Table: The Gay Individual in American Society* (New York: Touchstone Books, 1994); William N. Eskridge Jr., *The Case for Same-Sex Marriage: From Sexual Liberty to Civilized Commitment* (New York: Free Press, 1996); E. J. Graff, *What Is Marriage For?* (Boston: Beacon Press, 1999); Gabriel Rotello, *Sexual Ecology: AIDS and the Destiny of Gay Men* (New York: Dutton, 1997); and Andrew Sullivan, *Virtually Normal: An Argument about Homosexuality* (New York: Vintage, 1996). A more nuanced pro–same-sex marriage argument grounded in the right to assembly can be found in Morris Kaplan, *Sexual Justice* (Ithaca, N.Y.: Cornell University Press, 1997). For an argument supporting gay marriage rights as an analogue to interracial marriage, see James Trosino, "American Wedding: Same-Sex Marriage and the Miscegenation Analogy," *Boston University Law Review* 73, no. 1 (1993): 93–120.
4   Protestant Episcopal Church in the United States of America, in *The Book of Common Prayer* (1928) (Greenwich, Conn.: Seabury Press, 1953), 301.
5   Arguments made by lesbians and gays against legalizing same-sex marriage can be found in Robert M. Baird and Stuart E. Rosenbaum, eds., *Same-Sex Marriage: The Moral and Legal Debate* (Amherst, N.Y.: Prometheus Books, 1997); Lisa Duggan and Nan Hunter, eds., *Sex Wars: Sexual Dissent and Political Culture* (New York: Routledge, 1995); Jacqueline Stevens, "On the Marriage Question," in *Women Transforming Politics*, ed. Cathy J. Cohen, Kathleen B. Jones, and Joan C. Tronto (New York: New York University Press, 1997), 62–80; Andrew Sullivan, *Same-Sex Marriage: Pro and Con* (New York: Vintage, 1997); Urvashi Vaid, *Virtual*

Equality: The Mainstreaming of Lesbian and Gay Liberation (New York: Touchstone Books, 1996); and Warner, *The Trouble with Normal.*

6 Interestingly, progressive and reactionary politicians in parts of Europe have recently converged on the same solution to the problem of gay marriage: extending domestic partnership benefits to all kinds of cohabiting pairs—siblings, friends, adults and their elderly parents, and so forth. While this certainly accords state sanction and recognition to a multiplicity of relationships, it does not recognize the specifically sexual nature of gay couplehood. As the right wing has recognized, liberal domestic partnership politics have the effect of leaving heterosexual monogamy as the only state-sanctioned form of actual sex and putting gay couplehood into the same league as various platonic choices. It also doesn't negate a system in which the state rewards those who share property and caretaking with more resources, while it continues to decrease such things as public housing and health care. This is why I think the state should just stay out of the sex business altogether and allocate according to need.

7 See Lisa Duggan, "Queering the State," *Social Text* 39 (summer 1994): 9; and Nancy F. Cott, *Public Vows: A History of Marriage and the Nation* (Cambridge: Harvard University Press, 2000), 212.

8 Michel Foucault, *The History of Sexuality, Volume I: An Introduction*, trans. Robert Hurley (New York: Random House, 1978), 107.

9 Michel Foucault, "Friendship as a Way of Life," interview by R. de Caccaty, J. Danet, and J. Le Bitouz, trans. John Johnston, in *Ethics, Subjectivity, and Truth*, vol. 1 of *The Essential Works of Foucault*, ed. Paul Rabinow (New York: New York University Press, 1997), 135.

10 Ellen Lewin, *Recognizing Ourselves: Ceremonies of Lesbian and Gay Commitment* (New York: Columbia University Press, 1998). Other important articulations of how nonmarital affinities might be formalized include Esther D. Rothblum and Kathleen A. Brehony, eds., *Boston Marriages: Romantic but Asexual Relationships among Contemporary Lesbians* (Amherst: University of Massachusetts Press, 1993); and Kath Weston, *The Families We Choose: Lesbians, Gays, and Kinship* (New York: Columbia University Press, 1991).

11 Robert Brain, *Friends and Lovers* (New York: Basic Books, 1976). For a history of how erotic love became conceptually distinguished from friendship, see Jean H. Hagstrum, *Esteem Enlivened by Desire: The Couple from Homer to Shakespeare.* Chicago: University of Chicago Press, 1992.

12 See Northrop Frye, "The Mythos of Spring," in *The Anatomy of Criticism* (Princeton, N.J.: Princeton University Press, 1957), 163–86.

13 Joseph Allen Boone, *Tradition Counter Tradition: Love and the Form of Fiction* (Chicago: University of Chicago Press, 1987), 80.

14 See Boone, *Tradition Counter Tradition*; and Allen F. Stein, *After the Vows Were Spoken: Marriage and Literary Realism* (Columbus: Ohio State University Press,

1984). Other accounts of the relationship between the love plot and narrative form include Rachel Blau duPlessis, *Writing beyond the Ending: Narrative Strategies of Twentieth-Century Women Writers* (Bloomington: Indiana University Press, 1985); Teresa de Lauretis, *Alice Doesn't: Feminism, Semiotics, Cinema* (Bloomington: Indiana University Press, 1984); Alfred Habegger, *Gender, Fantasy, and Realism in American Literature* (New York: Columbia University Press, 1982); Evelyn J. Hinz, "Hierogamy vs. Wedlock: Types of Marriage Plots and Their Relationship to Genres of Prose Fiction," *PMLA* 19 (1976): 900–913; D. A. Miller, *Narrative and Its Discontents: Problems of Closure in the Traditional Novel* (Princeton, N.J.: Princeton University Press, 1981); Nancy K. Miller, *The Heroine's Text: Readings in the French and English Novel, 1722–1782* (New York: Columbia University Press, 1980); and Tony Tanner, *Adultery in the Novel: Contract and Transgression* (Baltimore, Md.: Johns Hopkins University Press, 1979).

15 George Eliot, *Middlemarch* (1874; reprint, New York: W. W. Norton, 1977), 136. See also Boone, *Tradition Counter Tradition*; and Habegger, *Gender, Fantasy, and Realism*.

16 *Sulka's Wedding*, dir. Kim Christy. Cabollero Home Video, Canoga Park, Calif., 1987.

17 Shyam Selvadurai, *Funny Boy: A Novel* (New York: William Morrow and Company, 1994). Gayatri Gopinath has written an elegant, much longer piece on *Funny Boy*; see "Nostalgia, Desire, Diaspora: South Asian Sexualities in Motion," in *New Formations, New Questions: Asian American Studies*, eds. Elaine Kim and Lisa Lowe, special issue of *positions: east asia cultures critique* 5 (fall 1997): 467–89.

18 Arjun Appadurai, "Disjuncture and Difference in the Global Cultural Economy," in *The Phantom Public Sphere*, ed. Bruce Robbins (Minneapolis: University of Minnesota Press, 1993), 272, 279.

19 See Judith Roof, *Come as You Are: Sexuality and Narrative* (New York: Columbia University Press, 1996).

20 *The Compact Edition of the Oxford English Dictionary* (New York: Oxford University Press, 1971), 11:3725.

21 See Walter Benjamin, "Allegory and Trauerspiel," in *The Origin of German Tragic Drama*, trans. John Osborne (London: Verso, 1985), 159–235, and "Theses on the Philosophy of History," in *Illuminations*, ed. Hannah Arendt, trans. Harry Zohn (New York: Schocken, 1968), 253–64. See also Lauren Berlant, " '68, or Something," *Critical Inquiry* 21 (1994): 124–55.

CHAPTER ONE Love among the Ruins

1 *The Mother of Us All: An Opera*, music by Virgil Thomson, text by Gertrude Stein (New York: Music Press, Inc., 1947), 92–93.

2 My list of media productions is partially indebted to Chrys Ingraham, *White Wedding: Romancing Heterosexuality in Popular Culture* (New York: Routledge, 1999), and conversations with Lauren Berlant and B. J. Wray. Even the art world joined the wedding frenzy with a 1992 showing at Filmforum in Los Angeles, titled "June Weddings: Six Matrimonial Shorts," which included *First Comes Love* (dir. Su Friedrich, 1991); *June Brides* (dirs. Cathy Cook and Claudia Looze, c. 1987); *Marriageable* (dir. David Jensen, n.d.); *Ricky and Rocky* (dirs. Jeff Kreines and Tom Palazollo, 1972); *Wedlock: An Intercourse* (dir. Stan Brakhage, 1959); and *With/out Regret(s)* (dir. Steve Anderson, n.d.). See Kevin Thomas, "Special Screenings: Adrift on a Sea of Matrimony," *Los Angeles Times*, 1 June 1992, sec. F, 4.

3 Title 1 of the U.S. Code, ch. 1, sec. 7, states that "in determining the meaning of any Act of Congress, or of any ruling regulation, or interpretation of the various administrative bureaus and agencies of the U.S., the word 'marriage' means only a legal union between one man and one woman as husband and wife, and the word 'spouse' refers only to a person of the opposite sex who is a husband or a wife" (cited in House of Representatives Report 104–664, 9 July 1996). The Vermont state legislature and governor's decision to legalize same-sex civil unions in 1999 was not the result of a popular referendum, and is limited by the Defense of Marriage Act's stipulation that no state must perforce recognize a same-sex union that is legitimate in another state. As of May 2001, over thirty states had enacted measures to ban same-sex marriage (Lambda Legal Defense, http://www.lambdalegal.org/cgi-bin/pages/documents/record?record=578).

4 For examples of this rhetoric, see especially Gabriel Rotello, *Sexual Ecology: AIDS and the Destiny of Gay Men* (New York: Dutton, 1997); and Andrew Sullivan, *Virtually Normal: An Argument about Homosexuality* (New York: Vintage, 1996).

5 Doris Sommer, *Foundational Fictions: The National Romances of Latin America* (Berkeley: University of California Press, 1991), 32.

6 Raymond Williams, "Structures of Feeling," in *Marxism and Literature* (New York: Oxford University Press, 1977), 132–33.

7 *First Comes Love*, dir. Su Friedrich. Women Make Movies, 1991.

8 Stuart Klawans, "First Comes Love," *Nation*, 23 September 1991, 351.

9 On the role of marriage law in regulating the membership of modern political societies, see Jacqueline Stevens, *Reproducing the State* (Princeton, N.J.: Princeton University Press, 1999).

10 Friedrich herself states in an interview that she is "more interested in finding the nuances, the subtle points which would undermine or recast . . . absolute feelings" (Su Friedrich, "Radical Form/Radical Content," *Millennium Film Journal* 22 [1989/1990]: 118). On Friedrich's formal tactics, see Chris Holmlund, "Fractured Fairytales and Experimental Identities: Looking for Lesbians in and around the Films of Su Friedrich," *Discourse* 17, no. 1 (fall 1994): 16–46; Liz Kotz, "An

Unrequited Desire for the Sublime: Looking at Lesbian Representation across the Works of Abigail Child, Cecilia Dougherty, and Su Friedrich," in *Queer Looks*, ed. Martha Gever, John Greyson, and Pratibha Parmar (New York: Routledge, 1993), 86–102; Liz Kotz, "Inside and Out: Lesbian and Gay Experimentals," *Afterimage* 19 (December 1991): 3–4; Su Friedrich, "Damned If You Don't: An Interview with Su Friedrich," interview by Scott MacDonald, *Afterimage* 15 (May 1988): 6–10; Scott MacDonald, "From Zygote to Global Cinema via Su Friedrich's Films," *Journal of Film and Video* 44 (1992): 30–41; Scott MacDonald, "Su Friedrich: Reappropriations," *Film Quarterly* 41 (winter 1987–1988): 34–43; and Erika Suderburg, "So Much for Pleasure," *Artweek*, 23 July 1988, 15.

11 Klawans, "First Comes Love," 351.

12 Barbara Kruger also notes that Friedrich uses the child as a figure of alienation. See Kruger's review "The Ties That Bind," *Artforum* 23 (October 1984): 89.

13 See Nayan Shah, "Asian Men, White Boys and the Policing of Sex in Early Twentieth-Century California," paper presented at Center for Lesbian and Gay Studies Colloquium Series in Lesbian and Gay Studies, City University of New York Graduate School and University Center, New York City, February 1998.

14 See John D'Emilio, "Capitalism and Gay Identity," in *The Lesbian and Gay Studies Reader*, ed. Henry Abelove, Michelle Aina Barale, and David Halperin (New York: Routledge, 1993), 467–76. See also David T. Evans, *Sexual Citizenship: The Material Construction of Sexualities* (New York: Routledge, 1993). On the role of capitalism in changes to the family form, see Philippe Ariès, *Centuries of Childhood: A Social History of Family Life*, trans. Robert Baldick (New York: Vintage, 1962); Michele Barrett and Mary McIntosh, *The Anti-Social Family* (London: Verso, 1982); Robert Brain, *Friends and Lovers* (New York: Basic Books, 1976); Stephanie Coontz, *The Social Origins of Private Life: A History of American Families, 1600–1900* (London: Verso, 1988); Stephanie Coontz, *The Way We Never Were: American Families and the Nostalgia Trap* (New York: Basic Books, 1992); John D'Emilio and Estelle B. Freedman, *Intimate Matters: A History of Sexuality in America* (New York: Harper and Row, 1988); Jonathan Ned Katz, *The Invention of Heterosexuality* (New York: Dutton, 1995); Friedrich Engels, *The Origins of the Family, Private Property, and the State* (1884; reprint, New York: Pathfinder Press, 1972); Steven Mintz and Susan Kellogg, *Domestic Revolutions: A Social History of American Family Life* (New York: Free Press, 1988); Ferdinand Mount, *The Subversive Family* (New York: Free Press, 1992); Mark Poster, *Critical Theory of the Family* (New York: Seabury Press, 1978); Edward Shorter, *The Making of the Modern Family* (New York: Basic Books, 1975); Lawrence Stone, *The Family, Sex, and Marriage in England, 1500–1800* (New York: Harper and Row, 1977); and Eli Zaretsky, *Capitalism, the Family, and Personal Life*, rev. ed. (New York: HarperPerennial, 1986).

15 Walter Edwards, *Modern Japan through Its Weddings: Gender, Person, and Society in Ritual Portrayal* (Stanford, Calif.: Stanford University Press, 1989). For an eth-

nographic study of English weddings in the 1970s, see Diana Leonard, *Sex and Generation: A Study of Courtship and Weddings* (London: Tavistock, 1980).

16 Ofra Goldstein-Gidoni, *Packaged Japaneseness: Weddings, Business, and Brides* (Honolulu: University of Hawaii Press, 1997); and Laurel Kendall, *Getting Married in Korea* (Berkeley: University of California Press, 1996), 67. On "invented traditions," see Eric Hobsbawm and Terence Ranger, eds. *The Invention of Tradition*. Cambridge: Cambridge University Press, 1983.

17 See the following sample of wedding ethnographies: Ruben R. Alcantara, "The Filipino Wedding in Waialua, Hawaii, *Amerasia Journal* 1, no. 6 (February 1972): 1–12; Luicija Baskauskas, "The Process of Ethnicity in the Structure of the Lithuanian Wedding," *Mankind Quarterly* 21, no. 3 (spring 1981): 227–57; Ann Bridgwood, "Dancing the Jar: Girls' Dress at Turkish Cypriot Weddings," in *Dress and Ethnicity: Change across Space and Time*, ed. Joanne B. Eicher (Oxford: Berg Publishers, 1995), 29–49; Susan Davis, "Old-Fashioned Polish Weddings in Utica, New York," *New York Folklore* 4 (1978): 1–4; Dennis Kolinski, "The Evolution of Polish-American Wedding Customs in Central Wisconsin," in vol. 2 of *The Polish Diaspora*, ed. James S. Pula and M. B. Biskupski (New York: Columbia University Press, 1993), 35–46; Caroline Lipson-Walker, "Weddings among Jews in the Post-World-War-II American South," in *Creative Ethnicity: Symbols and Strategies of Contemporary Ethnic Life*, ed. Stephen Stern and John Allan Cicala (Logan: Utah State University Press, 1991), 171–83; N. P. Lobacheva, "The Marriage Ritual as an Ethnographic Source for Historical Research: On the Example of the Khorezm Uzbeks," *Soviet Anthropology and Archaeology* 20, no. 3 (winter 1981–1982): 31–58; Elisah P. Renne, "Becoming a Bunu Bride: Bunu Ethnic Identity and Traditional Marriage Dress," in *Dress and Ethnicity: Change across Space and Time*, ed. Joanne B. Eicher (Oxford: Berg Publishers, 1995), 117–37; Balch Institute for Ethnic Studies, *Something Old, Something New: Ethnic Weddings in America; A Traveling Exhibition* (Philadelphia, Pa.: Balch Institute for Ethnic Studies, 1987); Janet S. Theophano, "'I Gave Him a Cake': An Interpretation of Two Italian-American Weddings," in *Creative Ethnicity: Symbols and Strategies of Contemporary Ethnic Life*, ed. Stephen Stern and John Allan Cicala (Logan: Utah State University Press, 1991), 44–54; and Philip V. R. Tilney, "The Immigrant Macedonian Wedding in Ft. Wayne," *Indiana Folklore* 3 (1970): 3–34.

18 See John R. Gillis, *For Better, for Worse: British Marriages, 1600 to the Present* (New York: Oxford University Press, 1985).

19 For an argument that the public processional constitutes the essential schema of the popular marriage ritual, see Nicole Belmont, "The Symbolic Function of the Wedding Procession in the Popular Rituals of Marriage," in *Ritual, Religion, and the Sacred*, ed. Robert Foster and Orest A. Ranum (Baltimore, Md.: Johns Hopkins University Press, 1982), 1–7.

20 See John Boswell, *Same-Sex Unions in Premodern Europe* (New York: Villard Books, 1994), 46–47.

21 Folklorists' compendiums of wedding traditions in England and the United States (generally undocumented) include Margaret Baker, *The Folklore and Customs of Love and Marriage* (Aylesbury, U.K.: Shire, 1974); Margaret Baker, *Wedding Customs and Folklore* (Totowa, N.J.: Rowman and Littlefield, 1977); Edson C. Eastman, *Curiosities of Matrimony* (Concord, N.H.: Republican Press, 1889); William J. Fielding, *Strange Customs of Courtship and Marriage* (New York: New Home Library, 1942); Madeleine Ginsburg, *Wedding Dress, 1740–1980* (London: Her Majesty's Stationery Office, 1981); Frank Haines and Elizabeth Haines, *Early American Brides: A Study of Costume and Tradition, 1594–1820* (Cumberland, Md.: Hobby House Press, 1982); Anthea Jarvis, *Brides: Wedding Clothes and Customs, 1850–1980* (Liverpool: Merseyside Country Museums, 1983); John Cordy Jeaffreson, *Brides and Bridals* (London: Hurst and Blackett, 1872); Leslie Jones, *Happy Is the Bride the Sun Shines On: Wedding Beliefs, Customs, and Traditions* (Chicago: Contemporary Books, 1995); Avril Landsdell, *Wedding Fashions, 1860–1980* (Aylesbury, U.K.: Shire, 1983); Peter Lacey, *The Wedding* (New York: Madison Square Press, 1969); Elizabeth Laverack, *With This Ring: One Hundred Years of Marriage* (London: Elm Tree Books, 1979); Elizabeth Hawkes (text) and Christopher Baker (photography), *Martha Stewart Weddings* (New York: Clarkson N. Potter, 1987); *Matrimonial Ceremonies Displayed* (London: Searjant, 1883); Ann Monsarrat, *And the Bride Wore . . . : The Story of the White Wedding* (New York: Dodd, Mead, and Company, 1973); Brian Murphy, *World of Weddings* (New York: Paddington Press, 1978); George Ryley Scott, *Curious Customs of Sex and Marriage* (London: Torchstream Books, 1953); Alice Lea Mast Tasman, *Wedding Album: Custom and Lore through the Ages* (New York: Walker and Company, 1982); and Barbara Tober, *The Bride: A Celebration* (New York: Harry N. Abrams, 1984).

22 See James A. Brundage, *Law, Sex, and Christian Society in Medieval Europe* (Chicago: University of Chicago Press, 1987), 128–29, George Elliot Howard, *The History of Matrimonial Institutions* (Chicago: University of Chicago Press), 1:258.

23 Boswell, *Same-Sex Unions*, 48–49; Brundage, *Law, Sex, and Christian Society*, 34. Phillip Lyndon Reynolds, *Marriage in the Western Church: The Christianization of Marriage during the Patristic and Early Medieval Periods* (New York: E. J. Brill, 1994), 30.

24 See Boswell, *Same-Sex Unions*, 48.

25 See John R. Gillis, "From Ritual to Romance: Toward an Alternative History of Love," in *Emotion and Social Change*, ed. Carol Z. Stearns and Peter N. Stearns (New York: Holmes and Meier, 1988), 87–121.

26 For historians' disputes as to the meaning of betrothal, see Howard, *The History of Matrimonial Institutions* 1:274–75. For descriptions of the exchanges of actual money, symbolic money, and gifts and tokens, see ibid., 258–76 and

Gillis, *For Better, for Worse*, 17–18. On the kiss, see Monsarrat, *And the Bride Wore*, 6.

27 See Gillis, 17–18; and Howard, *The History of Matrimonial Institutions* 1:273.

28 Howard, *History of Matrimonial Institutions*, 1:277–81. See also Andreas Fischer, *Engagement, Wedding, and Marriage in Old English* (Heidelberg: Carl Winter, 1986).

29 See Janet R. Jakobsen, "Can Homosexuality End Western Civilization As We Know It?" in *Queer Globalizations: Citizenship and the Afterlife of Colonialism*, ed. Arnaldo Cruz-Malave (New York: New York University Press, forthcoming 2002). I thank Janet for permission to discuss her unpublished manuscript.

30 Howard dates priestly benedictions at the first century A.D. (*The History of Matrimonial Institutions* 1:293); James A. Brundage dates the first priestly nuptial blessings in the fourth and fifth centuries A.D. (*Law, Sex, and Christian Society*, 88); Reynolds dates the earliest nuptial masses in the seventh and eighth centuries (*Marriage in the Western Church*, 323). Brundage (191) and Howard (1:295–96) concur that these blessings were extras, not essential for the validity of a union.

31 The history of sacramental marriage is briefly traced in Brundage, *Law, Sex, and Christian Society*, 433. Jack Goody argues that the system of impediments forced the breakup of vast tracts of feudal lands preserved through endogamous marriages and reduced the possibilities for inheritance among the aristocracy; these uninherited lands, in turn, defaulted to the church and expanded its holdings. See Jack Goody, *The Development of the Family and Marriage in Europe* (Cambridge: Cambridge University Press, 1983).

32 At the Council of Trent, between 1545 and 1563, the church finally voided all marriages except those contracted in the presence of a priest and two or three witnesses, but this edict was still ignored in England. See Howard, *History of Matrimonial Institutions*, 1:315.

33 See Howard, *History of Matrimonial Institutions*, 1:309–10, 315–16, 337–39. See also Frank Gaylord Cook, "The Marriage Celebration in Europe," *Atlantic Monthly* 61 (February 1888): 245–61.

34 On ceremonies between men in the early church, see Boswell, *Same-Sex Unions*, especially 80–83, 91–97, 106–7, 178–98, 267–70, 281. On the sacramental model, see John Witte Jr., *From Sacrament to Contract: Marriage, Religion, and Law in the Western Tradition* (Louisville, Ky.: Westminster John Knox Press, 1997). The more radical implications of Christian marriage theology are also explored in Adrian Thatcher, *Marriage after Modernity: Christian Marriage in Postmodern Times* (New York: New York University Press, 1999).

35 Howard, *History of Matrimonial Institutions*, 1:309–11.

36 See Michel Foucault, *The History of Sexuality, Volume I: An Introduction*, trans. Robert Hurley (New York: Random House, 1978).

37 See Jakobsen, "Can Homosexuality End Western Civilization?"

38 Howard, *History of Matrimonial Institutions*, 1:375.

39 Brundage, *Law, Sex, and Christian Society*, 571; Howard, *The History of Matrimonial Institutions*, 1:372.

40 Brundage, *Law, Sex, and Christian Society*, 571; Howard, *The History of Matrimonial Institutions*, 1:372.

41 The preceding account is drawn from Witte, *From Sacrament to Contract*. See also Cook, "Marriage Celebration"; and Howard, *History of Matrimonial Institutions*. On England, see Gillis, *For Better, for Worse*; and James T. Johnson, *A Society Ordained by God: English Puritan Marriage Doctrine in the First Half of the Seventeenth Century* (Nashville, Tenn.: Abingdon Press, 1970).

42 On dresses, see Monsarrat, *And the Bride Wore*, 20; Ginsburg, *Wedding Dress*; Jarvis, *Brides*; and Jeaffreson, *Brides and Bridals*. For a more scholarly examination of the wedding cake, see Simon R. Charsley, *Wedding Cakes and Cultural History* (New York: Routledge, 1992).

43 This is Charsley's primary argument about the wedding cake.

44 On clandestine marriages, see Gillis, *For Better, for Worse*; and Lawrence Stone, *Uncertain Unions: Marriage in England, 1660–1753* (New York: Oxford University Press, 1992), especially 92–98.

45 Gillis, *For Better, for Worse*, 140.

46 Howard, *History of Matrimonial Institutions*, 2:127, 131; Cook, "Marriage Celebration," 351. More generally, see Edmund Morgan, *The Puritan Family: Religion and Domestic Relations in Seventeenth-Century New England* (New York: Harper and Row, 1966). On Puritan objections, see Chilton L. Powell, "Marriage in Early New England," *New England Quarterly* 1 (1928): 327. On colonial laws, see Cook, "Marriage Celebration," 352–53; Powell, "Marriage," 328–29; Howard, *History of Matrimonial Institutions* 2:143–44, 180; and Michael Grossberg, *Governing the Hearth: Law and the Family in Nineteenth-Century America* (Chapel Hill: University of North Carolina Press, 1985), 67.

47 On the laws overturning the civil marriage requirement, see Cook, "Marriage Celebration," 352; Howard, *History of Matrimonial Institutions*, 2: 137–38; Powell, "Marriage," 330; and Grossberg, *Governing the Hearth*, 67–69. On the waning of banns, see Grossberg, 77 and Howard, 2:401.

48 See Howard, *History of Matrimonial Institutions*, 235; Henrik Hartog, *Man and Wife in America* (Cambridge: Harvard University Press, 2000), 63; and Katherine M. Franke, "Becoming a Citizen: Reconstruction Era Regulation of African-American Marriages," *Yale Journal of Law and the Humanities* 11 (1999): 252.

49 Grossberg, *Governing the Hearth*, 126.

50 See Martha Hodes, *White Women, Black Men: Illicit Sex in the Nineteenth-Century South* (New Haven, Conn.: Yale University Press, 1997).

51 Ibid., 21, 105; Hartog, *Man and Wife*, 34, 100; Cott, *Public Vows*, 133, 147.

52 See Virginia Sapiro, "Women, Citizenship, and Nationality: Immigration and Naturalization Policies in the United States," *Politics and Society* 13 (1984): 1–26; and Nancy F. Cott, "Marriage and Women's Citizenship in the United States, 1830–1934," *American Historical Review* 103 (1998): 1440–74. See also Candice Lewis Bredbenner, *A Nationality of Her Own: Women, Marriage, and the Law of Citizenship* (Berkeley: University of California Press, 1998).

53 See Cott, *Public Vows*, 85–93; Franke, "Becoming a Citizen," 251–309; and Amy Dru Stanley, *From Bondage to Contract: Wage Labor, Marriage, and the Market in the Age of Slave Emancipation* (New York: Cambridge University Press, 1998).

54 On property, see Cott, *Public Vows*, 99–102. More generally, see Robert J. Sickels, *Race, Marriage, and the Law* (Albuquerque: University of New Mexico Press, 1972).

55 Grossberg, *Governing the Hearth*, 149.

56 See Cott, *Public Vows*, 174–79.

57 The only scholarly history of marriage ceremonies in the United States is Ellen K. Rothman, *Hands and Hearts: A History of Courtship in America* (New York: Basic Books, 1984). On sentimental ritual, see Karen Halttunen, *Confidence Men and Painted Women: A Study of Middle-Class Culture in America, 1830–1870* (New Haven, Conn.: Yale University Press, 1982). Undocumented accounts of nineteenth-century etiquette in the U.S. can be found in Susannah A. Drive, ed., *I Do, I Do: American Wedding Etiquette of Yesteryear* (New York: Hippocrene Books, 1998). For a compendium of original nineteenth-century documents on wedding dresses and etiquette culled from *Godey's Lady's Book*, see Heidi Marsh, *Wedding Suggestions of the Era of the Hoop* (Greenville, Calif.: Heidi Marsh, 1992). On the history of wedding costumes in the United States, see Amy McKune, *To Love and to Cherish: The Great American Wedding* (New York: Museums at Stony Brook, 1991).

58 For a sociological examination of the wedding industry in the 1970s, see Trudy Nicely Henson, *The Wedding Complex: The Social Organization of a Rite of Passage* (Omaha, Nebr.: Park Bromwell, 1976), from which I borrowed the title.

59 Gillis, *For Better, for Worse.*

60 Rothman, *Hands and Hearts*, 176.

61 "Imagined communities" is Benedict Anderson's term. See Benedict Anderson, *Imagined Communities: Reflections on the Origin and Spread of Nationalism* (London: Verso, 1983).

62 Barbara Norfleet dates the invention of this particular pose as 1880 (see *Wedding* [New York: Simon and Schuster, 1979, n.p.]), but the photograph is undated. It was given to me by Molly McGarry, who found it at a flea market.

63 See "Brides and Your New Home," in *Women's Periodicals in the United States: Consumer Magazines*, ed. Kathleen L. Endres and Therese L. Lueck (Westport, Conn.: Greenwood Press, 1995), 38–43.

64 All quotations are taken from my examination of *Bride's* magazines published between 1934 and 1950, held at the New York Public Library.

65 Ibid.

66 For an intriguing discussion of bridal showers as interaction rituals that produce gender as a (heterosexual) form of membership rather than merely forging bonds between already fully gendered women, see David J. Cheal, "Women Together: Bridal Showers and Gender Membership," in *Gender in Intimate Relationships: A Microstructural Approach*, ed. Barbara J. Risman and Pepper Schwartz (Belmont, Calif.: Wadsworth Publishing Company, 1989), 87–93.

67 On the relationship between individualist self-making and the capitalist imperative to submit to factory discipline, see Mark Seltzer, *Bodies and Machines* (New York: Routledge, 1992).

68 J. L. Austin, *How to Do Things with Words*, ed. J. O. Urmson and Marina Sbisa, 2d ed. (Cambridge: Harvard University Press, 1962), 5.

69 Eve Sedgwick, "Queer Performativity," *GLQ (Gay and Lesbian Quarterly)* 1, no. 1 (1993): 1–16.

70 Judith Butler, "Performative Acts and Gender Constitution: An Essay in Phenomenology and Feminist Theory," in *Performing Feminisms*, ed. Sue-Ellen Case (Baltimore, Md.: Johns Hopkins University Press, 1990), 270–82.

71 Judith Butler, *The Psychic Life of Power* (Stanford, Calif.: Stanford University Press, 1997), 133.

72 Ibid., 146.

73 It's worth noting here that in his description of the rise of the allegory, C. S. Lewis connects it with both the rise of dyadic couplehood and incorporation of historically specific elements into present ones. For him, allegory is both the narrative mode that can exteriorize psychic conflicts by projecting them into personae and preserve the pagan gods in the form of these personae. See C. S. Lewis, *The Allegory of Love: A Study in Medieval Tradition* (New York: Oxford University Press, 1936).

74 See Judith Halberstam's *Female Masculinity* (Durham, N.C.: Duke University Press, 1998), the most complex treatment of female-to-male drag and the forms of masculinity it revives or reinvents. On camp as cultural recycling, see Andrew Ross, "The Uses of Camp," in *No Respect: Intellectuals and Popular Culture* (New York: Routledge, 1989), 135–70. I have worked out this argument in another published piece; see Elizabeth Freeman, "Packing History, Count(er)ing Generations." *New Literary History* 31, no. 4 (2000): 727–44.

75 See Judith Butler, *Antigone's Claim: Kinship Between Life and Death* (New York: Columbia University Press, 2000).

76 Mikhail Bakhtin, *Rabelais and His World* (Bloomington: Indiana University Press, 1984). For a call to reexamine ritual as an intersection with history, see John D. Kelly and Martha Kaplan, "History, Structure, and Ritual," *Annual Review of Anthropology* 19 (1990): 119–50.

77 Sommer, *Foundational Fictions*, 47.

78 See Morgan, *The Puritan Family*; John Demos, *A Little Commonwealth: Family Life in Plymouth Colony* (New York: Oxford University Press, 1970); and Melvin Yazawa, *From Colonies to Commonwealth: Familial Ideology and the Beginnings of the American Republic* (Baltimore, Md.: Johns Hopkins University Press, 1985).

79 See Jay Fliegelman, *Prodigals and Pilgrims: The American Revolution against Patriarchal Authority, 1750–1800* (Cambridge: Cambridge University Press, 1982); Shirley Samuels, *Romances of the Republic: Women, the Family, and Violence in the Literature of the Early American Nation* (New York: Oxford University Press, 1996); and Elizabeth Barnes, *States of Sympathy* (New York: Columbia University Press, 1997).

80 The paradox of illegitimate guarantee does not begin or end with the colonial era; Carole Pateman has demonstrated that the civil sphere is founded on primary sexual violence. What she calls the "sexual contract," or male right of sexual access to women, logically precedes and legitimates the Lockean "social contract" that serves as the raw material for state formation. See Carole Pateman, *The Sexual Contract* (Stanford, Calif.: Stanford University Press, 1988).

81 Karen Tracey, *Plots and Proposals: American Women's Fiction, 1850–1890* (Urbana: University of Illinois Press, 2000).

82 Stanley Cavell, *Pursuits of Happiness: The Hollywood Comedy of Remarriage* (Cambridge: Harvard University Press, 1981).

83 See Nancy Armstrong, *Desire and Domestic Fiction: A Political History of the Novel* (New York: Oxford University Press, 1987). For a similar discussion of modern romance novel reading, see Janice Radway, *Reading the Romance: Women, Patriarchy, and Popular Literature* (Chapel Hill: University of North Carolina Press, 1984).

84 See Gillian Brown, *Domestic Individualism: Imagining Self in Nineteenth-Century America* (Berkeley: University of California Press, 1990); Lora Romero, *Home Fronts: Domesticity and Its Critics in the Antebellum United States* (Durham, N.C.: Duke University Press, 1997); and Amy Kaplan, "Manifest Domesticity," *American Literature* 70, no. 3 (1998): 581–606.

85 See Joseph Allen Boone, *Tradition Counter Tradition: Love and the Form of Fiction* (Chicago: University of Chicago Press, 1987); and Leslie Fiedler, *Love and Death in the American Novel* (New York: Criterion Books, 1960).

86 Carson McCullers, *The Member of the Wedding* (1946; reprint, New York: Bantam Books, 1958), 110.

CHAPTER TWO *The We of Me:* The Member of the Wedding's *Novel Alliances*

1 Carson McCullers, *The Member of the Wedding* (1946; reprint, New York: Bantam Books, 1958), 102. Subsequent text references are designated MW.

2   Michel Foucault, "Friendship as a Way of Life," interview by R. de Caccaty, J. Danet, and J. Le Bitouz, trans. John Johnston, in *Ethics, Subjectivity, and Truth*, vol. 1 of *The Essential Works of Foucault*, ed. Paul Rabinow (New York: New York University Press, 1997), 140.

3   See, for instance, Frederic I. Carpenter, "The Adolescent in American Fiction," *English Journal* 46 (September 1957): 313–19; Elaine Ginsberg, "The Female Initiation Theme in American Fiction," *Studies in American Fiction* 3 (spring 1975): 27–37; Louise Westling, "Tomboys and Revolting Femininity," *Southern Humanities Review* 14 (1980): 339–50; and Barbara A. White, "Loss of Self in 'The Member of the Wedding,'" in *Carson McCullers*, ed. Harold Bloom (New York: Chelsea House, 1986), 125–38.

4   On the various titles, see Virginia Spencer Carr, *The Lonely Hunter: A Biography of Carson McCullers* (Garden City, N.Y.: Doubleday, 1975), 93, 138.

5   On World War II era dating patterns, see Beth L. Bailey, *From Front Porch to Back Seat: Courtship in Twentieth-Century America*. Baltimore, Md.: Johns Hopkins University Press, 1988.

6   Robert L. Westbrook, "'I Want a Girl, Just Like the Girl That Married Harry James': American Women and the Problem of Political Obligation in World War II," *American Quarterly* 42 (December 1990): 587–614.

7   A War Wife [Carson McCullers], "Love's Not Time's Fool," *Mademoiselle* 16 (April 1943): 166.

8   For a description of McCullers's household, see Carr, *The Lonely Hunter*, 120–26. Her letter to Reeves McCullers is cited in Carr, *Lonely Hunter*, 232.

9   On lesbian culture during World War II, see Lillian Faderman, *Odd Girls and Twilight Lovers: A History of Lesbian Life in Twentieth-Century America* (New York: Penguin, 1991). For lesbian readings of *The Member of the Wedding*, see Lee Lynch, "Cruising the Libraries," in *Lesbian Texts and Contexts*, ed. Karla Jay and Joanne Glasgow (New York: New York University Press, 1990), 39–48; and Lori J. Kenshaft, "Homoerotics and Human Connections: Reading Carson McCullers 'As a Lesbian,'" in *Critical Essays on Carson McCullers*, ed. Beverly Lyon Clark and Melvin J. Friedman (New York: G. K. Hall, 1996), 220–33.

10 Elspeth Probyn, *Outside Belongings* (New York: Routledge, 1996), 53. Though she articulates the problematic differently, Probyn's interest in uncoupling theories of queer desire from object choice has been influential to my thinking.

11 See Pamela R. Frese, "The Union of Nature and Culture: Gender Symbolism in the American Wedding Ritual," in *Transcending Boundaries: Multi-Disciplinary Approaches to the Study of Gender*, ed. Pamela R. Frese and John M. Coggeshall (New York: Bergin and Garvey, 1991), 97–112.

12 Benedict Anderson, *Imagined Communities: Reflections on the Origin and Spread of Nationalism* (London: Verso, 1983), 16.

13 Michael Warner, introduction to *Fear of a Queer Planet: Queer Politics and Social Theory*, ed. Michael Warner (Minneapolis: University of Minnesota Press, 1994), vii.

14 For a history of love that describes the transition from a symbolics of physical bonds to the wedding's more abstract formalization, see John R. Gillis, "From Ritual to Romance: Toward an Alternative History of Love," in *Emotion and Social Change*, ed. Carol Z. Stearns and Peter N. Stearns (New York: Holmes and Meier, 1988), 87–121.

15 For a related analysis of the relationship between Alaska and queer sexuality, see Sasha Torres, "Lesbische Migrationen, Televisuelle Frontiers: Northern Exposure," trans. Birgit Flos and Georg Tillner, *Montage* 4, no. 2 (1995): 40–62. My thanks to Sasha for sharing her unpublished English-language manuscript edition with me.

16 Lauren Berlant, "National Brands/National Body: 'Imitation of Life,'" in *Comparative American Identities: Race, Sex, and Nationality in the Modern Text*, ed. Hortense Spillers (New York: Routledge, 1991), 111.

17 See Claus-M. Naske, *An Interpretive History of Alaskan Statehood* (Anchorage: Alaska Northwest Publishing Company, 1973); Dorothy Tomhave, "Some Phases of the Alaskan Statehood Movement, 1867–1947" (master's thesis, University of Chicago, 1947); and John S. Whitehead, "Noncontiguous Wests: Alaska and Hawai'i," in *Many Wests: Place, Culture, and Regional Identity*, ed. David M. Wrobel and Mitchell C. Steiner (Lawrence: University of Kansas Press, 1997), 314–34.

18 On "cognitive mapping," see Fredric Jameson, "Cognitive Mapping," in *Marxism and the Interpretation of Culture*, eds. Cary Nelson and Lawrence Grossberg (Urbana: University of Illinois Press, 1988), 347–57. On space in postmodernity, see Fredric Jameson, *Postmodernism, or, the Cultural Logic of Late Capitalism* (Durham, N.C.: Duke University Press, 1991).

19 See the description of the first Queer Nation T-shirt, an outline of the U.S. map whose red and blue colors blur to make lavender, in Lauren Berlant and Elizabeth Freeman, "Queer Nationality," in *Fear of a Queer Planet*, ed. Michael Warner (Minneapolis: University of Minnesota Press, 1994), 205.

20 George and Ira Gershwin, "Love Is Sweeping the Country," on *Of Thee I Sing*, Broadway Angel Records, 1952; cited in Evan Wolfson, "Crossing the Threshold: Equal Marriage Rights for Lesbian and Gay Men, and the Intra-Community Critique," *New York University Review of Law and Social Change* 21, no. 3 (1994–1995): 571, 610.

21 See Ruth Tabrah, *Hawaii: A Bicentennial History* (New York: W. W. Norton and Company, 1980).

22 Randle Cotgrave, *A Dictionarie of the French and English Tongues (1611)* as cited in *The Compact Edition of Oxford English Dictionary* (New York: Oxford University Press, 1971), 1:590.

23 See, for instance, Edmund Wilson's review of *The Member of the Wedding*, "Two Books That Leave You Blank: Carson McCullers, Siegfried Sassoon," *New Yorker* 22, 30 March 1946, 87–88.

24 Thanks to Bill Brown for alerting me to the presence of Jane Addams in Frankie's renaming imaginary.

25 Walter Benjamin, "Allegory and Trauerspiel," in *The Origin of German Tragic Drama*, trans. John Osborne (London: Verso, 1985), 188.

26 Patricia White, *unInvited: Classical Hollywood Cinema and Lesbian Representability* (Bloomington: Indiana University Press, 1999), xii.

27 See Gilles Deleuze and Félix Guattari, "What Is a Minor Literature?" in *Out There: Marginalization and Contemporary Cultures*, ed. Russell Ferguson, Martha Gever, Trinh T. Minh-ha, and Cornel West (Cambridge: MIT Press, 1990), 59–69.

28 My thanks to Lauren Berlant for pointing out the significance of the "o" as both phoneme and emblem.

29 Walter Benjamin, "Theses on the Philosophy of History," in *Illuminations*, ed. Hannah Arendt, trans. Harry Zohn (New York: Schocken, 1968), 253–64.

30 Anderson, *Imagined Communities*, 31.

31 Thadious M. Davis, "Erasing 'the We of Me' and Rewriting the Racial Script: Carson McCullers Two 'Member[s] of the Wedding,'" *Critical Essays on Carson McCullers*, ed. Beverly Lyon Clark and Melvin J. Friedman (New York: G. K. Hall, 1996).

32 Leslie Fielder reads the relationship between Frankie and Berenice as a cross-race homosexual liaison on the model of Huck Finn and the slave Jim. See Leslie Fiedler, *Love and Death in the American Novel* (New York: Criterion Books, 1960), 479.

CHAPTER THREE *"That Troth Which Failed to Plight": Race, the Wedding, and Kin Aesthetics in* Absalom, Absalom!

1 William Shakespeare, *Henry V*, IV.i.232, in *The Oxford Shakespeare: Henry V*, ed. Gary Taylor (Oxford, U.K.: Clarendon Press, 1982), 217.

2 Hazel Carby, *Reconstructing Womanhood: The Emergence of the Afro-American Woman Novelist* (New York: Oxford University Press, 1987), 89.

3 Karen Sánchez-Eppler, *Touching Liberty: Abolition, Feminism, and the Politics of the Body* (Berkeley: University of California Press, 1993), 38–39.

4 See Lauren Berlant, "The Face of America and the State of Emergency," in *The Queen of America Goes to Washington City: Essays on Sex and Citizenship* (Durham, N.C.: Duke University Press, 1997), 175–220.

5 Robert J. C. Young, *Colonial Desire: Hybridity in Theory, Culture, and Race* (New York: Routledge, 1995), 25.

6   The fullest analysis of the effects of slavery on kinship, gendering, and narrative remains Hortense Spillers, "Mama's Baby, Papa's Maybe: An American Grammar Book," *diacritics* (summer 1987): 65–81.

7   In *The Coupling Convention: Sex, Text, and Tradition in Black Women's Fiction* (New York: Oxford University Press, 1993), Ann duCille usefully points out that African American women writers did not wait for legal marriage rights, or even stay within their terms, in order to represent heterosexual union as a marker of freedom, civic responsibility, and the transformative power of feelings. On "sentimental power," see Jane Tompkins, *Sensational Designs: The Cultural Work of American Fiction, 1790–1860* (New York: Oxford University Press, 1985), 122–46. Alex Haley's *Roots* (Garden City, N.Y.: Doubleday, 1976), with its straightforward story line of succeeding generations, is a paradigmatic example of the family dynasty narrative in African American literature.

8   Claudia Tate, *Domestic Allegories of Political Desire: The Black Heroine's Text at the Turn of the Century* (New York: Oxford University Press, 1992), 125.

9   See Tate's title above. On marriage and civic belonging see Virginia Sapiro, "Women, Citizenship, and Nationality: Immigration and Naturalization Policies in the United States," *Politics and Society* 13 (1984): 1–26; and especially Nancy Cott, "Marriage and Women's Citizenship in the United States, 1830–1934," *American Historical Review* 103 (December 1998): 1440–74.

10 Linda Brent [Harriet Jacobs], *Incidents in the Life of a Slave Girl, Written by Herself,* ed. Jean Fagan Yellin (Cambridge: Harvard University Press, 1987), 201. Subsequent text references are designated *I*.

11 Tate, *Domestic Allegories*, 32.

12 For similar suggestions about Jacobs / Brent's ambivalence toward marriage, see Amy Dru Stanley, *From Bondage to Contract: Wage Labor, Marriage, and the Market in the Age of Slave Emancipation* (New York: Cambridge University Press, 1998), 32; Carby, *Reconstructing Womanhood*, 36–61; and duCille, *Coupling Convention*, 4–5. The classic argument that enslaved African American families followed the two-parent, domestic reproductive household structure is Herbert G. Gutman, *The Black Family in Slavery and Freedom, 1750–1925* (New York: Vintage, 1976). For a revision of the Gutman thesis, see Brenda E. Stevenson, "Black Family Structure in Colonial and Antebellum Virginia: Amending the Revisionist Perspective," in *The Decline in Marriage among African Americans: Causes, Consequences, and Policy Implications*, ed. M. Belinda Tucker and Claudia Mitchell-Kernan (New York: Russell Sage Foundation, 1995), 27–56.

13 See Sara L. Zeigler, "Uniformity and Conformity: Regionalism and the Adjudication of Married Women's Property Acts," *Polity* 28, no. 4 (summer 1996): 467–95.

14 I follow Werner Sollors's definition of "interracial literature": "By 'interracial literature' I mean . . . works in all genres that represent love and family relations

involving black-white couples, biracial individuals, their descendants, and their larger kin—to all of whom the phrasing may be applied, be it as couples, as individuals, or as larger family units" (*Neither Black nor White yet Both: Thematic Explorations of Interracial Literature* [New York: Oxford University Press, 1997], 3). All the same, I prefer Martha Hodes's description of marriage across a historically variable color line. See Martha Hodes, *White Women, Black Men: Illicit Sex in the Nineteenth-Century South* (New Haven, Conn.: Yale University Press, 1997).

15 Eric Sundquist, "'Absalom, Absalom!' and the House Divided," in *William Faulkner's "Absalom, Absalom!"* ed. Harold Bloom (New York: Chelsea House Publishers, 1987), 92.

16 On miscegenation law as a means for controlling the distribution of property, see Eva Saks, "Representing Miscegenation Law," *Raritan* 8 (fall 1988): 39–69. On the relationship between queers and interracial couples as threats to a white supremacist system of property, see Phillip Brian Harper, "Gay Male Identities, Personal Privacy, and Relations of Public Exchange: Notes on Directions for Queer Critique," *Social Text* 15, nos. 3–4 (1997): 5–29.

17 See Saks, "Representing Miscegenation Law," and Randall Kennedy, "The Enforcement of Anti-Miscegenation Laws," in *Interracialism: Black-White Intermarriage in American Literature, History, and Law*, ed. Werner Sollors (New York: Oxford University Press, 2000), 144.

18 See Peter W. Bardaglio, "Shameful Matches: The Regulation of Interracial Sex and Marriage in the South before 1900," in *Sex, Love, Race: Crossing Boundaries in North American History*, ed. Martha Hodes (New York: New York University Press, 1999), 112–38. See also Peter W. Bardaglio, *Reconstructing the Household: Families, Sex, and the Law in the Nineteenth-Century South* (Chapel Hill: University of North Carolina Press, 1995); and Robert J. Sickels, *Race, Marriage, and the Law* (Albuquerque: University of New Mexico Press, 1972).

19 The case of Tempie James is recounted in Hodes, *White Women, Black Men*, 138. The second example is from David Dodge, "The Free Negroes of North Carolina," *Atlantic Monthly* 57 (January 1886): 20–30.

20 William Faulkner, *Absalom, Absalom!* (1936; reprint, New York: Vintage, 1990), 286. Subsequent references to this text appear within the body of the chapter as *A*.

21 See, for instance, Frederick R. Karl, "Race, History, and Technique in 'Absalom, Absalom!'" in *Faulkner and Race*, ed. Doreen Fowler and Ann Abadie (Jackson: University Press of Mississippi, 1987), 209–21; and James Snead, "The 'Joint' of Racism: Withholding the Black in 'Absalom, Absalom!'" in *William Faulkner's "Absalom, Absalom!"* ed. Harold Bloom (New York: Chelsea House Publishers, 1987), 129–41.

22 See Annette Gordon-Reid, *Thomas Jefferson and Sally Hemings: An American Controversy* (Charlottesville: University Press of Virginia, 1997).

23 On the arguments for whiteness as property in *Plessy*, see Amy Robinson, "Forms of Appearance of Value: Home Plessy and the Politics of Privacy," in *Performance and Cultural Politics*, ed. Elin Diamond (New York: Routledge, 1996), 237–61.

24 Gina L. Hicks, "Reterritorializing Desire: The Failure of Ceremony in 'Absalom, Absalom!'" *Faulkner Journal* 12, no. 2 (1997), 23–39, an admirable piece that I encountered partway through the writing of this chapter. Though we differ on several points, Hicks's contribution to my understanding of the Sutpen wedding is significant. On the channeling of desire, see Gilles Deleuze and Félix Guattari, *Anti-Oedipus: Capitalism and Schizophrenia*, trans. Robert Hurley, Mark Seem, and Helen R. Lane (Minneapolis: University of Minnesota Press, 1983).

25 See Richard Godden, "'Absalom, Absalom!' and Labor History: Reading Unreadable Relations," *ELH (English Literary History)* 61 (1994): 685–720.

26 On Haiti's three-caste racial system, see Laura Foner, "Free People of Color in Louisiana and St. Domingue: A Comparative Portrait of Two Three-Caste Slave Societies," *Journal of Social History* 3 (summer 1970): 406–30.

27 See Virginia R. Dominguez, *White by Definition: Social Classification in Creole Louisiana* (New Brunswick, N.J.: Rutgers University Press, 1986). For an important analysis of *Absalom, Absalom!* that focuses on the imposition of a binary race system onto Louisiana after 1803, see Barbara Ladd, "'The Direction of the Howling': Nationalism and the Color Line in 'Absalom, Absalom!'" in *Subjects and Citizens: Nation, Race, and Gender from Oroonoko to Anita Hill*, ed. Michael Moon and Cathy N. Davidson (Durham, N.C.: Duke University Press, 1995), 347–71.

28 A useful description of plaçage can be found in Carolyn Cossé Bell, *Revolution, Romanticism, and the Afro-Creole Protest Tradition in Louisiana, 1718–1868* (Baton Rouge: Louisiana State University Press, 1997), 112.

29 See Elizabeth Bowles Warbasse, *The Changing Legal Rights of Married Women, 1800–1861* (New York: Garland Publishers, 1987), 137–81.

30 Ibid., 48–56.

31 On Afro-Creole women's campaigns against plaçage, particularly that of Henriette DeLille, see Bell, *Revolution, Romanticism,* 128–34. It is beyond the scope of this project to do more than speculate about why Euramericans in Louisiana tolerated plaçage and what advantages African Americans may have gained from a system that was clearly so exploitative.

32 I have retained Faulkner's spelling of "Mr" without a period throughout this chapter.

33 See Alan Dundes, "'Jumping the Broom': On the Origin and Meaning of an African American Wedding Custom," *Journal of American Folklore* 109 (1996): 325.

34 See, for instance, Stevenson, "Black Family Structure."

35 Stanley, *From Bondage to Contract*, 44–45; see also Laura F. Edwards, *Gendered Strife and Confusion: The Political Culture of Reconstruction* (Urbana: University of Illinois Press, 1997), 45.

36 Katherine M. Franke, "Becoming a Citizen: Reconstruction Era Regulation of African-American Marriages," *Yale Journal of Law and the Humanities* 11, no. 2 (1999): 305.

37 See Edwards, *Gendered Strife and Confusion*, 54.

38 James Mellon, *Bullwhip Days: The Slaves Remember* (New York: Wiedenfeld and Nicholson, 1988), 352; cited in Dundes, "Jumping the Broom," 325. Given the female's subordinate status in the middle-class marriage contract, one wonders if any women similarly availed themselves of the same choice.

39 See, for instance, Harriette Cole, *Jumping the Broom: The African-American Wedding Planner* (New York: Henry Holt, 1993).

40 See Ingrid Sturges, *The Nubian Wedding Book* (New York: Crown, 1997), 71.

41 Dundes, "Jumping the Broom," 328. For an analysis of the Welsh origins of the custom, see C. W. Sullivan III, " 'Jumping the Broom': A Further Consideration of the Origins of an African American Wedding Custom," *Journal of American Folklore* 110 (spring 1997): 203–4.

42 See Ernst Kantrowics, "On the Golden Marriage Belt and the Marriage Rings of the Dumbarton Oaks Collection," *Dumbarton Oaks Papers* 14 (1960): 19; cited in John Boswell, *Same-Sex Unions in Premodern Europe* (New York: Villard Books, 1994), 213.

43 Boswell, *Same-Sex Unions*, 211–12.

44 John R. Gillis, "From Ritual to Romance: Toward an Alternative History of Love," in *Emotion and Social Change*, ed Carol Z. Stearns and Peter N. Stearns (New York: Holmes and Meier, 1988), 91.

45 Ibid., 87–121.

46 Boswell, *Same-Sex Unions*, 24.

47 James Snead, "Repetition as a Figure of Black Culture," in *Black Literature and Literary Theory*, ed. Henry Louis Gates Jr. (New York: Methuen, 1984), 59–60.

48 For an examination of the influence of black oral culture on another canonical novel by a white author, see Shelley Fisher Fishkin, *Was Huck Black? Mark Twain and African-American Voices* (New York: Oxford University Press, 1993).

49 See Gary Lee Stonum, "The Fate of Design," in *William Faulkner's "Absalom, Absalom!"* ed. Harold Bloom (New York: Chelsea House Publishers, 1987), 35–55.

50 On minstrelsy as a cultural performance of male-male, homoerotic miscegenation, see Eric Lott, *Love and Theft: Blackface Minstrelsy and the American Working Class* (New York: Oxford University Press, 1995).

1 e. e. Cummings, *Complete Poems, 1904–1962*, ed. George J. Furnage (New York: Liveright, 1994), 470.

2 See Carole Pateman, *The Sexual Contract* (Stanford, Calif.: Stanford University Press, 1988), 164. On various struggles to define the marriage contract, see Hendrik Hartog, *Man and Wife in America* (Cambridge: Harvard University Press, 2000).

3 Nancy F. Cott, " 'Giving Character to Our Whole Civil Polity': Marriage and the Public Order in the Late Nineteenth Century," in *U.S. History as Women's History: New Feminist Essays*, ed. Linda K. Kerber, Alice Kessler-Harris, and Kathryn Kish Sklar (Chapel Hill: University of North Carolina Press, 1995), 109.

4 See Jacqueline Stevens, "On the Marriage Question," in *Women Transforming Politics*, ed. Cathy J. Cohen, Kathleen B. Jones, and Joan C. Tronto (New York: New York University Press, 1997), 62–80.

5 See especially John Winthrop, "On Liberty" (1645), in *American Voices: Significant Speeches in American History*, ed. James R. Andrews and David Zarefsky (New York: Longman, 1989), 5–6.

6 See James T. Johnson, *A Society Ordained by God: English Puritan Marriage Doctrine in the First Half of the Seventeenth Century* (Nashville, Tenn.: Abingdon Press, 1970); Edmund Morgan, *The Puritan Family: Religion and Domestic Relations in Seventeenth-Century New England* (New York: Harper and Row, 1966); Mary Beth Norton, *Founding Mothers and Fathers: Gendered Power and the Formation of American Society* (New York: Knopf, 1996), 1–59; Mary Lyndon Shanley, "Marriage Contract and Social Contract in Seventeenth-Century English Political Thought," in *The Family in Political Thought*, ed. Jean Bethke Elshtain (Amherst: University of Massachusetts Press, 1982), 80–95; and John Witte Jr., *From Sacrament to Contract: Marriage, Religion, and Law in the Western Tradition* (Louisville, Ky.: Westminster John Knox Press, 1997).

7 See Witte, *From Sacrament to Contract*, 208.

8 On the popularity of wedding tableaux, see Alfred Habegger, *Gender, Fantasy, and Realism in American Literature* (New York: Columbia University Press, 1982), 20.

9 On the Oneidians, New Harmonites, Shakers, and Mormons, see Raymond Lee Muncy, *Sex and Marriage in Utopian Communities: Nineteenth-Century America* (Bloomington: Indiana University Press, 1973); John Spurlock, *Free Love: Marriage and Middle-Class Radicalism in America, 1825–1860* (New York: New York University Press, 1988); and Barbara Taylor, *Eve and the New Jerusalem* (New York: Pantheon, 1983).

10 As well as Norton, *Founding Mothers and Fathers*; and Witte, *From Sacrament to Contract*; see Amy Dru Stanley, "Legends of Contract Freedom," in *From Bondage*

to Contract: Wage Labor, Marriage, and the Market in the Age of Slave Emancipation (New York: Cambridge University Press, 1998), 1–59.

11   See Hartog, Man and Wife, 109, 117.

12   Nathaniel Hawthorne, The Scarlet Letter (1850; reprint, New York: W. W. Norton, 1988), 133.

13   Thomas Paine, "Reflections on Unhappy Marriage," Pennsylvania Magazine (June 1775); cited in Jay Fliegelman, Prodigals and Pilgrims: The American Revolution against Patriarchal Authority, 1750–1800 (New York: Cambridge University Press, 1982), 124.

14   Fliegelman, Prodigals and Pilgrims, 127. For a discussion of how structures of feeling such as compassion and identification linked the family to the nation, see Elizabeth Barnes, States of Sympathy (New York: Columbia University Press, 1997).

15   On sentimental ritual, see Karen Halttunen, Confidence Men and Painted Women: A Study of Middle-Class Culture in America, 1830–1870 (New Haven, Conn.: Yale University Press, 1982); and Mary Louise Kete, Sentimental Collaborations: Mourning and Middle-Class Identity in Nineteenth-Century America (Durham, N.C.: Duke University Press, 2000).

16   John Winthrop, "A Model of Christian Charity" (1630), in The Norton Anthology of American Literature, 3rd ed. (New York: W. W. Norton, 1989), 1:36.

17   See George Elliott Howard, The History of Matrimonial Institutions (Chicago: University of Chicago Press, 1979), 2:133.

18   See Ellen Rothman, Hands and Hearts: A History of Courtship in America (New York: Basic Books, 1984), especially 169.

19   Important studies linking Hawthorne to the production of "personal life" include Lauren Berlant, The Anatomy of National Fantasy: Hawthorne, Utopia, and Everyday Life (Chicago: University of Chicago Press, 1991); T. Walter Herbert, Dearly Beloved: The Hawthornes and the Making of the Middle-Class Family (Berkeley: University of California Press, 1993); and Joel Pfister, The Production of Personal Life: Class, Gender, and the Psychological in Hawthorne's Fiction (Stanford, Calif.: Stanford University Press, 1991).

20   See, for example, "The Shaker Bridal," "The Wedding-Knell," and The House of the Seven Gables.

21   Nathaniel Hawthorne, "The May-Pole of Merry Mount" (1837), in Hawthorne: Tales and Sketches, ed. Roy Harvey Pearce (New York: Library of America, 1982), 320. Subsequent text references are designated MPMM.

22   Johnson, A Society Ordained by God, 27; and Morgan, The Puritan Family, 144.

23   For a typical allegorical reading, see Sheldon Liebman, "Moral Choice in 'The Maypole of Merry Mount,'" Studies in Short Fiction 11 (1974): 173–80. Historical exegeses of "The May-Pole of Merry Mount" include Michael Colacurcio, The Province of Piety: Moral History in Hawthorne's Early Tales (Cambridge: Harvard University Press, 1984), 251–77; Richard Drinnon, "'The Maypole of Merry

Mount': Thomas Morton and the Puritan Patriarchs," *Massachusetts Review* 21 (1980): 382–410; John P. McWilliams Jr., "Fictions of Merry Mount," *American Quarterly* 29 (1977): 3–30; G. Harrison Orians, "Hawthorne and 'The Maypole of Merry Mount,'" *Modern Language Notes* 53, no. 3 (March 1938): 159–67; Etsuko Taketani, "Re-Narrativization of the Maypole Incident: Hawthorne and His New England Annalists," *Studies in English Literature* (Tokyo) 70, no. 2 (January 1994): 239–57; J. Golden Taylor, "'The Maypole of Merry Mount,'" in *Hawthorne's Ambivalence Toward Puritanism* (Logan: Utah State University Press, 1965), 25–33; J. Gary Williams, "History in Hawthorne's 'The Maypole of Merry Mount,'" *Essex Historical Collections* 108 (1972): 173–89; and Michael Zuckerman, "Pilgrims in the Wilderness: Community, Modernity, and the Maypole at Merry Mount," *New England Quarterly* 50 (1977): 255–77.

24 See Colacurcio, *The Province of Piety*, 251–77. The 1835 edition of "May-pole" accepted for publication in *The Token* for 1836 uses the name "Claxton"; Hawthorne appears to have changed the name to "Blackstone" when the tale was republished in *Twice-Told Tales* in 1837.

25 For the arguments outlined in the preceding two paragraphs, see Colacurcio, *The Province of Piety*, 251–77.

26 "Dr. James Savage is on record as having been unable to discover any marriage performed by a minister previous to 1686 except in Gorges's province" (*Proceedings of the Massachusetts Historical Society, 1858–1860*, 283; cited in Chilton L. Powell, "Marriage in Early New England," *New England Quarterly* 1 [1928]: 330). See also Frank Gaylord Cook, "The Marriage Celebration in the Colonies," *Atlantic Monthly* 61 (March 1888): 351.

27 See Johnson, *A Society Ordained by God*.

28 See Elizabeth Bowles Warbasse, *The Changing Legal Rights of Married Women, 1800–1861* (New York: Garland Publishers, 1987).

29 On the correspondence of Sophia and Nathaniel Hawthorne, see Herbert, *Dearly Beloved*. On radical reenvisionings of marriage during the Second Great Awakening, see Muncy, *Sex and Marriage*; Spurlock, *Free Love*; and Taylor, *Eve and the New Jerusalem*.

30 John E. Becker, "'The Maypole of Merry Mount,'" in *Hawthorne's Historical Allegory: An Examination of the American Conscience* (Port Washington, N.Y.: Kennikat Press, 1971), 25.

31 Cotton Mather, *Ratio Disciplinae Fratrum Nov-Anglorum* (1726; reprint, New York: Arno Press, 1972), 116.

32 Thomas Morton, *New English Canaan* (c. 1635), in *Publications of the Prince Society*, ed. Charles Francis Adams Jr. (New York: Burt Franklin, 1967), 14:330–31.

33 "An Admonition to Parliament" (1572), in *Puritan Manifestoes: A Study of the Origin of the Puritan Revolt*, ed. Walter Howard Frere and C. E. Douglas (London: Society for Promoting Christian Knowledge, 1907), 27.

34 Ibid., n. 4.

35 See Frederick Newberry, "Hawthorne's Knowledge of Blackstone: A Rebuttal," *The Nathaniel Hawthorne Review* 15 (fall 1989): 11–12; Orians, "Hawthorne and 'The Maypole of Merry Mount,'" 33; and Thomas Pribek, "Hawthorne's Blackstone," *American Notes and Queries* 24 (June 1986): 142–44.

36 See Stanley, *From Bondage to Contract*, 7; and Edmund Burke, "Speech Moving Resolutions for Conciliation with the Colonies," 22 March 1754, cited in Beverley Zweiben, *How Blackstone Lost the Colonies: English Law, Colonial Lawyers, and the American Revolution* (New York: Garland Publications, 1990), 2.

37 There are also more strictly literary-historical reasons for insisting that the Blackstone of Merry Mount is the Enlightenment lawyer and not the Anglican priest. A biography of Sir William Blackstone appears in the Valentine's Day entry of the 1824 edition of William Hone, *The Every-day Book, or Guide to the Year, Describing the Popular Amusements, Ceremonies, Manners, Customs, and Events, Incident to Three Hundred and Sixty-Five Days, in Past and Present Times* (1824; reprint, London: Hunt and Clarke, 1827). This book's hodgepodge of customs, literary and historiographical excerpts and analyses, and cultural frameworks may have informed "The Maypole of Merry Mount" as much as the text that the narrator actually cites in his pseudoscholarly preface, Joseph Strutt's *Book of English Sports and Pastime*. The Valentine's Day entry in *The Every-day Book* contains several images that resonate with those in "May-Pole": it juxtaposes a poem about Adam and Eve, whom Edith and Edgar clearly evoke, with a picture of a bear holding a heart in his mouth that recalls the dancing bear in "May-Pole." It refers to Bishop Valentine as "the only mitred priest upon the [Protestant] calendar" (Hone, *Every-day Book*, 219), which suspiciously prefigures the "canonically dressed" priest who so violates Endicott's sensibilities (MPMM, 362). Hawthorne critics disagree as to whether or not *The Every-day Book* influenced "The May-Pole of Merry Mount." While Daniel Hoffman insists that Hone was central to the tale's imagery and its metaphysical contest between "jollity and gloom," Neil Frank Doubleday refuses the connection, stating that Hawthorne did not check *The Every-day Book* out of the Salem Athanaeum library until September of 1835, too late for a tale published in *The Token* in 1836. See Daniel Hoffman, *Form and Fable in American Fiction* (New York: Oxford University Press, 1965), 134 n. 3; and Neal Frank Doubleday, *Hawthorne's Early Tales: A Critical Study* (Durham, N.C.: Duke University Press, 1972), 94 n. 16. Colacurcio, in *The Province of Piety*, calls the dispute irrelevant. For a list of Hawthorne's reading that includes the Hone books, see Marion L. Kesselring, *Hawthorne's Reading, 1828–1850* (New York: New York Public Library, 1949).

38 See Sara L. Zeigler, "Uniformity and Conformity: Regionalism and the Adjudication of Married Women's Property Act," *Polity* 28, no. 4 (summer 1996): 467–95.

39 William Blackstone, *Commentaries on the Laws of England* (1769; reprint, Chicago: University of Chicago Press, 1979), 1:421; and William Bradford, *Of Plimoth Plantation*, ed. Charles Deane (Boston: Massachusetts Historical Society, 1856), 101.

40 See Frederick G. Whelan, "Property as Artifice in Hume and Blackstone," in *Property*, ed. J. Roland Posnock and John W. Chapman (New York: New York University Press, 1980), 101–25. For a discussion of American revolutionaries' repudiation of the Blackstonian property doctrine as it pertained to the English colonies, see Zweiben, *How Blackstone Lost the Colonies*.

41 The clearest history of Morton's threats to the Massachusetts Bay Charter, from which this account is taken, can be found in Philip Ranlet, "The Lord of Misrule: Thomas Morton of Merry Mount," *New England Historical and Genealogical Register* 134 (1980): 282–90.

42 Ronald T. Takaki, *Iron Cages: Race and Culture in Nineteenth-Century America* (New York: Knopf, 1979), 99–100.

43 Richard Slotkin, *Regeneration through Violence: The Mythology of the American Frontier, 1600–1860* (Middletown, Conn.: Wesleyan University Press, 1983).

44 Michael Warner, "New English Sodom," *American Literature* 64, no. 1 (March 1992): 35.

45 Blackstone, *Commentaries*, 4:216.

46 Cited in Ed Cohen, "Legislating the Norm: From Sodomy to Gross Indecency," in *Displacing Homophobia: Gay Male Perspectives in Literature and Culture*, ed. Ronald R. Butters, John M. Clum, and Michael Moon (Durham, N.C.: Duke University Press, 1989), 173.

47 Ibid., 174.

48 See Jonathan Ned Katz, *The Gay/Lesbian Almanac: A New Documentary* (New York: Harper and Row, 1983), 88.

49 24 Henry VIII, c. 12, cited in Witte, *From Sacrament to Contract*, 139, 253 n. 8.

50 Cohen, "Legislating the Norm," 174.

51 This is clear in the use of *Bowers v. Hardwick* (1986), which upheld Georgia's anti-sodomy statutes, in arguments legitimating the Defense of Marriage Act (1996).

52 See Michael Grossberg, *Governing the Hearth: Law and the Family in Nineteenth-Century America* (Chapel Hill: University of North Carolina Press, 1985). On the Morrill Bill, see also David Bitten, *Historical Dictionary of Mormonism*, 2d ed. (Lanham, Md.: Scarecrow Press, 2000).

53 Mary Ryan, *Cradle of the Middle Class: The Family in Oneida County, New York, 1790–1865* (New York: Cambridge University Press, 1981).

54 Ryan uses this phrase and describes the period between 1825 and 1845. See *Cradle of the Middle Class*, chapter 3.

55 See Rothman, *Hands and Hearts*; and Ann Monsarrat, *And the Bride Wore . . . : The Story of the White Wedding* (New York: Dodd, Mead, and Company, 1973).

56 Nancy Bentley has persuasively argued that popular anti-Mormon novels of the late nineteenth century rhetorically resolved the contradiction of married women's subordinate status in a nation that was structured by both the social contract between free citizens and their government and a free market economy structured by the wage contract between employers and individuals free to sell their labor. By figuring polygamy as a form of slavery and Mormons as racially inferior, anti-Mormon novels promoted women's consent to heterosexual monogamy as the feminine form of Anglo-American freedom itself. See Nancy Bentley, "Marriage as Treason: Polygamy, Nation, and the Novel," in *The Futures of American Studies*, ed. Donald Pease and Robyn Wiegman (Durham, N.C.: Duke University Press, forthcoming September 2002). My thanks to her for permission to discuss this manuscript.

57 Nathaniel Hawthorne, *The Blithedale Romance* (1852; reprint, New York: Penguin, 1986), 24.

58 Ibid., 46–47.

59 Ibid., 53. For an analysis of the role of sexuality in utopian thought in the United States, see Lauren Berlant, "Fantasies of Utopia in 'The Blithedale Romance,'" *American Literary History* 1, vol. 1 (spring 1989): 30–62.

60 Joseph Kirkland, *Zury: The Meanest Man in Spring County* (1887; reprint, Urbana: University of Illinois Press, 1956). Subsequent text references are designated *z*.

61 Criticism of *Zury* includes John T. Flanagan's introduction to the 1956 reprint, v–xviii; John T. Flanagan, "Joseph Kirkland, Pioneer Realist," *American Literature* 11 (November 1939): 273–84; Clyde E. Henson, *Joseph Kirkland* (New York: Twayne Publishers, 1962); Kenneth J. LaBudde, "A Note on the Text of Joseph Kirkland's 'Zury,'" *American Literature* 20 (1949): 452–66; and Benjamin Lease, "Realism and Joseph Kirkland's 'Zury,'" *American Literature* 23 (1952): 464–66.

62 See Joseph Allen Boone, *Tradition Counter Tradition: Love and the Form of Fiction* (Chicago: University of Chicago Press, 1987); Habegger, *Gender, Fantasy, and Realism*; and Evelyn J. Hinz, "Hierogamy vs. Wedlock: Types of Marriage Plots and Their Relationship to Genres of Prose Fiction," *PMLA* 19 (1976): 900–913. For a discussion of the "marriage crisis" in realist novels, see Allen F. Stein, *After the Vows Were Spoken: Marriage in American Literary Realism* (Columbus: Ohio State University Press, 1984).

63 The contiguity between Fourierism and Mormonism in this passage illustrates the extent to which the Mormon crisis reshaped nineteenth-century views of earlier and concurrent socialist movements that included untraditional marriages. For an argument that nineteenth-century advocates of monogamy saw Mormon polygamy and Oneidian complex marriage in much the same light, see Carol Weisbrod and Pamela Sheingorn, "*Reynolds v. United States*: Nineteenth-Century Forms of Marriage and the Status of Women," in *The History of Women*

in the United States, Volume 3: Domestic Relations and Law, ed. Nancy Cott (New York: K. G. Saur, 1992), 345–75.

64 See John Hallwas, "Mormon Nauvoo from a Non-Mormon Perspective," in *Kingdom on the Mississippi Revisited: Nauvoo in Mormon History*, ed. Roger D. Launius and John E. Hallwas (Urbana: University of Illinois Press, 1996), 160–80.

65 William L. Snyder, *The Geography of Marriage, or, Legal Perplexities of Wedlock in the United States* (New York: G. P. Putnam's Sons, 1889), 137.

66 See Frank Gaylord Cook, "Reform in the Celebration of Marriage," *Atlantic Monthly* 61 (May 1888): 680–90.

67 This account of Mormon history is taken from Bitten, *Historical Dictionary of Mormonism* and Weisbrod and Sheingorn, *"Reynolds v. United States."*

68 Since they presume that all other men have been killed, Lot's daughters presumably see no other way to "preserve the seed" of their father.

69 See Robert Alter, "Sodom as Nexus: The Web of Design in Biblical Narrative," in *Reclaiming Sodom*, ed. Jonathan Goldberg (New York: Routledge, 1994), 28–42. I thank Molly McGarry for conversations about Lot and the cave.

70 See Ernest Cassara, *Universalism in America: A Documentary History* (Boston: Beacon Press, 1970).

71 Cited in "A Report of the Trial of Mrs. Anne Hutchinson before the Church in Boston," in *The Antinomian Controversy, 1636–1638: A Documentary History*, ed. David D. Hall (Durham, N.C.: Duke University Press, 1990), 372.

72 Ibid.

73 On the relationship between economic debt and the production of the social as such, see Friedrich Nietzsche, "On the Genealogy of Morals," in *On the Genealogy of Morals and Ecce Homo*, ed. Walter Kaufmann (New York: Vintage, 1989), 64–65. On the relationship between usury and sexual perversion, see Sander Gilman, *The Jew's Body* (New York: Routledge, 1991), 124. For analogies between polygamy and usury in seventeenth-century Catholic protests, see Benjamin N. Nelson, *The Idea of Usury: From Tribal Brotherhood to Universal Otherhood* (Princeton, N.J.: Princeton University Press, 1949), 104.

74 Nelson, *Idea of Usury*, xxiv and passim.

75 My thanks to Janet Jakobsen for help in untangling (or queering) the economics of Protestant marital doctrine.

76 See G. J. Barker-Benfield, *Horrors of the Half-Known Life: Male Attitudes toward Women and Sexuality in Nineteenth-Century America* (New York: Harper and Row, 1976), 221. Thanks to Molly McGarry and Christopher Looby for the reference.

77 For a discussion of midwestern agrarian money politics, see Henson, *Joseph Kirkland*. For explorations of the relationship between literary representation and the money form, see Walter Benn Michaels, *The Gold Standard and the Logic of Naturalism* (Berkeley: University of California Press, 1987); and John Vernon, *Money and Fiction: Literary Realism in the Nineteenth and Early Twentieth Centuries*

(Ithaca, N.Y.: Cornell University Press, 1984). The marriage plot of *Zury* complicates Michaels's statement that there was "nearly unanimous hostility to fiat
money" (*The Gold Standard,* 150).

CHAPTER FIVE *Honeymoon with a Stranger: Private Couplehood
and the Making of the National Subject*

1   Philip Larkin, "The North Ship" in *The North Ship* (London: Faber and Faber,
    1966), 46.
2   Some folklorists also link the modern honeymoon with Anglo-Saxon tribal prac-
    tices of marriage by abduction and English elopements to Gretna Green after the
    Hardwicke Act. See, for example, Ann Monsarrat, *And the Bride Wore . . . : The
    Story of the White Wedding* (New York: Dodd, Mead, and Company, 1973).
3   Ellen K. Rothman, *Hands and Hearts: A History of Courtship in America* (New
    York: Basic Books, 1984), 82.
4   On the history of the honeymoon in England, see John R. Gillis, *For Better, for
    Worse: British Marriages, 1600 to the Present* (New York: Oxford University Press,
    1985); and Monsarrat, *And the Bride Wore.* For histories emphasizing the United
    States, see Kris Bulcroft, Linda Smeins, and Richard Bulcroft, *Romancing the
    Honeymoon: Consummating Marriage in Modern Society* (New York: Sage Publica-
    tions, 1999); Karen Dubinsky, *The Second Greatest Disappointment: Honeymoon-
    ing and Tourism at Niagara Falls* (New Brunswick, N.J.: Rutgers University Press,
    1999); Patrick McGreevy, *Imagining Niagara: The Meaning and Making of Niagara
    Falls* (Amherst: University of Massachusetts Press, 1994); Elizabeth McKinsey,
    Niagara Falls: Icon of the American Sublime (New York: Cambridge University
    Press, 1985); and Rothman, *Hands and Hearts.* My thinking on honeymoons and
    travelogues was stimulated early on by Lisa Brawley, "From Niagara to Disney:
    American Travel as Family Practice" (paper presented at the Family Values con-
    ference, Chicago Humanities Center, University of Chicago, spring 1993).
5   See Dona Brown, *Inventing New England: Regional Tourism in the Nineteenth
    Century* (Washington, D.C.: Smithsonian Institution Press, 1995).
6   Helena Michie, "Looking at Victorian Honeymoons," *Common Knowledge* 6, no. 1
    (spring 1997): 130.
7   William Dean Howells, *Their Wedding Journey* (1871; reprint, Bloomington: Indi-
    ana University Press, 1968), 4.
8   Ibid., 179.
9   For Howells's description of *Their Wedding Journey,* see ibid., xxiii–xxxiii. On
    sentimental bonds, see Karen Sánchez-Eppler, *Touching Liberty: Abolition, Femi-
    nism, and the Politics of the Body* (Berkeley: University of California Press, 1993).
    On Howells's realism, see Amy Kaplan, *The Social Construction of American
    Realism* (Chicago: University of Chicago Press, 1988), 15–43.

10 Michie, "Looking at Victorian Honeymoons," 131.

11 See Bulcroft, Smeins, and Bulcroft, *Romancing the Honeymoon*, 24, 45.

12 See Susan Stewart, "Exogamous Relations: Travel Writing, the Incest Prohibition, and Hawthorne's 'Transformation,'" in *Culture/Contexture: Explorations in Anthropology and Literary Studies*, ed. E. Valentine Daniel and Jeffrey M. Peck (Berkeley: University of California Press, 1996), 132–55.

13 Howells, *Their Wedding Journey*, 59. The logic of fostering the couple's sexual intimacy through isolation from their larger, local affiliative network, on the one hand, and by contact with bodies and social systems coded as "primitive," on the other, culminated in the contemporary practice of honeymooning to locales such as Jamaica, Hawaii, and Puerto Rico. See Bulcroft, Smeins, and Bulcroft, *Romancing the Honeymoon*.

14 Nathaniel Hawthorne, "Little Annie's Ramble," in *Hawthorne: Tales and Sketches*, ed. Roy Harvey Pearce (New York: Library of America, 1982), 228–35. Subsequent text references are designated LAR.

15 Vladimir Nabokov, *Lolita* (1955; reprint, Middlesex, England: Harmondsworth, 1987). Subsequent text references are designated L. British spellings are retained.

16 Concerning Poe and Reid, see Elizabeth Hyde Reid, *Mayne Reid: A Memoir of His Life* (London: Ward and Downey, 1890); Joan Steele, *Captain Mayne Reid* (Boston: Twayne Publishers, 1978); and Joan Steele "The Image of America in the Novels of Mayne Reid" (Ph.D. diss., University of California at Los Angeles, 1970). For Mayne Reid's influence on Nabokov, see Brian Boyd, *Vladimir Nabokov: The Russian Years* (Princeton, N.J.: Princeton University Press, 1990); D. Barton Johnson, "Vladimir Nabokov and Captain Mayne Reid," *Cycnos* 10, no. 1 (January 1993): 99–106; and Vladimir Nabokov, *Speak, Memory: An Autobiography Revisited* (1947; reprint, New York: Vintage, 1989).

17 I use the terms "pedophilia" and "erotic child-loving" fairly interchangeably here. The term "pedophilia" has medical connotations that seem inappropriate to texts written before the late nineteenth century's "proliferation of perversions," yet it is less cumbersome than the phrase "erotic child-loving." The latter is less stigmatizing and historically broader, yet evacuates the sense of damage that pervades both "Little Annie's Ramble" and *Lolita*. I have chosen to use them interchangeably because I am less interested in the moral economy of erotic acts between adults and children here than their representational economies. On pedophilia, see *Semiotext(e) Special Large Type Edition: Loving Boys* (New York: Semiotexte, 1980); and James R. Kincaid, *Child-Loving: The Erotic Child and Victorian Culture* (New York: Routledge, 1992).

18 See Annette Kolodny, *The Lay of the Land: Metaphor as Experience and History in American Life and Letters* (Chapel Hill: University of North Carolina Press, 1975). For a related argument that focuses on the portrayal of women rather than on woman as a symbolic figure, see Carol Wershoven, "America's Child Brides: The

Price of a Bad Bargain," in *Portraits of Marriage in Literature*, ed. Anne C. Hargrove and Maurine Magliocco (Macomb: Western Illinois University Press, 1984), 151–57.

19 See Jacqueline Rose, *The Case of Peter Pan, or, the Impossibility of Children's Fiction* (London: Macmillan, 1984).

20 Barbara Babcock argues that "one of the major differences between the picaro and the hero, which is central to the former's maintenance of marginality, is his refusal or inability to reintegrate himself socially through marriage" ("Liberty's a Whore: Inversions, Marginalia, and Picaresque Narrative," in *The Reversible World: Symbolic Inversion in Art and Society*, ed. Barbara Babcock [Ithaca, N.Y.: Cornell University Press, 1978], 105.) On the erotic, racial, and gender politics of the captivity narrative, see Christopher Castiglia, *Bound and Determined: Captivity, Culture-Crossing, and White Womanhood from Mary Rowlandson to Patty Hearst* (Chicago: University of Chicago Press, 1996). On same-sex, cross-racial desire as central to U.S. literature, see Leslie Fiedler, *Love and Death in the American Novel* (New York: Criterion Books, 1960).

21 Nathaniel Hawthorne, "My Visit to Niagara" (1835), in *Hawthorne: Tales and Sketches*, ed. Roy Harvey Pearce (New York: Library of America, 1982), 244–50.

22 Nathaniel Hawthorne, "Sketches from Memory" (1835), in *Hawthorne: Tales and Sketches*, ed. Roy Harvey Pearce (New York: Library of America, 1982), 341.

23 Oscar Wilde, "Personal Impressions of America," lecture, 10 July 1883. Cited in Alvin Redman, ed., *The Wit and Wisdom of Oscar Wilde* (New York: Dover, 1959), 127.

24 Hawthorne, "My Visit to Niagara," 247.

25 See Mary M. Van Tassel, "Hawthorne, His Narrator, and His Readers in 'Little Annie's Ramble,'" *ESQ (English Studies Quarterly)* 33, no. 3 (1987): 172.

26 Samuel G. Goodrich [Nathaniel Hawthorne], *Peter Parley's Universal History on the Basis of Geography* (New York: Newman and Ivison, 1853). On Goodrich's denunciations of European fairy tales, see Gillian Avery, *Behold the Child: American Children and Their Books, 1621–1922* (Baltimore, Md.: Johns Hopkins University Press, 1994), 68. On the British conflicts over children's literature from which Goodrich drew his arguments, see the essays in James Holt McGavran Jr., ed., *Romanticism and Children's Literature in Nineteenth-Century England* (Athens: University of Georgia Press, 1991).

27 The phrase is Mary M. Van Tassel's; she reads the tale as an expression of Hawthorne's allegiance to juvenile literature—a reading that depends on overlooking the tale's more grotesque moments. For a similarly romantic interpretation of the tale, see Carol Billman, "Nathaniel Hawthorne: 'Revolutionizer' of Children's Literature," *Studies in American Fiction* 10 (spring 1982): 107–14. On Hawthorne as a juvenile writer, see Laura Laffrado, *Hawthorne's Literature for Children* (Athens: University of Georgia Press, 1992). For a more cynical vision of

Hawthorne's children's tales, see Lesley Ginsberg, " 'The Willing Captive': Narrative Seduction and the Ideology of Love in Hawthorne's 'A Wonder Book for Girls and Boys,' " *American Literature* 65, no. 2 (June 1993): 255–73.

28 The phrase "confusion of tongues," with all its connotations of flesh, languages, and the intermingling of the two, is Sandor Ferenczi's. See Sandor Ferenczi, "Confusion of Tongues between Adults and the Child" (1932), in *The Assault on Truth: Freud's Suppression of the Seduction Theory*, ed. Jeffrey Masson (New York: Farrar, Straus, and Giroux, 1984), 283–95.

29 Paula Marantz Cohen, *The Daughter's Dilemma: Family Process and the Nineteenth-Century Domestic Novel* (Ann Arbor: University of Michigan Press, 1993).

30 Karen Sánchez-Eppler, "Temperance in the Bed of a Child: Incest and Social Order in Nineteenth-Century America," *American Quarterly* 47 (March 1995): 1–33.

31 Edgar Allan Poe, "Annabel Lee" (1849), in *The Works of Edgar Allan Poe*, ed. Edmund Clarence Stedman and George Edward Woodberry (Chicago: Stone and Kimball, 1894–95), 10:41–42.

32 Edgar Allan Poe, "Three Sundays in a Week" (1841), in *The Works of Edgar Allan Poe*, ed. Edmund Clarence Stedman and George Edward Woodberry (Chicago: Stone and Kimball, 1894–95), 4:115–23. Subsequent text references are designated TSW.

33 On the standardization of U.S. time zones, see Alan Trachtenberg, *The Incorporation of America: Culture and Society in the Gilded Age* (New York: Hill and Wang, 1982), 60. On new technologies of travel along with the reorganization of time and space, see Wolfgang Schivelbusch, *The Railway Journey: The Industrialization of Time and Space in the Nineteenth Century* (Berkeley: University of California Press, 1987). On the application of temporal distance and proximity to human relationships, see Johannes Fabian, *Time and the Other: How Anthropology Makes Its Object* (New York: Columbia University Press, 1983).

34 See Gerald Dorset, "The Wonderful World of Captain Mayne Reid," *Journal of Irish Literature* 15, no. 1 (January 1986): 43–49. Dorset describes the huge popularity of Reid's work in czarist Russia and the international transformation of his novels from adult to juvenile literature. On dime novels, see Michael Denning, *Mechanic Accents: Dime Novels and Working-Class Culture in America* (New York: Verso, 1987).

35 Nabokov, *Speak, Memory*, 202.

36 For a discussion of how the Wild West show functioned as an exported advertisement for imperialist project of the United States, see Richard Slotkin, "Buffalo Bill's Wild West and the Mythologization of the American Empire," in *Cultures of United States Imperialism*, ed. Amy Kaplan and Donald Pease (Durham, N.C.: Duke University Press, 1993), 164–81. For an exploration of homosocial relations and the imagery of the U.S. West, see David Savran, *Communists, Cowboys,*

and Queers: The Politics of Masculinity in the Work of Arthur Miller and Tennessee Williams (Minneapolis: University of Minnesota Press, 1992).

37 A possibly apocryphal tale recounted in Steele, Captain Mayne Reid, 24.

38 Speech to the army and navy at American Thanksgiving Day in London, 1863, cite in ibid., 30.

39 Mayne Reid, The Child Wife: A Tale of the Two Worlds (1868; reprint, New York: Sheldon and Company, 1869), 218. Subsequent text references are designated CW.

40 Mayne Reid, The Headless Horseman: A Strange Tale of Texas (1865; reprint, London: R. Bentley, 1866). Subsequent text references are designated HH.

41 William Q. Boelhower, Through a Glass Darkly: Ethnic Semiosis in American Literature (New York: Oxford University Press, 1987), 50–51.

42 Myra Jehlen, American Incarnation: The Individual, the Nation, and the Continent (Cambridge: Harvard University Press, 1986), title and 1–21.

43 Kolodny, The Lay of the Land.

44 Mayne Reid, The Scalp-hunters or, Romantic Adventures in Northern Mexico (1851; reprint, as The Scalp-hunters: A Romance of the Plains, New York: Beadle and Adams, 1868), 56. Subsequent text references are designated SH.

45 I use "Hispanicize" rather than "Latinize" to emphasize the connection with Spain.

46 As Noel Ignatiev argues, Irish immigrants had to fight hard to be accepted as white people, and thereby eligible for naturalization, in the United States. Yet in Ignatiev's analysis, this battle was mainly fought in East Coast cities in relation to African Americans. A fuller history of the Southwest, relating the enfranchisement of Irish and other European immigrants to the disenfranchisement of Native Americans and descendants of Spanish conquerors, is outside the scope of this project. See Noel Ignatiev, How the Irish Became White (New York: Routledge, 1995).

47 Werner Sollors, Beyond Ethnicity (New York: Oxford University Press, 1986), 129.

48 This analysis has a certain debt to the film Chickenhawk: Men Who Love Boys (dir. Ari Seidman, 1994), whose creepiness derives from the pedophile's insistence that the child is reading sexual meaning into innocuous situations and initiating flirtatious contact. Dean MacCannell writes that tourism promotes the landscape as "a magical resource that can be used without actually possessing or diminishing it" (Empty Meeting Grounds: The Tourist Papers [New York: Routledge, 1992], 28).

49 See E. Reid, Mayne Reid, 208.

50 Frances Bartkowski, Travelers, Immigrants, Inmates: Essays in Estrangement (Minneapolis: University of Minnesota Press, 1995), 26–27. Homi K. Bhabha prefigures this analysis in his statement that "the scraps, patches, and rags of daily life must be repeatedly turned into the signs of a national culture" ("DissemiNa-

tion: Time, Narrative, and the Margins of the Modern Nation," in *Nation and Narration*, ed. Homi K. Bhabha [New York: Routledge, 1990], 297).

51 Vladimir Nabokov, *The Enchanter*, trans. Dmitri Nabokov (New York: Vintage, 1986).

52 Ibid., 54.

53 Ibid., 36.

54 My *New York Daily News* clippings file, from which the summary of the story is written, includes the following: Patricia Mangan and Virginia Breen, "Teacher, Student Flee over Forbidden Love" and "Straight Arrow Who Flew Astray," 11 May 1995, 3; Linda Yglesias and Virginia Breen, "Detectives Almost Got 'Em in Ala.," 11 May 1995, 3; Doreen C. Bowens et al., "Mom Begs Girl: 'Miss You,' She Cries," 12 May 1995, 5; Linda Yglesias, "Mississippi Lawyer: Teach Hunted for Marital Haven," 12 May 1995, 5; Corky Siemaszko, "Marrying Age Depends on What State You're In," 12 May 1995, 26; Patrice O'Shaughnessey, "Classanova Hunt in Nev.," 14 May 1995, 7; Corky Siemaszko, "Lovebird is Set to Land," 16 May 1995, 2; Juan Gonzales, "Classanova Sez He Did It for Her," 17 May 1995, 2–3; Patricia Mangan et al., "Gives Up, is Held on Kidnap Rap," 17 May 1995, 3; Mike McClary, "Girl Forgotten in Heat of Hunt," 17 May 1995, 3; Juan Gonzales, "Girl Lost in Adults' Madness," 18 May 1995, 2; Virginia Breen et al., "It's Splitsville: Teach to Jail, Teen to Godmom," 18 May 1995, 3; Mark Mooney, "Unromantic Night in Jail," 18 May 1995, 32; Virginia Breen et al., "Gym Teach out on Bail: Says He was Right to Escape with Teen to End Family Abuse," 19 May 1995, 7; Virginia Breen et al., "Classanova's Lesson," 23 May 1995, 3; Michael Daly, "Christina's Story: Why She Took Love Trek," 24 May 1995, 3; Juan Gonzales, "Scandal Teacher Tells His Side," 26 May 1995, 22; Virginia Breen and Jane Furse, "Classanova's Deal: Wins Girl, Loses Job," 26 July 1995, 5; Sandra Ormsbee et al., "Teacher's Still Her Pet," 27 July 1995, 3; and Linda Stasi, "DA's Slap on the Wrists for Classanova a Crime," 4 August 1995, 22.

55 Cited in Daly, "Christina's Story."

56 See Ian Hacking, "The Making and Molding of Child Abuse," *Critical Inquiry* 17 (winter 1991): 253–88; and James R. Kincaid, *Erotic Innocence: The Culture of Child Molesting* (Durham, N.C.: Duke University Press, 1998).

57 Thanks to Phillip Brian Harper for helping tease out the relationship between the two maps.

58 Cited in Ormsbee et al., "Teacher's Still Her Pet."

CHAPTER SIX *The Immediate Country, or, Heterosexuality in the Age of Mechanical Reproduction*

1 Michael Rossman, *The Wedding within the War* (Garden City, N.Y.: Doubleday, 1971), 385.

2 Shawn Smith, *American Archives* (Princeton, N.J.: Princeton University Press, 1999), esp. chaps. 1 and 2. On the relationship between the aura of heterosexuality and the still photograph, see Nita Rollins, "Something Borrowed, Something Taped: Video Nuptials," *Wide Angle* 13 (April 1991): 32–38. On the history of wedding photography, see Barbara Norfleet, *Wedding* (New York: Simon and Schuster, 1979).

3 See Hortense Spillers, "Mama's Baby, Papa's Maybe: An American Grammar Book," *diacritics* (summer 1987): 65–81. For an example of people with AIDS represented as lacking a kinship structure, see Nicholas Nixon and Bebe Nixon, *People with AIDS* (Boston: David Godine, 1991).

4 See Smith, *American Archives*, esp. chaps. 3 and 4.

5 Benedict Anderson, *Imagined Communities: Reflections on the Origin and Spread of Nationalism* (London: Verso, 1983), 140.

6 Anne McClintock has provided the key intervention into Anderson's linguistic model of nation formation. See her *Imperial Leather: Race, Gender, and Sexuality in the Colonial Contest* (New York: Routledge, 1995).

7 See Walter Benjamin, "A Short History of Photography," trans. Stanley Mitchell (1931; reprint, *Screen* 13 [spring 1972]: 5–26).

8 On the construction of dominant identities through the visual rhetoric of family photography, and the possible counternarratives invoked by the practices of reading photographs, see Marianne Hirsch, *Family Frames: Photography, Narrative, and Postmemory* (Cambridge: Harvard University Press, 1997).

9 The phrase "race into culture" is from Walter Benn Michaels, "Race into Culture: A Critical Genealogy of Cultural Identity," *Critical Inquiry* 18 (summer 1992): 655–85. Michaels argues that "culture" never moves beyond race, or completely turns biological "being" into social "doing," because one has to "be" a particular kind of subject in order to count as "doing" the things proper to one's culture—a position with which I tend to agree. My interest, though, is in the intersection between the visual technologies that have regulated the representation of "family" and the way that "family" contributes to what he calls "the rescue of race by culture" (658).

10 See Werner Sollors, *Beyond Ethnicity* (New York: Oxford University Press, 1986).

11 On the construction of national collectivity according to the logic of abstract citizenship, see Michael Warner, *The Letters of the Republic* (Cambridge: Harvard University Press, 1990). On the interventions of sentimental culture into that logic, see Lauren Berlant, "The Female Woman: Fanny Fern and the Form of Sentiment," *American Literary History* 3, no. 3 (fall 1991): 429–54.

12 William Q. Boelhower, *Through a Glass Darkly: Ethnic Semiosis in American Literature* (New York: Oxford University Press, 1987), 41 and passim. For another examination of how the fragments of mass culture coalesce into gestalts for group identity, see also Arjun Appadurai, "Disjuncture and Difference in the

Global Cultural Economy," in *The Phantom Public Sphere*, ed. Bruce Robbins (Minneapolis: University of Minnesota Press, 1993), 269–93.

13 Parley Ann Boswell, "The Pleasure of Our Company: Hollywood Throws a Wedding Bash," in *Beyond the Stars II: Plot Conventions in American Popular Film*, ed. Paul Loukides and Linda K. Fuller (Bowling Green, Ohio: Bowling Green State University Popular Press, 1991), 7.

14 See Angelika Bammer, introduction to *Displacements: Cultural Identities in Question*, ed. Angelika Bammer (Bloomington: Indiana University Press, 1994), xi.

15 See Werner Sollors, "Ethnicity," in *Critical Terms for Literary Study*, ed. Frank Letricchia and Thomas McLaughlin, 2d ed. (Chicago: University of Chicago Press, 1995), 289. See also Raymond Williams, "Ethnic," in *Keywords* (New York: Oxford University Press, 1983), 119–20.

16 See Warren Susman, "The Culture of the Thirties" in *Culture as History: The Transformation of American Society in the Twentieth Century* (New York: Pantheon, 1973), 150–83. Another excellent description of the transition from biological theories of race to "colorblind" theories of culture, is Peggy Pascoe, "Miscegenation Law, Court Cases, and Ideologies of 'Race' in Twentieth-Century America," *Journal of American History* 83 (June 1996): 44–69.

17 See Susan Davis, *Parades and Power: Street Theatre in Nineteenth-Century Philadelphia* (Philadelphia, Pa.: Temple University Press, 1985); and Kathleen Neils Conzen, "Ethnicity as Festive Culture: Nineteenth-Century German America on Parade," in *The Invention of Ethnicity*, ed. Werner Sollors (New York: Oxford University Press, 1989), 44–75.

18 On traditional folklorists' methodologies and assumptions, see Barbara Kirshenblatt-Gimblett, "Objects of Ethnography," in *Exhibiting Cultures: The Poetics and Politics of Museum Display*, ed. Ivan Karp and Steven D. Lavine (Washington, D.C.: Smithsonian Institution Press, 1991), 386–434.

19 In the 1991 remake, the character of the wedding director was cast as openly gay.

20 Boelhower, *Through a Glass Darkly*, 99.

21 In some ways, this return to the relationship between parents and children as a metaphor for, and defense against, shifts in cultural authority marks a return to a colonial model. See Jay Fliegelman, *Prodigals and Pilgrims: The American Revolution against Patriarchal Authority, 1750–1800* (New York: Cambridge University Press, 1982); and Sollors, *Beyond Ethnicity*.

22 Paul Simon and Art Garfunkel, "Mrs. Robinson," *Original Soundtrack Album to "The Graduate,"* Columbia LP OS 3180; CD CK 3180 (US:#1), track 13. The fact that Eleanor Roosevelt had female lovers makes the relationship between *The Graduate*'s love plot and U.S. nationality even more complicated in ways that go beyond the scope of this inquiry. Does the sarcastic entreaty to "Mrs. Robinson," thought in terms of "Mrs. Roosevelt," suggest an explicitly homophobic retreat from the socialized vision of the Roosevelt economy?

23 Details of Luci Baines Johnson's wedding are taken from the following bibliography: Hugh Sidey, "Great Society All Wound up in a Wedding," *Life*, 5 August 1966, 34B; "It's Wedding Week at the White House," *U.S. News and World Report*, 8 August 1966, 36–37; Cissy Morrisey, "Luci Gets Ready for a Family Affair," *Life*, 15 July 1966, 76–78; Mary Simmons and Marilyn Kayto, "Luci's White House Wedding," *Look*, August 1966, 34–39; "Romance and Courtship in the White House," *Saturday Evening Post*, spring 1972, 50–53; "The Splendor of Luci's Wedding," *Life*, 19 August 1966, 20– 27; "An Unusual Ceremony," *Time*, 12 August 1966, 9–11; "The Wedding in Washington," *Newsweek*, 15 August 1966, 17–21; and "When a President's Daughter Marries," *U.S. News and World Report*, 1 August 1966, 10. Details of Lynda Bird Johnson's wedding come from the following: "How Big a White House Wedding for Lynda?" *U.S. News and World Report*, 25 September 1967, 30; "When There's a White House Wedding . . . ," *U.S. News and World Report*, 18 December 1967, 16; and "White House Wedding," *Newsweek*, 18 December 1967, 28–32. The Tricia Nixon wedding bibliography is huge. It includes: "Behind the Main Event," *Life*, 18 June 1971, 40–49; Anne Coffin, "Father and the Bride," *Look*, 15 June 1971, 74–79; "A June Wedding in the White House," *Time*, 29 March 1971, 11– 12; "Mr. Cox Takes a June Bride," *Time*, 21 June 1971, 16; Marcia Seligson, "Tricia Got Her Rose Garden," *Life*, 25 June 1971, 32–35; "A Simple Spectacular at the White House," *Time*, 14 June 1971, 13–17; "The Wedding in the Garden," *Newsweek*, 21 June 1971, 20–21; "When Tricia Nixon Marries," *U.S. News and World Report*, 14 June 1971, 54; "White House Wedding," *Newsweek*, 14 June 1971, 30–34; and the NBC News special report, "The Rose Garden Wedding," 12 June 1971, narrated by Barbara Walters and Edwin Newman.

24 "A Simple Spectacular," *Time*, 15.

25 "White House Wedding," *Newsweek*, 30.

26 Tricia Nixon cited in ibid.; and Richard Nixon cited in Gil Troy, *Affairs of State: The Rise and Rejection of the Presidential Couple since World War II* (New York: Free Press, 1997), 193 (emphasis in original title).

27 For rich descriptions of nineteenth- and early-twentieth-century White House weddings, see Wilbur Cross and Ann Novotny, *White House Weddings* (New York: David McKay, 1967); and Marcia Seligson, "The American Spectacle: Hollywood and the White House," in *The Eternal Bliss Machine: America's Way of Wedding* (New York: Morrow, 1973), 163–80. For general examinations of the meaning and function of the presidential family, see Myra G. Gutin, *The President's Partner: The First Lady in the Twentieth Century* (New York: Greenwood Press, 1989); Sandra L. Quinn-Musgrove, *America's Royalty: All the President's Children* (Westport, Conn.: Greenwood Press, 1995); and Troy, *Affairs of State*.

28 Cited in Troy, *Affairs of State*, 193.

29 Cited in ibid., 158.

30 Cited in "A Simple Spectacular," *Time*, 17.

31 Cited in Troy, *Affairs of State*, 158.

32 Cited in "Romance and Courtship in the White House," 52.

33 "When There's a White House Wedding," *U.S. News and World Report*.

34 See, for instance, "The World of Jacqueline Kennedy" (written by Joseph Liss, dir. Eugene S. Jones, 1961).

35 See Troy, *Affairs of State*, 193–94.

36 See Daniel Dayan and Elihu Katz, "Electronic Ceremonies: Television Performs a Royal Wedding," in *On Signs*, ed. Marshall Blonsky (Baltimore, Md.: Johns Hopkins University Press, 1985), 16–32. I thank Scott Mendel for calling this article to my attention.

37 Cited in "White House Wedding," *Newsweek*, 31.

38 On-line fans continue to dispute whether more people tuned into the royal wedding or the nuptials between the fictional characters Luke Spencer and Laura Baldwin on the U.S. soap opera *General Hospital* in November of the same year.

39 On televisual wedding reception, see James M. Moran, "Wedding Video and Its Generation," in *Resolutions: Contemporary Video Practice*, ed. Michael Renov and Erica Suderburg (Minneapolis: University of Minnesota Press, 1996), 360–81. On labor protests during the royal wedding, see "Conditions Force People to Riot, Councilor Says," *London Times*, 29 July 1981, news sec., 28; "Labour Chooses Today to Start Campaign for Poor," *London Times*, 29 July 1981, news sec., 4; "Protest Fast over Pomp," *London Times*, 29 July 1981, news sec., 2; "Riots Flare in Toxteth," *London Times*, 29 July 1981, news sec., 1; and Donald Macintyre "Wedding Day Protest by Union at BL," *London Times*, 29 July 1981, news sec., 1. On the media portrayal of the courtship, see Anthony Holden, *A Princely Marriage* (London: Bantam, 1991).

40 Cited on CBS News special report, "The Royal Wedding," 29 July 1981. Subsequent text references are designated RW.

41 Lauren Berlant, *The Queen of America Goes to Washington City* (Durham, N.C.: Duke University Press, 1997).

42 For a description of the constitution of a mass public through identification with trauma, see Michael Warner, "The Mass Public and the Mass Subject," in *Habermas and the Public Sphere*, ed. Craig Calhoun (Cambridge: MIT Press, 1992), 377–401.

43 Sollors, *Beyond Ethnicity*, 227.

44 Details of *Tony 'n' Tina's Wedding* are taken from the performance I attended on 10 February 1994: *Tony 'n' Tina's Wedding*, produced by Joseph Corcoran, directed by Larry Pellegrini, at the Piper's Alley Theater, Chicago, Illinois. They also come from the following bibliography: Janice Arkatov, "Coping with 200 'Guests' a Night," *Los Angeles Times*, 25 March 1990, calendar sec., 49; Joseph N. Bell, "New Year's Calls for a Compulsory Good Time, No Matter How Tedious,"

Los Angeles Times, 30 December 1989, sec. N, 6; Louisa Benton, "A Marriage Off Broadway Takes the Cake," *New York Times*, 15 July 1990, late ed., sec. 2, 5; Thomas M. Disch, review of *Tony 'n' Tina's Wedding*, *Nation* 246, 5 March 1988, 317–18; Ellen Futterman, "The Honna of Your Presence is Requested," *Saint Louis Post-Dispatch*, 1 February 1996, get out sec., 23; Cheryl Johnson, "Nervous Suitor Receives Behind-the-Scenes Help," *Star-Tribune*, metro ed., 1 February 1996, news sec., 4B; Bruce McCabe, " 'Italian Weddings' Are Playing All over Town—With No Love Lost between Them," *Boston Globe*, 16 February 1996, living sec., 51; Julie Newmark, " 'Tony 'n' Tina': Campy Nuptials," *Saint Louis Post-Dispatch*, 5 February 1996, news sec., 2A; and Sid Smith, "With a Twist, 'Tony 'n' Tony' Recasts 'Tony 'n' Tina' as a Gay Wedding, with the Same Hilarity," *Chicago Tribune*, 10 April 1996, tempo sec., 2.

45 On the invention of the signs of national being such as "Italianicity," see Roland Barthes, *Mythologies*, trans. Annette Lavers (1957; reprint New York: Noonday Press, 1992).

46 See, for instance, Pauline Greenhill, "Folk Drama in Anglo Canada and the Mock Wedding: Transaction, Performance, and Meaning," *Canadian Drama* 14, no. 2 (1988): 169–205; and Jane Xenia Harris Woodside, "The Womanless Wedding: An American Folk Drama" (master's thesis, University of North Carolina, 1987).

47 This description comes from a survey of the following mock weddings: Esther C. Averill, *Henpeck at the Hitching Post* (Franklin, Ohio: Eldridge Entertainment, 1929); Mary Bonham, *The Kink in Kizzie's Wedding: A Mock Negro Wedding* (Dayton, Ohio: Payne Publishing Company, 1921); Ellen M. Gall, *My Wild Days Are Over: A Musical Mock Wedding in One Act* (San Francisco, Calif.: Banner Play Bureau, 1931); Marie Irish and Arthur Landis, *This Way to Matrimony: A Collection of Mock Weddings* (Syracuse, N.Y.: Willis N. Bugbee, 1934); Arthur LeRoy Kaser, *The Chocolate Cream Wedding: A Colored Mock Wedding* (Chicago: Dramatic Publishing Company, 1930); Arthur LeRoy Kaser, *For Men Only: A Mock Wedding Entertainment* (Chicago: T. S. Denison Company, 1949); Arthur LeRoy Kaser, *The Hitching Post: A Burlesque Mock Wedding* (Boston: Walter H. Baker Company, 1929); Arthur LeRoy Kaser, *Oh Promise Me! A Mock Wedding* (Chicago: Dramatic Publishing Company, 1930); Harriet Love, *The Coontown Wedding: A Mock Marriage in Blackface* (Boston: Walter H. Baker Company, 1925); Esther Phelps-Jones, *Mock Marriage in Rhyme* (New York: Fitzgerald Publishing Corporation, 1931); and Laura Kirkwood Plumb, *Down the Bridal Path: A Mock Wedding* (Boston: W. H. Baker Company, 1935). I thank Rosemary Cullen at the Harris Collection, Brown University, for helping me access this archive.

48 "So This is Marriage," in Irish and Landis, *This Way to Matrimony*, 18–19.

49 Cited in McCabe, "Italian Weddings."

50 Ibid.

51 Disch, review of *Tony 'n' Tina's Wedding*, 18.

52 Berlant, *The Queen of America*, 195.

53 Thomas J. Ferraro, "Blood in the Marketplace: The Business of Family in the 'Godfather' Narratives," in *The Invention of Ethnicity*, ed. Werner Sollors (New York: Oxford University Press, 1989), 176–207.

54 Bell, "New Year's Call for a Compulsory Good Time," 6.

55 Cited in Arkatov, "Coping with 200 'Guests,'" 49.

56 *Tony 'n' Tina's Wedding* (New York: Samuel French, 1994), 136; conceived by Nancy Cassaro, and created by Thomas Michael Allen, James Altuner, Mark Campbell, Nancy Cassaro, Patricia Cregan, Elizabeth Dennehy, Christopher Fracchiolla, Jack Fris, Kevin A. Leonidas, Mark Nassar, Larry Pellegrini, Susan Varon, and Moira Wilson. Originally produced by Joseph Corcoran and Daniel Corcoran in association with Artificial Intelligence. Subsequent text references are designated *TTWP*.

57 On the Gesamtkunstwerk, see Siegfried Kracauer, "Cult of Distraction: On Berlin's Picture Palaces," *New German Critique* 40 (winter 1987): 91–96. On the Aristotelianism of wedding videos, see Rollins, "Something Borrowed."

58 Moran, "Wedding Video," 371.

59 For an elegant analysis of the relationship between the concealment of directorial "cuts," the anal opening, and the homosexually panicked plotline of Alfred Hitchcock's *Rope*, see D. A. Miller, "Anal 'Rope,'" in *Inside/Out*, ed. Diana Fuss (New York: Routledge, 1991), 119–41.

CODA

1 "Forever and Always, Part I; Publishing the Banns: Challenging Same-Sex Marriage Laws," *CBC National Online News* (http://cbc.ca/national/news/gay/index.html), accessed 6 June 2001. A brief biographical note on Reverend Hawkes: In addition to having been Senior Pastor at the MCCT, he is a longtime activist for lesbian and gay rights, locally and nationally; his work has included AIDS and community care, membership in several rights groups, and outreach to Toronto police. See "Our Hero: Reverend Brent Hawkes," CANgay.com (http://www.cangay.com/people/hero/hawkes.htm), accessed 31 July 2001.

2 "Rev. Brent Hawkes, Paving the Way for Gay Marriage," Radio CBC, Toronto, 16 January 2001; producer Sian Jones, host Shelagh Rogers. See also "Forever and Always, Part I; Publishing the Banns: The Opposition," *CBC National Online News* (http://cbc.ca/national/news/gay/buckingham.html), accessed 6 June 2001; "Forever and Always, Part II; Publishing the Banns: The First Sunday," *CBC National Online News* (http://cbc.ca/national/news/gay/dec10.html), accessed 6 June 2001; "Gay and Lesbian Couples Wed in Double Ceremony," *CBC National Online News*, 15 January 2001 (http://cbc.ca/cgi-bin/templates/view.

cgi/news/2001/01/14/gay_marriage010114), accessed 6 June 2001; and Jean [pseud.], "Two Men Who Were Married," CANgay.com (http://www.cangay.com/ relation/partner/joe_kevin.htm), accessed 13 June 2001.

3   Cited in Jean [pseud.], "Interview with Reverend Brent Hawkes," CANgay.com (http://www.cangay.com/people/hero/brent_interv.htm), accessed 13 June 2001.

4   The Catholic Church first enforced the reading of the banns in France in its capitulary of 802, and the Fourth Lateral Council of 1215 enforced them for the rest of Europe (see George Elliott Howard, *The History of Matrimonial Institutions* [Chicago: University of Chicago Press, 1904], 2:258).

5   See Jean, "Interview."

6   Indeed, when the state "tolerates" a practice or belief, it explicitly trumps the power of that practice or belief to define relations of property, reproduction, or personhood (think, for instance, of freedom of expression or association, which allows speaking or gathering to take place, but does not automatically recognize the forms of being or belonging that result from these activities as ongoing rights-bearing entities). On *Reynolds*, see Carol Weisbrod and Pamela Sheingorn, "*Reynolds v. United States*: Nineteenth-Century Forms of Marriage and the Status of Women," in *The History of Women in the United States, Volume 3: Domestic Relations and the Law*, ed. Nancy Cott (New York: K. G. Saur, 1992).

7   On the preamble and MCCT lawyers' response to it, see "Gay and Lesbian Couples Wed in Double Ceremony."

8   Lisa Duggan, "Queering the State," *Social Text* 39 (summer 1994): 10.

9   See "Rev. Brent Hawkes, Paving the Way."

10 See Jean, "Two Men Who Were Married."

11 It is fair to say that Hawkes's intervention would not have worked without the rules of betrothal generated within small, face-to-face communities; thus, in some ways, it partakes in recent queer theorists' critiques of the urban bias in gay history (see, for example, John Howard, ed., *Carryin' On in the Lesbian and Gay South* [New York: New York University Press, 1997]). But the reading of the banns also might not have been effective without the prior presence of an extra-familial constituency whose ties with one another were as equally forged and mediated by wage work, the spaces of the modern city, and leisure activities as by religious practices or beliefs; the MCCT's status as a gay-friendly institution depended on Canadian gay migration patterns from rural areas to Toronto that are similar to those of San Francisco and New York.

12 Cited in Jean, "Two Men Who Were Married."

13 Ibid.

14 Cited in "Forever and Always, Part 1; Publishing the Banns: The Opposition."

15 Nancy Fraser, "Rethinking Recognition," *New Left Review* 3 (May 2000): 114. For an earlier argument about the distinction between redistribution and recogni-

tion, see Nancy Fraser, "From Redistribution to Recognition: Dilemmas of a 'Post-Socialist' Age," *New Left Review* 212 (July–August 1995): 68–93.

16   Fraser, "From Redistribution."

17   Essex Hemphill, "American Wedding," *Ceremonies: Prose and Poetry* (New York: Plume, 1992), 170–71. Reprinted in full by permission of Cleis Press and the Hemphill estate.

Selected Bibliography

"An Admonition to the Parliament." In *Puritan Manifestoes: A Study of the Origin of the Puritan Revolt*, edited by Walter Howard Frere and C. E. Douglas. London: Society for Promoting Christian Knowledge, 1907.

Anderson, Benedict. *Imagined Communities: Reflections on the Origin and Spread of Nationalism*. London: Verso, 1983.

Appadurai, Arjun. "Disjuncture and Difference in the Global Cultural Economy." In *The Phantom Public Sphere*, edited by Bruce Robbins. Minneapolis: University of Minnesota Press, 1993.

Ariès, Philippe. *Centuries of Childhood: A Social History of Family Life*. Translated by Robert Baldick. New York: Vintage, 1962.

Armstrong, Nancy. *Desire and Domestic Fiction: A Political History of the Novel*. New York: Oxford University Press, 1987.

Artificial Intelligence. *Tony 'n' Tina's Wedding*. New York: Samuel French, 1994. Conceived by Nancy Cassaro, created by Thomas Michael Allen, James Altuner, Mark Campbell, Nancy Cassaro, Patricia Cregan, Elizabeth Dennehy, Christopher Fracchiolla, Jack Fris, Kevin A. Leonidas, Mark Nassar, Larry Pellegrini, Susan Varon, and Moira Wilson. Originally produced by Joseph Corcoran and Daniel Corcoran in association with Artificial Intelligence.

Austin, J. L. *How to Do Things with Words*. Edited by J. O. Urmson and Marina Sbisa. 2d ed. Cambridge: Harvard University Press, 1962.

Ayers, Tess. *The Essential Guide to Lesbian and Gay Weddings*. Los Angeles, Calif.: Alyson, 1999.

Babcock, Barbara. "Liberty's a Whore: Inversions, Marginalia, and Picaresque Narrative." In *The Reversible World: Symbolic Inversion in Art and Society*, edited by Barbara Babcock. Ithaca, N.Y.: Cornell University Press, 1978.

Bailey, Beth L. *From Front Porch to Back Seat: Courtship in Twentieth-Century America*. Baltimore, Md.: Johns Hopkins University Press, 1988.

Baird, Robert M., and Stuart E. Rosenbaum, eds. *Same-Sex Marriage: The Moral and Legal Debate.* Amherst, N.Y.: Prometheus Books, 1997.

Baker, Margaret. *The Folklore and Customs of Love and Marriage.* Aylesbury, U.K.: Shire, 1974.

——. *Wedding Customs and Folklore.* Totowa, N.J.: Rowman and Littlefield, 1977.

Bammer, Angelika, ed. *Displacements: Cultural Identities in Question.* Bloomington: Indiana University Press, 1994.

Bardaglio, Peter W. *Reconstructing the Household: Families, Sex, and the Law in the Nineteenth-Century South.* Chapel Hill: University of North Carolina Press, 1995.

Barnes, Elizabeth. *States of Sympathy.* New York: Columbia University Press, 1997.

Barnett, James Harwood. *Divorce and the American Divorce Novel, 1858–1937.* New York: Russell and Russell, 1939.

Barrett, Michele, and Mary McIntosh. *The Anti-Social Family.* London: Verso, 1982.

Barthes, Roland. *Mythologies.* Translated by Annette Lavers. 1957. Reprint, New York: Noonday Press, 1992.

Bartkowski, Frances. *Travelers, Immigrants, Inmates: Essays in Estrangement.* Minneapolis: University of Minnesota Press, 1995.

Basch, Norma. *Framing American Divorce: From the Revolutionary Generation to the Victorians.* Berkeley: University of California Press, 1999.

Bawer, Bruce. *A Place at the Table: The Gay Individual in American Society.* New York: Touchstone Books, 1994.

Belmont, Nicole. "The Symbolic Function of the Wedding Procession in the Popular Rituals of Marriage." In *Ritual, Religion, and the Sacred,* edited by Robert Foster and Orest A. Ranum. Baltimore, Md.: Johns Hopkins University Press, 1982.

Benjamin, Walter. "Allegory and Trauerspiel." In *The Origin of German Tragic Drama,* translated by John Osborne. London: Verso, 1985.

——. "A Short History of Photography." Translated by Stanley Mitchell. 1931. Reprint, *Screen* 13 (spring 1972): 5–26.

——. "Theses on the Philosophy of History." In *Illuminations,* edited by Hannah Arendt, translated by Harry Zohn. New York: Schocken, 1968.

Bentley, Nancy. "Marriage as Treason: Polygamy, Nation, and the Novel." In *The Futures of American Studies,* edited by Donald Pease and Robyn Wiegman. Durham, N.C.: Duke University Press, 2002.

Berlant, Lauren. *The Anatomy of National Fantasy: Hawthorne, Utopia, and Everyday Life.* Chicago: University of Chicago Press, 1991.

——. "Fantasies of Utopia in 'The Blithedale Romance.'" *American Literary History* 1, vol. 1 (spring 1989): 30–62.

——. "The Female Woman: Fanny Fern and the Form of Sentiment." *American Literary History* 3, no. 3 (fall 1991): 429–54.

——. *The Queen of America Goes to Washington City: Essays on Sex and Citizenship.* Durham, N.C.: Duke University Press, 1997.

——. "'68, or Something." *Critical Inquiry* 21 (1994): 124–55.

Bhabha, Homi K. *The Location of Culture*. New York: Routledge, 1994.

——, ed. *Nation and Narration*. New York: Routledge, 1990.

Blackstone, William. *Commentaries on the Laws of England*. 4 Vols. 1769. Reprint, Chicago: University Chicago Press, 1979.

Boelhower, William Q. *Through a Glass Darkly: Ethnic Semiosis in American Literature*. New York: Oxford University Press, 1987.

Boone, Joseph Allen. *Tradition Counter Tradition: Love and the Form of Fiction*. Chicago: University of Chicago Press, 1987.

Bossen, Laurel. "Toward a Theory of Marriage: The Economic Anthropology of Marriage Transactions." *Ethnology* 27 (April 1988): 129–44.

Boswell, John. *Same-Sex Unions in Premodern Europe*. New York: Villard Books, 1994.

Boswell, Parley Ann. "The Pleasure of Our Company: Hollywood Throws a Wedding Bash." In *Beyond the Stars II: Plot Conventions in American Popular Film*, edited by Paul Loukides and Linda K. Fuller. Bowling Green, Ohio: Bowling Green State University Popular Press, 1991.

Brain, Robert. *Friends and Lovers*. New York: Basic Books, 1976.

Bredbenner, Candice Lewis. *A Nationality of Her Own: Women, Marriage, and the Law of Citizenship*. Berkeley: University of California Press, 1998.

Brent, Linda [Harriet Jacobs]. *Incidents in the Life of a Slave Girl, Written by Herself*. Edited by Jean Fagan Yellin. Cambridge: Harvard University Press, 1987.

Brown, Dona. *Inventing New England: Regional Tourism in the Nineteenth Century*. Washington, D.C.: Smithsonian Institution Press, 1995.

Brown, Gillian. *Domestic Individualism: Imagining Self in Nineteenth-Century America*. Berkeley: University of California Press, 1990.

Brundage, James A. *Law, Sex, and Christian Society in Medieval Europe*. Chicago: University of Chicago Press, 1987.

Bulcroft, Kris, Linda Smeins, and Richard Bulcroft. *Romancing the Honeymoon: Consummating Marriage in Modern Society*. New York: Sage Publications, 1999.

Butler, Becky. *Ceremonies of the Heart: Celebrating Lesbian Unions*. Seattle, Wash.: Seal Press, 1990.

Butler, Judith. *Antigone's Claim: Kinship between Life and Death*. New York: Columbia University Press, 2000.

——. "Performative Acts and Gender Constitution: An Essay in Phenomenology and Feminist Theory." In *Performing Feminisms*, edited by Sue-Ellen Case. Baltimore, Md.: Johns Hopkins University Press, 1990.

——. *The Psychic Life of Power*. Stanford, Calif.: Stanford University Press, 1997.

Calder, Jenni. *Women and Marriage in Victorian Fiction*. New York: Oxford University Press, 1976.

Carby, Hazel. *Reconstructing Womanhood: The Emergence of the Afro-American Woman Novelist*. New York: Oxford University Press, 1987.

Castiglia, Christopher. *Bound and Determined: Captivity, Culture-Crossing, and White Womanhood from Mary Rowlandson to Patty Hearst*. Chicago: University of Chicago Press, 1996.

Cavell, Stanley. *Pursuits of Happiness: The Hollywood Comedy of Remarriage*. Cambridge: Harvard University Press, 1981.

Charsley, Simon R. *Wedding Cakes and Cultural History*. New York: Routledge, 1992.

Cheal, David J. "Women Together: Bridal Showers and Gender Membership." In *Gender in Intimate Relationships: A Microstructural Approach*, edited by Barbara J. Risman and Pepper Schwartz. Belmont, Calif.: Wadsworth Publishing Company, 1989.

Clarke, Eric. "The Citizen's Sexual Shadow." *boundary 2*, 26, no. 2 (1999): 163–99.

Cohen, Ed. "Legislating the Norm: From Sodomy to Gross Indecency." In *Displacing Homophobia: Gay Male Perspectives in Literature and Culture*, edited by Ronald R. Butters, John M. Clum, and Michael Moon. Durham, N.C.: Duke University Press, 1989.

Cohen, Paula Marantz. *The Daughter's Dilemma: Family Process and the Nineteenth-Century Domestic Novel*. Ann Arbor: University of Michigan Press, 1993.

Colacurcio, Michael. *The Province of Piety: Moral History in Hawthorne's Early Tales*. Cambridge: Harvard Univerity Press, 1984.

Cole, Harriette. *Jumping the Broom: The African-American Wedding Planner*. New York: Henry Holt, 1993.

Cook, Frank Gaylord. "The Marriage Celebration in Europe." *Atlantic Monthly* 61 (February 1888): 245–61.

——. "The Marriage Celebration in the Colonies." *Atlantic Monthly* 61 (March 1888): 350–62.

——. "Reform in the Celebration of Marriage." *Atlantic Monthly* 61 (May 1888): 680–90.

Coontz, Stephanie. *The Social Origins of Private Life: A History of American Families, 1600–1900*. London: Verso, 1988.

——. *The Way We Never Were: American Families and the Nostalgia Trap*. New York: Basic Books, 1992.

Cott, Nancy F. " 'Giving Character to Our Whole Civil Polity': Marriage and the Public Order in the Late Nineteenth Century." In *U.S. History as Women's History: New Feminist Essays*, edited by Linda K. Kerber, Alice Kessler-Harris, and Kathryn Kish Sklar. Chapel Hill: University of North Carolina Press, 1995.

——. "Marriage and Women's Citizenship in the United States, 1830–1934." *American Historical Review* 103 (1998): 1440–74.

——. *Public Vows: A History of Marriage and the Nation*. Cambridge: Harvard University Press, 2000.

Cross, Wilbur, and Ann Novotny. *White House Weddings*. New York: David McKay, 1967.

Davis, Susan. *Parades and Power: Street Theatre in Nineteenth-Century Philadelphia.* Philadelphia, Pa.: Temple University Press, 1985.

Dayan, Daniel, and Elihu Katz. "Electronic Ceremonies: Television Performs a Royal Wedding." In *On Signs,* edited by Marshall Blonsky. Baltimore, Md.: Johns Hopkins University Press, 1985.

The Deer Hunter. Dir. Michael Cimino, 1978. Universal Studios Home Video, 1997.

de Lauretis, Teresa. *Alice Doesn't: Feminism, Semiotics, Cinema.* Bloomington: Indiana University Press, 1984.

Deleuze, Gilles, and Félix Guattari. *Anti-Oedipus: Capitalism and Schizophrenia.* Translated by Robert Hurley, Mark Seem, and Helen R. Lane. Minneapolis: University of Minnesota Press, 1983.

——. "What Is a Minor Literature?" In *Out There: Marginalization and Contemporary Cultures,* edited by Russell Ferguson, Martha Gever, Trinh T. Minh-ha, and Cornel West. Cambridge: MIT Press, 1990.

D'Emilio, John. "Capitalism and Gay Identity." In *The Lesbian and Gay Studies Reader,* edited by Henry Abelove, Michelle Aina Barale, and David Halperin. New York: Routledge, 1993.

D'Emilio, John, and Estelle B. Freedman. *Intimate Matters: A History of Sexuality in America.* New York: Harper and Row, 1988.

Demos, John. *A Little Commonwealth: Family Life in Plymouth Colony.* New York: Oxford University Press, 1970.

Denning, Michael. *Mechanic Accents: Dime Novels and Working-Class Culture in America.* New York: Verso, 1987.

Dominguez, Virginia R. *White by Definition: Social Classification in Creole Louisiana.* New Brunswick, N.J.: Rutgers University Press, 1986.

Drive, Susannah A., ed. *I Do, I Do: American Wedding Etiquette of Yesteryear.* New York: Hippocrene Books, 1998.

Dubinsky, Karen. *The Second Greatest Disappointment: Honeymooning and Tourism at Niagara Falls.* New Brunswick, N.J.: Rutgers University Press, 1999.

duCille, Ann. *The Coupling Convention: Sex, Text, and Tradition in Black Women's Fiction.* New York: Oxford University Press, 1993.

Duggan, Lisa. "Queering the State." *Social Text* 39 (summer 1994): 1–14.

Duggan, Lisa, and Nan Hunter, eds. *Sex Wars: Sexual Dissent and Political Culture.* New York: Routledge, 1995.

Dundes, Alan. " 'Jumping the Broom': On the Origin and Meaning of an African American Wedding Custom." *Journal of American Folklore* 109 (1996): 325.

duPlessis, Rachel Blau. *Writing beyond the Ending: Narrative Strategies of Twentieth-Century Women Writers.* Bloomington: Indiana University Press, 1985.

Eastman, Edson C. *Curiosities of Matrimony.* Concord, N.H.: Republican Press, 1889.

Edwards, Laura F. *Gendered Strife and Confusion: The Political Culture of Reconstruction.* Urbana: University of Illinois Press, 1997.

Edwards, Walter. *Modern Japan through Its Weddings: Gender, Person, and Society in Ritual Portrayal.* Stanford, Calif.: Stanford University Press, 1989.

Ellis, William. *The Theory of the American Romance: An Ideology in American Intellectual History.* Ann Arbor: University of Michigan Research Press, 1989.

Elshtain, Jean Bethke, ed. *The Family in Political Thought.* Amherst: University of Massachusetts Press, 1986.

Engels, Friedrich. *The Origins of the Family, Private Property, and the State.* 1884. Reprint, New York: Pathfinder Press, 1972.

Eskridge, William N., Jr. *The Case for Same-Sex Marriage: From Sexual Liberty to Civilized Commitment.* New York: Free Press, 1996.

Evans, David T. *Sexual Citizenship: The Material Construction of Sexualities.* New York: Routledge, 1993.

Fabian, Johannes. *Time and the Other: How Anthropology Makes Its Object.* New York: Columbia University Press, 1983.

Faderman, Lillian. *Odd Girls and Twilight Lovers: A History of Lesbian Life in Twentieth-Century America.* New York: Penguin, 1991.

Father of the Bride. Dir. Vincente Minnelli, 1950. Movies Unlimited, 1969.

Faulkner, William. *Absalom, Absalom!* 1936. Reprint, New York: Vintage, 1990.

Ferenczi, Sandor. "Confusion of Tongues between Adults and the Child." In *The Assault on Truth: Freud's Suppression of the Seduction Theory,* edited by Jeffrey Masson. New York: Farrar, Straus, and Giroux, 1984.

Ferraro, Thomas J. "Blood in the Marketplace: The Business of Family in the 'Godfather' Narratives." In *The Invention of Ethnicity,* edited by Werner Sollors. New York: Oxford University Press, 1989.

Fiedler, Leslie. *Love and Death in the American Novel.* New York: Criterion Books, 1960.

Fielding, William J. *Strange Customs of Courtship and Marriage.* New York: New Home Library, 1942.

First Comes Love. Dir. Su Friedrich. Women Make Movies, 1991.

Fischer, Andreas. *Engagement, Wedding, and Marriage in Old English.* Heidelberg: Carl Winter, 1986.

Fliegelman, Jay. *Prodigals and Pilgrims: The American Revolution against Patriarchal Authority, 1750–1800.* Cambridge: Cambridge University Press, 1982.

Foster, Shirley. *Victorian Women's Fiction: Marriage, Freedom, and the Individual.* Totowa, N.J.: Barnes and Noble, 1985.

Foucault, Michel. "Friendship as a Way of Life." Interview by R. de Caccaty, J. Danet, and J. Le Bitouz. Translated by John Johnston. In *Ethics, Subjectivity, and Truth.* Vol. 1 of *The Essential Works of Foucault,* edited by Paul Rabinow. New York: New York University Press, 1997.

——. *The History of Sexuality, Volume I: An Introduction.* Translated by Robert Hurley. New York: Random House, 1978.

Franke, Katherine M. "Becoming a Citizen: Reconstruction Era Regulation of African-

American Marriages. *Yale Journal of Law and the Humanities* 11, no. 2 (1999): 251–309.

Fraser, Nancy. "From Redistribution to Recognition: Dilemmas of a 'Post-Socialist' Age." *New Left Review* 212 (July–August 1995): 68–93.

———. "Heterosexism, Miscrecognition, and Capitalism: A Response to Judith Butler." *New Left Review* (1998): 140–49.

———. "Rethinking Recognition." *New Left Review* 3 (May 2000): 108–120.

Frese, Pamela R. "The Union of Nature and Culture: Gender Symbolism in the American Wedding Ritual." In *Transcending Boundaries: Multi-Disciplinary Approaches to the Study of Gender*, edited by Pamela R. Frese and John M. Coggeshall. New York: Bergin and Garvey, 1991.

Frye, Northrop. "The Mythos of Spring." In *The Anatomy of Criticism*. Princeton, N.J.: Princeton University Press, 1957.

Geertz, Clifford. "Deep Play: Notes on the Balinese Cock Fight." *Daedalus* 101 (1972): 1–38.

Gillis, John R. *For Better, for Worse: British Marriages, 1600 to the Present*. New York: Oxford University Press, 1985.

———. "From Ritual to Romance: Toward an Alternative History of Love." In *Emotion and Social Change*, edited by Carol Z. Stearns and Peter N. Stearns. New York: Holmes and Meier, 1988.

———. *A World of Their Own Making: Myth, Ritual, and the Quest for Family Values*. New York: Basic Books, 1996.

Ginsberg, Lesley. " 'The Willing Captive': Narrative Seduction and the Ideology of Love in Hawthorne's 'A Wonder Book for Girls and Boys.' " *American Literature* 65, no. 2 (June 1993): 255–73.

Ginsburg, Madeleine. *Wedding Dress, 1740–1980*. London: Her Majesty's Stationery Office, 1981.

The Godfather. Dir. Francis Ford Coppola. Paramount Home Entertainment, 1972.

Goldstein-Gidoni, Ofra. *Packaged Japaneseness: Weddings, Business, and Brides*. Honolulu: University of Hawaii Press, 1997.

Goodrich, Samuel G. [Nathaniel Hawthorne]. *Peter Parley's Universal History on the Basis of Geography*. New York: Newman and Ivison, 1853.

Goody, Jack. *The Development of the Family and Marriage in Europe*. Cambridge: Cambridge University Press, 1983.

Gordon, Sarah Barringer. " 'The Liberty of Self-Degradation': Polygamy, Woman Suffrage, and Consent in Nineteenth-Century America." *Journal of American History* 83 (December 1996): 815–47.

The Graduate. Dir. Mike Nichols, 1967. MGM Home Entertainment, 1999.

Graff, E. J. *What Is Marriage For?* Boston: Beacon Press, 1999.

Greenhill, Pauline. "Folk Drama in Anglo Canada and the Mock Wedding: Transaction, Performance, and Meaning." *Canadian Drama* 14, no. 2 (1988): 169–205.

Grossberg, Michael. *Governing the Hearth: Law and the Family in Nineteenth-Century America.* Chapel Hill: University of North Carolina Press, 1985.

Gutin, Myra G. *The President's Partner: The First Lady in the Twentieth Century.* New York: Greenwood Press, 1989.

Gutman, Herbert G. *The Black Family in Slavery and Freedom, 1750–1925.* New York: Vintage, 1976.

Habegger, Alfred. *Gender, Fantasy, and Realism in American Literature.* New York: Columbia University Press, 1982.

Hacking, Ian. "The Making and Molding of Child Abuse." *Critical Inquiry* 17 (winter 1991): 253–88.

Hagstrum, Jean H. *Esteem Enlivened by Desire: The Couple from Homer to Shakespeare.* Chicago: University of Chicago Press, 1992.

Haines, Frank, and Elizabeth Haines. *Early American Brides: A Study of Costume and Tradition, 1594–1820.* Cumberland, Md.: Hobby House Press, 1982.

Halberstam, Judith. *Female Masculinity.* Durham, N.C.: Duke University Press, 1998.

Halttunen, Karen. *Confidence Men and Painted Women: A Study of Middle-Class Culture in America, 1830–1870.* New Haven, Conn.: Yale University Press, 1982.

Hargrove, Anne C., and Maurine Magliocco, ed. *Portraits of Marriage in Literature.* Macomb: Western Illinois University Press, 1984.

Harper, Phillip Brian. "Gay Male Identities, Personal Privacy, and Relations of Public Exchange: Notes on Directions for Queer Critique." *Social Text* 15, nos. 3–4 (1997): 5–29.

Hartog, Hendrik. *Man and Wife in America.* Cambridge: Harvard University Press, 2000.

Hawkes, Elizabeth, and Christopher Baker. *Martha Stewart Weddings.* New York: Clarkson N. Potter, 1987.

Hawthorne, Nathaniel. *The Blithedale Romance.* 1852. Reprint, New York: Penguin, 1986.

——. "Little Annie's Ramble." In *Hawthorne: Tales and Sketches,* edited by Roy Harvey Pearce. New York: Library of America, 1982.

——. "The May-Pole of Merry Mount." In *Hawthorne: Tales and Sketches,* edited by Roy Harvey Pearce. New York: Library of America, 1982.

——. "My Visit to Niagara." In *Hawthorne: Tales and Sketches,* edited by Roy Harvey Pearce. New York: Library of America, 1982.

——. *The Scarlet Letter.* 1850. Reprint, New York: W. W. Norton, 1988.

——. "Sketches from Memory." In *Hawthorne: Tales and Sketches,* edited by Roy Harvey Pearce. New York: Library of America, 1982.

Herbert, T. Walter. *Dearly Beloved: The Hawthornes and the Making of the Middle-Class Family.* Berkeley: University of California Press, 1993.

Hinz, Evelyn J. "Hierogamy vs. Wedlock: Types of Marriage Plots and Their Relationship to Genres of Prose Fiction." *PMLA* 19 (1976): 900–913.

Hirsch, Marianne. *Family Frames: Photography, Narrative, and Postmemory.* Cambridge: Harvard University Press, 1997.

Hobsbawm, Eric, and Terence Ranger, eds. *The Invention of Tradition.* Cambridge: Cambridge University Press, 1983.

Hodes, Martha. *White Women, Black Men: Illicit Sex in the Nineteenth-Century South.* New Haven, Conn.: Yale University Press, 1997.

——, ed. *Sex, Love, Race: Crossing Boundaries in North American History.* New York: New York University Press, 1999.

Holden, Anthony. *A Princely Marriage.* London: Bantam, 1991.

Howard, George Elliott. *The History of Matrimonial Institutions.* 3 Vols. Chicago: University of Chicago Press, 1904.

Howells, William Dean. *Their Wedding Journey.* 1871. Reprint, Bloomington: Indiana University Press, 1968.

Ingraham, Chrys. *White Wedding: Romancing Heterosexuality in Popular Culture.* New York: Routledge, 1999.

Jakobsen, Janet R. "Can Homosexuality End Western Civilization As We Know It?" In *Queer Globalizations,* edited by Arnaldo Cruz-Malave and Martin Manalansan. New York: New York University Press, forthcoming 2002.

Jameson, Fredric. *Postmodernism, or, the Cultural Logic of Late Capitalism.* Durham, N.C.: Duke University Press, 1991.

Jarvis, Anthea. *Brides: Wedding Clothes and Customs, 1850–1980.* Liverpool: Merseyside Country Museums, 1983.

Jeaffreson, John Cordy. *Brides and Bridals.* London: Hurst and Blackett, 1872.

Jehlen, Myra. *American Incarnation: The Individual, the Nation, and the Continent.* Cambridge: Harvard University Press, 1986.

Johnson, James T. *A Society Ordained by God: English Puritan Marriage Doctrine in the First Half of the Seventeenth Century.* Nashville, Tenn.: Abingdon Press, 1970.

Jones, Leslie. *Happy Is the Bride the Sun Shines On: Wedding Beliefs, Customs, and Traditions.* Chicago: Contemporary Books, 1995.

Kaplan, Amy. "Manifest Domesticity." *American Literature* 70, no. 3 (1998): 581–606.

——. *The Social Construction of American Realism.* Chicago: University of Chicago Press, 1988.

Kaplan, Morris. *Sexual Justice.* Ithaca, N.Y.: Cornell University Press, 1997.

Katz, Jonathan Ned. *The Gay/Lesbian Almanac: A New Documentary.* New York: Harper and Row, 1983.

——. *The Invention of Heterosexuality.* New York: Dutton, 1995.

Kelly, John D., and Martha Kaplan. "History, Structure, and Ritual." *Annual Review of Anthropology* 19 (1990): 119–50.

Kendall, Laurel. *Getting Married in Korea.* Berkeley: University of California Press, 1996.

Kete, Mary Louise. *Sentimental Collaborations: Mourning and Middle-Class Identity in Nineteenth-Century America.* Durham, N.C.: Duke University Press, 2000.

Kincaid, James R. *Child-Loving: The Erotic Child and Victorian Culture.* New York: Routledge, 1992.

——. *Erotic Innocence: The Culture of Child Molesting.* Durham, N.C.: Duke University Press, 1998.

Kirkland, Joseph. *Zury: The Meanest Man in Spring County.* 1887. Reprint, Urbana: University of Illinois Press, 1956.

Kirshenblatt-Gimblett, Barbara. "Objects of Ethnography." In *Exhibiting Cultures: The Poetics and Politics of Museum Display,* edited by Ivan Karp and Steven D. Lavine. Washington, D.C.: Smithsonian Institution Press, 1991.

Koegel, Otto. *Common-Law Marriage and Its Development in the United States.* Washington, D.C.: John Byrne and Company, 1922.

Kolodny, Annette. *The Lay of the Land: Metaphor as Experience and History in American Life and Letters.* Chapel Hill: University of North Carolina Press, 1975.

Lacey, Peter. *The Wedding.* New York: Madison Square Press, 1969.

Laffrado, Laura. *Hawthorne's Literature for Children.* Athens: University of Georgia Press, 1992.

Landsdell, Avril. *Wedding Fashions, 1860–1980.* Aylesbury, U.K.: Shire, 1983.

Laverack, Elizabeth. *With This Ring: One Hundred Years of Marriage.* London: Elm Tree Books, 1979.

(Leonard) Barker, Diana. "A Proper Wedding." In *The Couple,* edited by Marie Corbin. London: Hammondsworth, 1978.

Leonard, Diana. *Sex and Generation: A Study of Courtship and Weddings.* London: Tavistock, 1980.

Levinton, G. A. "Male and Female Text in the Wedding Ritual: The Wedding as Dialogue." *Anthropology and Archaeology of Eurasia* 32 (1993): 47–73.

Lewin, Ellen. *Recognizing Ourselves: Ceremonies of Lesbian and Gay Commitment.* New York: Columbia University Press, 1998.

Lewis, C. S. *The Allegory of Love: A Study in Medieval Tradition.* New York: Oxford University Press, 1936.

Lott, Eric. *Love and Theft: Blackface Minstrelsy and the American Working Class.* New York: Oxford University Press, 1995.

MacCannell, Dean. *Empty Meeting Grounds: The Tourist Papers.* New York: Routledge, 1992.

Marsh, Heidi. *Wedding Suggestions of the Era of the Hoop.* Greenville, Calif.: Heidi Marsh, 1992.

Matrimonial Ceremonies Displayed. London: Searjant, 1883.

May, Elaine Tyler. *Great Expectations: Marriage and Divorce in Post-Victorian America.* Chicago: University of Chicago Press, 1980.

McClintock, Anne. *Imperial Leather: Race, Gender, and Sexuality in the Colonial Contest.* New York: Routledge, 1995.

McCullers, Carson. *The Member of the Wedding*. 1946. Reprint, New York: Bantam Books, 1958.

McGreevy, Patrick. *Imagining Niagara: The Meaning and Making of Niagara Falls*. Amherst: University of Massachusetts Press, 1994.

McKinsey, Elizabeth. *Niagara Falls: Icon of the American Sublime*. New York: Cambridge University Press, 1985.

McKune, Amy. *To Love and to Cherish: The Great American Wedding*. New York: Museums at Stony Brook, 1991.

Michaels, Walter Benn. *The Gold Standard and the Logic of Naturalism*. Berkeley: University of California Press, 1987.

———. *Our America: Nativism, Modernism, and Pluralism*. Durham, N.C.: Duke University Press, 1995.

———. "Race into Culture: A Critical Genealogy of Cultural Identity." *Critical Inquiry* 18 (summer 1992): 655–85.

Michie, Helena. "Looking at Victorian Honeymoons." *Common Knowledge* 6, no. 1 (spring 1997): 125–36.

Miller, D. A. *Narrative and Its Discontents: Problems of Closure in the Traditional Novel*. Princeton, N.J.: Princeton University Press, 1981.

Miller, Nancy K. *The Heroine's Text: Readings in the French and English Novel, 1722–1782*. New York: Columbia University Press, 1980.

Mintz, Steven, and Susan Kellogg. *Domestic Revolutions: A Social History of American Family Life*. New York: Free Press, 1988.

Monsarrat, Ann. *And the Bride Wore . . . : The Story of the White Wedding*. New York: Dodd, Mead, and Company, 1973.

Moran, James M. "Wedding Video and Its Generation." In *Resolutions: Contemporary Video Practice*, edited by Michael Renov and Erika Suderburg. Minneapolis: University of Minnesota Press, 1996.

Morgan, Edmund. *The Puritan Family: Religion and Domestic Relations in Seventeenth-Century New England*. New York: Harper and Row, 1966.

Morton, Thomas. *New English Canaan*. In *Publications of the Prince Society*, edited by Charles Francis Adams Jr. Vol. 14. New York: Burt Franklin, 1967.

Mount, Ferdinand. *The Subversive Family*. New York: Free Press, 1992.

Muncy, Raymond Lee. *Sex and Marriage in Utopian Communities: Nineteenth-Century America*. Bloomington: Indiana University Press, 1973.

Murphy, Brian. *World of Weddings*. New York: Paddington Press, 1978.

Nabokov, Vladimir. *The Enchanter*. Translated by Dmitri Nabokov. New York: Vintage, 1986.

———. *Lolita*. 1955. Reprint, New York: Penguin Books, 1987.

Nelson, Benjamin N. *The Idea of Usury: From Tribal Brotherhood to Universal Otherhood*. Princeton, N.J.: Princeton University Press, 1949.

Norfleet, Barbara. *Wedding.* New York: Simon and Schuster, 1979.

Norton, Mary Beth. *Founding Mothers and Fathers: Gendered Power and the Formation of American Society.* New York: Knopf, 1996.

O'Neill, William L. *Divorce in the Progressive Era.* New Haven, Conn.: Yale University Press, 1967.

Pascoe, Peggy. "Miscegenation Law, Court Cases, and Ideologies of 'Race' in Twentieth-Century America," *Journal of American History* 83 (June 1996): 44–69.

Pateman, Carole. *The Sexual Contract.* Stanford, Calif.: Stanford University Press, 1988.

Pfister, Joel. *The Production of Personal Life: Class, Gender, and the Psychological in Hawthorne's Fiction.* Stanford, Calif.: Stanford University Press, 1991.

Poe, Edgar Allan. "Annabel Lee." In *The Works of Edgar Allan Poe,* edited by Edmund Clarence Stedman and George Edward Woodberry. Vol. 10. Chicago: Stone and Kimball, 1894–95.

——. "Three Sundays in a Week." In *The Works of Edgar Allan Poe,* edited by Edmund Clarence Stedman and George Edward Woodberry. Vol. 4. Chicago: Stone and Kimball, 1894–95.

Poster, Mark. *Critical Theory of the Family.* New York: Seabury Press, 1978.

Powell, Chilton L. "Marriage in Early New England." *New England Quarterly* 1 (1928): 323–34.

Probyn, Elspeth. *Outside Belongings.* New York: Routledge, 1996.

Protestant Episcopal Church in the United States of America. "The Form of Solemnization of Matrimony." In *The Book of Common Prayer.* Greenwich, Conn.: Seabury Press, 1953.

Quale, G. Robina. *A History of Marriage Systems.* Westport, Conn.: Greenwood Press, 1988.

Radway, Janice. *Reading the Romance: Women, Patriarchy, and Popular Literature.* Chapel Hill: University of North Carolina Press, 1984.

Ranlet, Philip. "The Lord of Misrule: Thomas Morton of Merry Mount." *New England Historical and Genealogical Register* 134 (1980): 282–90.

Reid, Mayne. *The Child Wife: A Tale of the Two Worlds.* 1868. Reprint, New York: Sheldon and Company, 1869.

——. *The Headless Horseman: A Strange Tale of Texas.* 1865. Reprint, London: R. Bentley, 1866.

——. *The Scalp-hunters: Romantic Adventures in Northern Mexico.* 1851. Reprint, as *The Scalp-hunters: A Romance of the Plains,* New York: Beadle and Adams, 1868.

Reynolds, Philip Lyndon. *Marriage in the Western Church: The Christianization of Marriage during the Patristic and Early Medieval Periods.* New York: E. J. Brill, 1994.

Riley, Claire. "American Kinship: A Lesbian Account." *Feminist Studies* 8, no. 2: 75–94.

Rollins, Nita. "Something Borrowed, Something Taped: Video Nuptials." *Wide Angle* 13 (April 1991): 32–38.

Romero, Lora. *Home Fronts: Domesticity and Its Critics in the Antebellum United States.* Durham, N.C.: Duke University Press, 1997.

Roof, Judith. *Come as You Are: Sexuality and Narrative.* New York: Columbia University Press, 1996.

"The Rose Garden Wedding." NBC News special report, 12 June 1971, narrated by Barbara Walters and Edwin Newman.

Rose, Jacqueline. *The Case of Peter Pan, or, the Impossibility of Children's Fiction.* London: Macmillan, 1984.

Ross, Andrew. "The Uses of Camp." In *No Respect: Intellectuals and Popular Culture.* New York: Routledge, 1989.

Rossman, Michael. *The Wedding within the War.* Garden City, N.Y.: Doubleday, 1971.

Rotello, Gabriel. *Sexual Ecology: AIDS and the Destiny of Gay Men.* New York: Dutton, 1997.

Rothblum, Esther D., and Kathleen A. Brehony, eds. *Boston Marriages: Romantic but Asexual Relationships among Contemporary Lesbians.* Amherst: University of Massachusetts Press, 1993.

Rothman, Ellen K. *Hands and Hearts: A History of Courtship in America.* New York: Basic Books, 1984.

"The Royal Wedding." CBS News special report, 29 July 1981.

Rubin, Gayle. "The Traffic in Women: Notes on the Political Economy of 'Sex.' " In *Toward an Anthropology of Women,* edited by Rayna Reiter. New York: Monthly Review Press, 1975.

Ryan, Mary. *Cradle of the Middle Class: The Family in Oneida County, New York, 1790–1865.* New York: Cambridge University Press, 1981.

Saks, Eva. "Representing Miscegenation Law." *Raritan* 8 (fall 1988): 39–69.

Samuels, Shirley. *Romances of the Republic: Women, the Family, and Violence in the Literature of the Early American Nation.* New York: Oxford University Press, 1996.

Sánchez-Eppler, Karen. "Temperance in the Bed of a Child: Incest and Social Order in Nineteenth-Century America." *American Quarterly* 47 (March 1995): 1–33.

———. *Touching Liberty: Abolition, Feminism, and the Politics of the Body.* Berkeley: University of California Press, 1993.

Sapiro, Virginia. "Women, Citizenship, and Nationality: Immigration and Naturalization Policies in the United States." *Politics and Society* 13 (1984): 1–26.

Schivelbusch, Wolfgang. *The Railway Journey: The Industrialization of Time and Space in the Nineteenth Century.* Berkeley: University of California Press, 1987.

Schneider, David M. *American Kinship: A Cultural Account.* Englewood Cliffs, N.J.: Prentice Hall, 1968.

———. *A Critique of the Study of Kinship.* Ann Arbor: University of Michigan Press, 1984.

Scott, George Ryley. *Curious Customs of Sex and Marriage.* London: Torchstream Books, 1953.

Sedgwick, Eve. "Queer Performativity." *GLQ* (*Gay and Lesbian Quarterly*) 1, no. 1 (1993): 1–16.

Seidman, Steven. *Romantic Longings: Love in America, 1830–1980*. New York: Routledge, 1991.

Seligson, Marcia. *The Eternal Bliss Machine: America's Way of Wedding*. New York: Morrow, 1973.

Seltzer, Mark. *Bodies and Machines*. New York: Routledge, 1992.

Selvadurai, Shyam. *Funny Boy: A Novel*. New York: William Morrow and Company, 1994.

Semiotext(e) Special Large Type Edition: Loving Boys. New York: Semiotexte, 1980.

Shell, Marc. *The End of Kinship: "Measure for Measure," Incest, and the Ideal of Universal Siblinghood*. Stanford, Calif.: Stanford University Press, 1988.

Shorter, Edward. *The Making of the Modern Family*. New York: Basic Books, 1975.

Sickels, Robert J. *Race, Marriage, and the Law*. Albuquerque: University of New Mexico Press, 1972.

Slotkin, Richard. *Regeneration through Violence: The Mythology of the American Frontier, 1600–1860*. Middletown, Conn.: Wesleyan University Press, 1983.

Smith, Shawn. *American Archives*. Princeton, N.J.: Princeton University Press, 1999.

Snead, James. "Repetition as a Figure of Black Culture." In *Black Literature and Literary Theory*, edited by Henry Louis Gates Jr. New York: Methuen, 1984.

Snyder, William L. *The Geography of Marriage, or, Legal Perplexities of Wedlock in the United States*. New York: G. P. Putnam's Sons, 1889.

Sollors, Werner. *Beyond Ethnicity: Consent and Descent in American Culture*. New York: Oxford University Press, 1986.

——. "Ethnicity." In *Critical Terms for Literary Study*, edited by Frank Letricchia and Thomas McLaughlin. 2d ed. Chicago: University of Chicago Press, 1995.

——. *Neither Black nor White yet Both: Thematic Explorations of Interracial Literature*. New York: Oxford University Press, 1997.

——, ed. *Interracialism: Black-White Intermarriage in American Literature, History, and Law*. New York: Oxford University Press, 2000.

Sommer, Doris. *Foundational Fictions: The National Romances of Latin America*. Berkeley: University of California Press, 1991.

Spillers, Hortense. "Mama's Baby, Papa's Maybe: An American Grammar Book." *diacritics* (summer 1987): 65–81.

Spurlock, John. *Free Love: Marriage and Middle-Class Radicalism in America, 1825–1860*. New York: New York University Press, 1988.

Stanley, Amy Dru. *From Bondage to Contract: Wage Labor, Marriage, and the Market in the Age of Slave Emancipation*. New York: Cambridge University Press, 1998.

Stein, Allen F. *After the Vows Were Spoken: Marriage in American Literary Realism*. Columbus: Ohio State University Press, 1984.

Stern, Gail F., ed. *Something Old, Something New: Ethnic Weddings in America*. Philadelphia, Pa.: Balch Institute for Ethnic Studies, 1987.

Stevens, Jacqueline. "On the Marriage Question." In *Women Transforming Politics*, edited by Cathy J. Cohen, Kathleen B. Jones, and Joan C. Tronto. New York: New York University Press, 1997.

——. *Reproducing the State*. Princeton, N.J.: Princeton University Press, 1999.

Stevenson, Brenda E. "Black Family Structure in Colonial and Antebellum Virginia: Amending the Revisionist Perspective." In *The Decline in Marriage among African Americans: Causes, Consequences, and Policy Implications*, edited by M. Belinda Tucker and Claudia Mitchell-Kernan. New York: Russell Sage Foundation, 1995.

Stewart, Susan. "Exogamous Relations: Travel Writing, the Incest Prohibition, and Hawthorne's 'Transformation.'" In *Culture/Contexture: Explorations in Anthropology and Literary Studies*, edited by E. Valentine Daniel and Jeffrey M. Peck. Berkeley: University of California Press, 1996.

Stone, Lawrence. *The Family, Sex, and Marriage in England, 1500–1800*. New York: Harper and Row, 1977.

——. *Uncertain Unions: Marriage in England, 1660–1753*. New York: Oxford University Press, 1992.

Sturges, Ingrid. *The Nubian Wedding Book*. New York: Crown, 1997.

Sulka's Wedding. Dir. Kim Christy. Caballero Home Video, Canoga Park, Calif., 1987.

Sullivan, Andrew. *Same-Sex Marriage: Pro and Con*. New York: Vintage, 1997.

——. *Virtually Normal: An Argument about Homosexuality*. New York: Vintage, 1996.

Sullivan, C. W., III. "'Jumping the Broom': A Further Consideration of the Origins of an African American Wedding Custom." *Journal of American Folklore* 110 (spring 1997): 203–4.

Tanner, Tony. *Adultery in the Novel: Contract and Transgression*. Baltimore, Md.: Johns Hopkins University Press, 1979.

Tasman, Alice Lea Mast. *Wedding Album: Custom and Lore through the Ages*. New York: Walker and Company, 1982.

Tate, Claudia. *Domestic Allegories of Political Desire: The Black Heroine's Text at the Turn of the Century*. New York: Oxford University Press, 1992.

Taylor, Barbara. *Eve and the New Jerusalem*. New York: Pantheon, 1983.

Thorne, Bonnie, and Marilyn Yadom, ed. *Rethinking the Family*. New York: Longman, 1982.

Tober, Barbara. *The Bride: A Celebration*. New York: Harry N. Abrams, 1984.

Tompkins, Jane. *Sensational Designs: The Cultural Work of American Fiction, 1790–1860*. New York: Oxford University Press, 1985.

Tracey, Karen. *Plots and Proposals: American Women's Fiction, 1850–1890*. Urbana: University of Illinois Press, 2000.

Trachtenberg, Alan. *The Incorporation of America: Culture and Society in the Gilded Age*. New York: Hill and Wang, 1982.

Trosino, James. "American Wedding: Same-Sex Marriage and the Miscegenation Analogy." *Boston University Law Review* 73, no. 1 (1993): 93–120.

Troy, Gil. *Affairs of State: The Rise and Rejection of the Presidential Couple since World War II*. New York: Free Press, 1997.

Turner, Victor. *The Anthropology of Performance*. New York: P. A. J. Publications, 1986.

Urlin, Ethel L. *A Short History of Marriage*. Detroit: Singing Tree Press, 1969.

Vaid, Urvashi. *Virtual Equality: The Mainstreaming of Lesbian and Gay Liberation*. New York: Touchstone Books, 1996.

Vernon, John. *Money and Fiction: Literary Realism in the Nineteenth and Early Twentieth Centuries*. Ithaca, N.Y.: Cornell University Press, 1984.

Warbasse, Elizabeth Bowles. *The Changing Legal Rights of Married Women, 1800–1861*. New York: Garland Publishers, 1987.

Warner, Michael. Introduction to *Fear of a Queer Planet: Queer Politics and Social Theory*, edited by Michael Warner. Minneapolis: University of Minnesota Press, 1994.

——. *The Letters of the Republic*. Cambridge: Harvard University Press, 1990.

——. "The Mass Public and the Mass Subject." In *Habermas and the Public Sphere*, edited by Craig Calhoun. Cambridge: MIT Press, 1992.

——. "New English Sodom." *American Literature* 64, no. 1 (March 1992): 19–47.

——. *The Trouble with Normal*. New York: Free Press, 1999.

Weisbrod, Carol, and Pamela Sheingorn. "*Reynolds v. United States*: Nineteenth-Century Forms of Marriage and the Status of Women." In *The History of Women in the United States, Volume 3: Domestic Relations and the Law*, edited by Nancy Cott. New York: K. G. Saur, 1992.

Westbrook, Robert L. " 'I Want a Girl, Just Like the Girl That Married Harry James': American Women and the Problem of Political Obligation in World War II." *American Quarterly* 42 (December 1990): 587–614.

Weston, Kath. *Families We Choose: Lesbians, Gays, and Kinship*. New York: Columbia University Press, 1991.

Wexman, Virginia Wright. *Creating the Couple: Love, Marriage, and Hollywood Performance*. Princeton, N.J.: Princeton University Press, 1993.

Whelan, Frederick G. "Property as Artifice in Hume and Blackstone." In *Property*, edited by J. Roland Posnock and John W. Chapman. New York: New York University Press, 1980.

White, Patricia. *unInvited: Classical Hollywood Cinema and Lesbian Representability*. Bloomington: Indiana University Press, 1999.

Williams, Raymond. "Structures of Feeling." In *Marxism and Literature*. New York: Oxford University Press, 1977.

Wilson, Willie F. *The African American Wedding Manual*. Washington, D.C.: House of Knowledge Publishers, 1994.

Witte, John, Jr. *From Sacrament to Contract: Marriage, Religion, and Law in the Western Tradition*. Louisville, Ky.: Westminster John Knox Press, 1997.

Yazawa, Melvin. *From Colonies to Commonwealth: Familial Ideology and the Beginnings of the American Republic*. Baltimore, Md.: Johns Hopkins University Press, 1985.

Young, Robert J. C. *Colonial Desire: Hybridity in Theory, Culture, and Race*. New York: Routledge, 1995.

Zaretsky, Eli. *Capitalism, the Family, and Personal Life*. Rev. Ed. New York: Harper-Perennial, 1986.

Zeigler, Sara L. "Uniformity and Conformity: Regionalism and the Adjudication of Married Women's Property Acts." *Polity* 28, no. 4 (summer 1996): 467–95.

Index

Brides (*cont.*)
of, 11, 24–26, 28, 30–32, 34; bodies of,
10, 19–20, 31–32; child (*see* Child
brides); costumes of, 12, 19–20, 24–
25, 28–31, 127–28; demystification of,
205–6, 208; and honeymoons, 148–
50; imagined communities of, 27–32;
as national icons, 46; as objects of
transfer, 12–13, 186; and performativity, 31–32, 36–37; and photography,
28, 30–31, 173, 178–80; and the wedding industry, 27–32. *See also* Child
brides; Wedding rituals; White
weddings
Bride's Magazine, 28, 31–32
Bridesmaids. *See* Brides: attendants of
Butler, Judith, 35–37

Capitalism: and weddings, 9, 25–32, 131,
141–45. *See also* Advertisements; Com-
modities; Wedding industry
Captivity narratives, 153, 167–68
Carby, Hazel, 71
Catholic Church. *See* Roman
Catholicism
Cavell, Stanley, 40
Celibacy, 14, 16
Child brides: and honeymoons, 150–54,
171–76; and male subjectivity, 174–77;
and race, 166–72, 176–77; and U.S.
expansionism, 162–71. *See also* Brides;
Girls
Children: and affect, 158–60; and poly-
morphous desires, 6–8, 25, 68. *See
also* Child brides; Girls
Child Wife, The (Reid), 154, 164, 169–71
Christianity, 14, 25, 214. *See also* Protes-
tantism; Roman Catholicism
Church of Latter-Day Saints, The. *See*
Mormons
Citizenship: and affect, 109–10; and

homosexuality, 123–25; and marriage
law, 22–24, 72, 104; and monogamy,
136; and naturalization, 6, 22–23, 72;
and property, 124. *See also* National
belonging
"Classanova." *See* Harris, Glenn
Cohen, Ed, 123–24
Cohen, Paula Marantz, 158
Coke, Sir Edward, 118, 123
Colacurcio, Michael, 113–14, 118
Commodities, 3, 28, 34; and couplehood,
32; and honeymoons, 154, 156–59,
171–73. *See also* Capitalism; Wedding
industry
Complex marriages. *See* Marriages: plural; Polygamy
Contracts: marriage, 103–5, 107–11, 119,
122, 125–26; property, 120–21; sexual,
232 n.80; in wedding rituals, 13
Cott, Nancy, 104
Cotton, John, 139
Couplehood, 2–5; affective and economic functions of, 26; and allegory,
231 n.73; and commodities, 32; and
covenantal marriages, 125; and honeymoons, 146–50; as an object of desire,
49–51; privileges of, 2, 216, 219; in
slavery, 88; and videography, 204–6;
and wedding portraits, 178–79; and
wedding rituals, 35, 41–42, 128, 189–
90. *See also* Coverture
"The Courtship of Miles Standish"
(Longfellow), 105, 133–34
Covenantal marriages, 18, 107–8, 125–
29; Puritan, 39–40, 104–5, 110–12,
114–15, 118–19, 122–23, 131, 137–
40
Coverture, 91–92, 119–20
Creoles, 85, 163, 165–69, 172
Cross-dressing. *See* Drag
Currency. *See* Money

Marriage law (*cont.*)
and licenses, 18, 20, 24; *Loving v. Virginia* (1967), 74; Married Women's Property Acts, 85–86, 115, 119; medical tests and, 23–24; Morrill Act (1862), 126; Ontario Marriage Act, 212; and polygamy, 23, 126, 136–37; and property, 71, 73, 85–86, 115, 119; Puritan, 110, 118; and race, 71–74; *Reynolds v. United States* (1878), 212; and Roman Catholicism, 14–17, 19; and same-sex unions, 2, 24, 212, 224 n.3, 244 n.51; slaves and, 22, 68, 71–72, 88–89; and sodomy, 123–26 (*see also* Sodomy); state, movement to unify, 136; and women, 72–73, 85–86, 91–92, 115, 119–20

Marriages: in African American women's writing, 71–72, 236 n.7; and capitalism, 144; civil, 18, 20, 39–40, 102–8, 115, 117–26 (*see also* Marriage law: and civil unions; Weddings: civil); clandestine, 15–16, 20; common-law, 22, 133, 136–37; complex (*see* Marriages: plural); contractual, 103–5, 107–11, 119, 122, 125–26; covenantal, 18, 105, 107–8, 110–12, 114–15, 118–19, 122–23, 125–29, 131, 137–40; as different than weddings, 4–5, 74–75, 79–80, 100, 112–13; and families, 109, 213; and femininity, 72; and heterosexuality, 24; history of control over, 9, 11–24 (*see also* Marriage law); intergenerational, 150–51, 160–71 (*see also* Child brides); in monarchical Europe, 109, 228 n.31; monogamous (*see* Monogamy); *plaçage*, 85–88, 90; plural, 126–39, 144 (*see also* Polygamy); pre-Christian, 14; and the Protestant Reformation, 17–18; and race, 69–79, 85–86; in Roman Catholicism, 14–17, 19; as a sacrament, 14–15, 17; same-sex, 52, 56–57, 211–17 (*see also* Same-sex unions); in sentimental novels, 41. *See also* Marriage law; Marriage vows

Marriage vows: spoken, 15, 19, 32–35, 104, 134; symbolic, 13, 91

Masculinity: and adventure fiction, 41–42; African American, 72; and the gaze, 178; and gender development, 35–36; and honeymoons, 149–51; and performativity, 35–36 (*see also* Performativity); and subjectivity, 149–55, 164, 171, 173–77

Massachusetts Bay Colony, 105, 112–14, 116, 122, 130

Mather, Cotton, 116

"The May-Pole of Merry Mount" (Hawthorne), 23, 43, 111–27, 129–30, 137, 242 n.24, 243 n.37

McCullers, Carson, 45–47; "Letter From a War Wife," 46–47; *The Member of the Wedding*, 23, 43, 45–70, 102, 235 n.32

Melancholia: and allegory, 37–38; gender as a form of, 36–37; and queer desire, 48–51; weddings as scenes of, 9, 38, 40

Member of the Wedding, The (McCullers), 23, 43, 45–70, 102, 235 n.32

Metropolitan Community Church of Toronto, 211–17, 219–20, 259 n.11

Michaels, Walter Benn, 253 n.9

Michie, Helena, 148–49

Miscegenation, 70–71. *See also* Interracial marriages

Mixed-race body, 70–71, 74. *See also* Identity: racial; Race

Mock weddings. *See* Weddings: mock

Money, 141–44

Monogamy: and citizenship, 23, 136;

Protestantism: Anglican, 19–20, 112, 114, 116; Continental, 11, 16–19, 114; Puritan, 3, 12, 20, 22, 39–40, 105, 112, 114, 116 (*see also* Massachusetts Bay Colony). *See also* Antinomianism; Metropolitan Community Church of Toronto; Mormons; Universalism

Queer politics, 43, 56, 65; and gay marriage rights, 2, 4, 52, 56–57, 211–17, 219–20, 222 n.6, 224 n.3, 259 n.11; and imperialism, 56–57

Queers, and desire, 48–57; and heterosexual couplehood, 204–9; and name changes, 60; and national belonging, 47–69; and performativity, 36, 60; and politics (*see* Queer politics); and queer sex publics, 217–20; and sexual development, 45–49, 52–54, 64–66; as wedding guests, 2–3, 42, 202–4

Race: and child brides, 166–72, 176–77; and culture, 182–85, 253 n.9 (*see also* Ethnicity), and families, 80–84, 87–88, 92, 179–81; and femininity, 66–67, 72; and imperialism, 169–71; and kinship, 22, 71–75, 79; and marriages, 69–79, 85–86; and marriage law, 22–23, 71–76, 136; and *Plessy v. Ferguson* (1896), 78; and stereotypes, 206, 208; and wedding portraits, 179–85; and white weddings, 8–9, 70. *See also* African Americans; Asians; Creoles; Identity; racial; Interracial marriages; Latinos; Mixed-race body; Native Americans; Slavery

Realism, 131, 149

Receptions. *See* White weddings: receptions in

Reid, Mayne, 152–53, 161–63, 250 n.34;

The Child Wife, 154, 164, 169–71; *The Headless Horseman*, 162–67; *The Scalphunters*, 154, 164–69

Rings. *See* Wedding rings

Rituals: of affect, 109–10; funeral, 37, 48; queer, 216–20; wedding (*see* Wedding rituals)

Roman Catholicism, 11, 14–19, 212–14, 228 n.30, 228 n.31, 228 n.32

Rosado, Christina, 176–77

Rossman, Michael, 183

Rothman, Ellen, 26–27, 111, 128, 147

Royal Wedding, 1981 (CBS), 185, 195–98, 256 n.38; and Anglo-American kinship, 197–98; and participatory democracy, 196–97

Ryan, Mary, 127–28

Same-sex unions, 2, 16, 24, 52, 56–57, 91–94, 211–17, 224 n.3

Sánchez-Eppler, Karen, 71, 158

Scalp-hunters, The (Reid), 154, 164–69

Scarlet Letter, The (Hawthorne), 108–11

Sedgwick, Eve, 34

Sentimental novels, 41–42, 72, 153. *See also* Affect

Sexuality. *See* Heterosexuality; Queers

Slavery: and marriage law, 22, 68, 71–72, 88–89; unions in, 88–89; and wedding rituals, 85–90

Slotkin, Richard, 122

Smith, Shawn, 178–79

Sodomy: Blackstone on, 122–24; and civil marriages, 123–26; legal history of, 123–24, 244 n.51

Sollors, Werner, 167, 197–98, 236 n.14

Somers, Colin Magill, 204–9

Sommer, Doris, 4, 39

So You're Going to Be Married! See *Bride's Magazine*

*Elizabeth Freeman is Assistant Professor of English at
the University of California at Davis.*

Library of Congress Cataloging-in-Publication Data
Freeman, Elizabeth.
The wedding complex : forms of belonging in modern
American culture / Elizabeth Freeman.
p. cm.—(Series Q)
Includes bibliographical references and index.
ISBN 0-8223-2953-0 (cloth : acid-free paper)
ISBN 0-8223-2989-1 (pbk : acid-free paper)
1. American fiction—20th century—History and criticism.
2. Weddings in literature. 3. Same-sex marriage—United
States. 4. Popular culture—United States. 5. Sexual
orientation in literature. 6. Weddings in motion pictures.
7. Weddings in popular culture. 8. Weddings—United
States. I. Title. II. Series.
PS374.W39 F74 2002
813'.509355—dc21   2002003196